Encouraging Thoughtful Christians to be World Changers

American Literature
Teacher Edition

James P. Stobaugh

For Such A Time As This Ministries
Hollsopple, Pennsylvania

Acknowledgments

I wish to thank Mrs. Judy Kovalik, Dr. David Garber, and Mr. Jim Butti for their editorial assistance. Bob and Tina Farewell, Wade and Jessica Hulcy, and David and Shirley Quine have encouraged me in so many ways. My brother Bill and his wife Deborah and their family have been an incredible support to me. I also wish to thank my good friend Mr. Rick Patton for his support in this project. Thank you to the Aleithia Community for its inspiration for this particular work. Likewise, I thank my four children and my distance learning students who so graciously allowed me to use their essays. Finally, and most of all, I want to thank my best friend and editor, my wife, Karen. "Come let us glorify the Lord and praise His name forever . . ." Psalm 34:3.

Copyright © 2002, James P. Stobaugh. All rights reserved. No part of this book may be reproduced in any form or by any means, unless it is stated otherwise, without written permission from the publisher, For Such A Time As This Ministries, 510 Swank Rd., Hollsopple, PA 15935. Phone 814-479-7710, E-Mail JPSTOBAUGH@AOL.COM, Web-site: FORSUCHATIMEASTHIS.COM.

Scripture text is from The Holy Bible, *New International Version* ®, Copyright © 1973, 1978, 1984 by the International Bible Society, and is used by permission of Zondervan Publishing House, with all rights reserved. Other "Credits, Permissions, and Sources" are listed at the back of the book. Audio presentations of most of the readings in this book may be obtained from Blackstoneaudio.com.

AMERICAN LITERATURE, TEACHER EDITION
Copyright © 2002 by James P. Stobaugh
Published by For Such A Time As This Ministries
Printed in the United States of America
Book design by James P. Stobaugh
Cover design by James Butti

Printed in the United States of America.

International Standard Book Number: 0-9725890-1-5

10 9 8 7 6 5 4 3 2 1   11 10 09 08 07 06 05 04 03 02

This Book is gratefully dedicated to
Karen
and
our four children:
Rachel, Jessica, Timothy, and Peter.

He has given us a ministry of reconciliation . . .
2 Corinthians 5:18

Students, to you 'tis given to scan the heights
Above, to traverse the ethereal space,
And mark the systems of revolving worlds.
Still more, ye sons of science ye receive
The blissful news by messengers from heav'n,
How Jesus blood for your redemption flows . . .

--Phillis Wheatley

Table of Contents

I.	Preface	1
II.	Lesson One Various Puritan Writings	14
III.	Lesson Two World View	26
IV.	Lesson Three Jonathan Edwards	40
V.	Lesson Four Anne Bradstreet	53
VI.	Lesson Five Phillis Wheatley	63
VII.	Lesson Six 18th and 19th Century Poetry	74
VIII.	Lesson Seven Nathaniel Hawthorne, *The Scarlet Letter*	99
IX.	Lesson Eight Nathaniel Hawthorne, *The Scarlet Letter*	106
X.	Lesson Nine 19th Century Short Stories	119
XI.	Lesson Ten 19th Century Short Stories	138
XII.	Lesson Eleven 19th Century Short Stories	145
XIII.	Lesson Twelve Mark Twain, *The Adventures of Huckleberry Finn*	151
XIV.	Lesson Thirteen Mark Twain, *The Adventures of Huckleberry Finn*	157
XV.	Lesson Fourteen Mark Twain, *The Adventures of Huckleberry Finn*	167

XVI.	Lesson Fifteen . . . . .173 Herman Melville, *Billy Budd*
XVII.	Lesson Sixteen . . . . 178 Herman Melville, *Billy Budd*
XVIII.	Lesson Seventeen . . . . 205 Herman Melville, *Billy Budd*
XIX.	Lesson Eighteen . . . . 212 Stephen Crane, *The Red Badge of Courage*
XX.	Lesson Nineteen . . . . 262 Stephen Crane, *The Red Badge of Courage*
XXI.	Lesson Twenty . . . . .289 Edith Wharton, *Ethan Frome*
XXII.	Lesson Twenty-One . . . . 295 Edith Wharton, *Ethan Frome*
XXIII.	Lesson Twenty-Two . . . . .308 Edith Wharton, *Ethan Frome*
XXIV.	Lesson Twenty-Three . . . . .313 20th Century Poetry
XXV.	Lesson Twenty-Four . . . . .325 Ernest Hemingway, *A Farewell to Arms*
XXVI.	Lesson Twenty-Five . . . . 331 Ernest Hemingway, *A Farewell to Arms*
XXVII.	Lesson Twenty-Six . . . . .341 William Faulkner, *The Unvanquished*
XXVIII.	Lesson Twenty-Seven . . . . .352 20th Century Short Stories
XXIX.	Lesson Twenty-Eight . . . . 368 20th Century Short Stories
XXX.	Lesson Twenty-Nine . . . . .373 20th Century Short Stories
XXXI.	Lesson Thirty . . . . .379 20th Century Short Stories

XXXII.	Lesson Thirty-One 384
	20th Century Short Stories
XXXIII.	Lesson Thirty-Two 389
	20th Century Short Stories
XXXIV.	Lesson Thirty-Three 394
	20th Century Short Stories
XXXV.	Lesson Thirty Four 398
	John Knowles, *A Separate Peace*

Preface

These are exciting days in which we live! At the very time that Americans are searching for truth, at the very time they are hungry for things of the Lord, God is raising up a mighty generation! This is the generation God has called *for such a time as this* to bring a Spirit inspired revival.

The best lack all conviction, while the worst/Are full of passionate intensity, William Butler Yeats writes. *Turning and turning in the widening gyre,/The falcon cannot hear the falconer.* America in the beginning of the 21st century is spinning out of control. America is stretching its wings adventurously, but drifting farther away from its God. America is in trouble. This is the first generation to grow up when wholesale murder was legal; the first generation to access 130 channels and at the same time to access almost nothing of value; the first generation to see a lying U.S. President go unpunished. This is a time, William Bennett says, when outrage is dead. That is the challenge, the bad news as it were.

The good news is, at the beginning of this century, God is stirring the water. He is offering a new beginning for a new nation. The personification of that new beginning is this new generation.

The young people alive today are part of one of the most critical generations in the history of Western culture. Indeed, only the generation of which Augustine was a part, comes close in importance to this generation. In both cases--today and during the life of Augustine, Bishop of Hippo-- civilizations were in decline. Young Augustine lived through the decline of the Roman world; young Americans are living through the decline of American cultural superiority.

In spite of the terrible events of September 11, 2001, America's political dominance is uncontested. In the cultural and spiritual arenas, however, America is in serious trouble. As did Anne Bradstreet and other young Puritans who settled in 1630 Boston, this new generation will need to replace this old, tired culture with a new God-centered, God-breathed society. Or our nation may not survive another century.

To that end, all this writer's works are dedicated to the ambitious goal of preparing this generation to be twenty-first century world changers for Christ. *No other effort is worth the substantial commitment that these courses demand from you.*

The *Skills For Rhetoric* and *Skills For Literary Analysis* courses are middle school or early high school courses. Even the most reluctant writer or gifted wordsmith will find these courses useful. These are skill-based courses so you will need to complete the entire course.

The *American*, *British*, and *World Literature Critical Thinking* courses are content-based. Each literary work is treated individually, much like a unit study. Each author or work, therefore, can be studied independently from each other.

The Literature Critical Thinking courses are essay-based. Each lesson contains several critical thinking questions. Most students will write two or three essays per week. The student may answer the other questions orally. The Literature Critical Thinking Courses are whole book so the entire book/literary piece must be read before the lesson begins. Finally, when writing essays, context is as important as content. In other words, *how* a writer says something is as important as *what* he says.

How does one write a concise, well-written essay? Here are a few suggestions:

> ✓ Essays should be written in the context of the other social sciences.
> ✓ Some essays should be rewritten; some should not. Discuss this with your parents.
> ✓ Write something everyday; read something everyday.
> ✓ Begin writing assignments immediately and continue to write throughout the year. Write about one hour per day.
> ✓ Revise your papers as soon as they are corrected.

Every essay includes a *Pre-writing phase,* a *writing phase*, and a *revision phase.*

Pre-writing Phase

What is the topic? What questions must a student answer? A student should articulate a thesis (one sentence statement of purpose). A student should decide what sort of essay this is--a definition, expository, persuasive, etc.--and design a strategy. For instance, clearly a persuasive essay will demand that the student state the issue and give his opinion in the opening paragraph.

Next, after a thesis statement, the student must write an outline. *No matter what length the essay may be, 20 pages or one paragraph, the student should create an outline.*

> ## Outline
> Thesis: In his poem "The Raven," Edgar Allan Poe uses literary devices to describe weighty topics like death and unrequited love and these literary devices draw the reader to an insightful and emotional moment.
> I. Introduction
> II. Body
>   A. Imagining Death
>   B. Feeling Emotions
> III. Conclusions

One of the best ways to organize one's thoughts is to play the Thinking Game. The Thinking Game is a way to narrow one's topic.

The Thinking Game
Issues

✓ State problem/issue in five sentences.
✓ State problem/issue in two sentences.
✓ State problem/issue in one sentence.
✓ Name three or more subtopics of problem.
✓ Name three or more subtopics of the subtopics.
✓ What information must be known to solve the problem or to answer the question?
✓ State the answer to the question/problem
--in five sentences   --in two sentences   --in one sentence.
✓ Stated in terms of outcomes, what evidences will I see that confirm that I have made the right decision?
✓ Once the problem/question is answered/solved, what are one or two new problems/answers that will arise?

The Following is an example of a Thinking Game approach to Mark Twain's *The Adventures of Huckleberry Finn:*

The problem is: *Should Huck turn in his escaped slave friend Jim to the authorities?*
✓ Name the Issue
   State problem/issue in five sentences, then in two sentences, and, finally, in one sentence.
Five Sentences:
Huck runs away with Jim. He does so knowing that he is breaking the law. However, the lure of friendship overrides the perfidy he knows he is committing. As he floats down the Mississippi River he finds it increasingly difficult to hide his friend from the authorities and difficult to hide is own feelings of ambivalence. Finally he manages to satisfy both ambiguities.
Two Sentences:
Huck intentionally helps his friend and slave Jim escape from his servitude. As he floats down the Mississippi River he finds it increasingly difficult to hide his friend from the authorities and, at the same time, to hide his own feelings of ambivalence.
One Sentence:
After escaping with his friend and escaped slave Jim, as he floats down the Mississippi River he finds it increasingly difficult to hide his friend from the authorities and, at the same time, to hide his own feelings of ambivalence.
✓ Name three or more sub-topics of problem.
Are there times when we should disobey the law?
What responsibilities does Huck have to his family?
What should Huck do?
✓ Name three or more sub-topics of the subtopics.
Are there times when we should disobey the law?
   Who determines what laws are unjust?
   Should the law be disobeyed publicly?

> *Who is injured when we disobey the law?*
> *What responsibilities does Huck have to his family?*
> > *Who is his family? Jim? His dad?*
> > *Is allegiance to them secondary to Jim's needs?*
> > *Should his family support his civil disobedience?*
> *What should Huck do?*
> > *Turn in Jim?*
> > *Escape with Jim?*
> > *Both?*
>
> ✓ What information must be known?
> *Laws? Jim's character? If he is bad then should Huck save him.*
> ✓ State the answer to the question/problem in five, two, and one sentence(s).
> Five Sentences:
> Huck can escape with Jim with profound feelings of guilt. After all, he is helping a slave escape. This is important because it shows that Huck is still a moral, if flawed, character. Jim's freedom does outweigh any other consideration--including the laws of the land and his family's wishes. As the story unfolds the reader sees that Huck is indeed a reluctant criminal and the reader takes comfort in that fact.
> Two Sentences:
> Showing reluctance and ambivalence, Huck embarks on an arduous but moral adventure. Jim's freedom outweighs any other need or consideration.
> One Sentence:
> Putting Jim's freedom above all other considerations, Huck, the reluctant criminal, embarks on an arduous but moral adventure.
> ✓ Once the Problem is solved, what are one or two new problem that may arise? *What if Huck is wrong?*

Writing Phase

Every essay has a beginning (or introduction), a middle part (or body), and ending (or conclusion). The introduction must draw the reader into the topic. The body organizes the material and presents the thesis (a one sentence statement of purpose) in a cogent and inspiring way. The conclusion generally is merely a summary. Paragraphs in the body are connected with transitions: *furthermore, therefore, in spite of.* Another effective transition technique is to mention in the first sentence of a new paragraph a thought or word that occurs in the last sentence of the previous paragraph. In any event, the body should be intentionally organized to advance the purposes of the paper. And, by the way, a disciplined writer *always* writes a rough draft.

Writing Tips

✓ The writer must make the first paragraph grab the readers' attention.

✓ Write naturally, but not colloquially. In other words, the writer should not write as he would speak! *The football players blew it* is too colloquial.

✓ The writer should use as much visual imagery and precise detail as he can. He should assume nothing. He should explain everything.

Rewriting Phase

When the writer is satisfied that he has communicated effectively his subject, he is ready to write the final copy.

The top ten most frequent essay problems:

✓Agreement Between the Subject and Verb: Use singular forms of verbs with singular subjects and use plural forms of verbs with plural subjects.
  ✗Everyone finished their homework.
  ★Everyone finished his homework (*Everyone* is an indefinite singular pronoun.).

✓Using the Second Person Pronoun--"you" should rarely, if ever, be used in a formal essay.
  ✗You know what I mean (Too informal).

✓Redundancy: Never use "I think" or "It seems to me."
  ✗I think that it is true.
  ★That is true (We know you think it or you would not write it!)

✓Tense consistency: Use the same tense (usually present) throughout the paper.
  ✗ I was ready to go but my friend is tired.
  ★ I am ready to go but my friend is tired.

✓Misplaced Modifiers: Place the phrase or clause close to its modifier.
  ✗The man drove the car with a bright smile into the garage.
  ★The man with a bright smile drove the car into the garage.

✓ Antecedent Pronoun Problems: Make sure pronouns match in number and gender with their antecedents.
  ✗Mary and Susan both enjoyed her dinner.
  ★Mary and Susan both enjoyed their dinners.

✓ Parallelism: Make certain that your list includes similar phrase types.
  ✗I like to take a walk and swimming.
★I like walking and swimming.

✓ "Affect" vs. "Effect": "Affect" is a verb; "Effect" is a noun unless it means "to achieve".

✓ Dangling prepositions: Never end a sentence with an unmodified preposition.
  ✗Who were you speaking to?
★To whom were you speaking?

✓Transitions: Make certain that paragraphs are connected with transitions or other devices (e.g., furthermore, therefore, in spite of).
★Furthermore, Jack London loves to describe animal behavior.

Read the following essay written by Jessica (who was then 15). Note the corrections.

Literary Devices in Edgar Allen Poe's Poems

Edgar Allen Poe is a clever writer. To enhance his poetry, he **used** literary devices such as end rhyme, alliteration, assonance, and repetition. These devices are paths that one may follow while reading Poe's poetry.

Watch tense. Used is past tense but your paper exhibits present tense. Tense consistency is vitally important.

The reader is invited to walk with Poe as he describes weighty topics like death and unrequited love. The abovementioned literary devices draws the reader down Poe's trail to an insightful and many times emotional moment.

Watch verb agreement. Draws requires a singular subject but devices (the subject) is plural. Draw is the correct form of the verb to use.

For example, in his poem *The Sleeper* Poe uses end rhyme, alliteration, assonance, and repetition. *At midnight, in the month of June,/I stand beneath the mystic moon* (lines 1&2). Later in lines 25 and 26 he uses alliteration with laudable results. *And wave the curtain canopy/so fitfully-so carefully.* Lines 5 and 6 include assonance, alliteration, and end rhyme. *And, softly dripping, drop by drop./Upon the quiet mountain top.* These literary devices naturally help Poe describe a very emotional and existential experience; namely, death. These devices draw the reader along the path to visualizing and imagining what death is like--which is really all we can do. In that sense, these literary devices are particularly important.

Active voice is good.

Be more precise. Give more detail.

In the next two Poe poems, *Annabel Lee* and *To Helen*, Poe becomes romantic. He struggles with one of the most heart wrenching topics: unfulfilled or unrequited love. Literary devices are critical to Poe's overall effect. In fact, in **Annabel Lee** Poe uses alliteration in almost every verse. *It was many and many a year ago,/In a kingdom by the sea,/That a maiden there lived whom you may know/By the name of Annabel Lee;/And this maiden she lived with no other thought/Than to love and be loved by me.* Alliteration is important to **To Helen**. *Helen,* ~~they~~ *thy beauty is to me/Like those Nicean barks of yore,/That gently, o'er a perfumed sea,/The weary, wayworn wanderer bore/To his own native shore.* A powerful visual and olfactory metaphor like *perfumed sea* to describe death requires equally powerful literary devices. These draw the reader along the path to feeling the tremendous loss that Poe feels in each poem. His young wife, his beloved is dead. There is a chasm across which no man can cross. But Poe tries to cross and to take us with him. Literary devices pull us into that path by evoking feelings and emotions too deep to utter.

[Margin note: Needs a much stronger transition.]

I **don't** like Poe for the very reason he is so brilliant. I do not enjoy thinking about death. It is not a subject I enjoy exploring. It is not a road I am ready to walk. **But,** I must admit, by use of literary devices, Poe draws the reader into the dark maelstrom of death. His naked emotion and powerful images draw me into this vortex. However, I am glad that Jesus Christ is my savior and my death is **mitigated** by the fact that I shall live forever with our Lord.

[Margin note: Avoid using contractions and colloquialism. But is also a bad sentence transition.]

[Margin note: Usage problem. Wrong use of the word mitigated.]

7

Composition Evaluation

Based on 100 points: *95/A*

I. Grammar and Syntax: Is the composition grammatically correct?
   (25 points)

   Comments: *See Corrections! Watch Agreement! Your verb usage should be a lot more precise!*
   20/25

II. Organization: Does this composition exhibit well considered organization? Does it flow? Transitions? Introduction and a conclusion?
   (25 points)

   Comments: *Good Job! 25/25*

III. Content: Does this composition answer the question, argue the point well, and/or persuade the reader?
   (50 points)

   Comments: *Excellent insights.   50/50*

Composition Evaluation

Based on 100 points:

I. Grammar and Syntax: Is the composition grammatically correct?
   (25 points)

   Comments:

II. Organization: Does this composition exhibit well considered organization? Does it flow? Transitions? Introduction and a conclusion?
   (25 points)

   Comments:

III. Content: Does this composition answer the question, argue the point well, and/or persuade the reader?
      (50 points)

   Comments:

*To be duplicated and placed on each essay.

How To Write Literary Analysis

Literature is defined by Webster's Dictionary as "writings in prose or verse; especially : writings having excellence of form or expression and expressing ideas of permanent or universal interest."

The person who examines, interprets, and analyzes literature is a *critic*. A critic is a guide to the reader; he is not a prophet; he is not a therapist. While it is the critic's right to express his preferences, and even his privilege to influence others, it is not his job to tell that reader what he is to like or not like. However, the critic is a helper, a guide helping the reader understand better the author's intention and art.

In fact the critic is concerned about the structure, sound, and meaning of the literary piece. These structures are described as genres: prose, poetry, essays, drama.

Literary analysis or criticism is a way to talk about literature. Literary analysis, most feel, is a way to understand literature better. If one really wants to understand something, one needs to have a common language with everyone else. If one was talking about football, for instance, one would need to know about certain terminology and use it when describing the game. How lost one would be if he did not know what a tackle is! Or how could a person enjoy watching a game if he did not know what the referee meant when he says, "first and ten!" Literary analysis employs a common language to take apart and to discuss literary pieces.

The following is language that critics use to discuss literature.

Authors–especially poets–use sound to create a mood or to make a particularly important point. *Alliteration* is the repetition of initial consonant sounds. The repetition can be juxtaposed (side by side; e.g., simply sad). An Example would be "I conceive therefore, as to the business of being profound, that it is with writers, as with wells; a person with good eyes may see to the bottom of the deepest, provided any water be there; and that often, when there is nothing in the world at the bottom, besides dryness and dirt, though it be but a yard and a half under ground, it shall pass, however, for wondrous deep, upon no wiser a reason than because it is wondrous dark (Jonathan Swift)." Swift uses alliteration to create a satiric tone.

Allusion is a casual and brief reference to a famous historical or literary figure or event: "You must borrow me Gargantua's mouth first. 'Tis a word too great for any mouth of this age's size (Shakespeare)." Shakespeare uses a comparison to help the reader understand his point.

Characters who appear in the story may perform actions, speak to other characters, be described by the narrator, or be remembered. An *Antagonist* is the person with whom the main character has the most conflict. He is the enemy of the main character (*protagonist*). In *The Scarlet Letter*, by Nathaniel Hawthorne, for instance, Chillingsworth is the antagonist. Hester, Chillingsworth's wife, the person who wears the scarlet letter, is the protagonist. Characters who are introduced whose sole purpose is to develop the main character are called *foils*. Conflict often occurs within a character. This is called *internal conflict*. An example of this occurs in Mark Twain's *Huckleberry Finn*. In this novel Huck is struggling in his mind about whether to return an escaped slave and Huck's good friend, Jim, to the authorities. An *external conflict* is normally an obvious conflict between the protagonist and antagonist(s).

The plot is the story. The *Plot* includes the events of the story, in the order the story gives them. A typical plot has five parts: *Exposition, Rising Action, Crisis* or *Climax, Falling Action*, and *Resolution. Crisis* or *Climax* is the moment or event in the *Plot* in which the conflict is most directly addressed: the main character "wins" or "loses"; the secret is revealed. After the climax, the *denouement* or falling action occurs.

Metaphor is a comparison which creatively identifies one thing with another, dissimilar thing, and transfers or ascribes to the first thing some of the qualities of the second. Unlike a *simile* or *analogy*, metaphor asserts that one thing is another thing, not just that one is like another. Very frequently a metaphor is invoked by a *to be* verb: *Affliction then is ours; / We are the trees whom shaking fastens more.* --George Herbert. Then Jesus declared, *"I am the bread of life."* --John 6:35 (compare the use of metaphor in John 14)

The *Narration* of a story is the way the author chooses to tell the story. *First-person Narration:* a character refers to himself using "I." Example: Huck Finn in *The Adventures of Huckleberry Finn* tells the story from his perspective. This is a creative way to bring humor into the plot. *Second-person Narration*: addresses the reader and/or the main character as "you" (and may also use first-person narration, but not necessarily). One example is the opening of each of Rudyard Kipling's *Just-So Stories*, in which the narrator refers to the child-listener as "O Best-Beloved." *Third-person Narration*: not a character in the story; refers to the story's characters as "he" and "she." This is probably the most common form of narration, so I won't give a specific example. *Limited Narration:* is only able to tell what one person is thinking or feeling. Example: in *A Separate Peace*, by John Knowles, the reader only sees the story from Gene's perspective. *Omniscient Narration*: Charles Dickens in most of his novels employs this narration. *Reliable Narration*: everything this Narration says is true, and the Narration knows everything that is necessary to the story. *Unreliable Narrator*: may not know all the relevant information ; may be intoxicated or mentally ill; may lie to the audience. Example: Edgar Allan Poe's narrators are frequently unreliable. Think of the delusions that the narrator of "The Tell-Tale Heart" has about the old man.

Onomatopoeia is the use of words which in their pronunciation suggest their meaning. "Hiss," for example, when spoken is intended to resemble the sound of steam or of a snake. Other examples include these: *slam, buzz, screech, whirr, crush, sizzle, crunch, wring, wrench, gouge, grind, mangle, bang , pow, zap, fizz, roar, growl, blip, click, whimper*, and, of course, *snap, crackle, and pop*.

The *Setting* is the place(s) and time(s) of the story, including the historical period, social milieu of the characters, geographical location, descriptions of indoor and outdoor locales.

The *Theme* is the one sentence major purpose of a literary piece, rarely stated but implied. The theme is not a *Moral* which is a statement of the author's didactic purpose of his literary piece. A *Thesis Statement* is very similar to the theme. A *Precis* is a summary of the plot or a portion of the plot. A *Precis* interprets the literary work in a summary fashion; a *summary* merely states the general meaning of the literary work.

The *Tone* is the mood of a literary piece. For instance, the tone or mood of Poe's "Annabel Lee" is very somber.

These terms are the critic's tools to discuss and to analyze literature. Like a physician defines his patient in terms of this or that syndrome or physical attribute, the critic describes his literary piece in terms of a credible narrator or an exciting plot or an effective theme.

The following is a literary critical paper concerning the main character in the modern American novel *A Separate Peace*, by John Knowles.

John Knowles was a master at creating internal struggles with his characters. In *A Separate Peace* Gene, the protagonist and perfect student, struggles with his feelings about his best friend Finny and Gene's alter-ego/ antagonist. Knowles skillfully shows how Gene feels both love and hatred toward Finny. The following passage with Gene speaking to himself illustrates the ambiguity he is experiencing:

> *You are both driving ahead for yourselves alone. You did hate him for breaking that school swimming record, but so what? He hated your for getting and A in every course but one last term. You would have had an A in that one except for him. Except for him. Then a second realization broke as clearly and bleakly as dawn at the beach. Finny had deliberately set our to wreck my studies. That explained blitzball, that explained the nightly meetings of the Super Suicide Society, that explained his insistence that I share all his diversions.*

Gene and Finny are two extremes. Gene is excellent at scholarly activities. He has the best grades in Devon. Finny, however, is the best athlete. He breaks records and plays nearly every sport Devon has to offer. Thus, Finny and Gene are opposites.

Gene often is in trouble for things that Finny escapes. Finny is able to talk his way out of almost everything.

> *But Finny pressed his advantage. Not because he wanted to be forgiven for missing the meal- that didn't interest him at all, he might have enjoyed the punishment if it was done in some novel and unknown way. He pressed his advantage because he saw that Mr. Prud'homme was pleased, won over in spite of himself. The master was slipping from is official position momentarily, and it was just possible, if Phineas(Finny) pressed hard enough, that*

*there might be a flow of simple unregulated friendliness
between them and such flows were one of finny's reasons
for living.*

In spite of these substantial differences, Gene loves Finny and he is his best friend. Gene struggles with these two conflicting thoughts and it is this reader's opinion that his ambivalent feelings toward Finny that cause Gene to shake Finney out of the tree.

One final word: literary criticism papers are more frequently assigned than any other high school or college writing assignment. The student, therefore, must develop this craft and continue to refine it throughout his writing career.

LESSON ONE

Readings Due For This Lesson:
The History of Plimoth Plantation, William Bradford or excerpt in book.
A Quest for Godliness, J. I. Packer (optional)

Reading Ahead
Readings from John Smith and William Bradford are provided in Lesson Three.

Suggested Weekly Implementation

Day One	Day Two	Day Three	Day Four	Day Five
1 Students should have read the required reading(s) *before* the assigned lesson begins. 2. Teacher may want to discuss assigned reading(s) with student. 3. Teacher shall assign the required essays. Choose two or three. The rest of the essays can be outlined, answered with shorter answers, or skipped.	1. Student should begin reading(s) from next lesson. 2. Student should outline essays due at the end of the week. 3. Students should answer one or two of the essays that are not assigned as formal essays.	1. Students should write rough drafts of assigned essays. 2. The teacher should correct rough drafts.	Student will write final copy of essays due tomorrow.	1. Essays are due. 2. Students should take the Lesson One test. 3. Student should finish Lesson Two readings.

Various Puritan Writings
The History of Plymouth Plantation
by William Bradford

Critical Thinking

A. Pretend that you are part of an expedition to Mars. Write a one-page descriptive essay about your surroundings. What similarities do you find to Bradford's diary? *Answers will vary but all observations will be conceptualized by what your former experience has been. Such was the case with William Bradford. Bradford's understanding of history was unapologetically subjective--his experience tells him that God is alive, faithful, and ever-present in the lives of people. Subjectivity, at least in this case, is an asset. Bradford was able to see through the eyes of faith that brought the true story to his readers. This is not to imply that Bradford was inaccurate. On the contrary, his attention to detail combined with his acute sense of providence, evidence his skillful historical methods. The writing of history is the selection of information and the synthesis of this information into a narrative that will stand the critical eye of time. History, though, is never static. One never creates the definitive theory of an historical event. History invites each generation to re-examine its own story and to reinterpret past events in light of present circumstance. In this case, it was William Bradford's turn.*

The creation of this story is more difficult than it seems. From the beginning the historian is forced to decide what sort of human motivations matter most: Economic? Political? Religious?

While the historian knows that he can never be completely neutral about history, scholarly historical inquiry demands that he implement the following principles:

1. *The historian must evaluate the veracity of sources. There must be a hierarchy of historical sources.*

2. *The historian must be committed to telling both sides of the historical story. He may choose to lobby for one view over the other, but the historian must fairly present all theories.*

3. *He must avoid stereotypes and archetypes. He must overcome personal prejudices and dispassionately view history in ruthlessly objective terms.*

4. *He must be committed to the truth no matter where his scholarship leads him. At times the historian will discover unflattering information about his nation/state. He must not hesitate to accept and then to tell the truth.*

5. *Finally, the historian understands that real, abiding, and eternal history ultimately is made only by people who obey God at all costs.*

B. What was William Bradford's view of nature? *To William Bradford, nature was only an extension of God's creation. It is not alive; it was not even ubiquitous It was not friendly or unfriendly. God was alive. God is in control. And God loved Bradford very much–a fact of which Bradford was acutely aware. It is from this secure base that Bradford created his history. William Bradford, an English Separatist, was forced to reckon with awful conditions–1/2 of his Plymouth Pilgrims died the first winter. Nevertheless, Bradford continued to affirm God's basic goodness in the face of horrible conditions. William Bradford's state of mind was not dependent upon circumstances. Listen to Bradford's own words:*

> *But here I cannot but stay and make a pause, and stand half amazed at this poor people's present condition; and so I think will the reader too, when he well considers the same. Being thus passed the vast ocean, and a sea of troubles before in their preparation (as may be remembered by that which went before), they had now no friends to welcome them, nor inns to entertain or refresh their weather-beaten bodies, no houses or much less towns to repair to, to seek for succor. It is recorded in scripture as a mercy to the apostle and his shipwrecked company, that the barbarians showed no small kindness in refreshing them, but these savage barbarians, when they met with them (as after will appear) were readier to fill their sides full of arrows then otherwise. And for the season it was winter, and they that know the winters of that country know them to be sharp and violent and subject to cruel and fierce storms, dangerous to travel to known places, much more to search an unknown coast. Besides, what could they see but a hideous and desolate wilderness, full of wild beasts and wild men? and what multitudes there might be of them they knew not. Neither could they, as it were, go up to the top of Pigsah, to view from this wilderness a more goodly country to feed their hopes; for which way soever they turned their eyes (save upward to the heavens) they could have little solace or content in respect of any outward objects. For summer being done, all things stand upon them with a weather-beaten face; and the whole country, full of woods and thickets, represented a wild and savage hew. If they looked behind them, there was the mighty ocean which they had passed, and was now as a main bar and gulf to separate them from all the civil parts of the world. If it be said they had a ship to succor them, it is true; but what heard they daily from the master and company? But that with speed they should look out a place with their shallop, where they would be at some near distance; for the season was such as he would not stir from thence till a safe harbor was discovered by them where they would be, and he might go without danger; and that victuals consumed apace, but he must and would keep sufficient for themselves and their*

return. Yea, it was muttered by some, that if they got not a place in time, they would turn them and their goods ashore and leave them. Let it also be considered what weak hopes of supply and succor they left behind them, that might bear up their minds in this sad condition and trials they were under; and they could not but be very small. It is true, indeed, the affections and love of their brethren at Leyden was cordial and entire towards them, but they had little power to help them, or themselves; and how the case stood between them and the merchants at their coming away, hath already been declared. What could now sustain them but the spirit of God and his grace? Say not and ought not the children of these fathers rightly say: "Our fathers were Englishmen which came over this great ocean, and were ready to perish in this wilderness; but they cried unto the Lord, and he heard their voice, and looked on their adversity, etc. Let them therefore praise the Lord, because he is good, and his mercies endure forever. Yea, let them which have been redeemed of the Lord, show how he hath delivered them from the hand of the oppressor. When they wandered in the desert wilderness out of the way, and found no city to dwell in, both hungry, and thirsty, their soul was overwhelmed in them. Let them confess before the Lord his loving kindness, and his wonderful works before the sons of men.

C. An allusion is a brief, often indirect reference to a person, place, event, or artistic work which the author assumes the reader will recognize. To that end, Bradford uses many biblical allusions. Find two examples and in a one-page illustrative essay show how Bradford uses them. *There are several. For instance, on September 6, Bradford compares the Pilgrim's landing on Plymouth Rock to Paul's shipwreck on Malta in Acts 28:2: "And the natives showed us unusual kindness, for they kindled a fire and welcomed us all, because it had begun to rain and was cold."*

Challenge Questions

Challenge questions are more difficult critical thinking questions: synthesis, analysis, and evaluation; all students can answer these questions.

Read J. I. Packer, *A Quest For Godliness: The Puritan Vision of the Christian Life*. Packer argues that the depth and breadth of Puritan spiritual life stands in stark contrast to the facile and deadness of modern Western Christianity. He concludes that the main difference between the Puritans and us is spiritual maturity--the Puritans had it and we simply do not. The Puritans believed in an omnipotent God. They most certainly were not grouchy, legalistic, colorless settlers. They wore bright colors and enjoyed life. They had a passion for righteousness; they had a passion for God. "They were great souls," J. L. Packer writes, "serving a great God." In a one page essay, agree or disagree with Packer's thesis.

I most certainly agree with Packer. J.I. Packer, A Quest for Godliness (Wheaton, Ill: Crossway Books, Inc., 1990). My favorite quote is:

> *Puritans were not wild men, fierce and freaky, religious fanatics and social extremists, but sober, conscientious, and cultured citizens: persons of principle, devoted, determined, and disciplined, excelling in the domestic virtues, and with no obvious shortcomings save a tendency to run to words when saying anything important, whether to God or to man...They were great souls serving a great God. In them clear-headed passion and warm-hearted compassion combined.*

Supplemental Resources:

Arthur Bennet (Editor), *The Valley of Vision: A Collection of Puritan Prayers and Devotions*
    Bennet understands that the Puritans were men and women of God who were devoutly spiritual in their worship and fervently sincere in their faith. The reader will find these 17th century devotions to be surprisingly contemporary.

William Bradford, *Mourt's Relation: A Journal of the Pilgrims at Plymouth*
    A wonderful primary source description of the Plimoth pilgrims.

Horton Davies, *The Worship of the English Puritans*
    Davis shows that Puritan worship was not the lifeless, colorless experience that many suppose.

Andrew Delbanco, *The Puritan Ordeal*
    This book is about the experience of becoming American in the seventeenth century. It emphasizes what Delbanco calls renewal and risk. This is a distinctive of American history.

Morgan Edmund, *The Puritan Dilemma: The Story of John Winthrop*
    Morgan correctly argues that Winthrop and the Puritans were 17th century radicals.

Judith S. Graham, *Puritan Family Life: The Diary of Samuel Sewall*
    This book takes a close look at Judge Samuel Sewall, using his diary as an

example of Puritan family life. Sewall's experiences directly contradict the common understanding of the repressive and joyless Puritan household. His diaries show the reader that Puritans had a loving, vital relationship with their children.

Robert Middlekauff, *The Mathers: Three Generations of Puritan Intellectuals, 1596-1728*
Robert Middlekauff traces the evolution of Puritan thought and theology in America. He focuses on three generations of intellectual ministers--Richard, Increase, and Cotton Mather--in order to challenge the traditional telling of the secularization of Puritanism, a story of faith transformed by reason, science, and business.

Perry Miller *The American Puritans*
Without a doubt Perry Miller is the undisputed scholar in Puritan studies.

Perry Miller, *The New England Mind*: *The Seventeenth Century*

Gary D. Schmidt, *William Bradford: Plymouth's Faithful Pilgrim*
In very descriptive language Schmidt tells the reader about the horrible first winter in Plimoth and how the believing Pilgrims correctly conceptualized their ordeal in Christian concepts.

Notes:

Lesson One Test

True or False: (15 points)

_____ 1. The Boston Puritans loved the Church of England and only wished to "purify" it.

_____ 2. The Pilgrims were a special type of Puritan.

_____ 3. The Pilgrims lived in Northern Ireland before they traveled to America.

_____ 4. The Pilgrim landing in Cape Cod was really a mistake.

_____ 5. The Puritans' main motivation to traveling to America was to make money.

Explain what these quotes from *The History of Plimoth Plantation* mean and give their historical context: (30 points)

A. The one side (the Reformers) laboured to have ye* right worship of God & discipline of Christ established in ye church, according to ye simplicitie of ye gospell, without the mixture of mens inventions, and to have & to be ruled by ye laws of Gods word, dispensed in those offices, & by those officers of Pastors, Teachers, & Elders, according to ye Scripturs. The other partie (the Church of England), though under many colours & pretences, endevored to have ye episcopall dignitie (afftter ye popish maner) with their large power & jurisdiction still retained; with all those courts, cannons, & ceremonies, togeather with all such livings, revenues, & subordinate officers, with other such means as formerly upheld their antichristian greatnes, and enabled them with lordly & tyranous power to persecute ye poore servants of God.

B. Being thus arived in a good harbor and brought safe to land, they fell upon their knees & blessed ye God of heaven, who had brought them over ye vast & furious ocean, and delivered them from all ye periles & miseries therof, againe to set their feete on ye firme and stable earth, their proper elemente. And no marvell if they were thus joyfull, seeing wise Seneca was so affected with sailing a few miles on ye coast of his owne Italy; as he affirmed, that he had rather remaine twentie years on his way by land, then pass by sea to any place in a short time; so tedious & dreadfull was ye same unto him.

But hear I cannot but stay and make a pause, and stand half amased at this poore peoples presente condition; and so I thinke will the reader too, when he well considered ye same. Being thus passed ye vast ocean, and a sea of troubles before in their preparation (as may be remembred by yt which wente before), they had now no friends to wellcome them, nor inns to entertaine or refresh their weatherbeaten bodys, no houses or much less townes to repaire too, to seeke for succoure. ... Let it also be considred what weake hopes of supply & succoure they left behinde them, yt might bear up their minds in this sade condition and trialls they were under; and they could not but be very smale. It is true, indeed, ye affections & love of their brethren at Leyden was cordiall & entire towards them, but they had litle power to help them, or them selves; and how ye case stode betweene them & ye marchants at their coming away, hath already been declared. What could not sustaine them but ye spirite of God & his grace? May not & ought not the children of these fathers rightly say : *Our faithers were Englishmen which came over this great ocean, and were ready to perish in this willdernes; but they cried unto ye Lord, and he heard their voyce, and looked on their adversitie . . .*

C. They begane now to gather in ye small harvest they had, and to fitte up their houses and dwellings against winter, being all well recovered in health & strenght, and had all things in good plenty; fFor as some were thus imployed in affairs abroad, others were excersised in fishing, aboute codd, & bass, & other fish, of which yey tooke good store, of which every family had their portion. All ye somer ther was no want. And now begane to come in store of foule, as winter approached, of which this place did abound when they came first (but afterward decreased by degrees). And besids water foule, ther was great store of wild Turkies, of which they tooke many, besids venison, Besids, they had about a peck a meale a weeke to a person, or now since harvest, Indean corn to yt proportion. Which made many afterwards write so largly of their plenty hear to their freinds in England, which were not fained, but true reports.

*This "y" in Old English stood for "the."

Short Answer: (55 points)

Answer these questions in 75 words or less.

A. Compare William Bradford with a contemporary political or religious figure. (10 points)

B. Explain what the historian Perry Miller meant when he said, "Without some understanding of Puritanism. . . there is no understanding of America." (15 points)

C. Even though *Of Plimoth Plantation* is a nonfiction work, in many ways this book has more action than fiction novels. In that vein, take this literary work and discuss its plot. In other words, identify the rising action, climax, and falling action. (10 points)

D. Is (are) there antagonist(s) in *Of Plimoth*? Who is (are) it (they) and why? (10 points)

E. Explain why the Bible was so important to the Puritans? (10 points)

Lesson One Test Answers

True or False: (15 points)

T--The Boston Puritans loved the Church of England and only wished to "purify" it. *The Separatist Puritans at Plymouth, MA, sought to separate from the Church of England; the Puritans who settled in Boston wished merely to purify the Church of England.*

F--The Pilgrims were a special type of Puritan. *The Pilgrims included Separatist Puritans and secular settlers who immigrated to Plymouth, MA, in 1620.*

F--The Pilgrims lived in Northern Ireland before they traveled to America. *They stayed in Holland.*

T--The Pilgrim landing in Cape Cod was really a mistake. *They meant to settle in Virginia.*

F--The Puritans' main motivation to traveling to America was to make money.

Explain what these quotes from *The History of Plymouth Plantation* mean and give their historical context: (30 points)

A. The one side (the Reformers) laboured to have ye right worship of God & discipline of Christ established in ye church, according to ye simplicitie of ye gospell, without the mixture of mens inventions, and to have & to be ruled by ye laws of Gods word, dispensed in those offices, & by those officers of Pastors, Teachers, & Elders, according to ye Scripturs. The other partie (the Church of England), though under many colours & pretences, endevored to have ye episcopall dignitie (afftter ye popish maner) with their large power & jurisdiction still retained; with all those courts, cannons, & ceremonies, togeather with all such livings, revenues, & subordinate officers, with other such means as formerly upheld their antichristian greatnes, and enabled them with lordly & tyranous power to persecute ye poore servants of God.

Bradford is attacking the Church of England's "petences" and "tyranous power to persecute."

B. Being thus arived in a good harbor and brought safe to land, they fell upon their knees & blessed ye God of heaven, who had brought them over ye vast & furious ocean, and

23

delivered them from all ye periles & miseries therof, againe to set their feete on ye firme and stable earth, their proper elemente. And no marvell if they were thus joyefull, seeing wise Seneca was so affected with sailing a few miles on ye coast of his owne Italy; as he affirmed, that he had rather remaine twentie years on his way by land, then pass by sea to any place in a short time; so tedious & dreadfull was ye same unto him.

But hear I cannot but stay and make a pause, and stand half amased at this poore peoples presente condition; and so I thinke will the reader too, when he well considered ye same. Being thus passed ye vast ocean, and a sea of troubles before in their preparation (as may be remembred by yt which wente before), they had now no friends to wellcome them, nor inns to entertaine or refresh their weatherbeaten bodys, no houses or much less townes to repaire too, to seeke for succoure. ... Let it also be considred what weake hopes of supply & succoure they left behinde them, yt might bear up their minds in this sade condition and trialls they were under; and they could not but be very smale. It is true, indeed, ye affections & love of their brethren at Leyden was cordiall & entire towards them, but they had litle power to help them, or them selves; and how ye case stode betweene them & ye marchants at their coming away, hath already been declared. What could not sustaine them but ye spirite of God & his grace? May not & ought not the children of these fathers rightly say : *Our faithers were Englishmen which came over this great ocean, and were ready to perish in this willdernes; but they cried unto ye Lord, and he heard their voyce, and looked on their adversitie . . .*

This passage illustrates in broad relief the landing of the Pilgrims at Plymouth, MA, and how completely they conceptualized it as an act of God.

C. They begane now to gather in ye small harvest they had, and to fitte up their houses and dwellings against winter, being all well recovered in health & strenght, and had all things in good plenty; fFor as some were thus imployed in affairs abroad, others were excersised in fishing, aboute codd, & bass, & other fish, of which yey tooke good store, of which every family had their portion. All ye somer ther was no want. And now begane to come in store of foule, as winter approached, of which this place did abound when they came first (but afterward decreased by degrees). And besids water foule, ther was great store of wild Turkies, of which they tooke many, besids venison, Besids, they had about a peck a meale a weeke to a person, or now since harvest, Indean corn to yt proportion. Which made many afterwards write so largly of their plenty hear to their freinds in England, which were not fained, but true reports.

This is the story of the first Thanksgiving.

Short Answer (55 points)
Answer these questions in 75 words or less.

A. Compare William Bradford with a contemporary political or religious figure. (10 points)

Answers will vary. Bradford was a very Godly man who walked his talk!

B. Explain what the historian Perry Miller meant when he said, "Without some understanding of Puritanism... there is no understanding of America." (15 points)

The Puritans were the intellectual and spiritual epicenter of the American civilization for 150 years.

C. Even though *Of Plimoth Plantation* is a nonfiction work, in many ways this book has more action than fictional novels. In that vein, take this literary work and discuss its plot. In other words, identify the rising action, climax, and falling action. (10 points)

The trip over on the Mayflower certainly piqued the reader's interest (rising action). The climax would be the first winter when over half died. The falling action would be Thanksgiving. Of course answers will vary.

D. Is (are) there antagonist(s) in *Of Plimoth*? Who is (are) it (they) and why? (10 points)

It is insightful that nature is not the enemy (Naturalism) nor are the Native Americans. The enemy is the Devil.

E. Explain why the Bible was so important to the Puritans? (10 points)

The Bible was the inerrant, inspired Word of God. It was the basis for everything that the Puritans did. It was the guidebook for life itself.

Lesson Two

Readings Due For This Lesson

All readings are provided for the student.

Reading Ahead

Jonathan Edwards, *Religious Affections: A Christian's Character Before God* (portions are provided in Lesson Three) and *Sinners in the Hands of An Angry God* (provided in Lesson Three).

Suggested Weekly Implementation

Day One	Day Two	Day Three	Day Four	Day Five
1. Students will rewrite graded essays from last week and go over Lesson One test. 2. Students should have read the required reading(s) *before* the assigned lesson begins. 3. Teacher may want to discuss assigned reading(s) with student. 4. Teacher shall assign the required essays. Choose two or three. The rest of the essays can be outlined, answered with shorter answers, or skipped.	1. Student should begin reading(s) from next lesson. 2. Student should outline essays due at the end of the week. 3. Students should answer one or two of the essays that are not assigned as formal essays.	1. Students should write rough drafts of assigned essays. 2. The teacher should correct rough drafts.	Student will write final copy of essays due tomorrow.	1. Essays are due. 2. Students should take the test. 3. Student should finish Lesson Three reading.

Puritanism . . .

Throughout this course you will be challenged to analyze the world view of each writer. The following are several world views in literature.

A. Humans who bestow superior value on the lives of all human beings solely because they are members of our own species are judging along lines strikingly similar to those used by white racists who bestow superior value on the lives of other whites, merely because they are members of their own race.--P. Singer. *Naturalism. Equating animals and pets with human beings are dead giveaways to Romanticism.*

B. So God created man in His own image, in the image of God. *Theism. This passage is in Genesis.*

C. Gatsby believed...tomorrow we will run faster, stretch out our arms farther . . . And one fine morning--So we beat on, boats against the current, borne back ceaselessly into the past (Fitzgerald, *The Great Gatsby*, p. 121). *Fitzgerald is well known for his hopeless realism and unfocused Naturalism. There are hints, too, of Romanticism.*

D. Compare the world views represented in the next two passages. Which world view is obviously Christian? From these descriptions what generalizations can you draw about the Virginia and Plymouth settlement?

❀Being thus left to our fortunes, it fortuned that within ten dayes scarce ten amongst us could either goe, or well stand, such extreame weaknes and sicknes oppressed us. And thereat none need marvaile, if they consider the cause and reason, which was this; whiles the ships stayed, our allowance was somewhat bettered, by a daily proportion of Bisket, which the sailers would pilfer to sell, give, or exchange with us, for money, Saxefras, furres, or love. But when they departed, there remained neither taverne, beere house, nor place of reliefe, but the common Kettell. Had we beene as free from all sinnes as gluttony, and drunkennesse, we might have been canonized for Saints; But our President would never have beene admitted, for ingrossing to his private, Oatmeale, Sacke, Oyle, Aquavitae, Beefe, Egges, or what not, but the Kettell; that indeed he allowed equally to be distributed, and that was halfe a pint of wheat, and as much barely boyled with water for a man a day, and this having fryed some 26 weekes in the ships hold, contained as many wormes as graines; so that we might truely call it rather so much bran then corne, our drinke was water, our lodgings Castles in the ayre: with this lodging and dyet, our extreame toile in bearing and planting Pallisadoes, so strained and bruised us, and our continuall labour in the extremities of the heat had so weakned us, as were cause sufficient to have made us as miserable in our native Countrey, or any other place in the world. . . . The new president and Martin, being little beloved, of weake judgement in dangers, and less industrie in peace, committted managing of all things abroad to Captaine Smith: who by his owne example, good words, and faire promises, set some to mow, others to binde thatch, some to build houses, others to thatch them, himselfe always bearing the greatest taske for his own share, so that in short time, he provided most of them lodgings, neglecting any for himselfe. This done, seeing the Salvages superfluitie beginne to decrease (with some of his workmen) shipped himselfe in the Shallop to search the Country for trade. The want of the language, knowledge to mannage his boat without sailes, the want of a sufficient power, (knowing the multitude of the Salvages) apparell for his men, and other necessaries, were infinite impediments, yet no discouragement. -JOHN SMITH. *The General History of Virginia.* 1624 ❀

❀Ch.9: Sept 6: These troubles being blowne over, and now all being compacte togeather in one shipe, they put to sea againe with a prosperous winde, which continued diverce days togeather, which was some incouragement unto them; yet according to the usuall maner many were afflicted with sea-sicknes. And I may not omite hear a spetiall worke of Gods providence. There was a proud and very profane yonge man, one of the sea-men, of a lustie, able body, which made him the more hauty; he would allway be contemning the poore people in their sicknes, and cursing them dayly with greevous execrations, and did not let to tell them, that he hoped to help to cast halfe of them over board before they came to their jurneys end, and to make merry with what they had; and if he were by any gently reproved, he would curse and swear most bitterly. But it pleased God before they came halfe seas over, to smite this yong man with a greevous disease, of which he dyed in a desperate maner, and so was him self the first that was throwne overbord. Thus his curses light on his owne head; and it was an astonishment to all his fellow, for they noted it to be the just hand of God upon him. After they had injoyed faire winds and weather for a season, they were incountred many times with crosse winds, and mette with many feirce stormes, with which the shipe was shroudly shaken, and her upper works made very leakie; and one of the maine beames in the midd ships was bowed and craked, which put them in some fear that the shipe could not be able to performe the vioage. . . . . . --WILLIAM BRADFORD. *The History of Plimoth Plantation.* 1630-46. ❀

While both passages are Theistic, it seems to me, that Bradford's faith is stronger than Smith's. Smith begins, "left to our fortunes." Can you imagine Bradford talking about "fortune" or "luck?" Bradford refers to "a special act of God's Providence . . ."

E. If your parents will allow you to do so, watch the following movies and discuss the world view of each of them: *Star Wars, The Lion King, True Grit, Ice Age*, and *Hoosiers*. *Star Wars, True Grit,* and *Hoosiers* have a Theistic (but not necessarily Christian) message. The heroes uphold traditional, Judeo-Christian values. *Ice Age* advances Judeo-Christian Theistic values but exhibits Naturalistic tendencies (e.g., evolution). Likewise *The Lion King* celebrates Judeo-Christian values but advances a decidedly Existential agenda (e.g., the surrealistic dream sequences).

World View Development

To 500 A.D.	Classicism Christian Theism
Middle Ages, 500-1600	Christian Theism European Romanticism
1600-1865	Christian Theism Deism Transcendentalism (American Romanticism)
1865-Present	Naturalism Realism Absurdism Theism Revival

World View Review	
Theism	Christian Theism advances a world view that there is an omnipotent God Who has authored an inspired, authoritative work called the Bible, upon whose precepts mankind should base his society.
Deism	Deism advances a world view that accepts the notion that there is an authoritative, inspired source from which mankind should base his society (i.e., the Bible). Likewise the Deist is certain that there was once an omnipotent God. However, once the world was created, that very-same omnipotent God chose to absent Himself from His creation. The world, then, is like a clock. It was once created by an intelligent process. However, now the creator is absent. Thus, mankind, on his own, must find out how the clock works and go on living.
Romanticism	A natural companion to Deism was Rationalism. Rationalism (e.g., John Locke's philosophy) invited the Deist to see mankind as a "chalkboard" on which was written experience that ultimately created a personality. Thus, Rationalists/Deists were fond of speaking of "unalienable right" or "common sense." The Romantic (in American the Romantic would be called "the Transcendentalist") took issue with Deism and Theism. To the Romantic, Nature was God. Nature–an undefined indigenous, omnipotent presence–was very good. Original sin was man's separation from Nature. In fact, the degree to which mankind returned to Nature would determine his goodness and effectiveness. Thus, a man like Henry David Thoreau lived a year on Walden Pond so that he could find his God. In *Deerslayer*, James Fenimore Cooper, the protagonist is safe while he is on a lake separated from evil mankind. Only when he participates in human society is he in trouble. The Romantic was naturally suspicious of Theism because Theism appeared to be dogmatic and close-minded. The Romantics had confessions, but they had no dogma. Deism also bothered the Romantics. Romanticism emphasized the subjective; Deism emphasized the objective. In the Romantic novel *Frankenstein* the Deist/Rationalist Dr. Frankenstein creates a monster. Dr. Frankenstein, with disastrous results turns his back on the subjective and tries to use science to create life.

Naturalism	Naturalism was inclined to agree with Romanticism's criticism of Theism and Deism, but did not believe in a benevolent Nature. In fact, Nature, to the Naturalist, was malevolent, mischievous, and unpredictable. Mankind, as it were, lost control of the universe and the person who had control did not really care much for his creation. Theism of course was absurd. How could any sane person who experienced World War I believe in a loving, living God? Deism was equally wrong. God was not absent–he was present in an unpredictable, at times evil way. Or not. Romanticism was on the right track but terribly naive. God and His creation were certainly not "good" in any sense of the word. Nature was evil. Naturalism embraced a concept of fate not dissimilar to that held by the Greeks. In Homer's *Iliad*, for instance, the characters were subject to uncontrolled fate and pernicious gods and goddesses who inflicted terrible and good things on mankind with no apparent design or reason. No, to the Naturalist God was at best absent or wimpish. At worse, he was malevolent.
Realism	Realism was philosophically akin to Naturalism. In a sense, Naturalism was a natural companion Realism. Realism was different from Naturalism in degree, not in substance. Realism argued that it people were honest they would admit that God was not present at all. It there was anything worth embracing, it was reality. Realism advanced an in-your-face view of life. They prided themselves in "telling it like it is." They entered the cosmic arena and let the chips fall where they may. They shared the same criticisms of other world views that Naturalism held.
Absurdism	Absurdism certainly believed that Realism was on track. Where Realism erred, however, was its propensity to see meaning in life. Mind you, the meaning was tied to things one could see and one could feel–not in things that were abstract or immutable–but the Realist still sought some meaning in this life. The Absurdist abandoned all hope of finding meaning in life and embraced a sort of nihilism. The Absurdist was convinced that everything was meaningless and absurd. The subjectivity of a Romantic was appealing to the Absurd. However, even that implied that something was transcendent–a desire–and the Absurdist would have nothing to do with that. Billy Pilgrim, a protagonist in one of the Absurdist Kurt Vonnegut, Jr.'s novels, becomes "unhinged from time" and "wandered around in the cosmos. Things without meaning happen to him whose life has no meaning. Everything is absurd.

| Existentialism | Existentialism stepped outside the debate of meaning all together. Existentialism argued that the quest was futile. The only thing that matters was subjective feeling. "Experience" was a God at whose feet the Existentialist worshiped. Romanticism was on the right track in that it invited mankind to explore subjectivity. Where it erred was when it refused to give up the deity. Naturalism was an anomaly. It was too busy arguing with the cosmos to see that reality was in human desire not in providence. The degree to which mankind was to discover and to experience these desires determined the degree to which he participated in the divine. |

Enrichment Question

Most Americans obtain their world view from the television. The following advertisements represent a particular world view(s). What is(are) it (they)?

A.

B.

Picture A celebrates the innocence of youth. This is to invite the consumer to buy a particular product to create a "sunny meal." While there are some wholesome, perhaps Theistic implications to this advertisement, it also has a decidedly Romantic edge too. Notice the flowers. There is also evidence of Existentialism: the viewer cannot quite make out the faces of the children. They therefore have a universalist view and even appear a little surreal.

Picture B is clearly an Existentialist invitation. Its stoicism invites the reader to indulge nothing other than his appetite.

Picture C is a 19th century advertisement whose primary appeal is Theistic.

C.

The World's Great Timber Supply

From the great forests of the North and Northwest comes timber, which, converted into a diversity of forms, is used in all parts of the world. In this territory tributary to Chicago is one of the greatest of the world's timber supplies. Here every year are felled hundreds of thousands of towering trees to be transported by steam and river, lakes and railroads to the mills and factories of the manufacturing district centering in Chicago, where they are made into building materials, vehicles, implements, furniture and endless other products.

THE Continental & Commercial Banks for many years have assisted this great industry with dependable financial service. Today they are co-operating actively for its further development.

The CONTINENTAL and COMMERCIAL BANKS
CHICAGO

Invested capital more than 50 Million Dollars
Resources more than 500 Million Dollars

© Arttoday.com

33

Supplemental Reading:

Curtis Chang, *Engaging Unbelief: A Captivating Strategy from Augustine and Aquinas*
 Chang, InterVarsity Christian Fellowship chaplain at Tufts, M.I.T. and Harvard, urges the church to convert the post-Christian (1990 and beyond) world in the tradition of the theologians Augustine and Aquinas, whom he contends were missionary works-- Augustine to the pagan culture and Aquinas to the Islamic world. Both theologians were comfortable in the larger cultures of their audiences, able to draw non-Christian readers into the Gospel story by using their own familiar cultural authorities. Once they had engaged their audience, Augustine and Aquinas showed where their readers' cultures fell short, pointing to Christ as the answer. An must read for all students planning to attend secular universities.

John Jefferson Davis, *Evangelical Ethics*
 A comprehensive, readable overview of evangelical ethical positions concerning important issues such as abortion, euthanasia, and population control.

Os Guinness, *Fit Bodies, Fat Minds: Why Evangelicals Don't Think and What to Do about It*
 The title tells it all.

Os Guinness, *Long Journey Home: A Guide to Your Search for the Meaning of Life*
 The Christian scholar Os Guinness invites the student to articulate his own world view. Excellent!

Os Guinness, *Steering through Chaos: Vice and Virtue in an Age of Moral Confusion*
 One of the best anthologies of world view analysis on the market. Using anecdotes and case studies, Guinness challenges Evangelical Christians to take seriously their moral positions.

Mark A. Noll, *The Scandal of the Evangelical Mind.*
 Noll takes aim at lightweight Christians, stating that the scandal of the Evangelical mind is that they do not have a mind! In spite of this caustic comment, Noll makes some timely points.

Ronald L. Numbers, *The Creationists: The Evolution of Scientific Creationism*
 This reader appreciates Number's discussion of Creationism. Numbers believes in a literal flood and a relatively short life span for the earth (about 10,000 years). The rejection of Creationism teaching, Numbers believes, is at the heart of modernity and Post-Christian heresy.

David F. Wells, *God in the Wasteland: The reality of Truth in a World of Fading Dreams*
 Wells challenges the contemporary Evangelical community to examine honestly

its effect on the 21st century secular world. Wells is convinced that Modernity is now the Tempter seducing human pride to betray itself through a pawn-like participation in "an ironic recapitulation of the first dislocation in which God's creatures replaced their Creator and exiled Him from His own world."

Notes:

Lesson Two Test

Write responses to these statements according to each world view:
(80 points)

World View	Christian Theism	Romanticism/ Transcendentalism	Naturalism /Realism	Absurdism/ Existentialism
Jesus Christ is Lord.				
The world was created by God in six literal 24-hour days.				
If it feels good, do it.				
People would just be better off if society left them alone.				
Everyone will be saved as long as they are good people.				
I am not going to worry about the future; when my time is up, it is up.				
An animal is merely a person in animal garb.				
All I want to do is help people.				
God has a plan for us.				

Discussion Question: (20 Points)

Imagine that you have finished playing in a soccer game. You are walking across the field. Create conversations among players, parents, and spectators that exhibit at least four different world views.

Lesson Two Test Answers

Write responses to these statements according to each world view: (80 points)

Answers will vary.

World View	Christian Theism	Romanticism/ Transcendentalism	Naturalism/ Realism	Absurdism/ Existentialism
Jesus Christ is Lord.	Yes, He is.	Yes, and so are Buddha and the others.	He is not.	That statement has no meaning.
The world was created by God in six literal 24-hour days.	Absolutely!	I guess so–and didn't He do a great job. Nature is so beautiful!	No, that is religion. Science tells us that the world was created in a big bang.	Who cares?
If it feels good do it.	Whether it feels good or not, the wages of sin is death. Obedience to God and His Word is life.	Yes, and the more natural the feeling, the more spontaneous the response, the better.	Absolutely! Let it all hang out!	Yes and if it feels bad, do it too–who really cares what you do anyway? Leave me alone!
People would just be better off if society left them alone.	People will never be better off until they are in right relationship with God.	Surely that is true.	Yes, they may be better off for a while but sooner or later some rock will fall on their head or something bad will happen.	They will be better off if they stop pretending there is any reason to live.
Everyone will be saved as long as they are good people.	No, they will be saved only if they commit their lives to Jesus Christ.	Salvation occurs when people are in complete concert with nature.	There is no salvation; we all are doomed.	There is no future but nothingness.

I am not going to worry about the future; when my time is up, it is up.	If I don't worry about the future it is because my future is in the hands of the Lord.	Death is only a natural extension of life.	You got right! There is nothing we can do about the future except duck when it comes our way!	Our future is not even planned yet. It merely happens in a disorganized fashion.
An animal is merely a person in animal garb.	No, mankind is created in the image of God. Nothing else is.	No, that is not true. Although, I wish mankind acted more like animals–innocent and free.	Yes, makes sense to me.	Who really cares?
All I want to do is help people.	Nice idea; through God's love a person can help another person.	Nice idea.	Why?	What will you get out of it?
God has a plan for us.	Absolutely and everything works for good for those called by His name to His purposes.	Absolutely. He wants you to return to nature.	Absolutely. He means for you to be miserable.	If there was a God, and there really isn't, what makes you think He cares one iota about you?

Discussion Question: (20 Points)

Imagine that you have finished playing in a soccer game. You are walking across the field. Create conversations among players, parents, and spectators that exhibit at least four different world views.

"Good game!" I say to an opposing team member.
"Who really cares." He answers(Absurdism).
"God does–and He loves you!" I answer (Christian Theism).
"If there is a God, He must hate me," a bystander replies (Naturalism).
"How can He hate you? Just feel this grass, look at that sun!" another bystander retorts (Romanticism).

LESSON THREE

Readings Due For This Lesson
All readings are provided for the student. Before the lesson begins, students will read *Religious Affections: A Christian's Character Before God* (portions are provided in Lesson Three) and *Sinners in the Hands of An Angry God* (provided in Lesson Three).

Reading Ahead
Students should read poems by Anne Bradstreet (Lesson Four). All poems are provided in the text.

Suggested Weekly Implementation

Day One	Day Two	Day Three	Day Four	Day Five
1. Students will rewrite graded essays from last week and correct wrong answers from Lesson Two Test. 2. Students should have read the required reading(s) *before* the assigned lesson begins. 3. Teacher may want to discuss assigned reading(s) with student. 4. Teacher shall assign the required essays. Choose two or three. The rest of the essays can be outlined, answered with shorter answers, or skipped.	1. Student should begin reading(s) from next lesson. 2. Student should outline essays due at the end of the week. 3. Students should answer one or two of the essays that are not assigned as formal essays.	1. Students should write rough drafts of assigned essays. 2. The teacher should correct rough drafts.	Student will write final copy of essays due tomorrow.	1. Essays are due. 2. Students should take Lesson Three Test. 3. Over the weekend, student should finish readings due for the next lesson.

Puritanism. . .

Challenge Questions

A. Write a world view for yourself. In your composition, include your views on:

☞Authority--Is the Bible important to you? Do you obey God and other authority (your parents or guardians) even when doing so is uncomfortable?

☞Pleasure–What do you really enjoy doing? Does it please God?

☞Fate–What/who really determines your life? Chance? Circumstances? God?

☞Justice--What are the consequences of our actions? Is there some sort of judgement? Do bad people suffer? Why do good people suffer?

Answers will vary.

Biblical Application

You should answer biblical applications in essay form--usually about one-page--and should include biblical references.

A. Describe Edwards' religious affections and explain how they are evidences of true religion. *There are two kinds of true religion (p. 16): Love for Christ, Joy in Christ. Both grow out of suffering. Holy affections are evidence of a deeper piety and, to Edwards, personal piety is never so personal that it is not open to scrutiny by larger society. Edwards would be horrified with modern notions (i.e., Existentialism) that emphasizes privatism and the notion that "it is acceptable to do whatever pleases a person as long as it does not harm others."*

B. Read the following passage from Esther Edwards' diary entitled "...The Awful Sweetness of Walking With God." Esther, by the way, had a famous son, Aaron Burr (if you don't know who he was look him up!!!).

> *Though father is usually taciturn or preoccupied--my mother will call these large words--even when he takes one of us children with him, today he discoursed to me of the awful sweetness of walking with God in Nature. He seems to feel God in the woods, the sky, and the grand sweep of the river which winds so majestically through the woody silences here.*

Written in Northhampton, MA, 1741.

Compare and contrast the image we see of Jonathan Edwards through his sermon and the way Esther saw him. *Jonathan Edwards was a man of prayer and a very stern preacher. Ironically, he did not like people much–he much preferred to study the Word alone in his library. In fact, to many, he appeared cold. But to his family he was a warm, compassionate, vulnerable man--in an 18th century sort of way. He managed to be a great scholar, accomplished preacher, and devoted father and husband. Perhaps that is why he was so effective for God's kingdom. Unfortunately, those attributes were not valued by his congregation–who wished for Edwards to do more visitation–and Edwards was dismissed from his position.*

C. Describe your dad (or another parent or guardian) the same way Esther describes her dad. In what ways has the Lord used your father (or another adult) in your life? Compare your dad with King David, Joseph, or another dad in the Bible. *Answers will vary*

D. Jonathan Edwards gave his whole life to the Northhampton Church and was fired anyway. The following is his farewell sermon. Does he show any sign of bitterness?

I have just now said that I have had a peculiar concern for the young people, and in so saying I did not intend to exclude you. You are in youth, and in the most early youth. Therefore I have been sensible that if those that were young had a precious opportunity for their souls'' good, you who are very young had, in many respects, a peculiarly precious opportunity. And accordingly I have not neglected you. I have endeavored to do the part of a faithful shepherd, in feeding the lambs as well as the sheep. Christ did once commit the care of your souls to me as your minister; and you know, dear children, how I have instructed you, and warned you from time to time. You know how I have often called you together for that end, and some of you, sometimes, have seemed to be affected with what I have said to you. But I am afraid it has had no saving effect as to many of you, but that you remain still in an unconverted condition, without any real saving work wrought in your souls, convincing you thoroughly of your sin and misery, causing you to see the great evil of sin, and to mourn for it, and hate it above all things, and giving you a sense of the excellency of the Lord Jesus Christ, bringing you with all your hearts to cleave to him as your Savior, weaning your hearts from the world, and causing you to love God above all, and to delight in holiness more than in all the pleasant things of this earth. And I must now leave you in a miserable condition, having no interest in Christ, and so under the awful displeasure and anger of God, and in danger of going down to the pit of eternal misery. —— Now I must bid you farewell. I must leave you in the hands of God. I can do no more for you than to pray for you. Only I desire you not to forget, but often think of the counsels and warnings I have given you, and the endeavors I have used, that your souls might be saved from everlasting destruction.

Dear children, I leave you in an evil world, that is full of snares and temptations. God only knows what will become of you. This the Scripture has told us that there are but few saved, and we have abundant confirmation of it from what we see. This we see, that children die as well as others. Multitudes die before they grow up, and of those that grow up, comparatively few ever give good evidence of saving conversion to God. I pray God to pity you, and take care of you, and provide for you the best means for the good of your souls, and that God himself would undertake for you to be your heavenly Father, and the mighty Redeemer of your immortal souls. Do not neglect to pray for yourselves. Take heed you be not of the number of those who cast off fear, and restrain prayer before God. Constantly pray to God in secret, and often remember that great day when you must appear before the judgment seat of Christ, and meet your minister there, who has so often counseled and warned you.

Have you ever been disappointed? How did you keep from being bitter? Many Christian thinkers are calling brothers and sisters to forgiveness because forgiveness helps the person wronged more than the person who committed the wrong! Find Scriptural evidence that commands you to forgive those who have wronged you. *Edwards knew that he had to forgive others, or he himself would not be forgiven.*

For Enrichment
Read *Evangelical Ethics*, John Jefferson Davis, Ph.D., professor of ethics, Gordon Conwell Seminary, South Hamilton, MA. After reading Dr. Davis' book, state your position on these ethical issues: euthanasia, abortion, capital punishment, and others. *Dr. Davis feels that euthanasia and abortion are sinful. He is somewhat equivocal about capital punishment.*

Challenge Question
Summarize what Edwards says about the youth of his town in this passage from "A Faithful Narrative of the Surprising Work of God." Next, compare these youth to the youth in your church.

The people of the country, in general, I suppose, are as sober, orderly, and good sort of people, as in any part of New England; and I believe they have been preserved the freest by far of any part of the country, from error, and variety of sects and opinions. Our being so far within the land, at a distance from sea-ports, and in a corner of the country, has doubtless been one reason why we have not been so much corrupted with vice, as most other parts. But without question, the religion and good order of the county, and purity in doctrine, has, under God, been very much owing to the great abilities, and eminent piety of my venerable and honored grandfather Stoddard. I suppose we have been the freest of any part of the land from unhappy divisions and quarrels in our ecclesiastical and religious affairs, till the late lamentable Springfield contention. (The Springfield Contention relates to the settlement of a minister there, which occasioned too warm debates between some, both pastors and people, that were for it, and others that were against it, on account of their different apprehensions about his principles, and about some steps that were taken to procure his ordination.)

Being much separated from other parts of the province and having comparatively but little intercourse with them, we have always managed our ecclesiastical affairs within ourselves. It is the way in which the country, from its infancy, has gone on, by the practical agreement of all; and the way in which our peace and good order has hitherto been maintained.

The town of Northampton is of about 82 years standing, and has now about 200 families; which mostly dwell more compactly together than any town of such a size in these parts of the country. This probably has been an occasion, that both our corruptions and reformations have been, from time to time, the more swiftly propagated from one to another through the town. Take the town in general, and so far as I can judge, they are as rational and intelligent a people as most I have been acquainted with. Many of them have been noted for religion; and particularly remarkable for their distinct knowledge in things that relate to heart religion, and Christian experience, and their great regards thereto.

I am the third minister who has been settled in the town. The Rev. Mr. Eleazer Mather, who was the first, was ordained in July, 1669. He was one whose heart was much in his work, and abundant in labors for the good of precious souls. He had the high esteem and great love for his people, and was blessed with no small success. The Rev. Mr. Stoddard who succeeded him, came first to the town the November after his death; but was not ordained till September 11, 1672, and died February 11, 1728-9. So that he continued in the work of the ministry here, from his first coming to town, near 60 years. And as he was eminent and renowned for his gifts and grace; so he was blessed, from the beginning, with extraordinary success in his ministry, in the conversion of many souls. He had five harvests, as he called them. The first was about 57 years ago; the second about 53; the third about 40; the fourth about 24; the fifth and last about 18 years ago. Some of these times were much more remarkable than others, and the ingathering of souls more plentiful. Those about 53, and 40, and 24 years ago, were much greater than either the first or the last: but in each of them, I have heard my grandfather say, the greater part of the young people in the town, seemed to be mainly concerned for their eternal salvation.

After the last of these, came a far more degenerate time (at least among the young people), I suppose, than ever before. Mr. Stoddard, indeed, had the comfort, before he died, of seeing a time where there were no small appearances of a divine work among some, and a considerable ingathering of souls, even after I was settled with him in the ministry, which was about two years before his death; and I have reason to bless God for the great advantage I had by it. In these two years there were nearly twenty that Mr. Stoddard hoped to be savingly converted; but there was nothing of any general awakening. The greater part seemed to be at that time very insensible of the things of religion, and engaged in other cares and pursuits. Just after my grandfather's death, it seemed to be a time of extraordinary dullness in religion. Licentiousness for some years prevailed among the youth of the town; there were many of them very much addicted to night-walking, and frequenting the tavern, and lewd practices, wherein some, by their example, exceedingly corrupted others. It was their manner very frequently to get together, in conventions of both sexes for mirth and jollity, which they called frolics; and they would often spend the greater part of the night in them, without regard to any order in the families they belonged to: and indeed family government did too much fail in the town. It was become very customary with many of our young people to be indecent in their carriage at meeting, which doubtless would not have prevailed in such a degree, had it not been that my grandfather, through his great age (though he retained his powers surprisingly to the last), was not so able to observe them. There had also long prevailed in the town a spirit of contention between two parties, into which they had for many years been divided; by which they maintained a jealousy one of the other, and were prepared to oppose one another in all public affairs.

But in two or three years after Mr. Stoddard's death, there began to be a sensible amendment to these evils. The young people showed more of a disposition to hearken to counsel, and by degrees left off their frolics; they grew observably more decent in their attendance on the public worship, and there were more who manifested a religious concern than there used to be.

Answer: *Edwards was experienced problem with his youth. They were not showing the degree of commitment that he wished to see.*

Answer: *Edwards exhibited the magnanimity that would expect to see in a great man.*

Supplemental Reading:

John Jefferson Davis, *The Victorious Kingdom of Christ*.
    Post-millenialism offers a theological rubric that is important for serious Christian apologetics, in particular Christian missions. Optimism based on the Word of God--not on 17th century Enlightenment--is sorely needed in the Christian community as well as American society at large.

Marva J. Dawn (a pseudonym), *Reaching Out Without Dumbing Down: A Theology of Worship for the Turn-of-the-Century Culture*

Dr. Dawn uses the expression "dumbing down" to describe the status of most contemporary worship services--informal and formal, low and high, charismatic and traditional. Dawn draws many of her views about dumbing down from Jane Healey's book *Endangered Minds* (p. 6). It argues persuasively that many cultural forces are at work to sabotage people's abilities to think (p. 7).

George Marsden, *The Soul of the University*

Marsden traces the regrettable loss of influence that the Evangelical community once had on American Universities.

Alistair McGrath, *Evangelicalism and the Future of Christianity*

The idea of an established church situated in a friendly society is over. We need to rethink our evangelism strategies in that light. This reader likes the way McGrath calls us back to the 1st Century and Jonathan Edwards--in the same book!

Ian Murray, *Jonathan Edwards: A New Biography*

A wonderful historic narrative of the life of Jonathan Edwards.

Mark A. Noll, *America's God: From Jonathan Edwards to Abraham Lincoln*

A powerful, but readable story of how American' views of God and the worlds have changed over our the last 350 years.

Jaroslav Pelikan, *The Idea of the University*

Pelikan insists that intelligent discussion of the university requires an analysis of its most basic nature and a discussion of the role it can and should play among other institutions and communities within the local, national, and international community.

Notes:

Lesson Three Test

Discussion Question: (100 Points)

A. Define "religious affection" and discuss the religious affection Edwards highlights in this passage from *Religious Affections*:

Gracious affections are attended with evangelical humiliation. Evangelical humiliation is a sense that a Christian has of his own utter insufficiency, despicableness, and odiousnesss, with an answerable frame of heart.

There is a distinction to be made between a legal and evangelical humiliation. The former is what men may be the subjects of, while they are yet in a state of nature, and have no gracious affections; the latter is peculiar to true saints: the former is from the common influence of the Spirit of God, assisting natural principles, and especially natural conscience; the latter is from the special influences of the Spirit of God, implanting and exercising supernatural and divine principles: the former is from the mind's being assisted to a greater sense of the things of religion, as to their natural properties and qualities, and particularly of the natural perfections of God, such as his greatness, terrible majesty, , which were manifested to the congregation of Israel, in giving the law at mount Sinai; the latter is from a sense of the transcendent beauty of divine things in their moral qualities: in the former, a sense of the awful greatness, and natural perfections of God, and of the strictness of his law, convinces men that they are exceeding sinful, and guilty, and exposed to the wrath of God, as it will wicked men and devils at the day of judgment; but they do not see their own odiousness on the account of sin; they do not see the hateful nature of sin; a sense of this is given in evangelical humiliation, by a discovery of the beauty of God's holiness and moral perfection. In a legal humiliation, men are made sensible that they are little and nothing before the great and terrible God, and that they are undone, and wholly insufficient to help themselves; as wicked men will be at the day of judgment: but they have not an answerable frame of heart, consisting in a disposition to abase themselves, and exalt God alone; this disposition is given only in evangelical humiliation, by overcoming the heart, and changing its inclination, by a discovery of God's holy beauty: in a legal humiliation, the conscience is convinced; as the consciences of all will be most perfectly at the day of judgment; but because there is no spiritual understanding, the will is not bowed, nor the inclination altered: this is done only in evangelical humiliation. In legal humiliation, men are brought to despair of helping themselves; in evangelical, they are brought voluntarily to deny and renounce themselves: in the former, they are subdued and forced to the ground; in the latter, they are brought sweetly to yield, and freely and with delight to prostrate themselves at the feet of God. Legal humiliation has in it no spiritual good, nothing of the nature of true virtue; whereas evangelical humiliation is that wherein the excellent beauty of Christian grace does very much consist. Legal humiliation is useful, as a means in order to evangelical; as a common knowledge of the things of religion is a means requisite in order to spiritual knowledge. Men may be legally humbled and have no humility: as the wicked at the day of judgment will be thoroughly convinced that they have no righteousness, but are altogether sinful, and exceedingly guilty, and justly exposed to eternal damnation, and be fully sensible of their own helplessness, without the least mortification of the pride of their hearts: but the essence of evangelical humiliation consists in such humility, as becomes a creature, in itself exceeding sinful, under a dispensation of grace; consisting in a mean esteem of himself, as in himself nothing, and altogether contemptible and odious; attended with a mortification of a disposition to exalt himself, and a free renunciation of his own glory.

This is a great and most essential thing in true religion. The whole frame of the gospel, and everything appertaining to the new covenant, and all God's dispensations towards fallen man, are calculated to bring to pass this effect in the hearts of men. They that are destitute of this, have no true religion, whatever profession they may make, and how high soever their religious affections may be: Hab. 2:4, "Behold, his soul which is lifted up, is not upright in him; but the just shall live by his faith;" i.e., he shall live by his faith on God's righteousness and grace, and not his own goodness and excellency. God has abundantly manifested in his word, that this is what he has a peculiar respect to in his saints, and that nothing is acceptable to him without it. Psalm 34:18, "The Lord is nigh unto them that are of a broken heart, and saveth such as be of a contrite spirit." Psalm 51:17, "The sacrifices of God are a broken spirit: a broken and a contrite heart, O God, thou wilt not despise." Psalm 138:6, "Though the Lord be high, yet hath he respect unto the lowly." Prov. 3:34, "He giveth grace unto the lowly." Isa. 57:15, "Thus saith the high and lofty One who inhabiteth eternity, whose name is holy, I dwell in the high and holy place; with him also that is of a contrite and humble spirit, to revive the spirit of the humble, and to revive the heart of the contrite ones." Isa. 66:1, 2, "Thus saith the Lord, the heaven is my throne, and the earth is my footstool: but to this man will I look, even to him that is poor, and of a contrite spirit, and trembleth at my word." Micah 6:8, "He hath showed thee, O man, what is good; and what doth the Lord thy God require of thee; but to do justly, and to love mercy, and to walk humbly with thy God?" Matt. 5:3, "Blessed are the poor in spirit; for theirs is the kingdom of God." Matt. 18:3, 4, "Verily I say unto you, except ye be converted, and become as little children, ye shall not enter into the kingdom of heaven. Whosoever therefore shall humble himself as this little child, the same is greatest in the kingdom of heaven." Mark 10:15, "Verily I say unto you, Whosoever shall not receive the kingdom of God as a little child, he shall not enter therein." The centurion, that we have an account of, Luke 7, acknowledged that he was not worthy that Christ should enter under his roof, and that he was not worthy to come to him. See the manner of the woman's coming to Christ, that was a sinner, Luke 7:37, : "And behold, a woman in the city, which was a sinner, when she knew that Jesus sat at meat in the Pharisee's house, brought an alabaster box of ointment, and stood at his feet behind him weeping, and began to wash his feet with tears, and did wipe them with the hairs of her head." She did not think the hair of her head, which is the natural crown and glory of a woman (1 Cor. 11:15), too good to wipe the feet of Christ withal. Jesus most graciously accepted her, and says to her, "thy faith hath saved thee, go in peace." The woman of Canaan submitted to Christ, in his saying, "it is not meet to take the children's bread and cast it to dogs," and did as it were own that she was worthy to be called a dog; whereupon Christ says unto her, "O woman, great is thy faith; be it unto thee, even as thou wilt," Matt. 15:26, 27, 28. The prodigal son said, "I will arise and go to my father, and I will say unto him, Father, I have sinned against heaven and before thee, and am no more worthy to be called thy son: make me as one of thy hired servants," Luke 15:18. See also Luke 18:9: "And he spake this parable unto certain which trusted in themselves that they were righteous, and despised others, The publican, standing afar off, would not so much as lift up his eyes to heaven, but smote upon his breast, saying, God be merciful to me a sinner. I tell you, this man went down to his house justified rather than the other: for everyone that exalteth himself, shall be abased; and he that humbleth himself, shall be exalted." Matt. 28:9, "And they came, and held him by the feet and worshipped him." Col. 3:12, "Put ye on, as the elect of God, humbleness of mind." Ezek. 20:41, 42, "I will accept you with your sweet savor, when I bring you out from the people, And there shall ye remember your ways, and all your doings, wherein ye have been defiled, and ye shall loathe yourselves in your own sight, for all your evils that ye have committed." Chap. 36:26, 27, 31, "A new heart also will I give unto you-and I will put my Spirit within you, and cause you to walk in my statutes, Then shall ye remember your own evil ways, and your doings that were not good, and shall loathe yourselves in your own sight, for your iniquities, and for your abominations." Chap. 16:63, "That thou mayest remember and be confounded, and never open thy mouth any more because of thy shame, when I am pacified toward thee for all that thou hast done, saith the Lord." Job 42:6, "I abhor myself, and repent in dust and ashes."

As we would therefore make the holy Scriptures our rule in judging of the nature of true religion, and judging of our own religious qualifications and state; it concerns us greatly to look at this humiliation, as one of the most essential things pertaining to true Christianity. This is the principal part of the great Christian duty of self-denial. That duty consists in two things, viz., first, in a man's denying his worldly inclinations, and in forsaking and renouncing all worldly objects and enjoyments; and, secondly, in denying his natural self-exaltation, and renouncing his own dignity and glory and in being emptied of himself; so that he does freely and from his very heart, as it were renounce himself, and annihilate himself. Thus the Christian doth in evangelical humiliation. And this latter is the greatest and most difficult part of self-denial: although they always go together, and one never truly is, where the other is not; yet natural men can come much nearer to the former than the latter. Many Anchorites and Recluses have abandoned (though without any true mortification) the wealth, and pleasures, and common enjoyments of the world, who were far from renouncing their own dignity and righteousness; they never denied themselves for Christ, but only sold one lust to feed another, sold a beastly lust to pamper a devilish one; and so were never the better, but their latter end was worse than their beginning; they turned out one black devil, to let in seven white ones, that were worse than the first, though of a fairer countenance. It is inexpressible, and almost inconceivable, how strong a self-righteous, self-exalting disposition is naturally in man; and what he will not do and suffer to feed and gratify it: and what lengths have been gone in a seeming self-denial in other respects, by Essenes and Pharisees among the Jews, and by Papists, many sects of heretics, and enthusiasts, among professing Christians; and by many Mahometans; and by Pythagorean philosophers, and others among the Heathen; and all to do sacrifice to this Moloch of spiritual pride or self-righteousness; and that they may have something wherein to exalt themselves before God, and above their fellow creatures.

B. Outline a sermon that Edwards might preach. Include his favorite text, a title, and three points he would make.

Lesson Three Test Answers

Discussion Question: (100 Points)

A. Define "religious affection" and discuss the religious affection Edwards highlights in this passage from *Religious Affections*:

> *Gracious affections are attended with evangelical humiliation. Evangelical humiliation is a sense that a Christian has of his own utter insufficiency, despicableness, and odiousness, with an answerable frame of heart.*
> *There is a distinction to be made between a legal and evangelical humiliation. The former is what men may be the subjects of, while they are yet in a state of nature, and have no gracious affections; the latter is peculiar to true saints: the former is from the common influence of the Spirit of God, assisting natural principles, and especially natural conscience; the latter is from the special influences of the Spirit of God, implanting and exercising supernatural and divine principles: the former is from the mind's being assisted to a greater sense of the things of religion, as to their natural properties and qualities, and particularly of the natural perfections of God, such as his greatness, terrible majesty. . . men are made sensible that they are little and nothing before the great and terrible God, and that they are undone, and wholly insufficient to help themselves; as wicked men will be at the day of judgment: but they have not an answerable frame of heart, consisting in a disposition to abase themselves, and exalt God alone; this disposition is given only in evangelical humiliation, by overcoming the heart, and changing its inclination, by a discovery of God's holy beauty: in a legal humiliation, the conscience is convinced; as the consciences of all will be most perfectly at the day of judgment; but because there is no spiritual understanding, the will is not bowed, nor the inclination altered: this is done only in evangelical humiliation. In legal humiliation, men are brought to despair of helping themselves; in evangelical, they are brought voluntarily to deny and renounce themselves: in the former, they are subdued and forced to the ground; in the latter, they are brought sweetly to yield, and freely and with delight to prostrate themselves at the feet of God. Legal humiliation has in it no spiritual good, nothing of the*

Sidenotes:

- The religious affection Edwards described is humility.

- "True religion" is to be like Christ. To be humble like Christ.

- To Edwards the distinction between the natural mind and the evangelical or redeemed mind is great. He was not ready, however, to denigrate the natural mind.

51

nature of true virtue; whereas evangelical humiliation is that wherein the excellent beauty of Christian grace does very much consist. Legal humiliation is useful, as a means in order to evangelical; as a common knowledge of the things of religion is a means requisite in order to spiritual knowledge. Men may be legally humbled and have no humility: as the wicked at the day of judgment will be thoroughly convinced that they have no righteousness...

B. Outline a sermon that Edwards might preach. Include his favorite text, a title, and three points he would make.

I. Romans 8

II. More Than Conquerors

III. We are predestined ... but we need to respond in faith to God's grace.

LESSON FOUR

Readings Due For This Lesson
Before this lesson begins, students should have read poems by Anne Bradstreet. All poems are provided in the text.

Reading Ahead
Read background material on Phillis Wheatley and slavery and Phillis Wheatley, "On Being Brought to America From Africa" and "To His Excellency General Washington."

Suggested Weekly Implementation

Day One	Day Two	Day Three	Day Four	Day Five
1. Students will rewrite graded essays from last week and review Lesson Three test. 2. Students should have read the required reading(s) *before* the assigned lesson begins. 3. Teacher may want to discuss assigned reading(s) with student. 4. Teacher shall assign the required essays. Choose two or three. The rest of the essays can be outlined, answered with shorter answers, or skipped.	1. Student should begin reading(s) from next lesson. 2. Student should outline essays due at the end of the week. 3. Students should answer one or two of the essays that are not assigned as formal essays.	1. Students should write rough drafts of assigned essays. 2. The teacher should correct rough drafts.	Student will write final copy of essays due tomorrow.	1. Essays are due. 2. Students should take Lesson Four test. 3. Student should finish readings due for Lesson Five.

Puritanism...

Critical Thinking Question

Which poem is more hopeful?

Bradstreet's.

Why?

Bradstreet invites us to believe in a loving God. McCartney is full of hopelessness. The Beatles exhibited the self-serving, subjectivity of the 1960s. On the surface, however, they appeared harmless. And, in light of what follows (e.g., heavy metal bands) they appear mild indeed. But to their age, they were certainly radical. They also were the first of their genre. Ah, look at all the lonely people..." Many people would recognize this line as the beginning of the song "Eleanor Rigby" written by the Beatles. It continues, "Eleanor Rigby picks up the rice in the church where a wedding has been, lives in a dream, waits at the window wearing the face that she keeps in a jar by the door. Who is it for?" Then comes the chorus, a continual, unanswered question: "All the lonely people, where do they all come from? All the lonely people, where do they all belong?"

This song stands in stark contrast to the poem, "Upon the Burning of Our House", by Anne Bradstreet, a seventeenth century poet. She tells the story of waking in the middle of the night to find her house on fire and her earthly goods possessions destroyed. However, what is striking in her poem is not the story of the fire but the calmness, peace, and even joy with which she was enabled by her God to face the calamity.

> *"And when I could no longer look,*
> *I blest His name that gave and took,*
> *That laid my good now in the dust:*
> *Yea so it was, and so 'twas just.*
> *It was His own: it was not mine;*
> *Far be it that I should repine." V. 3*

Bradstreet's poem is more hopeful than "Eleanor Rigby" because, though she lost her home and precious possessions to fire, she knew that as a Christian she had "an house on high erect" which "stands permanent tho' this be fled". When her home was gone, it only reminded her that she had a home above that was unshakeable. Though her possessions were destroyed, she did not complain, but said, "The world no longer let me love, my hope and treasure lies above." She had her hope in God even in earthly despair. Not even the worst earthly tragedy could extinguish her hope in God. She had stability and steadfast joy in the

In contrast, Eleanor Rigby and Father McKenzie are completely trapped and controlled by their circumstances, and have no hope beyond the illusive dream of love, friendship, purpose, and happiness in this life. When Eleanor's fruitless life ends without the fulfillment of her dream of love, there is no further hope; she is "buried along with her name" and sinks into oblivion. Father McKenzie works hard, but for no purpose – "no one sees" and "no one is saved". The general tone is that of the hopelessness and despair of the "lonely people", coupled with the unending question, "Where do they come from - Where do they belong?" There is no place or purpose for them, and therefore no hope of joy and fulfillment.

    The difference between these two works is vast and clearly apparent: Bradstreet's poem is hopeful, even joyful, while the song by the Beatles is hopeless to the point of despair (Susanna).

Pretend that McCartney and Bradstreet meet. What would they say to each other? *I imagine Bradstreet would try to lead McCartney to a saving relationship to Jesus Christ.*

Compare Eleanor Rigby to the woman caught in adultery (John 8:2-11). *Poor Eleanor needed Christ not the empty cultic worship she found in this dreary poem. Rigby is captured in the hopelessness web of Naturalism (i.e., Nihilism and an impersonal god) and Existentialism (i.e., experience).*

For Enrichment

Modern Americans accuse the Puritans of being colorless and legalistic. Typically, to be "Puritan" means "to hide one's feelings." Yet, to read Anne Bradstreet, one is struck by the power of Puritan emotion! She never hesitated to share her heart with her reader.

To My Dear And Loving Husband

If ever two were one, then surely we.
If ever man were lov'd by wife, then thee.
If ever wife was happy in a man,
Compare with me, ye women, if you can.
I prize thy love more than whole Mines of gold
Or all the riches that the East doth hold.
My love is such that Rivers cannot quench,
Nor ought but love from thee give recompetence.
Thy love is such I can no way repay.
The heavens reward thee manifold, I pray.
Then while we live, in love let's so persever
That when we live no more, we may live ever.

Explore the genesis of the notion that Puritans were emotionless, colorless people.

Which historian/writer first advanced that idea? *During the middle of the 19th century several historians (e.g., Beard) advanced the notion that Puritans were unhappy, bigoted people. This particular viewpoint appealed a great deal to liberal, Romantic 19th century historians. The Harvard historians (e.g., Perry Miller, Douglas Edward Leech, Samuel Morison) reclaimed the Puritans as our spiritual ancestors.*

Supplemental Reading:

Anne Bradstreet, *The Works of Anne Bradstreet* (The John Harvard Library)
    The most complete edition of Anne Bradstreet's work. Annotated, these poems are imminently readable.

Anne Bradstreet, *To My Husband and Other Poems* (Dover Thrift Editions)
    A more affordable but equally fine edition of Bradstreet's poems.

David Freeman Hawke, *Everyday Life in Early America*
    Hawke uses anecdotes to tell the true story of early American life. This book is very readable.

Gary Nash, *Red, White, and Black: The Peoples of Early North America*
    Nash is a fine historian and his work reflects it. A book for the mature reader, *Red, White, and Black* describes the interactions of three cultures in early America.

Notes:

Lesson Four Test

Literary Analysis: (100 Points)

Paraphrase this poem. (30 Points)

What is its rhyme scheme in lines 1-20? (10 Points)

Identify four examples of figurative language. (30 Points)

To what animal(s) does she compare her children? (10 Points)

Explain what lines 75-77 mean. (10 Points)

What did Anne try to do for her children (lines 88-90)? (10 Points)

In Reference to Her Children, 23 June 1659
Anne Bradstreet

I had eight birds hatcht in one nest,
2 Four Cocks were there, and Hens the rest.
3 I nurst them up with pain and care,
4 No cost nor labour did I spare
5 Till at the last they felt their wing,
6 Mounted the Trees and learned to sing.
7 Chief of the Brood then took his flight
8 To Regions far and left me quite.
9 My mournful chirps I after send
10 Till he return, or I do end.
11 Leave not thy nest, thy Dame and Sire,
12 Fly back and sing amidst this Quire.
13 My second bird did take her flight
14 And with her mate flew out of sight.
15 *Southward* they both their course did bend,
16 And Seasons twain they there did spend,
17 Till after blown by *Southern* gales
18 They *Norward* steer'd with filled sails.
19 A prettier bird was no where seen,
20 Along the Beach, among the treen.
21 I have a third of colour white
22 On whom I plac'd no small delight,

57

23 Coupled with mate loving and true,
24 Hath also bid her Dame adieu.
25 And where *Aurora* first appears,
26 She now hath percht to spend her years.
27 One to the Academy flew
28 To chat among that learned crew.
29 Ambition moves still in his breast
30 That he might chant above the rest,
31 Striving for more than to do well,
32 That nightingales he might excell.
33 My fifth, whose down is yet scarce gone,
34 Is 'mongst the shrubs and bushes flown
35 And as his wings increase in strength
36 On higher boughs he'll perch at length.
37 My other three still with me nest
38 Until they're grown, then as the rest,
39 Or here or there, they'll take their flight,
40 As is ordain'd, so shall they light.
41 If birds could weep, then would my tears
42 Let others know what are my fears
43 Lest this my brood some harm should catch
44 And be surpris'd for want of watch
45 Whilst pecking corn and void of care
46 They fall un'wares in Fowler's snare;
47 Or whilst on trees they sit and sing
48 Some untoward boy at them do fling,
49 Or whilst allur'd with bell and glass
50 The net be spread and caught, alas;
51 Or lest by Lime-twigs they be foil'd;
52 Or by some greedy hawks be spoil'd.
53 O would, my young, ye saw my breast
54 And knew what thoughts there sadly rest.
55 Great was my pain when I you bred,
56 Great was my care when I you fed.
57 Long did I keep you soft and warm
58 And with my wings kept off all harm.
59 My cares are more, and fears, than ever,
60 My throbs such now as 'fore were never.
61 Alas, my birds, you wisdom want
62 Of perils you are ignorant.
63 Oft times in grass, on trees, in flight,
64 Sore accidents on you may light.
65 O to your safety have an eye,
66 So happy may you live and die.

67 Mean while, my days in tunes I'll spend
68 Till my weak lays with me shall end.
69 In shady woods I'll sit and sing
70 And things that past, to mind I'll bring.
71 Once young and pleasant, as are you,
72 But former toys (no joys) adieu!
73 My age I will not once lament
74 But sing, my time so near is spent,
75 And from the top bough take my flight
76 Into a country beyond sight
77 Where old ones instantly grow young
78 And there with seraphims set song.
79 No seasons cold, nor storms they see
80 But spring lasts to eternity.
81 When each of you shall in your nest
82 Among your young ones take your rest,
83 In chirping languages oft them tell
84 You had a Dame that lov'd you well,
85 That did what could be done for young
86 And nurst you up till you were strong
87 And 'fore she once would let you fly
88 She shew'd you joy and misery,
89 Taught what was good, and what was ill,
90 What would save life, and what would kill.
91 Thus gone, amongst you I may live,
92 And dead, yet speak and counsel give.
93 Farewell, my birds, farewell, adieu,
94 I happy am, if well with you.

Lesson Four Test Answers

Literary Analysis: (100 Points)

Paraphrase this poem. (30 Points)
Bradstreet takes each child and describes him/her as a type of bird. As she describes the life cycle of each bird, she is describing each child. She ends the poem by celebrating her future–which will be the satisfaction of rearing her children properly and then soaring to heaven!

What is its rhyme scheme in lines 1-20? (10 Points)
See below. It is aa, bb, cc, dd, and so on.

Identify four examples of figurative language. (30 Points)
See below.

To what animal(s) does she compare her children? (10 Points)
Birds.

Explain what lines 75-77 mean. (10 Points)
75 And from the top bough take my flight
76 Into a country beyond sight
77 Where old ones instantly grow young

Answer: Someday the mother will be going to heaven.

What did Anne try to do for her children (lines 88-90)? (10 Points)
88 She shew'd you joy and misery,
89 Taught what was good, and what was ill,
90 What would save life, and what would kill.

Answer: To prepare them for all of life–good and bad.

In Reference to Her Children, 23 June 1659
Anne Bradstreet

I had eight birds hatcht in one nest, a
2 Four Cocks were there, and Hens the rest. a
3 I nurst them up with pain and care, b
4 No cost nor labour did I spare b
5 Till at the last they felt their wing, c
6 Mounted the Trees and learned to sing. c
7 Chief of the Brood then took his flight d
8 To Regions far and left me quite. d
9 My mournful chirps I after send e

She uses the metaphor of a bird to describe her children.

10 Till he return, or I do end. e
11 Leave not thy nest, thy Dame and Sire, f
12 Fly back and sing amidst this Quire. f
13 My second bird did take her flight d
14 And with her mate flew out of sight. d
15 *Southward* they both their course did bend, e
16 And Seasons twain they there did spend, e
17 Till after blown by *Southern* gales g
18 They *Norward* steer'd with filled sails. g
19 A prettier bird was no where seen, h
20 Along the Beach, among the treen. h
21 I have a third of colour white
22 On whom I plac'd no small delight,
23 Coupled with mate loving and true,
24 Hath also bid her Dame adieu.
25 And where *Aurora* first appears,
26 She now hath percht to spend her years.
27 One to the Academy flew
28 To chat among that learned crew.
29 Ambition moves still in his breast
30 That he might chant above the rest,
31 Striving for more than to do well,
32 That nightingales he might excell.
33 My fifth, whose down is yet scarce gone,
34 Is 'mongst the shrubs and bushes flown
35 And as his wings increase in strength
36 On higher boughs he'll perch at length.
37 My other three still with me nest
38 Until they're grown, then as the rest,
39 Or here or there, they'll take their flight,
40 As is ordain'd, so shall they light.
41 If birds could weep, then would my tears
42 Let others know what are my fears
43 Lest this my brood some harm should catch
44 And be surpris'd for want of watch
45 Whilst pecking corn and void of care
46 They fall un'wares in Fowler's snare;
47 Or whilst on trees they sit and sing
48 Some untoward boy at them do fling,
49 Or whilst allur'd with bell and glass
50 The net be spread and caught, alas;
51 Or lest by Lime-twigs they be foil'd;
52 Or by some greedy hawks be spoil'd.
53 O would, my young, ye saw my breast

---

29 Ambition moves still in his breast
30 That he might chant above the rest,

This is personification (a type of metaphor)

---

17 Till after blown by *Southern* gales g
18 They *Norward* steer'd with filled sails.

Seasons are compared to sailing ships.

54 And knew what thoughts there sadly rest.
55 Great was my pain when I you bred,
56 Great was my care when I you fed.
57 Long did I keep you soft and warm
58 And with my wings kept off all harm.
59 My cares are more, and fears, than ever,
60 My throbs such now as 'fore were never.
61 Alas, my birds, you wisdom want
62 Of perils you are ignorant.
63 Oft times in grass, on trees, in flight,
64 Sore accidents on you may light.
65 O to your safety have an eye,
66 So happy may you live and die.
67 Mean while, my days in tunes I'll spend
68 Till my weak lays with me shall end.
69 In shady woods I'll sit and sing
70 And things that past, to mind I'll bring.
71 Once young and pleasant, as are you,
72 But former toys (no joys) adieu!
73 My age I will not once lament
74 But sing, my time so near is spent,
75 And from the top bough take my flight
76 Into a country beyond sight
77 Where old ones instantly grow young
78 And there with seraphims set song.
79 No seasons cold, nor storms they see
80 But spring lasts to eternity.
81 When each of you shall in your nest
82 Among your young ones take your rest,
83 In chirping languages oft them tell
84 You had a Dame that lov'd you well,
85 That did what could be done for young
86 And nurst you up till you were strong
87 And 'fore she once would let you fly
88 She shew'd you joy and misery,
89 Taught what was good, and what was ill,
90 What would save life, and what would kill.
91 Thus gone, amongst you I may live,
92 And dead, yet speak and counsel give.
93 Farewell, my birds, farewell, adieu,
94 I happy am, if well with you.

LESSON FIVE

Readings Due For This Lesson

Before this lesson begins, students should have read poems by Phillis Wheatley and the background narrative material on slavery. All poems and readings are provided in the text.

Reading Ahead

Read all narrative background and selections from 19th century poetry (Lesson Six). All poems are provided in the text. Students should also start reading Nathaniel Hawthorne's, *The Scarlet Letter* (Lesson Seven).

Suggested Weekly Implementation

Day One	Day Two	Day Three	Day Four	Day Five
1. Students will rewrite graded essays from last week and review Lesson Four test. 2. Students should have read the required reading(s) *before* the assigned lesson begins. 3. Teacher may want to discuss assigned reading(s) with student. 4. Teacher shall assign the required essays. Choose two or three. The rest of the essays can be outlined, answered with shorter answers, or skipped.	1. Student should begin reading(s) from next lesson. 2. Student should outline essays due at the end of the week. 3. Students should answer one or two of the essays that are not assigned as formal essays.	1. Students should write rough drafts of assigned essays. 2. The teacher should correct rough drafts.	Student will write final copy of essays due tomorrow.	1. Essays are due. 2. Students should take Lesson Five test. 3. Student should finish readings due for Lesson Six and continue to read Nathaniel Hawthorne, *The Scarlet Letter*.

Puritanism . . .

Challenge Question

A. Read the following two poems written by Phillis Wheatley. Historians have marveled at the fact that Phillis Wheatley, brought from Africa at the age of eight and enslaved nearly all her life, was able to acquire literary and scholastic acumen. Her avocation was certainly not typical of most colonial women of any race! Explore your own history texts and materials from your home and public libraries for accounts of the status of slaves and that of women in colonial America. Write a descriptive two-page essay about colonial women--both white and black, colonist and Indian or slave.... *Answers will vary. Colonial women had no spare time. They often died before they were thirty, and usually in child birth. They had no actual rights outside of their fathers and husbands. Yet, Bradstreet and Wheatley inspire us all!*

B. Read the two poems below. Some critics--especially of African-American descent-- have been critical of Phillis Wheatley. While they respect her achievements and writing ability, they wish that she would have used her talents to lead a slave revolt or to perform a Harriet Tubman-like role, at least not to extol the whites. She seemed too willing to accept her station in life. Do you agree? State your position and defend it in a one-page persuasive essay. *Because of her positive attitude in the face of her negative circumstances, Phillis Wheatley refused to give in to the anger, hatred, and unforgivingness which she would have been justified in feeling. She is to be commended and honored for her Christian witness. Phillis Wheatley was the first African-American writer of consequence in America and her life was an inspiring example to generations of Americans of all races. Abolitionists recognized this fact and reprinted her poetry. The powerful ideas contained in her deeply moving verse stood indirectly against the institution of slavery. Why would abolitionists publish an author's poetry if that author was not opposed to slavery? Clearly, Wheatley, opposed slavery, but saw in a place of adversity God's sovereignty in her life. She is to be applauded and immitated–not castigated–for such faith!*

On Being Brought to America From Africa

'TWAS mercy brought me from my Pagan land,
Taught my benighted soul to understand
That there's a God, that there's a Saviour too:
Once I redemption neither fought nor knew,
Some view our sable race with scornful eye,
"Their colour is a diabolic dye."
Remember, Christians, Negroes, black as Cain,
              May be refin'd, and join th' angelic train.

To His Excellency General Washington

Sir,
I Have taken the freedom to address your Excellency in the enclosed poem, and entreat your acceptance, though I am not insensible of its inaccuracies. Your being appointed by the Grand Continental Congress to be Generalissimo of the armies of North America, together with the fame of your virtues, excite sensations not easy to suppress. Your generosity, therefore, I presume, will pardon the attempt. Wishing your Excellency all possible success in the great cause you are so generously engaged in. I am, Your Excellency's most obedient humble servant,
Phillis Wheatley.

    Celestial choir! enthron'd in realms of light,
    Columbia's scenes of glorious toils I write.
While freedom's cause her anxious breast alarms,
    She flashes dreadful in refulgent arms.
    See mother earth her offspring's fate bemoan,
    And nations gaze at scenes before unknown!
See the bright beams of heaven's revolving light
    Involved in sorrows and the veil of night!
    The goddess comes, she moves divinely fair,
    Olive and laurel binds her golden hair;
    Wherever shines the native of the skies,
    Unnumber'd charms and recent graces rise.
    Muse! bow propitious while my pen relates
How pour her armies through a thousand gates,
    As when Eolus heaven's fair face deforms,
    Enwrapp'd in tempest and a night of storms;
    Astonish'd ocean feels the wild uproar,
    The refluent surges beat the sounding shore;
    Or thick as leaves in Autumn's golden reign,
Such, as so many, moves the warriors's train.
    In bright array they seek the work of war,
    Where high unfurl'd the ensign waves in air.
    Shall I to Washington their praise recite?
Enough thou know'st them in the fields of fight.
    Thee, first in peace and honours, -we demand
    The grace and glory of thy martial band.
    Fam'd for thy valour, for thy virtues more,
    Hear every tongue thy guardian aid implore!
    One century scarce perform'd its destined round,
    When Gallic powers Columbia's fury found;
    And so may you, whoever dares disgrace
    The land of freedom's heaven-defended race!
    Fix'd are the eyes of nations on the scales,

For in their hopes Columbia's arm prevails.
Anon Britannia droops the pensive head,
While round increase the rising hills of dead.
Ah! cruel blindness to Columbia's state!
Lament thy thirst of boundless power too late.
Proceed, great chief, with virtue on thy side,
Thy ev'ry action let the goddess guide.
A crown, a mansion, and a throne that shine,
With gold unfading, WASHINGTON! be thine. 1776.

For Further Enrichment

A. Research the Jamestown, VA, settlement. Contrast this settlement (1607) with the Pilgrim settlement (1620) and Puritan experiment (1630). *The Jamestown settlement was a commercial enterprise; the Plymouth/Boston settlements were started for religious reasons. Even a cursory examination of letters from Jamestown and Plymouth show the contrast of these two views. This is the tension played out throughout American history: commercialism/privatism/individualism vs. religious/spiritual agendas. One of the worst investments in the early 17th century was an investment in the Virginia Company. The Virginia company was a stock-option company set up to raise funds for new colonizing enterprises. Its first and only real undertaking was the Jamestown investment. The Jamestown settlement proved to be an extraordinarily bad investment because it lost vast amounts of money for its investors. This was principally due to the unwillingness of the early colonizers to do the necessary work of providing for themselves. At the same time, and in defense of the early settlers, the investors never really provided enough capital for supply of the venture. Nevertheless, how extraordinary that the United States--whose business is business President Calvin Coolidge once said--started as a bad business venture!*

Jamestown, Virginia, was the object of this investment venture and the site of the first permanent British settlement in North America. It was founded on May 14, 1607, and was located on a peninsula (later an island) in the James River in Virginia. It was named in honor of King James I.

From the beginning, the colony was unsure about its reason for existence. Ostensibly, it was founded for the sole purpose of making profit for its investors. One quick way to make money in the 17th century, of course, was to find gold. This method was especially appealing to the yeoman (middle class) farmer and second or third son of an aristocratic family (who had scant hope of inheriting any money in England), both of whom made up the majority element of early British settlers. Gold was and still is hard to come by in southeastern, tidewater Virginia. Finally, after starvation took over half the colony, the new colonists discovered that the cultivation of tobacco was about as good as gold. It was then grown everywhere–including the streets of Jamestown.

No one knows why the early profiteers would choose such an unhealthy place as

Jamestown for a settlement. No self-respecting Native American would be caught dead near the place. Situated in an unhealthful marshy area, the colony always had a small population because of a high death rate from disease. What disease did not kill, fire often did. In 1608 Jamestown was accidentally burned, and two years later it was about to be abandoned by its inhabitants when Thomas West, Lord De La Warr, arrived with new energy and new supplies. Other fires occurred in 1676 and 1698. Jamestown fell into decay when the seat of government of Virginia was moved in 1699 to the Middle Plantation (later Williamsburg). By this time quick profit had been abandoned for more long-term profit. However, from the beginning, Jamestown, was an experiment in profit making.

Meanwhile, in New England, Englishmen were starting a holy experiment. The historian Perry Miller wrote, "Without some understanding of Puritanism . . . there is no understanding of America." Indeed. But who were the Puritans? What is the difference between a Boston Puritan and a Plymouth Separatist? Were Puritans bigots? Saints? Puritanism, a movement arising within the Church of England in the latter part of the 16th century, sought to carry the reformation of that church beyond the point the early Anglican or Church of England had gone. The Church of England was attempting to establish a middle course between Roman Catholicism and the ideas of the Protestant reformers. This was unacceptable to a growing number of reformers, called Puritans, who wanted the Church of England to reject Anglicanism and embrace Calvinism. The term Puritanism was also used in a broader sense to refer to attitudes and values considered characteristic of these radical reformers. Thus, the Separatists (i.e., Pilgrims) in the 16th century, the Quakers in the 17th century, and Nonconformists after the Restoration were called Puritans, although they were no longer part of the established church. For our purposes, though, we shall refer to the Puritans in two ways: Puritans and Pilgrims.

The Pilgrims, Separatists, founders of Plymouth Colony in Massachusetts were, like their countrymen in Virginia, initially dependent upon private investments from profit-minded backers to finance their colony. In other ways, however, these intensely religious people were nothing like the Jamestown settlers.

B. Describe how it might have felt to be a member of the Lenape Indian tribe. Your name is Mary White Feather. You are a mother of three children. Your husband is an average Indian brave. You are watching these strange people in their big ships land at Jamestown. Describe your fears and hopes. *Answers will vary, but surely the Indians already knew from the beginning that these new Europeans were potentially a disastrous threat to their civilization. Their feelings were ambivalent, however. They recognized that there were advantages in trading with the Europeans. They also recognized that some of the technological advantages (e.g., guns) offered them an advantage over their enemies. Study Squanto to learn more about this tension. The main Native American tribe in the Virginia area in the early 17th century was the Lenape Powhatan Tribe. By the time the English colonists had arrived the chief of the Powhatans, Chief Powhatan, ruled a formidable 30-tribe confederacy. He allegedly controlled 128 villages with about 9,000 inhabitants. Powhatan initially opposed the English settlement at Jamestown.*

According to legend, he changed his policy in 1607 when he released the captured Smith. In April 1614, Pocahontas, Powhatan's daughter, married the planter John Rolfe, and afterwards Powhatan negotiated a peace agreement with his son-in-law's people. Peace reigned until after Powhatan died in 1618. In 1622 a great war broke out between the English settlers and the Powhatan Confederacy. Initially the Powhatan Confederation very nearly destroyed the Jamestown settlement. In the long term, however, the war destroyed the Confederacy as a viable entity.

C. C. Describe how you would feel if you were an Englishman named Ebenezer Davis. It is 1619. You have survived a long horrowing sea voyage and are now a settler in Jamestown. You have left your family behind in Yorkshire, England. You have never seen anything like America, much less a Lenape Indian! What are your fears and expectations? *Most Englishmen were lower middle class yeoman farmers. The excitement of owning one's own land was mitigated by the knowledge that you were in a dangerous, strange place. These fears were confirmed in the indian massacres of 1622.*

D. Pretend you are Joe Black (your English name) to your slave owners, but you know that your real name is Lomatata (your African name). You were captured and enslaved in West Africa two years ago. You have (had?) a wife and three children in Africa. You doubt that you will ever see them again. You have spent two years working in the West Indies. Now you are being sold to new owners in Jamestown, VA. It is 1619. How do you feel? What do you think about the Indians? *Slaves, from the beginning were treated poorly. Historians disagree whether racism preceded slavery or vice versa. But within a decade after the first English settlers came to Jamestown racism was a ubiquitous presence in American culture. Racism would surely have affected these early black Americans.*

E. Notwithstanding the somewhat fictionalized Disney version, Pocahontas was a real person. Research your history books and find out about this Indian princess! *Pocahontas was indeed a real person. who married an Englishman and died in England. It is interesting how Disney has made her into a feminist New-Ager who worshipped nature! She was born around 1595 to one of Powhatan's many wives. They named her Matoaka, though she is better known as Pocahontas, which means "Little Wanton," a playful, frolicsome little girl. Pocahontas probably saw Europeans before they settled in Jamestown in May 1607.*

    The first meeting of Pocahontas and John Smith is questionable if not entirely invented by Smith. He was leading an expedition in December 1607 when he was taken captive by some Indians. Days later, he was brought to Chief Powhatan where he was later saved by Pocahontas. There is some debate about whether this really happened. Nevertheless, Pocahontas and Smith soon became friends. In October 1609, John Smith was badly injured by a gunpowder explosion and was forced to return to England. When Pocahontas next came to visit the fort, she was told that her friend Smith was dead. Pocahontas apparently married an Indian named Kocoum in 1610. She lived in Potomac country among Indians, but her relationship with the Englishmen was not over. When an energetic and resourceful member of the Jamestown settlement, Captain Samuel Argall, learned where she was, he devised a plan to kidnap her and hold her for ransom. With the help of Japazaws, lesser chief of the Patowomeck Indians, Argall lured Pocahontas onto his ship. Argall sent word that he would return Chief Powhatan's beloved daughter only when the chief had returned to him the English prisoners he held, the arms and tools that the Indians had stolen, and also some corn. After some time Powhatan sent part of the ransom and asked that they treat his daughter well. Argall returned to Jamestown in April 1613 with Pocahontas. She eventually moved to a new settlement, Henrico, where she began her education in the Christian Faith, and that she met a successful tobacco planter named John Rolfe in July 1613. Pocahontas was allowed relative freedom within the settlement, and she began to enjoy her role in the relations between the colony and her people. She grew to love John Rolfe. John Rolfe, a committed Christian, agonized for many weeks over the decision to marry a "strange wife," a heathen Indian. He finally decided to marry Pocahontas after she had been converted to Christianity. Pocahontas was baptized, christened "Rebecca" and married John Rolfe on April 5, 1614. Rolfe returned to England, but in March 1617, he decided to return his family to Virginia. It was soon apparent, however, that Pocahontas would not survive the voyage home. She was ill from pneumonia or possibly tuberculosis. She was buried in a churchyard in Gravesend, England. She was 22 years old.

Supplemental Reading:

Molefi K. Asante, and Mark T. Mattson,. *Historical and Cultural Atlas of African-Americans*
   The single best resource of the African-American experience in America. It is full of pictures, graphs, and timely articles.

Robert N. Bellah, and Frederick E. Greenspahn, *Uncivil Religion: Interreligious Hostility in America*
   Bellah and Greenspahn are gifted sociologists who employ their ample skills to analyze cross-racial religious controversy in America–one of the most lamentable chapters in our history.

Andrew Billingsley, *Black Families in White America*
   A scholarly book that nonetheless is important to this area. Billingsley argues that the African-American family is the key to the slave's survival and the maintenance of African-American culture.

John W. Blassingame, *The Slave Community*
 Blassingame, like Billingsley, argues for the efficacy of the African-American slave family.

David Blankenhorn, Jr., *Fatherless America: Confronting Our Most Urgent Social Problem.*
 A scathing criticism of the American social welfare system. David Blankenhorn, in his revolutionary work of cultural criticism, asks an anti-modern, almost heretical question: "So the question is not, *What do men want?* but rather, *What do men do?*" Blankenhorn goes where very few social historians dare to go before: he argues that men should be, quite simply, good fathers--no matter how hard it is, or how foolish it may seem. "In a larger sense, the fatherhood story is the irreplaceable basis of a culture's most urgent imperative: the socialization of males." (p. 65). American children need fathers. American society needs fathers.

Ashley Bryan,, *Sing to the Sun*, *The Story of Lightning and Thunder*, *Climbing Jacob's Ladder: Heroes of the Bible in African-American Spirituals*, *Turtle Knows Your Name*, and *All Night, All Day: A Child's First Book of African-American Spirituals*
 The foremost African-American cultural historian in America. Using children's books as a vehicle, Bryan inspires his reader with fresh insights of African-American culture.

John Dawson, *Healing America's Wounds*
 Dawson explores the consequences of racism on American society and offers biblical solutions.

Robert William Fogel and Stanley L. Engerman, *Time on the Cross: The economics of American Negro Slavery*
 Fogel and Engerman argue persuasively that slavery was very profitable–which assured its duration.

Kenneth M. Stampp, *The Peculiar Institution: Slavery in the Ante-Bellum South*
 A seminal work on African-American history. The serious historian starts here.

Notes:

Lesson Five Test

Short Answer Questions. Answer in two or three sentences: (30 Points)

A. Did the Church support chattel slavery? Why?

B. Did slaves resist their masters? Why or why not? How did they resist?

C. Why did Phillis Wheatley so willingly accept her servitude?

Literary Analysis: (70 Points)

Read the following poem by Phillis Wheatley.

> To the University of Cambridge in New England (Harvard College)

> While an intrinsic ardor prompts to write,
> The muses promise to assist my pen;
> 'Twas not long since I left my native shore
> The land of errors, and *Egyptian* gloom:
> Father of mercy, 'twas thy gracious hand
> Brought me in safety from those dark abodes.
> Students, to you 'tis giv'n to scan the heights
> Above, to traverse the ethereal space,
> And mark the systems of revolving worlds.
> Still more, ye sons of science ye receive
> The blissful news by messengers from heav'n,
> How *Jesus'* blood for your redemption flows.
> See him with hands out-stretcht upon the cross;
> Immense compassion in his bosom glows;
> He hears revilers, nor resents their scorn:
> What matchless mercy in the Son of God!
> When the whole human race by sin had fall'n,
> He deign'd to die that they might rise again,
> And share with him in the sublimest skies
> Life without death, and glory without end.
> Improve your privileges while they stay,
> Ye pupils, and each hour redeem, that bears
> Or good or bad report of you to heav'n.

Let sin, that baneful evil to the soul,
By you be shun'd, nor once remit your guard;
Suppress the deadly serpent in its egg.
Ye blooming plants of human race divine,
An *Ethiop* tells you 'tis your greatest foe;
Its transient sweetness turns to endless pain,
And in immense perdition sinks the soul.

Summarize Wheatley's advice to Harvard College students.

Lesson Five Test Answers

Short Answer Questions. Answer in two or three sentences: (30 Points)

A. Did the Church support chattel slavery? Why?
Unfortunately, yes. Only the Mennonites and Quakers systematically opposed slavery.

B. Did slaves resist their masters? Why or why not? How did they resist?
Yes, they resisted in every way that they could: work slo downs and by sabotaging the crops. Most of all, they resisted by forming their own culture.

C. Why did Phillis Wheatley so willingly accept her servitude?
She saw it as being God's will for her life. That does no necessarily t mean, she enjoyed being a slave.

Literary Analysis: (70 Points)

Summarize Wheatley's advice to Harvard College students.
Wheatley advised college students to humble themselves before God and to learn knowledge to advance His kingdom. All other knowledge is useless. Students, to you 'tis giv'n to scan the heights/Above, to traverse the ethereal space,/And mark the systems of revolving worlds./Still more, ye sons of science ye receive/The blissful news by messengers from heav'n,/How Jesus' blood for your redemption flows./See him with hands out-stretcht upon the cross;/Immense compassion in his bosom glows;/He hears revilers, nor resents their scorn:/What matchless mercy in the Son of God!

Lesson Six

Readings Due For This Lesson

Students should have read all narrative background and selections from 19th century poetry in Lesson Six. All poems are provided in the text.

Reading Ahead

Students should finish reading Nathaniel Hawthorne's *The Scarlet Letter* (Lessons Seven & Eight).

Suggested Weekly Implementation

Day One	Day Two	Day Three	Day Four	Day Five
1. Students will rewrite graded essays from last week and review Lesson Five test. 2. Students should have read the required reading(s) *before* the assigned lesson begins. 3. Teacher may want to discuss assigned reading(s) with student. 4. Teacher shall assign the required essays. Choose two or three. The rest of the essays can be outlined, answered with shorter answers, or skipped.	1. Student should begin reading(s) from next lesson. 2. Student should outline essays due at the end of the week. 3. Students should answer one or two of the essays that are not assigned as formal essays.	1. Students should write rough drafts of assigned essays. 2. The teacher should correct rough drafts.	Student will write final copy of essays due tomorrow.	1. Essays are due. 2. Students should take Lesson Six test. 3. Student should read Nathaniel Hawthorne, *The Scarlet Letter*.

Eighteenth and Nineteenth Century Poetry

Critical Thinking

A. Read "The Snow-Storm," "Compensation," "Days," "The Rhodora," and "Forbearance," by the Transcendentalist writer Ralph Waldo Emerson. *Themes of Transcendentalism that should be identified include: absence of an omnipotent God; omniscient nature. The concept of a ubiquitous fate is absent (contrast this with the Greek concept of fate). Nature is venerated, if not worshiped. Subjectivity is celebrated–empiricism is suspect.*

B. Research Transcendentalism and the effect it had on American thought. *Transcendentalism was a major crack in the Theistic vision that was, until Emerson, endemic to the American ethos. For the first time there was a world view that invited men and women to follow their "feelings" and "intuition." In other words, to use Old Testament language, they felt justified in doing what was right in their own eyes.*

Challenge Questions

> In America, at least, in the past, God has primarily used the "revival" or "crusade" to bring great spiritual renewal. That is not true in other nations--like Korea where revival came through prayer and cell group house churches. These revival movements had a greater impact on America than any of the authors we are studying.

A. The last six lines of "The Snowstorm" contain a description of the events of the next morning. What is Emerson trying to say? What is his world view? Which does the author consider the true artist? Support your conclusions with references from the poem.

The Snow Storm

Announced by all the trumpets of the sky,
Arrives the snow, and, driving o'er the fields,
Seems nowhere to alight: the whited air
Hides hills and woods, the river, and the heaven,
And veils the farm-house at the garden's end.
The sled and traveller stopped, the courier's feet
Delayed, all friends shut out, the housemates sit

Around the radiant fireplace, enclosed
In a tumultuous privacy of storm.

Come see the north wind's masonry.
Out of an unseen quarry evermore
Furnished with tile, the fierce artificer
Curves his white bastions with projected roof
Round every windware stake, or tree, or door.
Speeding, the myriad-handed, his wild work
So fanciful, so savage, nought cares he
For number or proportion. Mockingly,
On coop or kennel he hangs Parian wreaths;

A swan-like form invests the hidden thorn;
Fills up the farmer's lane from wall to wall,
Maugre the farmer's sighs; and at the gate
A tapering turret overtops the work.
And when his hours are numbered, and the world
Is all his own, retiring, as he were not,
Leaves, when the sun appears, astonished Art
To mimic in slow structures, stone by stone,
Built in an age, the mad wind's night-work,
The frolic architecture of the snow.

The last six lines are: "And when his hours are numbered, and the world/Is all his own, retiring, as he were not,/Leaves, when the sun appears, astonished Art/To mimic in slow structures, stone by stone,/Built in an age, the mad wind's night-work,/The frolic architecture of the snow." The snowstorm is over. All creation is at rest. This scene evokes the same sobriety of the creation scene in Genesis 1. As God rested in Genesis 1, nature rests at the end of "The Snowstorm." Likewise, it was good–"The frolic architecture of the snow." Emerson is saying that the world is good, that God is good, and that man is good (so long as he behaves himself and does not intrude on nature's handiwork). The true artist is a mindless, benevolent deity called nature. Gone are the central tenants of Theism: an omnipotent, loving God, who created man in His own image. In theism, mankind is not an anemic version of creation, to be placed next to, or behind, the perfection of nature. Man is the ruler of, and separate from, nature. Nature to the Romantic is beautiful and inviting. To the Theist, God's order, His Word, and His Son Jesus Christ are beautiful and inviting. To Emerson, nature is the true artist. To the Theist, God of the Old and New Testament is the artist.

B. In Emerson's poem "Day," why is the day scornful? Write an essay explaining at whom the scorn is directed.

Days

DAUGHTERS of Time, the hypocritic Days,
Muffled and dumb like barefoot dervishes,
And marching single in an endless file,
Bring diadems and fagots in their hands.
To each they offer gifts after his will,
Bread, kingdoms, stars, and sky that holds them all.
I, in my pleached garden, watched the pomp,
Forgot my morning wishes, hastily
Took a few herbs and apples, and the Day
Turned and departed silent. I, too late,
Under her solemn fillet saw the scorn.

To the Transcendentalist time is the problem. Romanticism is able to address issues like the human soul, human life, and even human morality. Where Romanticism comes up short is in its discussion about death. Romanticism has no convincing answer to this question, "What happens to human beings when they die?" That is where the Christian Theistic world view is vastly superior.

C. Based on "The Rhodora," what is Emerson's idea of a god? Emerson could not accept the idea of a God separate from man and nature; in other words, Emerson was not a Christian believer. Yet, in his own way, he was a deeply religious person. How is this revealed in the last four lines of the poem? Using the poems above, and other Emerson writings, show how Emerson was "religious."

The Rhodora

ON BEING ASKED, WHENCE IS THE FLOWER?

IN May, when sea-winds pierced our solitudes,
I found the fresh Rhodora in the woods,
Spreading its leafless blooms in a damp nook,
To please the desert and the sluggish brook.
The purple petals, fallen in the pool,

Made the black water with their beauty gay;
Here might the red-bird come his plumes to cool,
And court the flower that cheapens his array.
Rhodora! if the sages ask thee why
This charm is wasted on the earth and sky,
Tell them, dear, that if eyes were made for seeing,

> Then Beauty is its own excuse for being:
>
> Why thou wert there, O rival of the rose!
> I never thought to ask, I never knew:
> But, in my simple ignorance, suppose
> The self-same Power that brought me there brought you.

Emerson was religious in that he fervently believed in transcendent truth but he was unwilling to put a specific name or classification on that truth. That meant very little to the American society that Emerson knew. In fact, at the time Emerson was writing, the great Charles Finney revival was spreading across upstate New York. America still basically embraced Judeo-Christian values. Transcendentalism was an aberration in the middle of the 19th century; it became the order of the day in the 20th century. By the way, Finney spoke to more folks and brought more social change in one city than Emerson did through his whole career!

D. Give several evidences of Transcendentalism from these poems. *The image of nature having a powerful presence and the celebration of the human spirit. The celebration of human subjectivity is advanced in every poem. Truth is uncovered by observing a snowstorm–not by reading the Word of God. Finally, man is equal–not superior–to nature. Why thou wert there, O rival of the rose!/I never thought to ask, I never knew: But, in my simple ignorance, suppose/The self-same Power that brought me there brought you.*

E. Transcendentalism is a sad commentary on the failure of American Puritanism. By the end of the 17th Century Puritanism was declining because of a lack of conversions and a disrespect for authority. As a result of this demise, American society lost a strong sense of community. Some thinkers, such as sociologist Peter Berger, argue that one feature of modern America has been the loss of mediating institutions, so that American is now full of increasingly atomistic individuals. This variety is maintained by a powerful state, with no buffers between government and people. Berger also argues that we Americans have lost all sense of community. Puritans rarely talked about themselves--they just lived their lives in the community of the Lord. Contemporary Americans talk about community so much because they experience it so little in their lives. The 17th and 18th Century Church ceased to be a mediating institution as it was in Puritan New England. As a result, Christianity lost credibility as a viable institution and Transcendentalism arose. Agree or disagree with this statement in an essay and offer evidence to support your answer. *A core of moral truth is at the center of all viable civilizations. Joshua knew that when he prepared the nation of Israel to enter the Promised Land in the last chapters of Deuteronomy. He urged his nation to choose this day whom they would serve . . . In our nation, as we reject our Judeo-Christian biblical roots, that moral core has been severely eroded. The Puritan vision, which was a decidedly Christian Theistic vision, lost its pervasive influence by the 19th century in all but the most covert ways.*

F. Compare the poetry of another New England poet, Ralph Waldo Emerson, with the poetry of Anne Bradstreet. *Ralph Waldo Emerson, while he is obviously a gifted poet, represents a Transcendentalist position. This view is in direct contradiction to Anne Bradstreet's viewpoint, a Christian view of life. In Emerson's poem "The Snowstorm" the reader sees a powerful, but impersonal, nature. Nature seems to be alive. In verses 10-15 nature is compared to a mason. "Come see the north wind's masonry..." vs. 10. Humankind is clearly not in control; nature is in control. There is no God in Emerson's poem or, if there is a God, he would be nature. In the poem "Days," nature is called fate. Fate is an impersonal force who seems to have no more interest in people than it would have in a rainstorm. "Daughters of Time, the hypocritic Days,/Muffled and dumb like barefoot dervishes." vs.1-2. Nature unites people with all creatures. There seems to be no difference, for instance, between a flower--the Rhodora--and a man. "The self-same Power that brought me there brought you."--verse. 16 in "The Rhodora." There is a power outside humankind that exists to Bradstreet, but it is not impersonal. It is intimately involved with everything that happens to people. "It" is a loving God. "Shall I then praise the earth, the trees, the earth?"--section 20, v. 2. Of course Bradstreet would say no, she does not praise nature. She praises God. "to My Dear and Loving Husband" she recognizes that human relationships require perseverance (vs 11). But, while pain and misery are part of life they are not inflicted by an impersonal force like fate. They are allowed to happen by a loving God. Bradstreet feels pain, disappointment, and disaster but she finds hope in God not in her earthly belongings or circumstances. There is no fate to Bradstreet. She believes in providence, not fate. For instance, she is not worried about her house burning down, growing old, leaving her beloved husband. She does not sentimentalize flowers or snowy days. Why? Because beautify to her is to be found in relationship with her God. Besides, temporal things have relatively no interest to her when they are compared to the future. While she may suffer now, and will experience physical death, she is nonetheless acutely aware that she will live forever with God in heaven. She is forever separated from "flowers" and "snowstorms" because she is created in the image of God. They are not. She does not need to paint pretty pictures of bad things in her life. Because she knows that God loves her and has great plans for her life. In Emerson's poetry and in Bradstreet's poetry we see two entirely different world views. One celebrates a loving, personal God. Another reaches for meaning in nature. One is fearful of fate. Another rests in an all powerful God. Carl H. Henry in his book* <u>Toward a Recovery of Christian Belief</u> *(1990) tells a story that illustrates what happens when Romanticism replaces Theism as the main cultural world view of our nation. When flying with a friend the pilot announces that their spotter had just died. "What does that mean?" Henry asked. "It means no one knows where we are," the pilot answered. "With the rise of Romanticism America lost its moral and epistemic (i.e., knowledge) moral compass bearings," Henry concludes.*

G. At the same time that Emerson was writing the well-attended revivals led by Charles Finney were being held in upstate New York. In fact, this revival had a greater impact than Emerson's essays and poetry on American society. Write a one-page report on this revival. *Finney's upstate New York revivals were epic in proportion to Emerson's influence on America. Thousands of people committed their lives to Christ. In fact, the entire sociological structure of upstate New York was indelibly changed by Finney's revivals. His revivals became part of what was called the Second Great Awakening.*

H. Read four or five essays that Emerson wrote and compare and contrast the themes of these essays with his poetry. *Answers will vary, but the student should highlight themes from Transcendentalism.*

Puritans saw the world in terms of individual sin and of principalities and powers. They always saw themselves as being part of a larger, more important cosmological story. They knew, without a doubt, that every knee would bow, every tongue confess . . . With the rise of Lockian (i.e., John Locke) rationalism and its emphasis on individual rights, supported so vigorously by men such as Thomas Jefferson, Americans privatized its faith and morality. Morality was defined according to each individual preference and Americans avoided static moral biblical structures. For the first time in American thought, man's agendas were more important than the Word of God. Theism was still everywhere present in America, but for the first time morality was loosed from its biblical moorings–with disastrous results.

An Overview of 18th and 19th Century Poetry

Edward Taylor

Edward Taylor (1642-1729) was a New England Puritan's Puritan. Taylor was a colleague of famous Increase Mather and Charles Chauncey, and corresponded with Richard Baxter and other English Puritan Calvinists. American critic Donald Stanford says, "Taylor seems to have been endowed with most of those qualities usually connoted by the word *puritan*. He was learned, grave, severe, stubborn, and stiff-necked. He was very, very pious. But his piety was sincere. It was fed by a long continuous spiritual experience arising, so he felt, from a mystical communion with Christ. The reality and depth of this experience is amply witnessed by his poetry."

It was his custom to write a poem ("Meditation") before each Lord's Supper. These poems are wonderful examples of spiritual experience and devotion. Some readers are embarrassed by Taylor's raw intimacy with our Lord!

Meditation 1

What Love is this of thine, that Cannot bee
In thine Infinity, O Lord, Confinde,

Unless it in thy very Person see,
Infinity, and Finity Conjoyn'd?
What hath thy Godhead, as not satisfide
Marri'de our Manhood, making it its Bride?

Oh, Matchless Love! filling Heaven to the brim!
O're running it: all running o're beside
This World! Nay Overflowing Hell; wherein
For thine Elect, there rose a mighty Tide!
That there our Veans might through thy Person bleed,
To quench those flames, that else would on us feed.

Oh! that thy Love might overflow my Heart!
To fire the same with Love: for Love I would.
But oh! my streight'ned Breast! my Lifeless Sparke!
My Fireless Flame! What Chilly Love, and Cold?
In measure small! In Manner Chilly! See.
Lord blow the Coal: Thy Love Enflame in mee.

Edgar Allan Poe

Edgar Allan Poe, the greatest American short story writer, invented the modern detective story. His poetry, too, was extraordinary. In fact, Poe was perhaps the first and greatest poet America produced. In Poe's poems, like his tales, his characters were tortured by nameless fears and longings. Today Poe is acclaimed as one of America's greatest writers, but in his own unhappy lifetime he knew little but failure. Struggling with ill-health, and later drug and alcoholic addiction, Poe was a broken man. The untimely death of his young wife was the last straw. It broke his heart and perhaps drove him mad.

The Raven

Once upon a midnight dreary, while I pondered, weak and weary,
Over many a quaint and curious volume of forgotten lore,
While I nodded, nearly napping, suddenly there came a tapping,
As of some one gently rapping, rapping at my chamber door.
"'Tis some visitor," I muttered, "tapping at my chamber door--
Only this, and nothing more."

Ah, distinctly I remember it was in the bleak December,
And each separate dying ember wrought its ghost upon the floor.

Eagerly I wished the morrow;- -vainly I had sought to borrow
From my books surcease of sorrow- sorrow for the lost Lenore-
For the rare and radiant maiden whom the angels name Lenore-
    Nameless here for evermore.

And the silken sad uncertain rustling of each purple curtain
Thrilled me- filled me with fantastic terrors never felt before;
So that now, to still the beating of my heart, I stood repeating,
"'Tis some visitor entreating entrance at my chamber door--
Some late visitor entreating entrance at my chamber door;--
    This it is, and nothing more."

Presently my soul grew stronger; hesitating then no longer,
"Sir," said I, "or Madam, truly your forgiveness I implore;
But the fact is I was napping, and so gently you came rapping,
And so faintly you came tapping, tapping at my chamber door,
That I scarce was sure I heard you"-- here I opened wide the door;--
    Darkness there, and nothing more.

Deep into that darkness peering, long I stood there wondering, fearing,
Doubting, dreaming dreams no mortals ever dared to dream before;
But the silence was unbroken, and the stillness gave no token,
And the only word there spoken was the whispered word, "Lenore!"
This I whispered, and an echo murmured back the word, "Lenore!"--
    Merely this, and nothing more.

Back into the chamber turning, all my soul within me burning,
Soon again I heard a tapping somewhat louder than before.
"Surely," said I, "surely that is something at my window lattice:
Let me see, then, what the threat is, and this mystery explore--
Let my heart be still a moment and this mystery explore;--
    'Tis the wind and nothing more."

Open here I flung the shutter, when, with many a flirt and flutter,
In there stepped a stately raven of the saintly days of yore;
Not the least obeisance made he; not a minute stopped or stayed he;
But, with mien of lord or lady, perched above my chamber door--
Perched upon a bust of Pallas just above my chamber door--
    Perched, and sat, and nothing more.

Then this ebony bird beguiling my sad fancy into smiling,

By the grave and stern decorum of the countenance it wore.
"Though thy crest be shorn and shaven, thou," I said, "art sure no craven,
Ghastly grim and ancient raven wandering from the Nightly shore-
Tell me what thy lordly name is on the Night's Plutonian shore!"
Quoth the Raven, "Nevermore."

Much I marvelled this ungainly fowl to hear discourse so plainly,
Though its answer little meaning- little relevancy bore;
For we cannot help agreeing that no living human being
Ever yet was blest with seeing bird above his chamber door--
Bird or beast upon the sculptured bust above his chamber door,
With such name as "Nevermore."

But the raven, sitting lonely on the placid bust, spoke only
That one word, as if his soul in that one word he did outpour.
Nothing further then he uttered-- not a feather then he fluttered--
Till I scarcely more than muttered, "other friends have flown before-
On the morrow he will leave me, as my hopes have flown before."
Then the bird said, "Nevermore."

Startled at the stillness broken by reply so aptly spoken,
"Doubtless," said I, "what it utters is its only stock and store,
Caught from some unhappy master whom unmerciful Disaster
Followed fast and followed faster till his songs one burden bore--
Till the dirges of his Hope that melancholy burden bore
Of 'Never-- nevermore'."

But the Raven still beguiling all my fancy into smiling,
Straight I wheeled a cushioned seat in front of bird, and bust and door;
Then upon the velvet sinking, I betook myself to linking
Fancy unto fancy, thinking what this ominous bird of yore-
What this grim, ungainly, ghastly, gaunt and ominous bird of yore
Meant in croaking "Nevermore."

This I sat engaged in guessing, but no syllable expressing
To the fowl whose fiery eyes now burned into my bosom's core;
This and more I sat divining, with my head at ease reclining
On the cushion's velvet lining that the lamplight gloated o'er,
But whose velvet violet lining with the lamplight gloating o'er,
She shall press, ah, nevermore!

Then methought the air grew denser, perfumed from an unseen censer
Swung by Seraphim whose footfalls tinkled on the tufted floor.
"Wretch," I cried, "thy God hath lent thee-- by these angels he hath sent thee
Respite- respite and nepenthe, from thy memories of Lenore!
Quaff, oh quaff this kind nepenthe and forget this lost Lenore!"
Quoth the Raven, "Nevermore."

"Prophet!" said I, "thing of evil!-- prophet still, if bird or devil!--
Whether Tempter sent, or whether tempest tossed thee here ashore,
Desolate yet all undaunted, on this desert land enchanted-
On this home by horror haunted- tell me truly, I implore-
Is there- is there balm in Gilead?-- tell me-- tell me, I implore!"
Quoth the Raven, "Nevermore."

"Prophet!" said I, "thing of evil- prophet still, if bird or devil!
By that Heaven that bends above us-- by that God we both adore-
Tell this soul with sorrow laden if, within the distant Aidenn,
It shall clasp a sainted maiden whom the angels name Lenore-
Clasp a rare and radiant maiden whom the angels name Lenore."
Quoth the Raven, "Nevermore."

"Be that word our sign in parting, bird or fiend," I shrieked, upstarting--
"Get thee back into the tempest and the Night's Plutonian shore!
Leave no black plume as a token of that lie thy soul hath spoken!
Leave my loneliness unbroken!- quit the bust above my door!
Take thy beak from out my heart, and take thy form from off my door!"
Quoth the Raven, "Nevermore."

And the Raven, never flitting, still is sitting, still is sitting
On the pallid bust of Pallas just above my chamber door;
And his eyes have all the seeming of a demon's that is dreaming,
And the lamplight o'er him streaming throws his shadow on the floor;
And my soul from out that shadow that lies floating on the floor
Shall be lifted--nevermore!

Emily Dickinson

Emily Dickinson,"the belle of Amherst", is almost as famous for her mysteriously secluded life as for her poetry, which ranks her with Walt Whitman as one of the most gifted poets in modern American literature. In fact, she and Whitman introduced "Realism in poetry." She never married, and after age 30 she became a recluse. Some scholars believe that this was her response to the narrow literary establishment of her time, which expected female writers to limit their subjects to home life and romance. Dickinson, on the other hand, preferred images of real life.

Of Dickinson's 1700 plus poems, only 10 were published in her lifetime, and those without her permission. After her death, however, her sister found and published the body of her work. Dickinson wrote from a Romantic world view in a decidedly modern way.

Emancipation

No rack can torture me,
My soul's at liberty
Behind this mortal bone
There knits a bolder one

You cannot prick with saw,
Nor rend with scymitar.
Two bodies therefore be;
Bind one, and one will flee.

The eagle of his nest
No easier divest
And gain the sky,
Than mayest thou,

Except thyself may be
Thine enemy;
Captivity is consciousness,
So's liberty.

I'm nobody! Who are you?

I'm nobody! Who are you?
Are you nobody, too?
Then there 's a pair of us -- don't tell!
They 'd banish us, you know.

How dreary to be somebody!
How public, like a frog
To tell your name the livelong day
To an admiring bog!

Henry Wadsworth Longfellow

Probably the best loved of American poets is Henry Wadsworth Longfellow. Many of his lines are as familiar to us as rhymes from Mother Goose or the words of nursery songs learned in early childhood. Longfellow wrote on archetype themes which appeal to all kinds of people. His poems are easily understood and full of rime and meter. Above all, though, Longfellow wrote with optimism and hope uncharacteristic of the post-Civil War.

Paul Revere's Ride

Listen my children and you shall hear
Of the midnight ride of Paul Revere,
On the eighteenth of April, in Seventy-five;
Hardly a man is now alive
Who remembers that famous day and year.

He said to his friend, "If the British march
By land or sea from the town to-night,
Hang a lantern aloft in the belfry arch
Of the North Church tower as a signal light,--
One if by land, and two if by sea;
And I on the opposite shore will be,
Ready to ride and spread the alarm
Through every Middlesex village and farm,
For the country folk to be up and to arm."

Then he said "Good-night!" and with muffled oar
Silently rowed to the Charlestown shore,
Just as the moon rose over the bay,
Where swinging wide at her moorings lay
The Somerset, British man-of-war;
A phantom ship, with each mast and spar
Across the moon like a prison bar,
And a huge black hulk, that was magnified
By its own reflection in the tide.

Meanwhile, his friend through alley and street
Wanders and watches, with eager ears,

Till in the silence around him he hears
The muster of men at the barrack door,
The sound of arms, and the tramp of feet,
And the measured tread of the grenadiers,
Marching down to their boats on the shore.

Then he climbed the tower of the Old North Church,
By the wooden stairs, with stealthy tread,
To the belfry chamber overhead,
And startled the pigeons from their perch
On the sombre rafters, that round him made
Masses and moving shapes of shade,--
By the trembling ladder, steep and tall,
To the highest window in the wall,
Where he paused to listen and look down
A moment on the roofs of the town
And the moonlight flowing over all.

Beneath, in the churchyard, lay the dead,
In their night encampment on the hill,
Wrapped in silence so deep and still
That he could hear, like a sentinel's tread,
The watchful night-wind, as it went
Creeping along from tent to tent,
And seeming to whisper, "All is well!"
A moment only he feels the spell
Of the place and the hour, and the secret dread
Of the lonely belfry and the dead;
For suddenly all his thoughts are bent
On a shadowy something far away,
Where the river widens to meet the bay,--
A line of black that bends and floats
On the rising tide like a bridge of boats.

Meanwhile, impatient to mount and ride,
Booted and spurred, with a heavy stride
On the opposite shore walked Paul Revere.
Now he patted his horse's side,
Now he gazed at the landscape far and near,
Then, impetuous, stamped the earth,
And turned and tightened his saddle girth;
But mostly he watched with eager search
The belfry tower of the Old North Church,
As it rose above the graves on the hill,

Lonely and spectral and sombre and still.
And lo! as he looks, on the belfry's height
A glimmer, and then a gleam of light!
He springs to the saddle, the bridle he turns,
But lingers and gazes, till full on his sight
A second lamp in the belfry burns.

A hurry of hoofs in a village street,
A shape in the moonlight, a bulk in the dark,
And beneath, from the pebbles, in passing, a spark
Struck out by a steed flying fearless and fleet;
That was all! And yet, through the gloom and the light,
The fate of a nation was riding that night;
And the spark struck out by that steed, in his flight,
Kindled the land into flame with its heat.
He has left the village and mounted the steep,
And beneath him, tranquil and broad and deep,
Is the Mystic, meeting the ocean tides;
And under the alders that skirt its edge,
Now soft on the sand, now loud on the ledge,
Is heard the tramp of his steed as he rides.

It was twelve by the village clock
When he crossed the bridge into Medford town.
He heard the crowing of the cock,
And the barking of the farmer's dog,
And felt the damp of the river fog,
That rises after the sun goes down.

It was one by the village clock,
When he galloped into Lexington.
He saw the gilded weathercock
Swim in the moonlight as he passed,
And the meeting-house windows, black and bare,
Gaze at him with a spectral glare,
As if they already stood aghast
At the bloody work they would look upon.

It was two by the village clock,
When he came to the bridge in Concord town.
He heard the bleating of the flock,
And the twitter of birds among the trees,
And felt the breath of the morning breeze
Blowing over the meadow brown.

And one was safe and asleep in his bed
Who at the bridge would be first to fall,
Who that day would be lying dead,
Pierced by a British musket ball.

You know the rest. In the books you have read
How the British Regulars fired and fled,---
How the farmers gave them ball for ball,
From behind each fence and farmyard wall,
Chasing the redcoats down the lane,
Then crossing the fields to emerge again
Under the trees at the turn of the road,
And only pausing to fire and load.

So through the night rode Paul Revere;
And so through the night went his cry of alarm
To every Middlesex village and farm,---
A cry of defiance, and not of fear,
A voice in the darkness, a knock at the door,
And a word that shall echo for evermore!
For, borne on the night-wind of the Past,
Through all our history, to the last,
In the hour of darkness and peril and need,
The people will waken and listen to hear
The hurrying hoof-beats of that steed,
And the midnight message of Paul Revere.

Walt Whitman

Whitman was one of the first American poets to abandon most of the Romanticism of earlier poetry and create a distinctly American idiom to address those he celebrated as the "American masses." Walt Whitman, and later Carl Sandburg, spoke for a nation. Whitman and Emily Dickinson were the first modern American poets.

O Captain! My Captain!

O CAPTAIN! my Captain! our fearful trip is done;
The ship has weather'd every rack, the prize we sought is won;
The port is near, the bells I hear, the people all exulting,

While follow eyes the steady keel, the vessel grim and daring:
But O heart! heart! heart!
O the bleeding drops of red,
Where on the deck my Captain lies,
Fallen cold and dead.

O Captain! my Captain! rise up and hear the bells;
Rise up--for you the flag is flung--for you the bugle trills;
For you bouquets and ribbon'd wreaths--for you the shores a-crowding;
For you they call, the swaying mass, their eager faces turning;
Here Captain! dear father!
This arm beneath your head;
It is some dream that on the deck,
You've fallen cold and dead.

My Captain does not answer, his lips are pale and still;
My father does not feel my arm, he has no pulse nor will;
The ship is anchor'd safe and sound, its voyage closed and done;
From fearful trip, the victor ship, comes in with object won;
Exult, O shores, and ring, O bells!
But I, with mournful tread,
Walk the deck my Captain lies,
Fallen cold and dead.

Biblical Application

A. In what way is this statement by the Transcendentalist/ Romantic Emerson about Jesus inconsistent with a Christian Theistic world view? *"An immense progress in natural and religious knowledge has been made since his death. Even his genius cannot quicken all that stark nonsense about the blessed and the damned. Yet in the' Life of Christ' I have thought him a Christian Plato; so rich and great was his philosophy. Is it possible the intellect should be so inconsistent with itself? It is singular also that the bishop's morality should sometimes trip, as in his explanation of false witness."*
Answer: *Jesus Christ is not a rationalistic perfect man; he is the Son of God.*

B. Born in 1803, Emerson began his working life as a Unitarian preacher. Early widowhood plunged him into a crisis of faith (already weakened by Unitarian Universalism), and he resigned his ministry in 1832. He abandoned any semblance of Theism. In Nature alone he found his comfort and direction. But Emerson had an ambivalent viewpoint towards nature. He loved and respected Nature but he also, to

Emerson, Nature was all-powerful and reverent. Emerson's faith ultimately strayed into pantheistic nature-worship. Pantheism argues that god is alive everywhere–in animate and inanimate objects alike. There is nothing new under the sun! Emerson and his pantheism was very common in the Bible. In the Old Testament BAAL worship (attacked by Elijah) was very similar to Emerson's Transcendentalism. Compare and contrast the BAAL worship that men such as Joshua and Elijah fought so vigorously and the Nature worship that Transcendentalism advanced. Use the following passages as a guide for your discussion. Refute Emerson's world view by advancing the truth as you find it in the Bible.

The texts below are from *Nature* (1836).

> *The Lie: Direct revelation comes to man through nature.*
> The foregoing generations beheld God face to face; we, through their eyes. Why should not we also enjoy an original relation to the universe? Why should not we have . . . a religion by revelation to us, and not the history of theirs? Embosomed for a season in nature, whose floods of life stream around and through us, and invite us by the powers they supply, to action. . .?
> *The Truth: Revelation comes to man through God; He has chosen to speak most definitively to us through the Word of God.*

> *The Lie: "God" exists everywhere--but especially in Nature.*
> One might think the atmosphere was made transparent with this design, to give man, in the heavenly bodies, the perpetual presence of the sublime. . . If the stars should appear one night in a thousand years, how would men believe and adore; and preserve for many generations the remembrance of the City of God which had been shown! . . But all natural objects make a kindred impression, when the mind is open to their influence. . .Nature says, -- he is my creature . . .
> *The Truth: God is omniscient, but He is also omnipotent. He is not to be sentimentalized. He is to be worshiped. He is no man's creature!*

> *The Lie: Nature unifies us all.*
> A leaf, a drop, a crystal, a moment of time is related to the whole, and partakes of the

> perfection of the whole. Each particle is a microcosm, and faithfully renders the likeness of the world. . . . So intimate is this Unity, that, it is easily seen, it lies under the undermost garment of nature, and betrays its source in the Universal Spirit. . .
>
> *The Truth: Man is hopelessly lost without the Lord Jesus Christ. All have sinned, all are separated from God and one another without the miraculous intervention of God. Furthermore, man is separate from animals. He has a soul and was commanded by God in the Bible to rule over the other animals. Only man is created in the image of God.*

C. Find instances in the Bible where nature is controlled by God. *Creation, The Red Sea, Mt. Carmel--among others. God is very much in control of all elements of His creation.*

For Enrichment

Henry David Thoreau was born in 1817 to an ordinary family in Concord, Massachusetts, and lived most of his life in the Northeast. He was the third child of a small businessman named John Thoreau and his sanguine, talkative wife, Cynthia Dunbar Thoreau. His parents sent him in 1828 to Concord Academy where he impressed his teachers and so was permitted to prepare for college. Upon graduating from the academy, he entered Harvard in 1833. Graduating in the middle ranks of the class of 1837, he searched for a teaching job and secured one in Concord at his old grammar school. He was not successful at these jobs until he embraced the Romanticism of his good friend Ralph Waldo Emerson and started writing verse. "Civil Disobedience" grew out of a jail term that Thoreau was forced to serve because he refused to pay taxes that supported the Mexican War. Thoreau is best known, however, for his book *On Walden Pond* where he described his one-year sojourn next to Walden Pond. Thoreau's pacifism and environmentalism were popular in the 1960's. Read "Civil Disobedience" and outline its argument.

"Civil Disobedience" clearly exemplifies the Romantic tendency to extol the individual above society and tradition. "That government is best that governs not at all . . ." The idea is that people do not need restraints; do not need limits. The goodness in man, unshackled by federal limits will carry the day. "Can there not be a government in which majorities do not virtually decide right and wrong . . . but the conscience decides." This view sounds good to the Christian--until the conscience part. The fact is, the Word of God is absolutely true and right for people--however the conscience feels. Concerning Thoreau's arguments, he feels that civil disobedience is acceptable when the action proposed by the state is immoral. However, the person committing the act should accept the consequences of the act and should commit the act publically.

Challenge Question

Edward Taylor's poetry displays the influence of English metaphysical poets. Research the metaphysical poets in England and compare and contrast their writings with Taylor's. *Metaphysical English poets include Andrew Marvell and John Donne (see British Literature). Both Metaphysical poets and Puritan poets emphasize the supernatural (in a good way). Their works often reflect a religious theme; however, some of the Metaphysical poets (e.g., John Vaughn) are not Calvinistic Puritans–as Edward Taylor is.*

For Enrichment

Compare "Sleepy Hollow" by Washington Irving with "The Devil and Tom Walker." *Both short stories exhibit a Romantic vision and style of writing. The subject matter is drawn from the unusual and from the supernatural (compare to James Fenimore Cooper, Edgar Allan Poe, and the English novelist Mary Shelley). On the other hand, the Theistic moral vision of "The Devil and Tom Walker" is absent from "Sleepy Hollow." The tone too is far less serious in "Sleepy Hollow" than it is in "The Devil and Tom Walker."*

Supplemental Reading:

Lawrence Buell (Editor), *Ralph Waldo Emerson: A Collection of Critical Essays*
    A great overview of scholarship surrounding Emerson's works.

Vincent Buranelli, *Edgar A. Poe*
    A readable, but scholarly study of Poe's life and works.

Herbert S. Gorman, *A Victorian American*
    An intriguing study on Henry W. Longfellow.

William R. Hutchison, *The Transcendentalist Ministers; Church Reform in the New England Renaissance*
    A Harvard professor who knows more about the Transcendentalists than anyone alive.

Alfred Habegger, *My Wars Are Laid Away in Books: The Life of Emily Dickinson*
    Even though Habegger makes too much of Emily Dickinson's feminism, she was not a feminist at all, his biography of Dickinson is one of the best on the market.

Susan Howe, *My Emily Dickinson*

A poet's bird's eye view of the very elusive Emily Dickinson.

Milton Meltzer, *Walt Whitman: A Biography*

Louise Hall Tharp, *The Peabody Sisters of Salem*
    The Peabody sisters had a profound impact on America through their influence on the Alcott sisters and N. Hawthorne.

Notes:

Lesson Six Test

Discussion Questions: (100 Points)

A. Paraphrase "A Psalm of Life" and explain why you agree or disagree with its world view. What are Longfellow's favorite words and metaphors?

The Psalm of Life
by Henry Wadsworth Longfellow

Tell me not, in mournful numbers,
Life is but an empty dream!
For the soul is dead that slumbers,
And things are not what they seem.

Life is real! Life is earnest!
And the grave is not its goal;
Dust thou art, to dust returnest,
Was not spoken of the soul.

Not enjoyment, and not sorrow,
Is our destined end or way;
But to act, that each tomorrow
Find us farther than today.

Art is long, and Time is fleeting,
And our hearts, though stout and brave,
Still, like muffled drums, are beating
Funeral marches to the grave.

In the world's broad field of battle,
In the bivouac of Life,
Be not dumb, driven cattle!
Be a hero in the strife!

Trust no Future, howe'er pleasant!
Let the dead Past bury its dead!
Act,~act in the living Present!
Heart within, and God o'erhead!

Lives of great men all remind us
We can make our lives sublime,
And, departing, leave behind us

> Footprints on the sands of time;
>
> Footprints, that perhaps another,
> Sailing o'er life's solemn main,
> A forlorn and shipwrecked brother,
> Seeing, shall take heart again.
>
> Let us, then, be up and doing,
> With a heart for any fate;
> Still achieving, still pursuing,
> Learn to labor and to wait

B. Discuss the way Americans view themselves in Transcendentalism and contrast it to Puritanism. Cite several poems to argue your case.

C. Some critics find Longfellow's poetry to be simple and colorless concluding that it is for children, not adults. Other critics, while conceding that Longfellow uses a simple style and rhyme, argue that such simplicity makes his whole enterprise, overall, more profound. Agree or disagree with one of these positions.

D. Transcendentalism became, by and large, a northeastern phenomenon centered in the Boston area. It was very much an elitist movement. There were many critics of this movement. "I was given to understand that whatever was unintelligible would be certainly Transcendental," Charles Dickens wrote. Define Transcendentalism and then evaluate its credibility as a world view.

E. Compare and contrast Edgar Allan Poe and Edward Taylor.

Lesson Six Test Answers

Discussion Questions: (100 Points)

A. Paraphrase "A Psalm of Life" and explain why you agree or disagree with its world view. What are Longfellow's favorite words and metaphors?
This poem is a typical Romantic response to life. It invites the reader to make the most of time–carpe diem—without adequately addressing the consequences nor the after life. Certainly the poem has merit–but ultimately it falls short in its quest for eternal meaning to life. Longfellow's favorite metaphor is sand on a beach washed by the ocean of time.

The Psalm of Life
by Henry Wadsworth Longfellow

Tell me not, in mournful numbers,
   Life is but an empty dream!
For the soul is dead that slumbers,
   And things are not what they seem.

Life is real! Life is earnest!
   And the grave is not its goal;
Dust thou art, to dust returnest,
   Was not spoken of the soul.

Not enjoyment, and not sorrow,
   Is our destined end or way;
But to act, that each tomorrow
   Find us farther than today.

Art is long, and Time is fleeting,
And our hearts, though stout and brave,
Still, like muffled drums, are beating
   Funeral marches to the grave.

In the world's broad field of battle,
   In the bivouac of Life,
Be not dumb, driven cattle!
   Be a hero in the strife!

Trust no Future, howe'er pleasant!
Let the dead Past bury its dead!
Act,~act in the living Present!
Heart within, and God o'erhead!

> Lives of great men all remind us
> We can make our lives sublime,
> And, departing, leave behind us
> Footprints on the sands of time;
>
> Footprints, that perhaps another,
> Sailing o'er life's solemn main,
> A forlorn and shipwrecked brother,
> Seeing, shall take heart again.
>
> Let us, then, be up and doing,
> With a heart for any fate;
> Still achieving, still pursuing,
> Learn to labor and to wait

B. Discuss the way Americans view themselves in Transcendentalism and contrast it to Puritanism. Cite several poems to argue your case. *Transcendentalists are humanists–man centered. They worship intuition and subjectivity. They are in stark contrast to the Puritans who worship and glorify y God.*

C. Some critics find Longfellow's poetry to be simple and colorless, concluding that it is for children, not adults. Other critics, while conceding that Longfellow uses a simple style and rhyme, argue that such simplicity makes his whole enterprise, overall, more profound. Agree or disagree with one of these positions. *Answers will vary. This reader finds Longfellow to be simplistic and trite.*

D. Transcendentalism became, by and large, a northeastern phenomenon centered in the Boston area. It was very much an elitist movement. There were many critics of this movement. "I was given to understand that whatever was unintelligible would be certainly Transcendental," Charles Dickens wrote. Define Transcendentalism and then evaluate its credibility as a world view. *Transcendentalists are very subjective and then somewhat vague in their pursuit of truth. I agree with Dickens.*

E. Compare and contrast Edgar Allan Poe and Edward Taylor. *Poe is a Romantic; Taylor is a Puritan.*

Lesson Seven

Readings Due For This Lesson

Students should have read Nathaniel Hawthorne's *The Scarlet Letter*.

Reading Ahead

Students should begin reading the short story "The Devil and Tom Walker" by Washington Irving in Lesson Nine. Looking ahead, student should begin reading "Fall of the House of Usher" and "The Tell Tale Heart" both by Edgar Allan Poe. Finally, students should begin reading "The Birthmark" by Nathaniel Hawthorne.

Suggested Weekly Implementation

Day One	Day Two	Day Three	Day Four	Day Five
1. Students will rewrite graded essays from last week and review Lesson Six test. 2. Students should have read the required reading(s) *before* the assigned lesson begins. 3. Teacher may want to discuss assigned reading(s) with student. 4. Teacher shall assign the required essays. Choose two or three. The rest of the essays can be outlined, answered with shorter answers, or skipped.	1. Student should begin reading(s) from next lesson. 2. Student should outline essays due at the end of the week. 3. Students should answer one or two of the essays that are not assigned as formal essays.	1. Students should write rough drafts of assigned essays. 2. The teacher should correct rough drafts.	Student will write final copy of essays due tomorrow.	1. Essays are due. 2. Students should take Lesson Seven test. 3. Student should read review the novel *Scarlet Letter* and read short stories in Lessons Nine, Ten, and Eleven.

Book Checkup

__c__ 1. __a__ 2. __b__ 3. __d__ 4. __a__ 5.

Suggested Vocabulary Words

<u>Word</u>
ignominy *(disgrace)*
heterogeneous *(mixed)*
iniquity *(evil)*
imperious *(contemptuous)*
dauntless *(fearless)*
odious *(detestable)*
forlorn *(dejected)*
efficacious *(useful)*
expiation *(do penance)*
scurrilous *(crude and offensive)*
misanthropy *(hate of people)*
effluence *(flowing out)*
choleric *(peevish)*
vicissitude *(change)*

Supplemental Reading:

Nathaniel Hawthorne, Millicent Bell (Editor), *Nathaniel Hawthorne : Collected Novels: Fanshawe, The Scarlet Letter, The House of the Seven Gables, The Blithedale Romance*
    An excellent collection of Hawthorne's five novels with editorial helps. The reader's choice of a version for young readers.

Nathaniel Hawthorne, Roy Harvey Pearce (Editor) *Nathaniel Hawthorne : Tales and Sketches*
    Tales and Sketches offers young readers an authoritative edition of Hawthorne's complete stories in a single comprehensive volume.

LouAnn Gaeddert. *A New England Love Story: Nathaniel Hawthorne and Sophia Peabody*
    For mature readers, Gaeddert gives great insights into the relationship of Sophia

Peabody and Nathaniel Hawthorne.

Bradley Sculley, ed. *The Scarlet Letter: Backgrounds and Sources, Criticism.*
    One of the best scholarly resources on Hawthorne and his works.

Arlin Turner, *Nathaniel Hawthorne: A Biography*
    An unpretentious but readable biography of Hawthorne.

Notes:

Lesson Seven Test

Discussion Questions: (100 Points)

A. What is the purpose of the introductory chapter "The Custom House" in Hawthorne's *The Scarlet Letter*?

B. Discuss Pearl's role in *The Scarlet Letter*?

C. *The Scarlet Letter* is a battleground between two world views: Christian Theism (Puritanism) and Romanticism. Give examples of both world views in this novel.

D. What is the significance of these passages:

> This rose-bush, by a strange chance, has been kept alive in history; but whether it had merely survived out of the stern old wilderness, so long after the fall of the gigantic pines and oaks that originally overshadowed it, or whether, as there is far authority for believing, it had sprung up under the footsteps of the sainted Ann Hutchinson as she entered the prison-door, we shall not take upon us to determine. Finding it so directly on the threshold of our narrative, which is now about to issue from that inauspicious portal, we could hardly do otherwise than pluck one of its flowers, and present it to the reader. It may serve, let us hope, to symbolize some sweet moral blossom that may be found along the track, or relieve the darkening close of a tale of human frailty and sorrow . . . Ch. 1.

> We have as yet hardly spoken of the infant, that little creature, whose innocent life had sprung, by the inscrutable decree of Providence, a lovely and immortal flower, out of the rank luxuriance of a guilty passion. How strange it seemed to the sad woman, as she watched the growth, and the beauty that became every day more brilliant, and the intelligence that threw its quivering sunshine over the tiny features of this child! Her Pearl--for so had Hester called her; not as a name expressive of her aspect, which had nothing of the calm, white, unimpassioned lustre that would be indicated by the comparison. But she named the infant "Pearl," as being of great price--purchased with all she had--her mother's only treasure! How strange, indeed! Man had marked this woman's sin by a scarlet letter, which had such potent and disastrous efficacy that no human sympathy could reach her, save it were sinful like herself. God, as a direct

consequence of the sin which man thus punished, had given her a lovely child, whose place was on that same dishonoured bosom, to connect her parent for ever with the race and descent of mortals, and to be finally a blessed soul in heaven! Yet these thoughts affected Hester Prynne less with hope than apprehension. She knew that her deed had been evil; she could have no faith, therefore, that its result would be good. Day after day she looked fearfully into the child's expanding nature, ever dreading to detect some dark and wild peculiarity that should correspond with the guiltiness to which she owed her being. (Ch. 6)

E. In this passage, Dimmesdale visits the platform where Hester stood at the beginning of the novel. " Why, then, had he come hither?"

It was an obscure night in early May. An unwearied pall of cloud muffled the whole expanse of sky from zenith to horizon. If the same multitude which had stood as eye-witnesses while Hester Prynne sustained her punishment could now have been summoned forth, they would have discerned no face above the platform nor hardly the outline of a human shape, in the dark grey of the midnight. But the town was all asleep. There was no peril of discovery. The minister might stand there, if it so pleased him, until morning should redden in the east, without other risk than that the dank and chill night air would creep into his frame, and stiffen his joints with rheumatism, and clog his throat with catarrh and cough; thereby defrauding the expectant audience of to-morrow's prayer and sermon. No eye could see him, save that ever-wakeful one which had seen him in his closet, wielding the bloody scourge. Why, then, had he come hither? (Ch. 12)

Lesson Seven Test Answers

Discussion Questions

A. What is the purpose of the introductory chapter "The Custom House" in Hawthorne's *The Scarlet Letter*? *There is some debate about that. Some critics argue that it is supercilious. Others insist that it is a vital door through with the reader must walk. On the surface, it is the place where the author discovers the story that is related in The Scarlet Letter.*

B. Discuss Pearl's role in *The Scarlet Letter*? *This is also much debated. Is she Hester's alter-ego? Is she the "wild side" of Hester kept under control by Puritan laws? In any event, Pearl is the quintessential foil.*

C. *The Scarlet Letter* is a battleground between two world views: Christian Theism (Puritanism) and Romanticism. Give examples of both world views in this novel. *The community is a place of laws, order, and safety (Puritanism). Nature, while it is appealing and beautiful, is dangerous because it is outside the laws of man (Romanticism). Stylistically it is a Romantic novel–Hawthorne describes an aberration vs. ordinary events (Realism). The world view, however, is clearly Christian Theism.*

D. What is the significance of these passages:

> This rose-bush, by a strange chance, has been kept alive in history; but whether it had merely survived out of the stern old wilderness, so long after the fall of the gigantic pines and oaks that originally overshadowed it, or whether, as there is far authority for believing, it had sprung up under the footsteps of the sainted Ann Hutchinson as she entered the prison-door, we shall not take upon us to determine. Finding it so directly on the threshold of our narrative, which is now about to issue from that inauspicious portal, we could hardly do otherwise than pluck one of its flowers, and present it to the reader. It may serve, let us hope, to symbolize some sweet moral blossom that may be found along the track, or relieve the darkening close of a tale of human frailty and sorrow . . . Ch. 1.

This of course is the famous scene in which the present events are tied symbolically to the Puritan past. Hester stands with the scarlet A that ties her to the rose planted by the Puritans. Both symbols imply life and hope.

> We have as yet hardly spoken of the infant, that little creature, whose innocent life had sprung, by the inscrutable decree of Providence, a lovely and immortal flower, out of the rank luxuriance of a guilty passion. How strange it seemed to the sad woman, as she watched the growth, and the beauty that became every day more brilliant, and the intelligence that

> threw its quivering sunshine over the tiny features of this child! Her Pearl-
> -for so had Hester called her; not as a name expressive of her aspect,
> which had nothing of the calm, white, unimpassioned lustre that would be
> indicated by the comparison. But she named the infant "Pearl," as being of
> great price--purchased with all she had--her mother's only treasure! How
> strange, indeed! Man had marked this woman's sin by a scarlet letter,
> which had such potent and disastrous efficacy that no human sympathy
> could reach her, save it were sinful like herself. God, as a direct
> consequence of the sin which man thus punished, had given her a lovely
> child, whose place was on that same dishonoured bosom, to connect her
> parent for ever with the race and descent of mortals, and to be finally a
> blessed soul in heaven! Yet these thoughts affected Hester Prynne less
> with hope than apprehension. She knew that her deed had been evil; she
> could have no faith, therefore, that its result would be good. Day after day
> she looked fearfully into the child's expanding nature, ever dreading to
> detect some dark and wild peculiarity that should correspond with the
> guiltiness to which she owed her being. (Ch. 6)

This is the scene in which Pearl is introduced. She is an enigma. On one hand, she is wildly beautiful; but she lies outside the bounds of Puritan society. See comments above.

E. In this passage, Dimmesdale visits the platform where Hester stood at the beginning of the novel. " Why, then, had he come hither?"

> It was an obscure night in early May. An unwearied pall of cloud muffled
> the whole expanse of sky from zenith to horizon. If the same multitude
> which had stood as eye-witnesses while Hester Prynne sustained her
> punishment could now have been summoned forth, they would have
> discerned no face above the platform nor hardly the outline of a human
> shape, in the dark grey of the midnight. But the town was all asleep. There
> was no peril of discovery. The minister might stand there, if it so pleased
> him, until morning should redden in the east, without other risk than that
> the dank and chill night air would creep into his frame, and stiffen his
> joints with rheumatism, and clog his throat with catarrh and cough;
> thereby defrauding the expectant audience of to-morrow's prayer and
> sermon. No eye could see him, save that ever-wakeful one which had seen
> him in his closet, wielding the bloody scourge. Why, then, had he come
> hither? (Ch. 12)

He futilely tried to atone for his sins privately.

LESSON EIGHT

Readings Due For This Lesson

Students should have read Nathaniel Hawthorne's *The Scarlet Letter*.

Reading Ahead

Students should read the short story "The Devil and Tom Walker" by Washington Irving (Lesson Nine). Looking ahead, student should begin reading "Fall of the House of Usher" and "The Tell Tale Heart" both by Edgar Allan Poe (Lesson Ten). Finally, students should begin reading "The Birthmark" by Nathaniel Hawthorne (Lesson Eleven).

Suggested Weekly Implementation

Day One	Day Two	Day Three	Day Four	Day Five
1. Students will rewrite graded essays from last week and review Lesson Seven test. 2. Students should have read the required reading(s) *before* the assigned lesson begins. 3. Teacher may want to discuss assigned reading(s) with student. 4. Teacher shall assign the required essays. Choose two or three. The rest of the essays can be outlined, answered with shorter answers, or skipped.	1. Student should begin reading(s) from next lesson. 2. Student should outline essays due at the end of the week. 3. Students should answer one or two of the essays that are not assigned as formal essays.	1. Students should write rough drafts of assigned essays. 2. The teacher should correct rough drafts.	Student will write final copy of essays due tomorrow.	1. Essays are due. 2. Students should take Lesson Eight test. 3. Student should read review the novel *Scarlet Letter* and read short stories in Lessons Nine, Ten, and Eleven.

Hawthorne. . .

Biblical Application

A. Contrast the way Hester's community handles her adultery and the way Jesus dealt with the adulterous woman who was brought to Him (John 8). *Hester's community was unable to forgive her. Nonetheless, Hester found forgiveness and wholeness through her contrite heart. Jesus announced the adulterous woman's forgiveness and invited others to forgive her too. Whether they did or not, the woman at the well, and Hester Prynne, found forgiveness. Undeserved, unconditional loves invited both heroines to be His disciple. Both individuals manifested a decidedly Theistic response to bad choices!*

B. While we many agree that Hester's community was somewhat rough on her, are we willing to say that she should not have been punished? Do a Bible study on the whole topics of *sin*, *repentance*, and *restoration*. Start in Matthew 18. *Answers will vary. The purpose of Christian discipline is expressly to bring restoration. It is never punitive. Therefore, holding someone responsible for his/her actions is necessary for restoration to occur. If there is no moral standard to be upheld, there can be no sin, and therefore no restoration. This is the concern of the psychologist Karl Menninger when he wrote his influential work* <u>Whatever Happened to Sin</u>?

Literary Criticism

In *The Scarlet Letter*, as Hawthorne did in most of his books, he combined historical truth with imaginative detail to create an allegory. An allegory is a narrative in which characters, action, and sometimes setting represent abstract concepts or moral qualities. What moral qualities are represented by Arthur? Hester? Roger? Write an illustrative essay describing the moral qualities each character represents. *Arthur Dimmesdale represents the flawed religious community. He is not hypocritical--he deeply feels his crime--but he is pusillanimous. Roger Chillingsworth is the villain of this novel. He is amoral. He is the cold, technical, bureaucrat who judges but refuses to get involved. He is only concerned about himself. He represents the Yankee commercialism that is overtaking Hawthorne's community. He represents the cold, dispassionate scientist (e.g., Dr. Frankenstein in Shelley's* <u>Frankenstein</u>) *Hester is a true heroine. Refusing to flee her punishment, she realizes that repentance brings restoration. She is the strongest member of her community. True, strong, and faithful Hester inspires us all. She is a repentant, forgiven sinner who, ironically, is the only person who survives and is stronger for the journey.*

Critical Thinking

A. *The Scarlet Letter* was one of the last books in American literature that had a Theistic moral vision. Although Hawthorne never hinted that Prynne's punishment was unjust, he seemed far more disturbed by Dimmesdale's deception and Chillingway's evil ways. Using this book as a metaphor for the tensions existing in American society c. 1850, in a two-page essay, discuss these tensions and evidence them from the text. Who is the victim in this book? *Surely the setting of <u>The Scarlet Letter</u>--the stern, joyless world of Puritan New England--appears to have very little potential for joy. Why did Hawthorne choose this dark world for his masterpiece? Why did Hawthorne reject the contemporary scene? Hawthorne reached back to Salem in the 1600s to find men and women who would speak directly to his creative imagination. The Puritan world of the mid-17th century apparently gave Hawthorne something he badly needed--people who lived their lives to the full. In the pages of <u>The Scarlet Letter</u>, the Puritans emerge from the shadows of an earlier time, direct of speech, and full of integrity. The Puritans had a moral vitality never again found on the American scene. For a writer like Hawthorne, intrigued with the subject of conscience, here were people with conscience to spare. The Puritans at least knew the difference between right and wrong. Hawthorne made no apologies for Hester's punishment. Likewise, Hawthorne clearly thought that Dimmesdale deserved his punishment too. If there was ambivalence in Hawthorne's world view–between Theism and Transcendentalism–it came forth honestly. Hawthorne, a Theist, was married to a beautiful Transcendentalist, Sophia Peabody. Their friends included Transcendentalists Melville, the Alcott sisters, Emerson, and Thoreau. Hawthorne, the Theist, was no doubt influenced by these individuals. In the life of Hawthorne the reader observes the movement of America's cultural world view from Puritanism to Transcendentalism. By the time Melville wrote <u>Billy Budd</u> the protagonist was "saved" through good works and the Puritan theistic vision appeared to be dead. Hester Prynne was no Billy Budd. Hester Prynne committed adultery, repented, and was forgiven. In summary, what bothered Hawthorne was that Dr. Chillingsworth and Pastor Dimmesdale were unrepentant hypocrites. Chillingsworth, the realist (as Alymer in "The Birthmark"), and Dimmesdale, the coward/hypocrite, would not stand with Hester on the scaffold (until the end when Dimmesdale owned his sin). Hawthorne's characters knew no redemption until they understood and accepted the antidote to sin–the sacrifice of Jesus Christ at calvary which is only accessible to a repentant heart. Really, Hawthorne would say we all are standing on the scaffold with Hester . . . All have sinned and fallen short . . . Ergo, in 1820-1850, when American society was changing so much, and there were so many alternative world views (viz., Realism, Transcendentalism, and Romanticism), Hawthorne, for the last time, promoted a Theistic/Puritan vision. Hawthorne, who wrote like a Romantic but believed like a Christian Theist, was making one last literary effort to make a stand for morality in the face of situation ethics (Realism), an unfeeling angry God (Naturalism), an impersonal God (Deism), a Nature powered world (Romanticism), and a world that emphasizes human intuition (Transcendentalism). For the last time in American literature for two generations, a character stood up and takes responsibility for her moral choices. Contrast this with a later novel <u>A Farewell to Arms</u> where the* *protagonist blamed fate for his problems! The world of which Hawthorne was a part invited him to step away from his Christian beliefs. He chose not to do so. That is the genius of his book. There were no victims--only men and women making decisions that have eternal consequences!*

B. A recent television commercial argued, "Doesn't everyone deserve a second chance?" Do you agree with this statement? Does this book offend your sense of justice? *As long as the person confesses his sin and takes measures to make sure that he does not repeat the offense. Christians should be anxious to forgive the repentant sinner.*

C. Pretend that Hester Prynne lived in City Anywhere, USA. How would she be treated at a public school? At the grocery story? At your church? Defend your answer. *Answers will vary.*

D. Give a characterization of Hester. What sort of woman is she? She could have run away with Arthur. Why doesn't she? *Hester recognizes the value of her punishment. She does not judge others, though. In her attempt to be humble before God, referring to guilt and responsibilities of others, "I know not. I know not."*

E. Pearl functions as a foil (a character whose primary purpose is to develop the main character). Give evidence of this purpose. *Pearl is a wild, impish character who represents the fruit of Hester's and Arthur's sin. She is an invitation, that Hester never takes, to be wild and unholy.*

F. In another essay, compare the use of a foil in this book with another foil in another piece of literature. *One of the best foils in American literature is Jim in Huckleberry Finn. In the movie* Chariots of Fire *Aubrey functions as a foil.*

G. Compare Pearl to a foil in your favorite movie (e.g. the way Aubrey is used in the movie *Chariots of Fire*). *An excellent foil in the movie* Iron Will *is the Native American Companion of Will Stoner.*

H. Many scholars find evidence that Nathaniel Hawthorne was a believer. While there were evidences of Transcendentalism in his writings, Hawthorne admired and advanced the Puritan Theistic vision. The ambivalence in his writing may have been from his Transcendalist/Universalist wife Sophia Peabody Hawthorne who no doubt influenced him . What do you think? Offer evidence in your essay from the *The Scarlet Letter* and other writings. *Hawthorne came dangerously close to Transcendentalism. His use of the rose, for instance, and other symbolism resembled Emerson's writing. Also, Hawthorne seemed to borrow symbols of light and darkness which were powerful Transcendental symbols. On the other hand, he did not deify nature nor did he prosper immoral characters.*

Historical Setting

A. Hawthorne, with friends, explored utopian living. This early 19th- century generation that so closely resembled the generation of the 1960s, dabbled in utopia, or a perfect society. In 1516 an Englishman named Sir Thomas More had coined the word *Utopia* when he wrote his book by the same name. Between 1840 and 1850, Americans founded 40 utopian communities. These early attempts at perfection were founded on the notion that mankind could be perfect if it lived in a cooperative–not competitive–community.

One notable attempt to live this life was Brook Farm. This experiment in communal living was both scandalous and revolutionary. The founder, George Ripley, described it this way:

Our objectives, as you know are to insure a more natural union between intellectual and manual labor than now exists; to combine the thinker and the worker, as far as possible, in the same individual; to guarantee the highest mental freedom, by proving all with labor, adapted to their tastes and talents, and securing to them the fruits of their industry; to do away with the necessity of menial services, by opening the benefits of education and the profits of labor to all; and thus to prepare a society of liberal, intelligent and cultivated persons, whose relations with each other would permit a more simple and wholesome life than can be lead amidst the pressure of our competitive institutions.

Founded in 1841, Brook Farm existed for only a few years, but more than anything else, it represented the hope and optimism of Hawthorne and his friends.

In a two-page essay, explore the similarities between artists of the 1960s (Dylan, Hendrix, Warhol) and artists of the 1830s (Emerson, Hawthorne, Thoreau, and Melville). *Both groups celebrated individuality and subjectivity. It is fair to say, however, that the 19th century reformers never dreamed of participating in the hedonistic excesses that 1960 artists experienced. The difference, however, is more in degree than in substance. Both were very radical groups.*

B. The Puritans of Boston, Massachusetts Bay sailed to America in 1630, as had the Separatist Puritans, to worship God freely. Unlike the Separatists, the Puritans did not desire to separate themselves from the Church of England but hoped instead to reform it. Nonetheless, the notions of freedom and equality, so precious to later New England patriots, were completely foreign to Puritan leaders. The leaders of the Massachusetts Bay enterprise never intended their colony to be a bastion of freedom and toleration in the New World; rather, they intended it to be a "City on a Hill," a model of Christian felicity and fervency.

Massachusetts Bay was not a democracy; it was an autocracy under the law of the land and the perceived laws of the Bible. This was one of the first efforts to create a new society entirely on the Word of God. The first governor, John Winthrop, believed that it was not the duty of the public officials of the commonwealth to act as the direct representatives of their constituents but rather to act entirely according to the laws of the land and the laws of the World of God. The will of the people was suspect and even spurious when stacked against the Bible.

Nonetheless, in 1634 the General Court, the ruling body of Massachusetts Bay, under the stated authority of Scripture, adopted a new plan of representation that became a prototype for American representative democracy. Each town was allowed to send representatives to a sort of legislature. This was a new phenomenon, even in British political history.

However, the world in which Hester Prynne lived did not practice wholesale equality, and several disenchanted Puritans moved on to found other colonies, notably Connecticut and Rhode Island. In fact, Roger Williams ironically founded Rhode Island as a religious sanctuary from the orthodox Massachusetts Bay Colony!

How accurate is Hawthorne's image of Puritan New England?

It is fairly accurate.

Challenge Questions

A. Read *The Crucible*, by the playwright Arthur Miller. Compare the view of Puritanism in Arthur Miller's *The Crucible* and Nathaniel Hawthorne's *The Scarlet Letter*. *Arthur Miller rejects "sin" as a legitimate category in human ethics. He embraces psychology and rejects theology. "Evil" to Miller is defined as "close-mindedness." <u>The Crucible</u> was written during the McCarthy Era in the 1950's. The McCarthy Era was a sort of witch trial.*

B. Do you really think that there were witches in Salem? *One of the most remarkable and bizarre–depending on the reader's perspective–events in early colonial history occurred during May through October 1692. Around Salem Village, Massachusetts, north of Boston, 19 convicted "witches" were hanged and many other suspects were imprisoned in the town of Salem in the Massachusetts Bay Colony. Alarmed by tales told by a West Indian slave named Tituba, local officials, encouraged by Pastor Samuel Parris, set up a special court in Salem to try those accused of practicing witchcraft. The list of the accused increased (even Massachusetts governor William Phips's wife was implicated) until over a 100 people were put in jail. While there could well have been witches among the accused, this whole affair was reflective more of the growing concern that the hold of Puritanism was being replaced rapidly by a growing Yankee spirit of commercialism and secularism than it was about the punishment of witches.*

C. Allan Bloom has written in *The Closing of the American Mind*:

> *As it now stands, students have a powerful image of what a perfect body is and pursue it incessantly. But deprived of ...guidance they no longer have any image of a perfect soul...the eternal conflict between good and evil has been replaced with "I'm okay, you're okay." Men and women once paid for difficult choices with their reputations, their sanity, and even their lives. But no more...America has no-fault automobile accidents, no fault insurance...no consequence choices.*

How accurate is this quote? Have we moved too far from Hester Prynne's world? Answer in a two-page essay. *We are too much a reflection of our culture and not enough of our Lord. We should be countercultural subversives. We must break the hold that Satan has on our world. We must tear up the culture of disbelief (Carter) and culture of hopelessness (Bruggemann). The Christian teacher Os Guinness writes, "It is now questionable whether America's cultural order is capable of nourishing the freedom, responsibility, and civility that Americans require to sustain democracy. Modernity creates problems far deeper than drugs, etc. It creates a crisis of cultural authority in which America's beliefs, ideals, and traditions are losing their compelling power in society."*

For Further Enrichment

A. *The Scarlet Letter* is a classic read by millions of American students every year. How do you account for the book's continued relevance? In your response, consider such matters such as style, setting, plot, theme, point of view, and moral vision. If you were a teacher, would you want your students to read this book? Why or why not? Write a two-page essay. *Like most classics, the <u>Scarlet Letter</u>, presents themes of universal and timeless importance.*

B. *The Scarlet Letter* was a critical success but not a best seller. In American society today, so structured around entertainment, one wonders if Hawthorne could find a publisher. In his book *Amusing Ourselves to Death* Neil Postman argues that television is transforming our culture into one vast arena for show business (p. 80). TV is the highest order of abstract thinking and consistently undermines critical thinking (p.41). The message has become the medium. What do you think? Read Postman or use other material and write an essay explaining how our culture has been transformed by television and the entertainment industry. *Clearly Postman is correct.*

C. Compare and contrast Hester Prynne in *The Scarlet Letter* and Phoebe Pyncheon in *House of the Seven Gables*. *Both Phoebe and Prynne are strong , female, Theistic characters in a dark, Romantic world.*

Supplemental Reading:

Nathaniel Hawthorne, Millicent Bell (Editor), *Nathaniel Hawthorne : Collected Novels: Fanshawe, The Scarlet Letter, The House of the Seven Gables, The Blithedale Romance*

    An excellent collection of Hawthorne's five novels with editorial helps. The reader's choice of a version for young readers.

Nathaniel Hawthorne, Roy Harvey Pearce (Editor) *Nathaniel Hawthorne : Tales and Sketches*
    Tales and Sketches offers young readers an authoritative edition of Hawthorne's complete stories in a single comprehensive volume.

LouAnn Gaeddert. *A New England Love Story: Nathaniel Hawthorne and Sophia Peabody*
    For mature readers, Gaeddert gives great insights into the relationship of Sophia Peabody and Nathaniel Hawthorne.

Bradley Sculley, ed. *The Scarlet Letter: Backgrounds and Sources, Criticism.*
> One of the best scholarly resources on Hawthorne and his works.

Arlin Turner, *Nathaniel Hawthorne: A Biography*
> An unpretentious but readable biography of Hawthorne.

Notes:

Lesson Eight Test

Discussion Questions: (100 Points)

The following are quotes from critics about *The Scarlet Letter*. Paraphrase each criticism and agree or disagree with each one.

A. The personages in it with whom the reader will interest himself are four--the husband, the minister who has been the sinful lover, the woman, and the child. The reader is expected to sympathize only with the woman--and will sympathize only with her. The husband, an old man who has knowingly married a young woman who did not love him, is a personification of that feeling of injury which is supposed to fall upon a man when his honor has been stained by the falseness of a wife. He has left her and has wandered away, not even telling her of his whereabouts. He comes back to her without a sign. The author tells us that he had looked to find his happiness in her solicitude and care for him. The reader, however, gives him credit for no love. But the woman was his wife, and he comes back and finds that she had gone astray. Her he despises, and is content to leave herto the ascetic cruelty of the town magistrates; but to find the man out and bring the man to his grave by slow torture is enough of employment for what is left to him of life and energy (1879).

B. Above all it is Hester Prynne whose passion and beauty dominate every other person, and color each event. Hawthorne has conceived her as he has conceived his scene, in the full strength of his feeling for ancient New England. He is the Homer of that New England, and Hester is its most heroic creature. Tall, with dark and abundant hair and deep black eyes, a rich complexion that makes modern women (says Hawthorne) pale and thin by comparison, and a dignity that throws into low relief the "delicate, evanescent, and indescribable grace" by which gentility in girls has since come to be known, from the very first--and we believe it--she is said to cast a spell over those who behold her (Martin Van Doren, 1949).

C. "The Custom House" throws light on a theme in The Scarlet Letter which is easily overlooked amid the ethical concerns of the book. Every character, in effect, re-enacts "The Custom House" scene in which Hawthorne himself contemplated the letter, so that the entire "romance" becomes a kind of exposition on the nature of symbolic perception. Hawthorne's subject is not only the meaning of adultery but also meaning in general; not only what the focal symbol means but also how it gains significance. (Charles Feidelson, Jr., 1953)

D. Hawthorne was morally, in an appreciative degree, a chip off the old block. His forefathers crossed the Atlantic for conscience sake, and it was the idea of the urgent conscience that haunted the imagination of their so-called degenerate successor. The Puritan strain in his blood ran clear--there are passages in his diaries, kept during his residence in Europe, which might almost have been written by the grimmest of the old Salem worthies. (Henry James, 1879)

E. In *The Scarlet Letter*, passion justifies nothing, while its denial justifies all. The fallen Eden of this world remains fallen; but the sinful priest purges himself by public confession, becomes worthy of his sole remaining way to salvation, death. Even Hester, though sin and suffering have made her an almost magical figure, a polluted but still terrible goddess, must finally accept loneliness and self-restraint instead of the love and freedom she dreamed. (Leslie A. Fiedler, 1968).

Lesson Eight Test Answers

Discussion Questions: (100 Points)

The following are quotes from critics about *The Scarlet Letter*. Paraphrase each criticism and agree or disagree with each one.

A. The personages in it with whom the reader will interest himself are four--the husband, the minister who has been the sinful lover, the woman, and the child. The reader is expected to sympathize only with the woman--and will sympathize only with her. The husband, an old man who has knowingly married a young woman who did not love him, is a personification of that feeling of injury which is supposed to fall upon a man when his honor has been stained by the falseness of a wife. He has left her and has wandered away, not even telling her of his whereabouts. He comes back to her without a sign. The author tells us that he had looked to find his happiness in her solicitude and care for him. The reader, however, gives him credit for no love. But the woman was his wife, and he comes back and finds that she had gone astray. Her he despises, and is content to leave her to the ascetic cruelty of the town magistrates; but to find the man out and bring the man to his grave by slow torture is enough of employment for what is left to him of life and energy (1879). *First, Hawthorne does not "pity" Hester. He respects and honors her. She is the person of integrity and honor–not desirous of pity. She deserves none–she is redeemed by her walk with God. Secondly, Chillingworth, full of unforgivingness is neither a victim nor a hero. He is despicable. He could have forgiven his wife and had her as his wife again–but chose to participate in evil machinations and rejected her.*

B. Above all it is Hester Prynne whose passion and beauty dominate every other person, and color each event. Hawthorne has conceived her as he has conceived his scene, in the full strength of his feeling for ancient New England. He is the Homer of that New England, and Hester is its most heroic creature. Tall, with dark and abundant hair and deep black eyes, a rich complexion that makes modern women (says Hawthorne) pale and thin by comparison, and a dignity that throws into low relief the "delicate, evanescent, and indescribable grace" by which gentility in girls has since come to be known, from the very first--and we believe it--she is said to cast a spell over those who behold her (Martin Van Doren, 1949). *This is accurate.*

C. "The Custom House" throws light on a theme in The Scarlet Letter which is easily overlooked amid the ethical concerns of the book. Every character, in effect, re-enacts "The Custom House" scene in which Hawthorne himself contemplated the letter, so that the entire "romance" becomes a kind of exposition on the nature of symbolic perception. Hawthorne's subject is not only the meaning of adultery but also meaning in general; not only what the focal symbol means but also how it gains significance. (Charles Feidelson,

Jr., 1953) *Intriguing idea, but perhaps this critic is making too much of the custom house since Hawthorne only mentions it in the beginning of the novel and never again.*

D. Hawthorne was morally, in an appreciative degree, a chip off the old block. His forefathers crossed the Atlantic for conscience sake, and it was the idea of the urgent conscience that haunted the imagination of their so-called degenerate successor. The Puritan strain in his blood ran clear--there are passages in his diaries, kept during his residence in Europe, which might almost have been written by the grimmest of the old Salem worthies. (Henry James, 1879) *A bit harsh, this critic nonetheless is correct in saying that Hawthorne advanced Puritan/Christian Theist values.*

E. In *The Scarlet Letter*, passion justifies nothing, while its denial justifies all. The fallen Eden of this world remains fallen; but the sinful priest purges himself by public confession, becomes worthy of his sole remaining way to salvation, death. Even Hester, though sin and suffering have made her an almost magical figure, a polluted but still terrible goddess, must finally accept loneliness and self-restraint instead of the love and freedom she dreamed. (Leslie A. Fiedler, 1968). *He is right on target with Dimmesdale but misses Hester all together. In fact, she is happy, and more than that. She experiences the pleasure of living a Christian Theistic life.*

LESSON NINE

Readings Due For This Lesson
Students should have read the short story "The Devil and Tom Walker" by Washington Irving.

Reading Ahead
Students should read Fall of the House of Usher and "The Tell Tale Heart" both by Edgar Allan Poe (Lesson Ten) and "The Birthmark" by Nathaniel Hawthorne (Lesson Eleven).

Suggested Weekly Implementation

Day One	Day Two	Day Three	Day Four	Day Five
1. Students will rewrite graded essays from last week and review Lesson Eight test. 2. Students should have read the required reading(s) *before* the assigned lesson begins. 3. Teacher may want to discuss assigned reading(s) with student. 4. Teacher shall assign the required essays. Choose two or three. The rest of the essays can be outlined, answered with shorter answers, or skipped.	1. Student should begin reading(s) from next lesson. 2. Student should outline essays due at the end of the week. 3. Students should answer one or two of the essays that are not assigned as formal essays.	1. Students should write rough drafts of assigned essays. 2. The teacher should correct rough drafts.	Student will write final copy of essays due tomorrow.	1. Essays are due. 2. Students should take Lesson Nine test. 3. Student should read short stories in Lessons Ten and Eleven. Stories are provided in text.

Nineteenth Century Short Stories

Literary Criticism

A. In "The Devil and Tom Walker" Irving used an extensive vocabulary. Define each word and use it in a sentence.

parsimonious (miserly)

propitiatory (fortunate)

ostentatious (showy)

superfluous (unnecessary)

melancholy (sad)

B. The use of these difficult words makes his short story more humorous. How? *To the unsophisticated 19th century audience, pretentious language would have portrayed Tom Walker as the pompous, self-centered, shallow man that he was. The audience would have loved it.*

C. Find the sentence in the conclusion of the short story where Tom makes an ironic statement. *"The devil take me if I have made a farthing." That is of course exactly what happened.*

D. What is the meaning of the Woodman's scoring of the trees in *The Devil and Tom Walker? This foreshadows the mark of the devil on Tom Walker.* What do the trees symbolize? *Just as the trees burn, so shall Walker someday.*

E. As Tom ages, he becomes "a violent churchgoer." Is Tom's conversion genuine? Offer evidence to support your answer. *Clearly, Tom was seeking "fire insurance." It was to no avail, however."*

F. *Hyperbole* is a figure of speech in which exaggeration of fact is used in order to produce humor. Give an example of hyperbole in *The Devil and Tom Walker? "...female scold is generally considered a match for the devil.*

G. The theme of this book--selling one's soul to the devil--is a common theme in world literature. Offer at least one other example. *The Tragedy of Faust, Goethe, but there are many other examples too. Marlowe wrote an English play about the same theme.*

Biblical Application

A. Write an expository essay describing two or three biblical characters who compromised their faith for fame, fortune, or other reasons. *Possible choices include Samson, Saul, and Soloman.*

B. Create a modern version of "The Devil and Tom Walker." Your short story should be about five to ten pages. *Answers will vary.*

Challenge Question

A. Compare and contrast Irving's short story with Goethe's *Faust*. *Faust is a similar story, but much longer, and much more complicated. than "The Devil and Tom Walker." There is no person quite like Goethe's Gretchen in Irving's "The Devil and Tom Walker." Also, the ending is much different in Goethe's Faust. Faust is allowed to escape eternal damnation; Walker does not escape antyhing.*

B. Critic Harold Bloom in *The Western Canon* laments the propensity for other critics to discuss world view in literary works. He argues that suggesting that literary works have a world view cheapens their artistic value. Is it possible to read literature as if it does not have a world view? Do you agree with Bloom? *At the beginning of the 21st century, in the midst of a culture war, to suggest that one should read books, watch movies, and pretend that they are only "art" is absurd. Christians, especially, must be careful to guard their hearts.*

Supplemental Reading:

Nathaniel Hawthorne, Millicent Bell (Editor), *Nathaniel Hawthorne : Collected Novels: Fanshawe, The Scarlet Letter, The House of the Seven Gables, The Blithedale Romance*

An excellent collection of Hawthorne's five novels with editorial helps. The reader's choice of a version for young readers.

Nathaniel Hawthorne, Roy Harvey Pearce (Editor) *Nathaniel Hawthorne : Tales and Sketches*

Tales and Sketches offers young readers an authoritative edition of Hawthorne's complete stories in a single comprehensive volume.

LouAnn Gaeddert. *A New England Love Story: Nathaniel Hawthorne and Sophia Peabody*

For mature readers, Gaeddert gives great insights into the relationship of Sophia Peabody and Nathaniel Hawthorne.

Bradley Sculley, ed. *The Scarlet Letter: Backgrounds and Sources, Criticism.*

One of the best scholarly resources on Hawthorne and his works.

Arlin Turner, *Nathaniel Hawthorne: A Biography*

An unpretentious but readable biography of Hawthorne.

Notes:

Lesson Nine Test

Discussion Questions: (100 Points)

Read the following short story and complete the accompanying worksheet.

Great Stone Face
Nathaniel Hawthorne

One afternoon, when the sun was going down, a mother and her little boy sat at the door of their cottage, talking about the Great Stone Face. They had but to lift their eyes, and there it was plainly to be seen, though miles away, with the sunshine brightening all its features. And what was the Great Stone Face? Embosomed amongst a family of lofty mountains, there was a valley so spacious that it contained many thousand inhabitants. Some of these good people dwelt in loghuts, with the black forest all around them, on the steep and difficult hillsides. Others had their homes in comfortable farm houses, and cultivated the rich soil on the gentle slopes or level surfaces of the valley. Others, again, were congregated into populous villages, where some wild, highland rivulet, tumbling down from its birthplace in the upper mountain region, had been caught and tamed by human cunning, and compelled to turn the machinery of cotton factories. The inhabitants of this valley, in short, were numerous, and of many modes of life. But all of them, grown people and children, had a kind of familiarity with the Great Stone Face, although some possessed the gift of distinguishing this grand natural phenomenon more perfectly than many of their neighbors.

The Great Stone Face, then, was a work of Nature in her mood of majestic playfulness, formed on the perpendicular side of a mountain by some immense rocks, which had been thrown together in such a position as, when viewed at a proper distance, precisely to resemble the features of the human countenance. It seemed as if an enormous giant, or a Titan, had sculptured his own likeness on the precipice. There was the broad arch of the forehead, a hundred feet in height; the nose, with its long bridge; and the vast lips, which, if they could have spoken, would have rolled their thunder accents from one end of the valley to the other. True it is, that if the spectator approached too near, he lost the outline of the gigantic visage, and could discern only a heap of ponderous and gigantic rocks, piled in chaotic ruin one upon another. Retracing his steps, however, the wondrous features would again be seen; and the farther he withdrew from them, the more like a human face, with all its original divinity intact, did they appear; until, as it grew dim in the distance, with the clouds and glorified vapor of the mountains clustering about it, the Great Stone Face seemed positively to be alive.

It was a happy lot for children to grow up to manhood or womanhood with the Great Stone Face before their eyes, for all the features were noble, and the expression was at once grand and sweet, as if it were the glow of a vast, warm heart, that embraced all mankind in its affections, and had room for more. It was an education only to look at it. According to the belief of many people, the valley owed much of its fertility to this benign aspect that was continually beaming over it, illuminating the clouds, and infusing its tenderness into the sunshine.

As we began with saying, a mother and her little boy sat at their cottage door, gazing at the Great Stone Face, and talking about it. The child's name was Ernest.

"Mother," said he, while the Titanic visage milled on him, "I wish that it could speak, for it looks so very kindly that its voice must needs be pleasant. If I were to See a man with such a face, I should love him dearly." "If an old prophecy should come to pass," answered his mother, "we may see a man, some time, for other, with exactly such a face as that." "What prophecy do you mean, dear mother?" eagerly inquired Ernest. "Pray tell me all about it!" So his mother told him a story that her own mother had told to her, when she herself was younger than little Ernest; a story, not of things that were past, but of what was yet to come; a story, nevertheless, so very old, that even the Indians, who formerly inhabited this valley, had heard it from their forefathers, to whom, as they affirmed, it had been murmured by the mountain streams, and whispered by the wind among the treetops. The purport was, that, at some future day, a child should be born hereabouts, who was destined to become the greatest and noblest personage of his time, and whose countenance, in manhood, should bear an exact resemblance to the Great Stone Face. Not a few old-fashioned people, and young ones likewise, in the ardor of their hopes, still cherished an enduring faith in this old prophecy. But others, who had seen more of the world, had watched and waited till they were weary, and had beheld no man with such a face, nor any man that proved to be much greater or nobler than his neighbors, concluded it to be nothing but an idle tale. At all events, the great man of the prophecy had not yet appeared."

O mother, dear mother!" cried Ernest, clapping his hands above his head, "I do hope that I shall live to see him!

His mother was an affectionate and thoughtful woman, and felt that it was wisest not to discourage the generous hopes of her little boy. So she only said to him, "Perhaps you may."

And Ernest never forgot the story that his mother told him. It was always in his mind, whenever he looked upon the Great Stone Face. He spent his childhood in the log cottage where he was born, and was dutiful to his mother, and helpful to her in many things, assisting her much with his little hands, and more with his loving heart. In this manner, from a happy yet often pensive child, he grew up to be a mild, quiet, unobtrusive boy, and sun-browned with labor in the fields, but with more intelligence brightening his aspect than is seen in many lads who have been taught at famous schools. Yet Ernest had had no teacher, save only that the Great Stone Face became one to him. When the toil of the day was over, he would gaze at it for hours, until he began to imagine that those vast features recognized him, and gave him a smile of kindness and encouragement, responsive to his own look of veneration. We must not take upon us to affirm that this was a mistake, although the Face may have looked no more kindly at Ernest than at all the world besides. But the secret was that the boy"s tender and confiding simplicity discerned what other people could not see; and thus the love, which was meant for all, became his peculiar portion.

About this time there went a rumor throughout the valley, that the great man, foretold from ages long ago, who was to bear a resemblance to the Great Stone Face, had appeared at last. It seems that, many years before, a young man had migrated from the valley and settled at a distant seaport, where, after getting together a little money, he had set up as a shopkeeper. His name but I could never learn whether it was his real one, or a nickname that had grown out of his habits and success in life was Gathergold.

Being shrewd and active, and endowed by Providence with that inscrutable faculty which develops itself in what the world calls luck, he became an exceedingly rich merchant, and owner of a whole fleet of bulky bottomed ships. All the countries of the globe appeared to join hands for the mere purpose of adding heap after heap to the mountainous accumulation of this one man's wealth. The cold regions of the north, almost within the gloom and shadow of the Arctic Circle, sent him their tribute in the shape of furs; hot Africa sifted for him the golden sands of her rivers, and gathered up the ivory tusks of her great elephants out of the forests; the east came bringing him the rich shawls, and spices, and teas, and the effulgence of diamonds, and the gleaming purity of large pearls. The ocean, not to be behindhand with the earth, yielded up her mighty whales, that Mr. Gathergold might sell their oil, and make a profit on it. Be the original commodity what it might, it was gold within his grasp. It might be said of him, as of Midas, in the fable, that whatever he touched with his finger immediately glistened, and grew yellow, and was changed at once into sterling metal, or, which suited him still better, into piles of coin. And, when Mr. Gathergold had become so very rich that it would have taken him a hundred years only to count his wealth, he bethought himself of his native valley, and resolved to go back thither, and end his days where he was born. With this purpose in view, he sent a skillful architect to build him such a palace as should be fit for a man of his vast wealth to live in.

As I have said above, it had already been rumored in the valley that Mr. Gathergold had turned out to be the prophetic personage so long and vainly looked for, and that his visage was the perfect and undeniable similitude of the Great Stone Face. People were the more ready to believe that this must needs be the fact, when they beheld the splendid edifice that rose, as if by enchantment, on the site of his father's old weatherbeaten farmhouse. The exterior was of marble, so dazzlingly white that it seemed as though the whole structure might melt away in the sunshine, like those humbler ones which Mr. Gathergold, in his young playdays, before his fingers were gifted with the touch of transmutation, had been accustomed to build of snow. It had a richly ornamented portico supported by tall pillars, beneath which was a lofty door, studded with silver knobs, and made of a kind of variegated wood that had been brought from beyond the sea. The windows, from the floor to the ceiling of each stately apartment, were composed, respectively of but one enormous pane of glass, so transparently pure that it was said to be a finer medium than even the vacant atmosphere. Hardly anybody had been permitted to see the interior of this palace; but it was reported, and with good semblance of truth, to be far more gorgeous than the outside, insomuch that whatever was iron or brass in other houses was silver or gold in this; and Mr. Gathergold's bedchamber, especially, made such a glittering appearance that no ordinary man would have been able to close his eyes there. But, on the other hand, Mr. Gathergold was now so inured to wealth, that perhaps he could not have closed his eyes unless where the gleam of it was certain to find its way beneath his eyelids.

In due time, the mansion was finished; next came the upholsterers, with magnificent furniture; then, a whole troop of black and white servants, the haranguers of Mr. Gathergold, who, in his own majestic person, was expected to arrive at sunset. Our friend Ernest, meanwhile, had been deeply stirred by the idea that the great man, the noble man, the man of prophecy, after so many ages of delay, was at length to be made manifest to his native valley. He knew, boy as he was, that there were a thousand ways in which Mr. Gathergold, with his vast wealth, might transform himself into an angel of beneficence, and assume a control over human affairs as wide and benignant as the smile of the Great Stone Face. Full of faith and hope, Ernest doubted not that what the people said was true, and that now he was to behold the living likeness of those wondrous features on the mountainside. While the boy was still gazing up the valley, and fancying, as he always did, that the Great Stone Face returned his gaze and looked kindly at him, the rumbling of wheels was heard, approaching swiftly along the winding road.

"Here he comes!" cried a group of people who were assembled to witness the arrival. "Here comes the great Mr. Gathergold!"

A carriage, drawn by four horses, dashed round the turn of the road. Within it, thrust partly out of the window, appeared the physiognomy of the old man, with a skin as yellow as if his own Midas hand had transmuted it. He had a low forehead, small, sharp eyes, puckered about with innumerable wrinkles, and very thin lips, which he made still thinner by pressing them forcibly together.

"The very image or the Great Stone Face!" shouted the people. "Sure enough, the old prophecy is true; and here we have the great man come, at last!"

And, what greatly perplexed Ernest, they seemed actually to believe that here was the likeness which they spoke of. By the roadside there chanced to be an old beggar woman and two little beggar children, stragglers from some far-off region, who, as the carriage rolled onward, held out their hands and lifted up their doleful voices, most piteously beseeching charity. A yellow claw the very same that had dawed together so much wealth poked itself out of the coach window, and dropped some copper coins upon the ground; so that, though the great man's name seems to have been Gathergold, he might just as suitably have been nicknamed Scatter copper. Still, nevertheless, with an earnest shout, and evidently with as much good faith as ever, the people bellowed "He is the very image of the Great Stone Face!" But Ernest turned sadly from the wrinkled shrewdness of that sordid visage, and gazed up the valley, where, amid a gathering mist, gilded by the last sunbeams, he could still distinguish those glorious features which had impressed themselves into his soul. Their aspect cheered him. What did the benign lips seem to say?

"He will come! Fear not, Ernest; the man will come! "

The years went on, and Ernest ceased to be a boy. He had grown to be a young man now. He attracted little notice from the other inhabitants of the valley; for they saw nothing remarkable in his way of life, save that, when the labor of the day was over, he still loved to go apart and gaze and meditate upon the Great Stone Face. According to their idea of the matter, it was a folly, indeed, but pardonable, inasmuch as Ernest was industrious, kind, and neighborly, and neglected no duty for the sake of indulging this idle habit. They knew not that the Great Stone Face had become a teacher to him, and that the sentiment which was expressed in it would enlarge the young man's heart, and fill it with wider and deeper sympathies than other hearts. They knew not that thence would come a better wisdom than could be learned from books, and a better life than could be molded on the defaced example of other human lives. Neither did Ernest know that the thoughts and affections which came to him so naturally, in the fields and at the fireside, and wherever he communed with himself, were of a higher tone than those which all men shared with him. A simple soul simple as when his mother first taught him the old prophecy he beheld the marvelous features beaming down the valley, and still wondered that their human counterpart was so long in making his appearance.

By this time poor Mr. Gathergold was dead and buried; and the oddest part of the matter was, that his wealth, which was the body and spirit of his existence, had disappeared before his death, leaving nothing of him but a living skeleton, covered over with a wrinkled, yellow skin. Since the melting away of his gold, it had been very generally conceded that there was no such striking resemblance, after all, betwixt the ignoble features of the ruined merchant and that majestic face upon the mountainside. So the people ceased to honor him during his lifetime, and quietly consigned him to forgetfulness after his decease. Once in a while, it is true, his memory was brought up in connection with the magnificent palace which he had built, and which had long ago been turned into a hotel for the accommodation of strangers, multitudes of whom came, every summer, to visit that famous natural curiosity, the Great Stone Face. Thus, Mr. Gathergold being discredited and thrown into the shade, the man of prophecy was yet to come.

It so happened that a native-born son of the valley, many years before, had enlisted as a soldier, and, after a great deal of hard fighting, had now become an illustrious commander. Whatever he may be called in history, he was known in camps and on the battlefield under the nickname of Old Blood and Thunder. This war worn veteran, being now infirm with age and wounds, and weary of the turmoil of a military life, and of the roll of the drum and the clangor of the trumpet, that had so long been ringing in his ears, had lately signified a purpose of returning to his native valley, hoping to find repose where he remembered to have left it. The inhabitants, his old neighbors and their grownup children, were resolved to welcome the renowned warrior with a salute of cannon and a public dinner; and all the more enthusiastically, it being affirmed that now, at last, the likeness of the Great Stone Face had actually appeared. An aide camp of Old Blood and Thunder, traveling through the valley, was said to have been struck with the resemblance. Moreover the schoolmates and early acquaintances of the general were ready to testify, on oath, that, to the best of their recollection, the aforesaid general had been exceedingly like the majestic image, even when a boy, only that the idea had never occurred to them at that period. Great, therefore, was the excitement throughout the valley; and many people, who had never once thought of glancing at the Great Stone Face for years before, now spent their time in gazing at it, for the sake of knowing exactly how General Blood and Thunder looked.

On the day of the great festival, Ernest, with all the other people of the valley, left their work, and proceeded to the spot where the sylvan banquet was prepared. As he approached, the loud voice of the Rev. Dr. Battleblast was heard, beseeching a blessing on the good things set before them, and on the distinguished friend of peace in whose honor they were assembled. The tables were arranged in a cleared space of the woods, shut in by the surrounding trees, except where a vista opened eastward, and afforded a distant view of the Great Stone Face. Over the general's chair, which was a relic from the home of Washington, there was an arch of verdant boughs, with the laurel profusely intermixed, and surmounted by his country's banner, beneath which he had won his victories. Our friend Ernest raised himself on his tiptoes, in hopes to get a glimpse of the celebrated guest; but there was a mighty crowd about the tables anxious to hear the toasts and speeches, and to catch any word that might fall from the general in reply; and a volunteer company, doing duty as a guard, pricked ruthlessly with their bayonets at any particularly quiet person among the throng. So Ernest, being of an unobtrusive character, was thrust quite into the background, where he could see no more of Old Blood and Thunder's physiognomy than if it had been still blazing on the battlefield. To console himself, he turned towards the Great Stone Face, which, like a faithful and long remembered friend, looked back and smiled upon him through the vista of the forest. Meantime, however, he could overhear the remarks of various individuals, who were comparing the features of the hero with the face on the distant mountainside.

"T is the same face, to a hair!" cried one man, cutting a caper for joy.

"Wonderfully like, that's a fact!" responded another.

"Like! why, I call it Old Blood and Thunder himself, in a monstrous looking-glass!" cried a third.

"And why not? He's the greatest man of this or any other age, beyond a doubt."

And then all three of the speakers gave a great shout, which communicated electricity to the crowd, and called forth a roar from a thousand voices, that went reverberating for miles among the mountains, until you might have supposed that the Great Stone Face had poured its thunder breath into the cry. All these comments, and this vast enthusiasm, served the more to interest our friend; nor did he think of questioning that now, at length, the mountain visage had found its human counterpart. It is true, Ernest had imagined that this long looked for personage would appear in the character of a man of peace, uttering wisdom, and doing good, and making people happy. But, taking an habitual breadth of view, with all his simplicity, he contended that providence should choose its own method of blessing mankind, and could conceive that this great end might be effected even by a warrior and a bloody sword, should inscrutable wisdom see fit to order matters SO.

"The general! the general!" was now the cry. " Hush! silence! Old Blood and Thunder's going to make a speech."

Even so; for, the cloth being removed, the general's health had been drunk, amid shouts of applause, and he now stood upon his feet to thank the company. Ernest saw him. There he was, over the shoulders of the crowd, from the two glittering epaulets and embroidered collar upward, beneath the arch of green boughs with intertwined laurel, and the banner drooping as if to shade his brow! And there, too, visible in the same glance, through the vista of the forest, appeared the Great Stone Face! And was there, indeed, such a resemblance as the crowd had testified? Alas, Ernest could not recognize it! He beheld a war worn and weatherbeaten countenance, full of energy, and expressive of an iron will; but the gentle wisdom, the deep, broad, tender sympathies, were altogether wanting in Old Blood and Thunder's visage; and even if the Great Stone Face had assumed his look of stern command, the milder traits would still have tempered it.

" This is not the man of prophecy," sighed Ernest to himself, as he made his way out of the throng. "And must the world wait longer yet?"

The mists had congregated about the distant mountainside, and there were seen the grand and awful features of the Great Stone Face, awful but benignant, as if a mighty angel were sitting among the hills, and enrobing himself in a cloudvesture of gold and purple. As he looked, Ernest could hardly believe but that a smile beamed over the whole visage, with a radiance still brightening, although without motion of the lips. It was probably the effect of the western sunshine, melting through the thinly diffused vapors that had swept between him and the object that he gazed at. But as it always did the aspect of his marvelous friend made Ernest as hopeful as if he had never hoped in vain.

"Fear not, Ernest," said his heart, even as if the Great Face were whispering himself, "fear not, Ernest; he will come."

More years sped swiftly and tranquilly away. Ernest still dwelt in his native valley, and was now a man of middle age. By imperceptible degrees, he had become known among the people. Now, as heretofore, he labored for his bread, and was the same simple-hearted man that he had always been. But he had thought and felt so much, he had given so many of the best hours of his life to unworldly hopes for some great good to mankind, that it seemed as though he had been talking with the angels, and had imbibed a portion of their wisdom unawares. It was visible in the calm and well-considered beneficence of his daily life, the quiet stream of which had made a wide green margin all along its course. Not a day passed by, that the world was not the better because this man, humble as he was, had lived. He never stepped aside from his own path, yet would always reach a blessing to his neighbor. Almost involuntarily, too, he had become a preacher. The pure and high simplicity of his thought, which, as one of its manifestations, took shape in the good deeds that dropped silently from his hand, flowed also forth in speech. He uttered truths that wrought upon and molded the lives of those who heard him. His auditors, it may be, never suspected that Ernest, their own neighbor and familiar friend, was more than an ordinary man; least of all did Ernest himself suspect it; but, inevitably as the murmur of a rivulet, came thoughts out of his mouth that no other human lips had spoken.

When the people's minds had had a little time to cool, they were ready enough to acknowledge their mistake in imagining a similarity between General Blood and Thunder's truculent physiognomy and the benign visage on the mountainside. But now, again, there were reports and many paragraphs in the newspapers, affirming that the likeness of the Great Stone Face had appeared upon the broad shoulders of a certain eminent statesman. He, like Mr. Gathergold and old Blood-and-Thunder, was a native of the valley, but had left it in his early days, and taken up the trades of law and politics. Instead of the rich man's wealth and the warrior's sword, he had but a tongue, and it was mightier than both together. So wonderfully eloquent was he, that whatever he might choose to say, his auditors had no choice but to believe him; wrong looked like right, and right like wrong; for when it pleased him, he could make a kind of illuminated fog with his mere breath, and obscure the natural daylight with it. His tongue, indeed, was a magic instrument: sometimes it rumbled like the thunder; sometimes it warbled like the sweetest music. It was the blast of war the song of peace; and it seemed to have a heart in it, when there was no such matter. In good truth, he was a wondrous man; and when his tongue had acquired him all other imaginable success when it had been heard in halls of state, and in the courts of princes and potentates after it had made him known all over the world, even as a voice crying from shore to shore it finally persuaded his countrymen to select him for the Presidency. Before this time indeed, as soon as he began to grow celebrated his admirers had found out the resemblance between him and the Great Stone Face; and so much were they struck by it, that throughout the country this distinguished gentleman was known by the name of Old Stony Phiz. The phrase was considered as giving a highly favorable aspect to his political prospects; for, as is likewise the case with the Popedom, nobody ever becomes President without taking a name other than his own.

While his friends were doing their best to make him President, Old Stony Phiz, as he was called, set out on a visit to the valley where he was born. Of course, he had no other object than to shake hands with his fellow citizens, and neither thought nor cared about any effect which his progress through the country might have upon the election. Magnificent preparations were made to receive the illustrious statesman; a cavalcade of horsemen set forth to meet him at the boundary line of the State, and all the people left their business and gathered along the wayside to see him pass. Among these was Ernest. Though more than once disappointed, as we have seen, he had such a hopeful and confiding nature, that he was always ready to believe in whatever seemed beautiful and good.

He kept his heart continually open, and thus was sure to catch the blessing from on high when it should come. So now again, as buoyantly as ever, he went forth to behold the likeness of the Great Stone Face.

The cavalcade came prancing along the road, with a great clattering of hoofs and a mighty cloud of dust, which rose up so dense and high that the visage of the mountainside was completely hidden from Ernest's eyes. All the great men of the neighborhood were there on horseback; militia officers, in uniform; the member of Congress; the sheriff of the county; the editors of newspapers; and many a farmer, too, had mounted his patient steed, with his Sunday coat upon his back. It really was a very brilliant spectacle, especially as there were numerous banners flaunting over the cavalcade, on some of which were gorgeous portraits of the illustrious statesman and the Great Stone Face, smiling familiarly at one another, like two brothers. If the pictures were to be trusted, the mutual resemblance, it must be confessed, was marvelous. We must not forget to mention that there was a band of music, which made the echoes of the mountains ring and reverberate with the loud triumph of its strains; so that airy and soul-thrilling melodies broke out among all the heights and hollows, as if every nook of his native valley had found a voice, to welcome the distinguished guest. But the grandest effect was when the far-off mountain precipice flung back the music; for then the Great Stone Face itself seemed to be swelling the triumphant chorus, in acknowledgment, that, at length, the man of prophecy was come.

All this while the people were throwing up their hats and shouting, with enthusiasm so contagious that the heart of Ernest kindled up, and he likewise threw up his hat, and shouted, as loudly as the loudest, "Huzza for the great man! Huzza for Old Stony Phiz!" But as yet he had not seen him.

"Here he is, now!" cried those who stood near Ernest. "There! There! Look at Old Stony Phiz and then at the Old Man of the Mountain, and see if they are not as like as two twin brothers!"

In the midst of all this gallant array came an open barouche, drawn by four white horses; and in the barouche, with his massive head uncovered, sat the illustrious statesman, Old Stony Phiz himself.

"Confess it," said one of Ernest's neighbors to him, "the Great Stone Face has met its match at last!"

Now, it must be owned that, at his first glimpse of the countenance which was bowing and smiling from the barouche, Ernest did fancy that there was a resemblance between it and the old familiar face upon the mountainside. The brow, with its massive depth and loftiness, and all the other features, indeed, were boldly and strongly hewn, as if in emulation of a more than heroic, of a Titanic model. But the sublimity and stateliness, the grand expression of a divine sympathy, that illuminated the mountain visage and etherealized its ponderous granite substance into spirit, might here be sought in vain. Something had been originally left out, or had departed. And therefore the marvelously gifted statesman had always a weary gloom in the deep caverns of his eyes, as of a child that has outgrown its playthings or a man of mighty faculties and little aims, whose life, with all its high performances, was vague and empty, because no high purpose had endowed it with reality.

Still, Ernest's neighbor was thrusting his elbow into his side, and pressing him for an answer.

"Confess! confess! Is not he the very picture of your Old Man of the Mountain?"

"No!" said Ernest, bluntly, "I see little or no likeness."

"Then so much the worse for the Great Stone Face!" answered his neighbor; and again he set up a shout for Old Stony Phiz.

But Ernest turned away, melancholy, and almost despondent: for this was the saddest of his disappointments, to behold a man who might have fulfilled the prophecy, and had not willed to do so. Meantime, the cavalcade, the banners, the music, and the barouches swept past him, with the vociferous crowd in the rear, leaving the dust to settle down, and the Great Stone Face to be revealed again, with the grandeur that it had worn for untold centuries.

"Lo, here I am, Ernest!" the benign lips seemed to say. "I have waited longer than thou, and am not yet weary. Fear not; the man will come."

The years hurried onward, treading in their haste on one another's heels. And now they began to bring white hairs, and scatter them over the head of Ernest; they made reverend wrinkles across his forehead, and furrows in his cheeks. He was an aged man. But not in vain had he grown old: more than the white hairs on his head were the sage thoughts in his mind; his wrinkles and furrows were inscriptions that Time had engraved, and in which he had written legends of wisdom that had been tested by the tenor of a life. And Ernest had ceased to be obscure. Unsought for, undesired, had come the fame which so many seek, and made him known in the great world, beyond the limits of the valley in which he had dwelt so quietly. College professors, and even the active men of cities, came from far to see and converse with Ernest; for the report had gone abroad that this simple husbandman had ideas unlike those of other men, not gained from books, but of a higher tone a tranquil and familiar majesty, as if he had been talking with the angels as his daily friends. Whether it were sage, statesman, or philanthropist, Ernest received these visitors with the gentle sincerity that had characterized him from boyhood, and spoke freely with them of whatever came uppermost, or lay deepest in his heart or their own. While they talked together, his face would kindle, unawares, and shine upon them, as with a mild evening light. Pensive with the fulness of such discourse, his guests took leave and went their way; and passing up the valley, paused to look at the Great Stone Face, imagining that they had seen its likeness in a human countenance, but could not remember where.

While Ernest had been growing up and growing old, a bountiful Providence had granted a new poet to this earth. He, likewise, was a native of the valley, but had spent the greater part of his life at a distance from that romantic region, pouring out his sweet music amid the bustle and din of cities. Often, however, did the mountains which had been familiar to him in his childhood lift their snowy peaks into the clear atmosphere of his poetry. Neither was the Great Stone Face forgotten, for the poet had celebrated it in an ode, which was grand enough to have been uttered by its own majestic lips. This man of genius, we may say, had come down from heaven with wonderful endowments. If he sang of a mountain, the eyes of all mankind beheld a mightier grandeur reposing on its breast, or soaring to its summit, than had before been seen there. If his theme were a lovely lake, a celestial smile had now been thrown over it, to gleam forever on its surface. If it were the vast old sea, even the deep immensity of its dread bosom seemed to swell the higher, as if moved by the emotions of the song. Thus the world assumed another and a better aspect from the hour that the poet blessed it with his happy eyes. The Creator had bestowed him, as the last best touch to his own handiwork. Creation was not finished till the poet came to interpret, and so complete it.

The effect was no less high and beautiful, when his human brethren were the subject of his verse. The man or woman, sordid with the common dust of life, who crossed his daily path, and the little child who played in it, were glorified if they beheld him in his mood of poetic faith. He showed the golden links of the great chain that intertwined them with an angelic kindred; he brought out the hidden traits of a celestial birth that made them worthy of such kin. Some, indeed, there were, who thought to show the soundness of their judgment by affirming that all the beauty and dignity of the natural world existed only in the poet's fancy. Let such men speak for themselves, who undoubtedly appear to have been spawned forth by Nature with a contemptuous bitterness; she plastered them up out of her refuse stuff, after all the swine were made. As respects all things else, the poet's ideal was the truest truth.

The songs of this poet found their way to Ernest. He read them after his customary toil, seated on the bench before his cottage door, where for such a length of time he had filled his repose with thought, by gazing at the Great Stone Face. And now as he read stanzas that caused the soul to thrill within him, he lifted his eyes to the vast countenance beaming on him so benignantly.

"O majestic friend," he murmured, addressing the Great Stone Face, "is not this man worthy to resemble thee?"

The face seemed to smile, but answered not a word.

Now it happened that the poet, though he dwelt so far away, had not only heard of Ernest, but had meditated much upon his character, until he deemed nothing so desirable as to meet this man, whose untaught wisdom walked hand in hand with the noble simplicity of his life.

One summer morning, therefore, he took passage by the railroad, and, in the decline of the afternoon, alighted from the cars at no great distance from Ernest's cottage. The great hotel, which had formerly been the palace of Mr. Gathergold, was close at hand, but the poet, with his carpetbag on his arm, inquired at once where Ernest dwelt, and was resolved to be accepted as his guest.

Approaching the door, he there found the good old man, holding a volume in his hand, which alternately he read, and then, with a finger between the leaves, looked lovingly at the Great Stone Face.

"Good evening," said the poet. "Can you give a traveler a night's lodging?"

"Willingly," answered Ernest; and then he added, smiling, "Methinks I never saw the Great Stone Face look so hospitably at a stranger."

The poet sat down on the bench beside him, and he and Ernest talked together. Often had the poet held intercourse with the wittiest and the wisest, but never before with a man like Ernest, whose thoughts and feelings gushed up with such a natural feeling, and who made great truths so familiar by his simple utterance of them. Angels, as had been so often said, seemed to have wrought with him at his labor in the fields; angels seemed to have sat with him by the fireside; and, dwelling with angels as friend with friends, he had imbibed the sublimity of their ideas, and imbued it with the sweet and lowly charm of household words. So thought the poet. And Ernest, on the other hand, was moved and agitated by the living images which the poet flung out of his mind, and which peopled all the air about the cottage door with shapes of beauty, both gay and pensive. The sympathies of these two men instructed them with a profounder sense than either could have attained alone. Their minds accorded into one strain, and made delightful music which neither of them could have claimed as all his own, nor distinguished his own share from the other's. They led one another, as it were, into a high pavilion of their thoughts, so remote, and hitherto so dim, that they had never entered it before, and so beautiful that they desired to be there always.

As Ernest listened to the poet, he imagined that the Great Stone Face was bending forward to listen too. He gazed earnestly into the poet's glowing eyes.

"Who are you, my strangely gifted guest?" he said.

The poet laid his finger on the volume that Ernest had been reading.

"You have read these poems," said he. "You know me, then for I wrote them."

Again, and still more earnestly than before, Ernest examined the poet's features; then turned towards the Great Stone Face; then back, with an uncertain aspect, to his guest. But his countenance fell; he shook his head, and sighed.

"Wherefore are you sad?" inquired the poet. "Because," replied Ernest, "all through life I have awaited the fulfilment of a prophecy; and, when I read these poems, I hoped that it might be fulfilled in you."

"You hoped," answered the poet, faintly smiling, "to find in me the likeness of the Great Stone Face. And you are disappointed, as formerly with Mr. Gathergold, and old Blood-and-Thunder, and Old Stony Phiz. Yes, Ernest, it is my doom.

You must add my name to the illustrious three, and record another failure of your hopes. For in shame and sadness do I speak it, Ernest I am not worthy to be typified by yonder benign and majestic image."

"And why?" asked Ernest. He pointed to the volume. "Are not those thoughts divine?"

"They have a strain of the Divinity," replied the poet. "You can hear in them the far-off echo of a heavenly song. But my life, dear Ernest, has not corresponded with my thought. I have had grand dreams, but they have been only dreams, because I have lived and that, too, by my own choice among poor and mean realities. Sometimes, even shall I dare to say it? I lack faith in the grandeur, the beauty, and the goodness, which my own works are said to have made more evident in nature and in human life. Why, then, pure seeker of the good and true, shouldst thou hope to find me, in yonder image of the divine?"

The poet spoke sadly, and his eyes were dim with tears. So, likewise, were those of Ernest.

At the hour of sunset, as had long been his frequent custom, Ernest was to discourse to an assemblage of the neighboring inhabitants in the open air. He and the poet, arm in arm, still talking together as they went along, proceeded to the spot. It was a small nook among the hills, with a gray precipice behind, the stern front of which was relieved by the pleasant foliage of many creeping plants that made a tapestry for the naked rock, by hanging their festoons from all its rugged angles. At a small elevation above the ground, set in a rich framework of verdure, there appeared a niche, spacious enough to admit a human figure, with freedom for such gestures as spontaneously accompany earnest thought and genuine emotion. Into this natural pulpit Ernest ascended, and threw a look of familiar kindness around upon his audience. They stood, or sat, or reclined upon the grass, as seemed good to each, with the departing sunshine falling obliquely over them, and mingling its subdued cheerfulness with the solemnity of a grove of ancient trees, beneath and amid the boughs of which the golden rays were constrained to pass. In another direction was seen the Great Stone Face, with the same cheer, combined with the same solemnity, in its benignant aspect.

"Ernest began to speak, giving to the people of what was in his heart and mind. His words had power, because they accorded with his thoughts; and his thoughts had reality and depth, because they harmonized with the life which he had always lived. It was not mere breath that this preacher uttered; they were the words of life, because a life of good deeds and holy love was melted into them. Pearls, pure and rich, had been dissolved into this precious draught. The poet, as he listened, felt that the being and character of Ernest were a nobler strain of poetry than he had ever written.

His eyes glistening with tears, he gazed reverentially at the venerable man, and said within himself that never was there an aspect so worthy of a prophet and a sage as that mild, sweet, thoughtful countenance, with the glory of white hair diffused about it. At a distance, but distinctly to be seen, high up in the golden light of the setting sun, appeared the Great Stone Face, with hoary mists around it, like the white hairs around .the brother of Ernest. Its look of grand beneficence seemed to embrace the world.
At that moment, in sympathy with a thought which he was about to utter, the face of Ernest assumed a grandeur of expression, so imbued with benevolence, that the poet, by an irresistible impulse, threw his arms aloft and shouted

"Behold! Behold! Ernest is himself the likeness of the Great Stone Face!"

Then all the people looked and saw that what the deep sighted poet said was true. The prophecy was fulfilled. But Ernest, having finished what he had to say, took the poet's arm, and walked slowly homeward, still hoping that some wiser and better man than himself would by and by appear, bearing a resemblance to the GREAT STONE FACE.

Short Story Checkup

NAME OF SHORT STORY: *Great Stone Face*

NAME OF AUTHOR: *Nathaniel Hawthorne*

I. BRIEFLY DESCRIBE: (20 Points)

PROTAGONIST–

ANTAGONIST-

OTHER CHARACTERS USED TO DEVELOP PROTAGONIST--

DO ANY OF THE CHARACTERS REMIND ME OF A BIBLE CHARACTER? WHO? WHY?

II. SETTING: (10 Points)

III. POINT OF VIEW: CIRCLE ONE: FIRST PERSON, THIRD PERSON, THIRD PERSON OMNISCIENT (10 Points)

IV. BRIEF SUMMARY OF THE PLOT: (20 Points)

    IDENTIFY THE CLIMAX OF THE SHORT STORY. (10 Points)

V. THEME (THE QUINTESSENTIAL MEANING/PURPOSE OF THE BOOK IN ONE OR TWO SENTENCES): (10 Points)

VI. AUTHOR'S WORLD VIEW:

HOW DO YOU KNOW THIS? WHAT BEHAVIORS DO(ES) THE CHARACTER(S) MANIFEST THAT LEAD YOU TO THIS CONCLUSION?
(10 Points)

VII. WHY DID YOU LIKE/DISLIKE THIS SHORT STORY? (10 Points)

Lesson Nine Test Answers

Short Story Checkup

NAME OF SHORT STORY: *Great Stone Face*

NAME OF AUTHOR: Nathaniel Hawthorne

I. BRIEFLY DESCRIBE: (20 Points)

  PROTAGONIST– *Ernest*

  ANTAGONIST-- *None*

  OTHER CHARACTERS USED TO DEVELOP PROTAGONIST--*Mr. Gathergold, and old Blood-and-Thunder, Old Stony Phiz, and the Poet.*

  DO ANY OF THE CHARACTERS REMIND ME OF A BIBLE CHARACTER? WHO? WHY? *Ernest appears to be a Christlike figure; the Poet is perhaps John the Baptist.*

II. SETTING: (10 Points) *White Mountains in New Hampshire*

III. POINT OF VIEW: CIRCLE ONE: FIRST PERSON, THIRD PERSON, <u>THIRD PERSON OMNISCIENT</u> (10 Points)

IV. BRIEF SUMMARY OF THE PLOT: (20 Points) *A young man grows up wondering who is the Great Stone Face. Eventually, he himself is the stone face by virtue of his imagination, hard work, and embrace of his community.*

  IDENTIFY THE CLIMAX OF THE SHORT STORY. (10 Points) *When the poet visits at the end.*

V. THEME (THE QUINTESSENTIAL MEANING/PURPOSE OF THE BOOK IN ONE OR TWO SENTENCES): (10 Points) *A young man perseveres in his dreams and hopes and is rewarded by finding meeting the stone face–himself.*

VI. AUTHOR'S WORLD VIEW:

  HOW DO YOU KNOW THIS? WHAT BEHAVIORS DO(ES) THE CHARACTER(S) MANIFEST THAT LEAD YOU TO THIS CONCLUSION?

(10 Points) *There are elements of Romanticism but the embrace of community and ethical values indicates that Theism is the predominant world view.*

VII. WHY DID YOU LIKE/DISLIKE THIS SHORT STORY? (10 Points)

Lesson Ten

Readings Due For This Lesson

Students should have read "Fall of the House of Usher" and "The Tell Tale Heart" both by Edgar Allan Poe.

Reading Ahead

Students should read "The Birthmark" by Nathaniel Hawthorne (Lesson Eleven) and begin to read *Huckleberry Finn*, by Mark Twain (Lesson Twelve).

Suggested Weekly Implementation

Day One	Day Two	Day Three	Day Four	Day Five
1. Students will rewrite graded essays from last week and review Lesson Nine test. 2. Students should have read the required reading(s) *before* the assigned lesson begins. 3. Teacher may want to discuss assigned reading(s) with student. 4. Teacher shall assign the required essays. Choose two or three. The rest of the essays can be outlined, answered with shorter answers, or skipped.	1. Student should begin reading(s) from next lesson. 2. Student should outline essays due at the end of the week. 3. Students should answer one or two of the essays that are not assigned as formal essays.	1. Students should write rough drafts of assigned essays. 2. The teacher should correct rough drafts.	Student will write final copy of essays due tomorrow.	1. Essays are due. 2. Students should take Lesson Ten test. 3. Student should read short stories in Lesson Eleven. The material is provided in text.

Literary Criticism

A. Part of Poe's genius is his ability to create mood by the use of connotative language(language that suggests more than the words explicitly express). Write an essay describing how this literary technique is employed by Poe in "The Fall of the House of Usher." *There are innumerable examples. One is "...dull, dark, and soundless day in the autumn of the year...*

B. Write a characterization of Roderick Usher. *Usher is a very bright but disturbed man. Usher is an injured, lifeless man. He is at the end of a declining, aristocratic family. He has no heirs and now his sister is apparently ill. Or so we think. In my opinion, Usher is representative of the old, dysfunctional life style/world view that Poe finds objectionable. The visitor is the fresh, neutral observer who interprets the story.*

C. In the third paragraph of the short story, Poe identifies the Usher family with what structure? Why? *A wealthy, but flawed line of aristocrats, the Usher family is represented by the physical structure, the Usher mansion, which itself is in disrepair.*

D. How does first-person narration enhance Poe's purposes to scare his readers? Who is the narrator? Is he reliable? Why or why not? *We are drawn into the story through first-person narrator. We sense that he is reliable. The narrator is an observer, not a participant, in the story. This is a very common technique to enhance the credibility of the narration.*

E. Find the narrator's description of Roderick's picture. How does this foreshadow future events? *Throughout the short story the reader wonders if Usher is mad. The painting presented an Usher whose countenance had an expression of "low cunning and perplexity."*

Supplemental Resources:

Eric W. Carlson, Editor, *The fall of the house of Usher*
　　A critical analysis of this best of Poe short stories.
Arthur Hobson Quinn, *Edgar Allan Poe: A Critical Biography*
　　One of the best biographies on the market.

Joseph Wood Krutch, *Edgar Allan Poe: A Study in Genius*
　　A very readable but well-considered biography of Poet.

Vincent Price (Reader), Basil Rathbone (Reader), *Edgar Allan Poe Audio Collection*
　　An excellent audio adaptation of Poe's short stories.

Notes:

Lesson Ten Test

Discussion Questions: (100 Points)

A. Poe believed in what he called "unity of effect." "Unity of effect" to Poe meant that the short story could be read at a single sitting.. To Poe, tone was everything. He would deliberately subordinate everything in the story to tone. As a result, the short story became "poetic." Give examples of this effect in our two short stories. (20 Points)

B. Poe was accused of being a detective and horror story writer. However, in fact, he was a Romantic writer. Explain and give examples of Romanticism in these two short stories.
(20 Points)

C. Poe was fond of creating paradoxes in his short stories. Explain and give examples from these two short stories. (20 Ponts)

D. Describe Roderick. Why does he both repel and attract the reader? (20 Points)

E. Compare and contrast "Usher" to "Tell Tale Heart." (10 Points)

F. Which passage is from Poe? How do you know? (10 Points)

♣I was sick, sick unto death, with that long agony, and when they at length unbound me, and I was permitted to sit, I felt that my senses were leaving me. The sentence, the dread sentence of death, was the last of distinct accentuation which reached my ears. After that, the sound of the inquisitorial voices seemed merged in one dreamy indeterminate hum. It conveyed to my soul the idea of Revolution, perhaps from its association in fancy with the burr of a mill-wheel. This only for a brief period, for presently I heard no more. Yet, for a while, I saw, but with how terrible an exaggeration ! I saw the lips of the black-robed judges. They appeared to me white -- whiter than the sheet upon which I trace these words -- and thin even to grotesqueness; thin with the intensity of their expression of firmness, of immovable resolution, of stern contempt of human torture. I saw that the decrees of what to me was fate were still issuing from those lips. I saw them writhe with a deadly locution. I saw them fashion the syllables of my name, and I shuddered, because no sound succeeded. I saw, too, for a few moments of delirious horror, the soft and nearly imperceptible waving of the sable draperies which enwrapped the walls of the apartment; and then my vision fell upon the seven tall candles upon the table. At first they wore the aspect of charity, and seemed white slender angels who would save me: but then all at once there came a most deadly nausea over my spirit, and I felt every fibre in my frame thrill, as if I had touched the wire of a galvanic battery, while the angel forms became

141

meaningless specters, with heads of flame, and I saw that from them there would be no help. And then there stole into my fancy, like a rich musical note, the thought of what sweet rest there must be in the grave. The thought came gently and stealthily, and it seemed long before it attained full appreciation; but just as my spirit came at length properly to feel and entertain it, the figures of the judges vanished, as if magically, from before me; the tall candles sank into nothingness; their flames went out utterly; the blackness of darkness superceded ; all sensations appeared swallowed up in a mad rushing descent as of the soul into Hades. Then silence, and stillness, and night were the universe.

♣And I would have you believe, my sons, that the same Justice which punishes sin may also most graciously forgive it, and that no ban is so heavy but that by prayer and repentance it may be removed. Learn then from this story not to fear the fruits of the past, but rather to be circumspect in the future, that those foul passions whereby our family has suffered so grievously may not again be loosed to our undoing. "Know then that in the time of the Great Rebellion (the history of which by the learned Lord Clarendon I most earnestly commend to your attention) this . . . was held by Hugo of that name, nor can it be gainsaid that he was a most wild, profane, and godless man. This, in truth, his neighbour might have pardoned, seeing that saints have never flourished in those parts, but there was in him a certain wanton and cruel humor which made his name a byword through the West. It chanced that this Hugo came to love (if, indeed, so dark a passion may be known under so bright a name) the daughter of a yeoman who held lands near the Baskerville estate. But the young maiden, being discreet and of good repute, would ever avoid him, for she feared his evil name. So it came to pass that one Michaelmas this Hugo, with five or six of his idle and wicked companions, stole down upon the farm and carried off the maiden, her father and brothers being from home, as he well knew. When they had brought her to the Hall the maiden was placed in an upper chamber, while Hugo and his friends sat down to a long carouse, as was their nightly custom. Now, the poor lass upstairs was like to have her wits turned at the singing and shouting and terrible oaths which came up to her from below. . .

Lesson Ten Answers

Discussion Questions: (100 Points)

A. Poe believed in what he called "unity of effect." "Unity of effect" to Poe meant that the short story could be read at a single sitting.. To Poe, tone was everything. He would deliberately subordinate everything in the story to tone. As a result, the short story became "poetic." Give examples of this effect in "Usher" and "Tell Tale." (20 Points) *"Usher" has symmetry–the decaying owner lives in the decaying house. "During the whole of a dull, dark, and soundless day in the autumn of the year, when the clouds hung oppressively low in the heavens, had been passing alone, on horseback, through a singularly dreary tract of country; and at length found myself, as the shades of the evening drew on, within view of the melancholy House of Usher." "Tell Tale Heart" also has a unity of effect: "Presently, I heard a slight groan, and I knew it was the groan of mortal terror. It was not a groan of pain or of grief -- oh, no! It was the low stifled sound that arises from the bottom of the soul when overcharged with awe. I knew the sound well."*

B. Poe was accused of being a detective and horror story writer. However, in fact, he was a Romantic writer. Explain and give examples of Romanticism in these two short stories. (20 Points)

1. Appeals to imagination; use of the "willing suspension of disbelief."
2. Stress on emotion and imagination rather than reason; optimism, geniality.
3. Subjectivity in form and meaning.
4. Prefers the remote setting in time and space.
5. Prefers the exotic and improbable plots.
6. Prefers aberrant characterization.
7. Form rises out of content, non-formal.
8. Prefers individualized, subjective writing.

C. Poe was fond of creating paradoxes in his short stories. Explain and give examples from these two short stories. (20 Points) *His life was basically insecure and highly emotional, but his writing is structured. Poe was a Romantic writer, but he emphasized rationality. He presented realistic details in Romantic/horror settings.*

D. Describe Roderick. Why does he both repel and attract the reader? (20 Points) *Roderick is erudite, well-educated but also very disturbed. His physical appearance, both fascinating and repulsive, declines as the story progresses.*

E. Compare and contrast "Usher" to "Tell Tale Heart." (10 Points) *Both employ*

Romantic writing principles. Both build suspense. Both protagonists seem to be insane. "Tell Tale" however employs first person narration. "Usher" also is first person but he functions as a neutral observer.

F. Which passage is from Poe? How do you know? (10 Points) *The first is from "Pit and Pendulum." The second is Arthur Conan Doyle's The Hounds of the Baskerville. The language and images in Poe are significantly more pronounced than in Hounds.*

LESSON ELEVEN

Readings Due For This Lesson
Students should have read "The Birthmark" by Nathaniel Hawthorne.

Reading Ahead

Read *Huckleberry Finn*, by Mark Twain (Lesson Twelve).

Suggested Weekly Implementation

Day One	Day Two	Day Three	Day Four	Day Five
1. Students will rewrite graded essays from last week and review Lesson Ten test. 2. Students should have read the required reading(s) *before* the assigned lesson begins. 3. Teacher may want to discuss assigned reading(s) with student. 4. Teacher shall assign the required essays. Choose two or three. The rest of the essays can be outlined, answered with shorter answers, or skipped.	1. Student should begin reading(s) from next lesson. 2. Student should outline essays due at the end of the week. 3. Students should answer one or two of the essays that are not assigned as formal essays.	1. Students should write rough drafts of assigned essays. 2. The teacher should correct rough drafts.	Student will write final copy of essays due tomorrow.	1. Essays are due. 2. Students should take Lesson Eleven test. 3. Student should read *Huckleberry Finn*, Mark Twain.

Critical Thinking

A. As stated previously, Hawthorne flirted with Transcendentalism but never left his Theistic Romanticism. Find examples of Theistic Romanticism in *The Birthmark*. *Evidences of Romanticism are abundant. The use of the forest; the juxtaposition of nature and the personality of Aylmer; etc. Theism is also evident but in more subtle ways. Again, as Hawthorne wrote in The Scarlet Letter, Birthmark has a moral vision. There is only one God in Hawthorne's world and He is not Chillingsworth or Aylmer.*

B. *Answers will vary.*

C. How can Aylmer love both science and Georgiana? Are these loves mutually contradictory? *To Hawthorne they are. Either man will worship the Creator or the creation. Science is the creation; God is the Creator. Aylmer most certainly cannot improve on God's handiwork--that is Georgiana.*

D. What basic differences are there between Aylmer's world view and Transcendentalism? *Aylmer is truly an interesting nineteenth century character. He is the rationalist; a Chillingsworth, a scientist. He is a type of modern man. Transcendentalism, while celebrating "the human spirit" and "relativism" also tries to embrace science rationalism. But, the essence of Transcendentalism is the opposite of scientific rationalism: experience verses empiricism. It is a conflict as old as Aristotle and Plato. Plato argued that the metaphysical realm (that is, God) controls the natural world; Aristotle believed that the natural world defined God. All contemporary world view discussions can be traced one way or another to Plato and Aristotle. Plato was the Pharisee of his day, the conservative, the one who believed that the gods were intimately involved with human beings. His "Republic" was a perfect society based on the notion that mankind was creating a city based on the word of the gods. Cosmology, or the presence of supernatural being(s), in other words, was very important to Plato. Likewise, to the Pharisee, who believed strongly in the Resurrection, the supernatural was very involved in human life. To Plato, the gods defined reality. Aristotle, on the other hand, in his important essay Poeticus argued that the world was governed by impersonal laws. Aristotle argued that mankind defined who the gods were. While the gods are alive and well, they do not much concern themselves with the world. Therefore, mankind should be concerned about finding out about his world without worrying about the gods. This view was evident again in the Sadducees--who rejected the supernatural--and later philosophers like David Hume. I am not discussing Hellenistic philosophy for any other reason than to point out that the struggle in which our children will participate is over three thousand years old. It is the struggle that Elijah joined when he fought King Ahab. King Ahab was a good Jew; the problem was he did not live his life as if God was actually alive. Is God intentionally involved in the affairs of mankind or not? The answer to this question is more or less the battle that is raging on college campuses today. Paul, a student of Greek philosophy, was deeply effected by Plato. The Holy Spirit led Paul to write: "So we fix our eyes not on what is seen, but on what is unseen. For what is seen is temporary, but what is unseen is eternal." (2 Cor. 4:18).*

E. In the final analysis, Aylmer's attempts to perfect Georgiana are doomed to failure. Why? *Georgiana could not be changed by anyone but God. In the short story "The Birth Mark" by Nathaniel Hawthorne the main character is a scientist named Aylmer. Aylmer has a gentle, loving wife named Georgiana who has a birth mark on her cheek. Aylmer cannot stand this birth mark. Therefore, he convinces his wife to let him remove it. In the end, he removes the mark but he kills her. Aylmer is the antithesis of a world view/movement of the middle 19th century called Transcendentalism. What is Transcendentalism? It is a 19th-century movement of writers and philosophers in New England who were loosely bound together by adherence to an idealistic system of thought based on a belief in the essential unity of all creation, the innate goodness of man, and the supremacy of insight over logic and experience for the revelation of the deepest truths (Encyclopedia Britannica). In other words, Transcendentalism reveres subjectivity. Subjectivity celebrates individuality and creativity. It is a reality that grows from the heart of man; not from science. Aylmer can not understand, much less appreciate his beautiful Transcendental wife. Georgiana loves gardens, flowers, and anything else that draws out her innate feelings of goodness. The scientist Alymer does not have a clue.*

Georgiana's birthmark is certainly something that sets her a part from a genus or phallum. "Georgiana," said he, "has it ever occurred to you that the mark upon your cheek might be removed?" "No, indeed," she said, smiling; but perceiving the seriousness of his manner she blushed deeply. "To tell you the truth, it has been so often called a charm that I was simple enough to imagine it might be so." The Transcendentalist Georgiana values what is unique, different. It is a "charm." The scientist Aylmer who is always looking for the usual, the pattern, the repeated behavior cannot value or chooses not to value an aberration.

Aylmer also has a drive for every thing to be perfect. Everything must be in perfect order. Every little thing filed away. But on his wife, whom he loves greatly, there is a imperfect spot. This spot drives him crazy. He will do anything to get rid of it.

In this short story, Nathaniel Hawthorne shows how this beautiful woman, with a birth mark that some would say it was a "charm", was destroyed by this literalist, this empiricist monster, Aylmer. Beauty was destroyed for the passion of perfection. (Peter Stobaugh, age 15)

F. This story is an *allegory*. What moral quality is represented by Aylmer? *Well intentioned but misplaced rationalism. He is the scientist, the empiricist.* By Georgiana? *Romanticism.* Aminadab? *Cautious rationalism.*

Challenge Question

Compare the theme(s) of this short story with the theme(s) of Mary Shelley's *Frankenstein (English Literature Critical Thinking* Vol. 4).
Dr. Frankenstein sought to create perfect life and he created a monster. Alymer could

not accept limits on his science and he killed the person he most loved. Both were betrayed by their modern tendencies to worship science/rationalism–a typical Romantic theme of both Shelley and Hawthorne.

Supplemental Reading:

Nathaniel Hawthorne, Millicent Bell (Editor), *Nathaniel Hawthorne : Collected Novels: Fanshawe, The Scarlet Letter, The House of the Seven Gables, The Blithedale Romance*
    An excellent collection of Hawthorne's five novels with editorial helps. The reader's choice of a version for young readers.

Nathaniel Hawthorne, Roy Harvey Pearce (Editor) *Nathaniel Hawthorne : Tales and Sketches*
    Tales and Sketches offers young readers an authoritative edition of Hawthorne's complete stories in a single comprehensive volume.

LouAnn Gaeddert. *A New England Love Story: Nathaniel Hawthorne and Sophia Peabody*
    For mature readers, Gaeddert gives great insights into the relationship of Sophia Peabody and Nathaniel Hawthorne.

Bradley Sculley, ed. *The Scarlet Letter: Backgrounds and Sources, Criticism.*
    One of the best scholarly resources on Hawthorne and his works.

Arlin Turner, *Nathaniel Hawthorne: A Biography*
    An unpretentious but readable biography of Hawthorne.

Notes:

Lesson Eleven Test

Identification: (90 Points)

Which themes appeared in what writings?

Theme	*The Scarlet Letter*	*Birthmark*	*Old Stone Face*
Alienation			
Science vs. Romanticism			
Allegory			
Unforgivingness			
Individual vs. society			
Problem of Guilt			
Fate vs. free will			
Pride			
Hypocrisy			

Discussion Question: (10 Points)

What does this quote mean and how does it apply to *The Birthmark*?
"I have sometimes produced a singular and not unpleasing effect, so far as my own mind was concerned, by imagining a train of incidents in which the spirit and mechanism of the fairyland should be combined with the characters and manners of familiar life."
N. Hawthorne

Lesson Eleven Test Answers

Identification: (90 Points)

Which themes appeared in what writings?

Theme	*The Scarlet Letter*	*Birthmark*	*Old Stone Face*
Alienation	Yes	No	No
Science vs. Romanticism	Yes	Yes	No
Allegory	Yes	Yes	Yes
Unforgivingness	Yes	No	No
Individual vs. society	Yes	No	No
Problem of Guilt	Yes	No	No
Fate vs. free will	Yes	Yes	No
Pride	Yes	Yes	Yes
Hypocrisy	Yes	Yes	No

Discussion Question: (10 Points)

What does this quote mean and how does it apply to *The Birthmark*?
"I have sometimes produced a singular and not unpleasing effect, so far as my own mind was concerned, by imagining a train of incidents in which the spirit and mechanism of the fairyland should be combined with the characters and manners of familiar life."
N. Hawthorne

An ordinary birthmark is the occasion for Hawthorne to discuss metaphysical issues that relate to human experience: What is beauty? Must everything be analyzed and/or controlled? Realism–a marriage, a birthmark, a scientist–all are made extraordinary by the inherent tension in this clash between two world views.

Lesson Twelve

Readings Due For This Lesson

Students should have read *The Adventures of Huckleberry Finn,* by Mark Twain.

Reading Ahead

Read *Billy Budd*, Herman Melville (Lesson Fifteen)

Suggested Weekly Implementation

Day One	Day Two	Day Three	Day Four	Day Five
1. Students will rewrite graded essays from last week and review Lesson Eleven test. 2. Students should have read the required reading(s) *before* the assigned lesson begins. 3. Teacher may want to discuss assigned reading(s) with student. 4. Teacher shall assign the required essays. Choose two or three. The rest of the essays can be outlined, answered with shorter answers, or skipped.	1. Student should begin reading(s) from next lesson. 2. Student should outline essays due at the end of the week. 3. Students should answer one or two of the essays that are not assigned as formal essays.	1. Students should write rough drafts of assigned essays. 2. The teacher should correct rough drafts.	Student will write final copy of essays due tomorrow.	1. Essays are due. 2. Students should take Lesson Twelve test. 3. Student should read *Billy Budd*, Herman Melville

The Adventures of Huckleberry Finn

Twain was the first major writer to use real American speech (and not only in dialogue), to deal with themes and topics that were important to Americans, and to assume that the concerns of Americans were as worthy of serious treatment. One critic observed that one of the reasons we classify some writers as great is that they alter the consciousness of the people they write for; another is that they redefine the terrain for all writers who come after them. On both counts, Mark Twain is a greater writer. He made Americans aware of their surroundings and their heritage. At the same time he featured a hero who could barely read and write, whose language was peppered with vulgar expressions and figures of speech.

Book Checkup

__a__ 1. _c__ 2. __b__ 3. __b__ 4. __c__ 5.

Biblical Application

Compare Huckleberry Finn to the young Samuel (1 Samuel 1-3). *Huck Finn was a moralistic young man. Samuel was a man who followed God's laws. There is a significant difference. Huck did what seemed right to him; Samuel obeyed God's Word. Huck's vision was a Realistic vision; Samuel has a Theistic vision. Huck basically responded to each situation and made his choices; Samuel obeyed God at all costs.*

Suggested Vocabulary Words--

<u>Word</u>

    temperance *(abstinence)*
    reticule *(handbag)*
    wince *(draw back)*
    pensive *(thoughtful)*
    degraded *(debased)*
    histrionic *(theatrical)*
    obsequies *(funeral rites)*
    ingenious *(inventive)*

Supplemental Resources:

Ken Burns, *Mark Twain* (PBS Program)
    A wonderful documentary on the life of Mark Twain.

Ken Burns, Dayton Duncan, and Geoffrey C. Ward. *Mark Twain, An Illustrated Biography.*
    The book version of the PBS documentary.

Forrest G. Robinson, ed. *The Cambridge Companion to Mark Twain*
    Single best secondary resource on Mark Twain.

Hal Holbrook, *Mark Twain Tonight* (DVD)
    Hal Holbrook is the perfect Mark Twain in this 1967 television special.

Notes:

Lesson Twelve Test

Discussion Questions: (100 Points)

A. Most critics agree that *The Adventures of Huckleberry Finn* is one of the best, if not the best, American novel ever written. Yet, at the same time, it is a deceptively easy book to read. In fact, the same critics argue that it is one of the most difficult books really to understand and to analyze effectively. Why?

B. One must be skeptical about most of what Huck says in order to hear what Twain is saying. Why?

C. Is Twain speaking through Huck or Jim?

D. "All right, then, I'll go to Hell," Huck says when he decides not to return Jim to slavery. Huck is convinced that his reward for defying the moral norms of his society will be eternal damnation. What is the right thing for Huck to do?

E. *The Adventures of Huckleberry Finn* really is a different kind of book from what we have read so far this year. Explain.

F. Most readers assume that Huck is the hero and center of the story and consider Jim to be a foil. Is it possible they are wrong, and Jim is the main character with Huck as a foil?

G. One of the major criticisms of *Huck Finn* has been that the Jim is a racist stereotype and that the implication is that African-Americans are stupid, superstitious, and passive. To what extent is Jim a stereotype? Does he break out of this role?

H. What do you think is the climax of the novel? Why?

I. Why do you think the author chose a carefree, but uneducated character as the voice through which to tell this story?

J. Do you think it was necessary for Twain to use the word "nigger?" Why or why not?

Lesson Twelve Test Answers

Discussion Questions: (100 Points)

A. Most critics agree that *The Adventures of Huck Finn* is one of the best, if not the best, American novel ever written. Yet, at the same time, it is a deceptively easy book to read. In fact, the same critics argue that it is one of the most difficult books really to understand and to analyze effectively. Why? *There are so many layers of meaning in this novel. On one hand, it appears to be a children's story–the continuation of the Tom Sawyer saga–which is a children's story. On the other hand, it is the first major Realistic (world view) novel written in America. While Melville is a transition writer, there is no doubt that Twain is breaking new ground with this novel.*

B. One must be skeptical about most of what Huck says in order to hear what Twain is saying. Why? *Twain teases his reader by understatement, hyperbole, and irony. These literary elements all conspire to warn the reader to read between the lines to hear really what Twain is saying.*

C. Is Twain speaking through Huck or Jim? *I believe that he is speaking through Huck because Huck is the main character (in my opinion) and we see the story unfold through Huck's mind.*

D. "All right, then, I'll go to Hell," Huck says when he decides not to return Jim to slavery. Huck is convinced that his reward for defying the moral norms of his society will be eternal damnation. What is the right thing for Huck to do? *Yes, when man's laws (e.g., abortion) violate God's laws, man should obey God's laws.*

E. *The Adventures of Huck Finn* really is a different kind of book from what we have read so far this year. Explain. *Romanticism–both as a world view and as a literary technique-- is dead in this novel. Especially in the scene where Huck is in Arkansas, we see the consequences of Romanticism–a crazy feud murders a generation. The characterizations are real; the setting is real too–not an aberration.*

F. Most readers assume that Huck is the hero and center of the story and consider Jim to be a foil. Is it possible they are wrong, and Jim is the main character with Huck as a foil? *As I said above, I believe Huck is the protagonist. Frankly I do not think that Twain was an anti-slavery person, nor do I see evidence that he was any different from other 19th century Americans–he also exhibited some racism. Jim was merely there to develop Huck.*

G. One of the major criticisms of *Huck Finn* has been that the Jim is a racist stereotype and that the implication is that African-Americans are stupid, superstitious, and passive. To what extent is Jim a stereotype? Does he break out of this role? *He breaks out of his role at the end while he is in prison. Twain is no different than his contemporaries in his views of African-Americans.*

H. What do you think is the climax of the novel? Why? *The whole novel is about a journey, an escape, and the climax occurs when Jim is released at the end.*

I. Why do you think the author chose a carefree, but uneducated character as the voice through which to tell this story? *This is a brilliant way to poke fun at Romanticism and to take the focus off Huck and onto the matter at hand. His lack of sophistication is disarming and charming!*

J. Do you think it was necessary for Twain to use the word "nigger?" Why or why not? *This novel is a realistic novel; therefore, it requires the use of this pejorative expression.*

LESSON THIRTEEN

Readings Due For This Lesson

Students should have read *The Adventures of Huckleberry Finn*, by Mark Twain.

Reading Ahead

Read *Billy Budd*, Herman Melville (Lesson Fifteen)

Suggested Weekly Implementation

Day One	Day Two	Day Three	Day Four	Day Five
1. Students will rewrite graded essays from last week and review Lesson Twelve test. 2. Students should have read the required reading(s) *before* the assigned lesson begins. 3. Teacher may want to discuss assigned reading(s) with student. 4. Teacher shall assign the required essays. Choose two or three. The rest of the essays can be outlined, answered with shorter answers, or skipped.	1. Student should begin reading(s) from next lesson. 2. Student should outline essays due at the end of the week. 3. Students should answer one or two of the essays that are not assigned as formal essays.	1. Students should write rough drafts of assigned essays. 2. The teacher should correct rough drafts.	Student will write final copy of essays due tomorrow.	1. Essays are due. 2. Students should take Lesson Thirteen test. 3. Student should read *Billy Budd*, Herman Melville

Critical Thinking

A. Jim and Huck are ironically trying to escape from slavery by floating down the Mississippi River. Why is this escape ironic? *They are floating southward. To escape slavery, Jim and Huck need to escape to the North.*

B. Mark Twain used several literary devices. Look up the meaning of each of the following literary terms and find at least one example for the book.
    1. satire *(the description of the people at the camp meeting)*
    2. symbolism *(the way the two confidence men "pay" for their escape)*
    3. allegory *(the journey downriver, the story of the Duke and the Dauphin)*
    4. foreshadowing *(Huck's early thoughts about helping a runaway slave)*

C. Twain uses first person point of view to tell his story. What advantages and disadvantages does this present Twain? *We have more intimate details and in that sense they are reliable. On the other hand, we see everything from Huck's viewpoint--hardly a reliable witness. Everything is colored by the eyes of a young, ambivalent, moralistic white southern boy. This viewpoint is especially evident in Huck's ambivalence about escaping with Jim.*

Supplemental Resources:

Ken Burns, *Mark Twain* (PBS Program)
    A wonderful documentary on the life of Mark Twain.

Ken Burns, Dayton Duncan, and Geoffrey C. Ward. *Mark Twain, An Illustrated Biography.*
    The book version of the PBS documentary.

Forrest G. Robinson, ed. *The Cambridge Companion to Mark Twain*
    Single best secondary resource on Mark Twain.

Hal Holbrook, *Mark Twain Tonight* (DVD)
    Hal Holbrook is the perfect Mark Twain in this 1967 television special.

Notes:

Lesson Thirteen Test

Discussion Questions: (100 Points)

State what world view–Romanticism or Realism–is exhibited in each passage below. Defend your answer.

A. It was Sunday, and, according to his custom on that day, McTeague took his dinner at two in the afternoon at the car conductors' coffee-joint on Polk Street. He had a thick gray soup; heavy, underdone meat, very hot, on a cold plate; two kinds of vegetables; and a sort of suet pudding, full of strong butter and sugar. On his way back to his office, one block above, he stopped at Joe Frenna's saloon and bought a pitcher of steam beer. It was his habit to leave the pitcher there on his way to dinner. *McTeague*, Frank Norris.

B. I am by birth a Genevese; and my family is one of the most distinguished of that republic. My ancestors had been for many years counselors and syndics; and my father had filled several public situations with honor and reputation. He was respected by all who knew him for his integrity and indefatigable attention to public business. He passed his younger days perpetually occupied by the affairs of his country; a variety of circumstances had prevented his marrying early, nor was it until the decline of life that he became a husband and the father of a family. *Frankenstein*, Mary Shelley.

C. The village lay under two feet of snow, with drifts at the windy corners. In a sky of iron the points of the Dipper hung like icicles and Orion flashed his cold fires. The moon had set, but the night was so transparent that the white house-fronts between the elms looked gray against the snow, clumps of bushes made black stains on it, and the basement windows of the church sent shafts of yellow light far across the endless undulations. Young Ethan Frome walked at a quick pace along the deserted street, past the bank and Michael Eady's new brick store and Lawyer Varnum's house with the two black Norway spruces at the gate. Opposite the Varnum gate, where the road fell away toward the Corbury valley, the church reared its slim white steeple and narrow peristyle. As the young man walked toward it the upper windows drew a black arcade along the side wall of the building, but from the lower openings, on the side where the ground sloped steeply down to the Corbury road, the light shot its long bars, illuminating many fresh furrows in the track leading to the basement door, and showing, under an adjoining shed, a line of sleighs with heavily blanketed horses. *Ethan Frome*, Edith Wharton.

D. The little farmers watched debt creep up on them like the tide. They sprayed the trees and sold no crop, they pruned and grafted and could not pick the crop. And the men of knowledge have worked, have considered, and the fruit is rotting on the ground, and the decaying mash in the wine vats is poisoning the air. And taste the wine--no grape flavor at all, just sulphor and tannic acid and alcohol. This little orchard will be part of a great holding next year, for the debt will have choked the owner. This vineyard will belong to the bank. Only the great owners can survive, for they won the canneries too. And four pears peeled and cut in half, cooked and canned, still cost fifteen cents. And the canned pears do not spoil. They will last for years. The decay spreads over the State, and the sweet smell is a great sorrow on the land. Men who can graft the trees and make the seed fertile and big can find no way to let the hungry people eat their produce. men who have created new fruits in the world cannot create a system whereby their fruits may be eaten. and the failure hangs over the State like a great sorrow. The works of the roots of the vines, of the trees, must be destroyed to keep up the price, and this is the saddest, bitterest thing of all. Carloads of oranges dumped on the ground. The people come from miles to take the fruit, but this could not be. How would they buy oranges at twenty cents a dozen if they could drive out and pick them up? And men with hoses squirt kerosine on the oranges, and they are angry at the crime, angry at the people who have come to take the fruit. A million people hungry, needing the fruit--and kerosine sprayed over the golden mountains. And the smell of rot fills the country. Burn coffee for fuel in the ships. Burn corn to keep warm, it makes a hot fire. Dump potatoes in the rivers and place guards along the banks to keep the hungry people from fishing them out. Slaughter the pigs and bury them, and let the putrescence drip down into the earth. *Grapes of Wrath*, John Steinbeck.

E. On the human imagination, events produce the effects of time. Thus, he who has traveled far and seen much, is apt to fancy that he has lived long; and the history that most abounds in important incidents, soonest assumes the aspect of antiquity. In no other way can we account for the venerable air that is already gathering around American annals. When the mind reverts to the earliest days of colonial history, the period seems remote and obscure, the thousand changes that thicken along the links of recollections, throwing back the origin of the nation to a day so distant as seemingly to reach the mists of time; and yet four lives of ordinary duration would suffice to transmit, from mouth to mouth, in the form of tradition, all that civilized man has achieved within the limits of the republic. Although New York, alone, possesses a population materially exceeding that of either of the four smallest kingdoms of Europe, or materially exceeding that of the entire Swiss Confederation, it is little more than two centuries since the Dutch commenced their settlement, rescuing region from the savage state. Thus, what seems venerable by an accumulation of changes, is reduced to familiarity when we come seriously to consider it solely in connection with time. *Deerslayer*, James Fenimore Cooper.

F. Found among the papers of the late Diedrech Knickerbocker. A pleasing land of drowsy head it was, Of dreams that wave before the half-shut eye; And of gay castles in the clouds that pass, Forever flushing round a summer sky. Castle of Indolence. In the bosom of one of those spacious coves which indent the eastern shore of the Hudson, at that broad expansion of the river denominated by the ancient Dutch navigators the Tappan Zee, and where they always prudently shortened sail and implored the protection of St. Nicholas when they crossed, there lies a small market town or rural port, which by some is called Greensburgh, but which is more generally and properly known by the name of Tarry Town. This name was given, we are told, in former days, by the good housewives of the adjacent country, from the inveterate propensity of their husbands to linger about the village tavern on market days. Be that as it may, I do not vouch for the fact, but merely advert to it, for the sake of being precise and authentic. Not far from this village, perhaps about two miles, there is a little valley or rather lap of land among high hills, which is one of the quietest places in the whole world. A small brook glides through it, with just murmur enough to lull one to repose; and the occasional whistle of a quail or tapping of a woodpecker is almost the only sound that ever breaks in upon the uniform tranquillity. *The Legend of Sleep Hollow*, Washington Irving.

G. I'm not! And if turning up my hair makes me one, I'll wear it in two tails till I'm twenty, cried Jo, pulling off her net, and shaking down a chestnut mane. I hate to think I've got to grow up, and be Miss March, and wear long gowns, and look as prim as a China Aster! It's bad enough to be a girl, anyway, when I like boy's games and work and manners! I can't get over my disappointment in not being a boy. And it's worse than ever now, for I'm dying to go and fight with Papa. And I can only stay home and knit, like a poky old woman! *Little Women*, Lousia Alcott

H. Shaking off the sleet from my ice-glazed hat and jacket, I seated myself near the door, and turning sideways was surprised to see Queequeg near me. Affected by the solemnity of the scene, there was a wondering gaze of incredulous curiosity in his countenance. This savage was the only person present who seemed to notice my entrance; because he was the only one who could not read, and, therefore, was not reading those frigid inscriptions on the wall. Whether any of the relatives of the seamen whose names appeared there were now among the congregation, I knew not; but so many are the unrecorded accidents in the fishery, and so plainly did several women present wear the countenance if not the trappings of some unceasing grief, that I feel sure that here before me were assembled those, in whose unhealing hearts the sight of those bleak tablets sympathetically caused the old wounds to bleed afresh. *Moby Dick*, Herman Melville

I. The Time Traveler (for so it will be convenient to speak of him) was expounding a recondite matter to us. His grey eyes shone and twinkled, and his usually pale face was flushed and animated. The fire burned brightly, and the soft radiance of the incandescent lights in the lilies of silver caught the bubbles that flashed and passed in our glasses. Our chairs, being his patents, embraced and caressed us rather than submitted to be sat upon, and there was that luxurious after-dinner atmosphere when thought roams gracefully free of the trammels of precision. And he put it to us in this way--marking the points with a lean forefinger--as we sat and lazily admired his earnestness over this new paradox (as we thought it:) and his fecundity. *The Time Machine*, H. G. Wells

J. On an exceptionally hot evening early in July a young man came out of the garret in which he lodged in S. Place and walked slowly, as though in hesitation, towards K. bridge. He had successfully avoided meeting his landlady on the staircase. His garret was under the roof of a high, five-storied house, and was more like a cupboard than a room. The landlady, who provided him with garret, dinners, and attendance, lived on the floor below, and every time he went out he was obliged to pass her kitchen, the door of which invariably stood open. And each time he passed, the young man had a sick, frightened feeling, which made him scowl and feel ashamed. He was hopelessly in debt to his landlady, and was afraid of meeting her. *Crime and Punishment*, Fydor Doestoevsky

Lesson Thirteen Test Answers

Discussion Questions: (100 Points)

State what world view–Romanticism or Realism–that is exhibited in each passage below. Defend your answer.

A. It was Sunday, and, according to his custom on that day, McTeague took his dinner at two in the afternoon at the car conductors' coffee-joint on Polk Street. He had a thick gray soup; heavy, underdone meat, very hot, on a cold plate; two kinds of vegetables; and a sort of suet pudding, full of strong butter and sugar. On his way back to his office, one block above, he stopped at Joe Frenna's saloon and bought a pitcher of steam beer. It was his habit to leave the pitcher there on his way to dinner. *McTeague*, Frank Norris. *Realism (and Naturalism). Notice the every day details, the unadorned writing, and the ordinary setting.*

B. I am by birth a Genevese; and my family is one of the most distinguished of that republic. My ancestors had been for many years counselors and syndics; and my father had filled several public situations with honor and reputation. He was respected by all who knew him for his integrity and indefatigable attention to public business. He passed his younger days perpetually occupied by the affairs of his country; a variety of circumstances had prevented his marrying early, nor was it until the decline of life that he became a husband and the father of a family. *Frankenstein*, Mary Shelley. *Romanticism. Shelley chooses the extraordinary setting to develop her protagonist. In fact, Dr. Frankenstein is a sort of Alymer (in Birthmark).*

C. The village lay under two feet of snow, with drifts at the windy corners. In a sky of iron the points of the Dipper hung like icicles and Orion flashed his cold fires. The moon had set, but the night was so transparent that the white house-fronts between the elms looked gray against the snow, clumps of bushes made black stains on it, and the basement windows of the church sent shafts of yellow light far across the endless undulations. Young Ethan Frome walked at a quick pace along the deserted street, past the bank and Michael Eady's new brick store and Lawyer Varnum's house with the two black Norway spruces at the gate. Opposite the Varnum gate, where the road fell away toward the Corbury valley, the church reared its slim white steeple and narrow peristyle. As the young man walked toward it the upper windows drew a black arcade along the side wall of the building, but from the lower openings, on the side where the ground sloped steeply down to the Corbury road, the light shot its long bars, illuminating many fresh furrows in the track leading to the basement door, and showing, under an adjoining shed, a line of sleighs with heavily blanketed horses. *Ethan Frome*, Edith Wharton. *Realism. The realistic, cold, unappetizing setting is a metaphor for the empty lives we shall soon observe unfold in this novel.*

D. The little farmers watched debt creep up on them like the tide. They sprayed the trees and sold no crop, they pruned and grafted and could not pick the crop. And the men of knowledge have worked, have considered, and the fruit is rotting on the ground, and the decaying mash in the wine vats is poisoning the air. And taste the wine--no grape flavor at all, just sulphor and tannic acid and alcohol. This little orchard will be part of a great holding next year, for the debt will have choked the owner. This vineyard will belong to the bank. Only the great owners can survive, for they won the canneries too. And four pears peeled and cut in half, cooked and canned, still cost fifteen cents. And the canned pears do not spoil. They will last for years. The decay spreads over the State, and the sweet smell is a great sorrow on the land. Men who can graft the trees and make the seed fertile and big can find no way to let the hungry people eat their produce. men who have created new fruits in the world cannot create a system whereby their fruits may be eaten. and the failure hangs over the State like a great sorrow. The works of the roots of the vines, of the trees, must be destroyed to keep up the price, and this is the saddest, bitterest thing of all. Carloads of oranges dumped on the ground. The people come from miles to take the fruit, but this could not be. How would they buy oranges at twenty cents a dozen if they could drive out and pick them up? And men with hoses squirt kerosine on the oranges, and they are angry at the crime, angry at the people who have come to take the fruit. A million people hungry, needing the fruit--and kerosine sprayed over the golden mountains. And the smell of rot fills the country. Burn coffee for fuel in the ships. Burn corn to keep warm, it makes a hot fire. Dump potatoes in the rivers and place guards along the banks to keep the hungry people from fishing them out. Slaughter the pigs and bury them, and let the putrescence drip down into the earth. *Grapes of Wrath*, John Steinbeck. *Realism. Steinbeck is one of the most famous American Realism writers. Notice the earthy details.*

E. On the human imagination, events produce the effects of time. Thus, he who has traveled far and seen much, is apt to fancy that he has lived long; and the history that most abounds in important incidents, soonest assumes the aspect of antiquity. In no other way can we account for the venerable air that is already gathering around American annals. When the mind reverts to the earliest days of colonial history, the period seems remote and obscure, the thousand changes that thicken along the links of recollections, throwing back the origin of the nation to a day so distant as seemingly to reach the mists of time; and yet four lives of ordinary duration would suffice to transmit, from mouth to mouth, in the form of tradition, all that civilized man has achieved within the limits of the republic. Although New York, alone, possesses a population materially exceeding that of either of the four smallest kingdoms of Europe, or materially exceeding that of the entire Swiss Confederation, it is little more than two centuries since the Dutch commenced their settlement, rescuing region from the savage state. Thus, what seems venerable by an accumulation of changes, is reduced to familiarity when we come seriously to consider it solely in connection with time. *The Deerslayer,* James Fenimore Cooper. *Romanticism. To Cooper, nature is ubiquitous. In fact, Native Americans are "noble" and nature in its pure form (i.e., untouched by human civilization) is pristine.*

F. Found among the papers of the late Diedrech Knickerbocker. A pleasing land of drowsy head it was, Of dreams that wave before the half-shut eye; And of gay castles in the clouds that pass, Forever flushing round a summer sky. Castle of Indolence. In the bosom of one of those spacious coves which indent the eastern shore of the Hudson, at that broad expansion of the river denominated by the ancient Dutch navigators the Tappan Zee, and where they always prudently shortened sail and implored the protection of St. Nicholas when they crossed, there lies a small market town or rural port, which by some is called Greensburgh, but which is more generally and properly known by the name of Tarry Town. This name was given, we are told, in former days, by the good housewives of the adjacent country, from the inveterate propensity of their husbands to linger about the village tavern on market days. Be that as it may, I do not vouch for the fact, but merely advert to it, for the sake of being precise and authentic. Not far from this village, perhaps about two miles, there is a little valley or rather lap of land among high hills, which is one of the quietest places in the whole world. A small brook glides through it, with just murmur enough to lull one to repose; and the occasional whistle of a quail or tapping of a woodpecker is almost the only sound that ever breaks in upon the uniform tranquillity. *The Legend of Sleep Hollow*, Washington Irving. *Romanticism–nature has a powerful effect on the setting.*

G. I'm not! And if turning up my hair makes me one, I'll wear it in two tails till I'm twenty, cried Jo, pulling off her net, and shaking down a chestnut mane. I hate to think I've got to grow up, and be Miss March, and wear long gowns, and look as prim as a China Aster! It's bad enough to be a girl, anyway, when I like boy's games and work and manners! I can't get over my disappointment in not being a boy. And it's worse than ever now, for I'm dying to go and fight with Papa. And I can only stay home and knit, like a poky old woman! *Little Women*, Lousia Alcott *Romanticism. The characters and setting conspire to celebrate the extraordinary–the family is extraordinary, the setting is extraordinary.*

H. Shaking off the sleet from my ice-glazed hat and jacket, I seated myself near the door, and turning sideways was surprised to see Queequeg near me. Affected by the solemnity of the scene, there was a wondering gaze of incredulous curiosity in his countenance. This savage was the only person present who seemed to notice my entrance; because he was the only one who could not read, and, therefore, was not reading those frigid inscriptions on the wall. Whether any of the relatives of the seamen whose names appeared there were now among the congregation, I knew not; but so many are the unrecorded accidents in the fishery, and so plainly did several women present wear the countenance if not the trappings of some unceasing grief, that I feel sure that here before me were assembled those, in whose unhealing hearts the sight of those bleak tablets sympathetically caused the old wounds to bleed afresh. *Moby Dick*, Herman Melville

This is a tough call. Melville is a Romantic writer but this book is a transition from Romanticism to Realism.

I. The Time Traveler (for so it will be convenient to speak of him) was expounding a recondite matter to us. His grey eyes shone and twinkled, and his usually pale face was flushed and animated. The fire burned brightly, and the soft radiance of the incandescent lights in the lilies of silver caught the bubbles that flashed and passed in our glasses. Our chairs, being his patents, embraced and caressed us rather than submitted to be sat upon, and there was that luxurious after-dinner atmosphere when thought roams gracefully free of the trammels of precision. And he put it to us in this way--marking the points with a lean forefinger--as we sat and lazily admired his earnestness over this new paradox (as we thought it:) and his fecundity. *The Time Machine*, H. G. Wells *Realism. While Wells wrote science fiction, in fact the images are ordinary, the main characters are ordinary.*

J. On an exceptionally hot evening early in July a young man came out of the garret in which he lodged in S. Place and walked slowly, as though in hesitation, towards K. bridge. He had successfully avoided meeting his landlady on the staircase. His garret was under the roof of a high, five-storied house, and was more like a cupboard than a room. The landlady, who provided him with garret, dinners, and attendance, lived on the floor below, and every time he went out he was obliged to pass her kitchen, the door of which invariably stood open. And each time he passed, the young man had a sick, frightened feeling, which made him scowl and feel ashamed. He was hopelessly in debt to his landlady, and was afraid of meeting her. *Crime and Punishment*, Fydor Doestoevsky *Realism. While this is a Theistic novel, Doestoevsky writes in a Realistic style.*

LESSON FOURTEEN

Readings Due For This Lesson
Students should have read *The Adventures of Huckleberry Finn,* by Mark Twain.

Reading Ahead
Read *Billy Budd*, Herman Melville (Lesson Fifteen)

Suggested Weekly Implementation

Day One	Day Two	Day Three	Day Four	Day Five
1. Students will rewrite graded essays from last week and review Lesson Thirteen test. 2. Students should have read the required reading(s) *before* the assigned lesson begins. 3. Teacher may want to discuss assigned reading(s) with student. 4. Teacher shall assign the required essays. Choose two or three. The rest of the essays can be outlined, answered with shorter answers, or skipped.	1. Student should begin reading(s) from next lesson. 2. Student should outline essays due at the end of the week. 3. Students should answer one or two of the essays that are not assigned as formal essays.	1. Students should write rough drafts of assigned essays. 2. The teacher should correct rough drafts.	Student will write final copy of essays due tomorrow.	1. Essays are due. 2. Students should take Lesson Fourteen test. 3. Student should read *Billy Budd*, Herman Melville

Twain...

A. In many ways I find the end of the novel to be very disappointing...*Answers will vary. Critics usually like Huck Finn better than Tom Sawyer. Tom is a rascally boy who is silly and terribly predictable. He is also incorrigibly a Romantic.*

B. Twain's handling of Christianity wavers... *Obviously Huck did not have a vital, living faith. "After supper she (Widow Douglas) learned me about Moses . . . but when I discovered he had been dead a considerable long time . . . I don't take no stock in dead people (p. 2)." The whole novel, in effect, is the story of a boy in conflict with and fleeing from ever increasing deadly forms of sin. Perhaps the only real change in Huck Finn during the course of the book is his duty to Jim, a morality loosely based on New Testament ethic.*

C. Give at least one example of Twain's cynicism. *When he had Colonel Sherburn taunt the mob. When he described the Duke putting up the notice, "Ladies and Children not Admitted." "There, if that line don't fetch them, I don't know Arkansaw." The contempt for humanity that Twain exhibits are only two examples.*

D. Every journey must have a goal. What is the goal of Huck's journey? *Throughout the book there is an ever increasing engagement between the world of the raft and the world on shore. As the book progresses there is less and less notice taken of the raft and more and more of the river bank world. The world on shore--the real world--is singularly unsatisfactory, disingenuous, and immoral. The world on the raft--exhibited by the friendship of Huck and Jim is genuine and wholesome.*

Challenge Question

Huck's decision to run away with Jim--a slave--is an unlawful act. Huck, though, decides to commit civil disobedience act. When, if ever, is civil disobedience appropriate? *When man's laws violate God's laws Christians are obligated to follow God's laws no matter what the consequences. Thus, since chattel slavery, I believe, is against God's laws Huck has every right to violate that law; however, once an act of civil disobedience is committed, the perpetrator of the act is obligated to accept the punishment for the crime. Civil disobedience <u>never</u> justifies an act of violence.*

Supplemental Resources:

Ken Burns, *Mark Twain* (PBS Program)
    A wonderful documentary on the life of Mark Twain.

Ken Burns, Dayton Duncan, and Geoffrey C. Ward. *Mark Twain, An Illustrated Biography.*
    The book version of the PBS documentary.

Forrest G. Robinson, ed. *The Cambridge Companion to Mark Twain*
    Single best secondary resource on Mark Twain.

Hal Holbrook, *Mark Twain Tonight* (DVD)
    Hal Holbrook is the perfect Mark Twain in this 1967 television special.

Notes:

Lesson Fourteen Test

Discussion Questions: (100 Points)

A. Agree or disagree with these critics: (60 Points)

☞All modern American literature comes from one book by Mark Twain called Huckleberry Finn. If you read it you must stop where the Nigger Jim is stolen from the boys. That is the real end. The rest is just cheating. But it's the best book we've had. All American writing comes from that. There was nothing before. There has been nothing as good since. –Ernest Hemingway (1959).

☞Huck Finn is alone: there is no more solitary character in fiction. The fact that he has a father only emphasizes his loneliness; and he views his father with a terrifying detachment. So we come to see Huck himself in the end as one of the permanent symbolic figures of fiction; not unworthy to take a place with Ulysses, Faust, Don Quixote, Don Juan, Hamlet and other great discoveries that man has made about himself. –T. S. Eliot (1959)

☞In one sense, Huckleberry Finn seems a circular book, ending as it began with a refused adoption and a projected flight; and certainly it has the effect of refusing the reader's imagination passage into the future. But there is a break-through in the last pages, especially in the terrible sentence which begins,"But I reckon I got to light out for the territory ahead of the rest...." In these words, the end of childhood is clearly signaled; and we are forced to ask the question, which, duplicitously, the book refuses to answer: what will become of Huck if he persists in his refusal to return to the place where he has been before? -Leslie A. Fiedler (1982)

B. The following was quoted in an 1885 newspaper, "The Concord Public Library committee has decided to exclude Mark Twain's latest book from the library. One member of the committee says that, while he does not wish to call it immoral, he thinks it contains but little humor, and that of a very coarse type. He regards it as the veriest trash. The librarian and the other members of the committee entertain similar views, characterizing it as rough, coarse and inelegant, dealing with a series of experiences not elevating, the whole book being more suited to the slums that to intelligent, respectable people." Agree or disagree with the Concord Public Library. (20 Points)

C. One newspaper editor observed in an obituary that "in ages to come, if historians and archaeologists would know the thoughts, the temper, the characteristic psychology of the American of the latter half of the nineteenth century, he will need only to read *Innocents Abroad, Tom Sawyer,* and *Huckleberry Finn.*" What is the "characteristic psychology" to which he is referring?(20 Points)

Lesson Fourteen Test Answers

Discussion Questions: (100 Points)

A. Agree or disagree with these critics: (60 Points)

♣All modern American literature comes from one book by Mark Twain called Huckleberry Finn. If you read it you must stop where the Nigger Jim is stolen from the boys. That is the real end. The rest is just cheating. But it's the best book we've had. All American writing comes from that. There was nothing before. There has been nothing as good since. –Ernest Hemingway (1959). *I categorically disagree. At this point the climax has not occurred—Jim's struggle from freedom in the prison is a great opportunity for Twain to develop Jim and Huck.*

♣Huck Finn is alone: there is no more solitary character in fiction. The fact that he has a father only emphasizes his loneliness; and he views his father with a terrifying detachment. So we come to see Huck himself in the end as one of the permanent symbolic figures of fiction; not unworthy to take a place with Ulysses, Faust, Don Quixote, Don Juan, Hamlet and other great discoveries that man has made about himself. –T. S. Eliot (1959) *I agree. Huck, in spite of his proximity to other characters, is actually very alone. Twain creates Huck this way so that his journey, so to speak, belongs to the reader and Huck and to no one else.*

♣In one sense, Huckleberry Finn seems a circular book, ending as it began with a refused adoption and a projected flight; and certainly it has the effect of refusing the reader's imagination passage into the future. But there is a break-through in the last pages, especially in the terrible sentence which begins,"But I reckon I got to light out for the territory ahead of the rest...." In these words, the end of childhood is clearly signaled; and we are forced to ask the question, which, duplicitously, the book refuses to answer: what will become of Huck if he persists in his refusal to return to the place where he has been before? -Leslie A. Fiedler (1982) *This is a critical question whose answer is pure speculation. The sense is that Huck is a changed young man and cannot return to the racism and duplicity that was the ante-bellum South.*

B. The following was quoted in an 1885 newspaper, "The Concord Public Library committee has decided to exclude Mark Twain's latest book from the library. One member of the committee says that, while he does not wish to call it immoral, he thinks it contains but little humor, and that of a very coarse type. He regards it as the veriest trash. The librarian and the other members of the committee entertain similar views, characterizing it as rough, coarse and inelegant, dealing with a series of experiences not elevating, the whole book being more suited to the slums that to intelligent, respectable people." Agree or disagree with the Concord Public Library. (20 Points) *We must be careful to place present moral standards on 1885 America. At that time, according to their standards, it probably was obscene. However, I found the novel to mild compared to a Hemingway, Steinbeck, or Salinger.*

C. One newspaper editor observed in an obituary that "in ages to come, if historians and archaeologists would know the thoughts, the temper, the characteristic psychology of the American of the latter half of the nineteenth century, he will need only to read *Innocents Abroad*, *Tom Sawyer*, and *Huckleberry Finn*." What is the "characteristic psychology" to which he is referring?(20 Points) *Realism, Social Darwinism (i.e., the feud in Arkansas), and racism were all a part of the cultural scene of post-Civil War America.*

Lesson Fifteen

Readings Due For This Lesson
Students should have read *Billy Budd*, Herman Melville.

Reading Ahead
Students should begin to read *The Red Badge of Courage*, Stephen Crane (Lesson Eighteen)

Suggested Weekly Implementation

Day One	Day Two	Day Three	Day Four	Day Five
1. Students will rewrite graded essays from last week and review Lesson Fourteen test. 2. Students should have read the required reading(s) *before* the assigned lesson begins. 3. Teacher may want to discuss assigned reading(s) with student. 4. Teacher shall assign the required essays. Choose two or three. The rest of the essays can be outlined, answered with shorter answers, or skipped.	1. Student should begin reading(s) from next lesson. 2. Student should outline essays due at the end of the week. 3. Students should answer one or two of the essays that are not assigned as formal essays.	1. Students should write rough drafts of assigned essays. 2. The teacher should correct rough drafts.	Student will write final copy of essays due tomorrow.	1. Essays are due. 2. Students should take Lesson Fifteen test. 3. Student should read *The Red Badge of Courage*, Stephen Crane.

173

Book Checkup

__b___ 1.__b___ 2. __b___ 3. __c___ 4.__a___ 5.

Suggested Vocabulary Words

    <u>Word</u>
    motley *(many colored)*
    retinue *(escort)*
    genial *(cordial)*
    decorum *(propriety)*
    deference *(submission)*
    appellation *(name)*
    felonious *(criminal)*
    comely *(handsome)*
    clandestine *(secret)*
    immured *(confined)*

Supplemental Resources:

W. H. Auden, "The Christian Tragic Hero." In *New York Times Book Review*, December 16, 1945
    Auden is an incredible poet and not half-bad critic. This article is seminal in studies on Romanticism.

Consider the Sea (VHS Tape)
    This is another very fine video on Melville, et al.

Famous Authors: Herman Melville (VHS Tape)
    This is an exhaustive video presentation of Melville's life.

Field Trip Possibility: The New Bedford Whaling Museum (New Bedford, MA)
    This museum is located across from the famous chapel in *Moby Dick*.

Leslie Fiedler, *Love and Death in the American Novel*
    This book is only tangentially connected to Melville but I really like Fiedler's criticisms of literary works.

Harry Levin, *The Power of Blackness: Hawthorne, Poe, Melville*
    The use of darkness in Romantic writers. Interesting.

Perry Miller,"Melville and Transcendentalism." In *Virginia Quarterly Review*, 29 (Autumn 1953)
    Perhaps no one is better able to speak to the tension in Melville's transition from

Romanticism to Realism.

Carl Van Doren, *The American Novel*
    A great, general overview of the rise of the American novel (of which *Billy Budd* help prominence).

Nathalia Wright, *Melville's Use of the Bible*
    Hard to find resource that discusses Melville's biblical motifs.

Notes:

Lesson Fifteen Test

Discussion Questions: (100 Points)

A. Like so much of Romantic literature, *Billy Budd* examines in great detail the problem of good and evil. Explain.

B. Hawthorne undertook a similar quest in his books. Compare and contrast the views of Hawthorne and Melville on this important problem.

C. Several of the characters have biblical parallels. Compare at least three characters to biblical characters.

D. Likewise, the plot itself, parallels several biblical references/stories. Identify at least three.

E. The protagonist Billy Budd is a quintessential Romantic man. Explain.

Lesson Fifteen Test Answers

Discussion Questions: (100 Points)

A. Like so much of Romantic literature, *Billy Budd* examines in great detail the problem of Good and Evil. Explain. *A young man is unjustly accused of a crime he did not commit (Evil). He is executed because of a greater Good–the need for wartime discipline. Ultimately, though, the implication that Good overcomes Evil in the person of Billy Budd.*

B. Hawthorne undertook a similar quest in his books. Compare and contrast the views of Hawthorne and Melville on this important problem of Good and Evil. *Hawthorne's Billy Budd figure would be Hester Prynne–but Hawthorne, who is essentially a Theist, accepts that Hester is really guilty. There can be no redemption without a willing admission of guilt, Hawthorne argues. Melville, on the other hand, is a truer Romantic: Good is the absence of intrusive human moral structure.*

C. Several of the characters have biblical parallels. Compare at least three characters to biblical characters. *Billy Budd = Jesus Christ (although I vehemently disagree with this comparison), Captain Vere= Pilate, and Captain Vere = Abraham sacrificing his favorite son Isaac (Billy Budd).*

D. Likewise, the plot itself, parallels several biblical references/stories. Identify at least three. *Billy would be Adam before the fall; Saul (Claggart) and David (Billy Budd) story about jealousy; the story of Ananias (conspiracy).*

E. The protagonist Billy Budd is a quintessential Romantic man. Explain. *Billy is the natural, naive, man, unpolluted by human machination and intrigue.*

Lesson Sixteen

Readings Due For This Lesson
Students should have read *Billy Budd*, Herman Melville.

Reading Ahead
Students should begin to read *The Red Badge of Courage*, Stephen Crane (Lesson Eighteen)

Suggested Weekly Implementation

Day One	Day Two	Day Three	Day Four	Day Five
1. Students will rewrite graded essays from last week and review Lesson Fifteen test. 2. Students should have read the required reading(s) *before* the assigned lesson begins. 3. Teacher may want to discuss assigned reading(s) with student. 4. Teacher shall assign the required essays. Choose two or three. The rest of the essays can be outlined, answered with shorter answers, or skipped.	1. Student should begin reading(s) from next lesson. 2. Student should outline essays due at the end of the week. 3. Students should answer one or two of the essays that are not assigned as formal essays.	1. Students should write rough drafts of assigned essays. 2. The teacher should correct rough drafts.	Student will write final copy of essays due tomorrow.	1. Essays are due. 2. Students should take Lesson Sixteen test. 3. Student should read *The Red Badge of Courage*, Stephen Crane.

Biblical Application

A. Billy Budd is obviously a Christlike figure. Find evidence to support this idea from the book. Contrast that view with the New Testament account of Christ's crucifixion. *Innocent Billy dies for another's sin. He struggles a night before he dies. An unnatural event occurs at his burial. Billy cries "God bless Captain Vere" at his death. This is similar to Christ's cry on the cross (Luke 23:34).*

B. Billy finds salvation...*See Chapter 25. Jesus Christ is the way and the truth and the life.*

Literary Criticism

A. *Billy Budd* is a tragedy...*American society is beginning to be confused about sin, morality, and truth. For the first time the happiness of a central character is more important than the propagation of truth.*

B. Give...symbolism in this book. *There are several. Begin by looking at the names of the ships.*

C. Melville intentionally rejects Judeo-Christian notions of sin and depravity...*The Bible has lost its central importance to Melville's life and understanding.*

D. How does Melville create character? *Inevitably Melville introduces his characters through the medium of an introductory description and narrative.*

E. In what way is *Billy Budd* autobiographical? *Melville spent many years on the sea and was very familiar with ship politics.*

For Enrichment
In the following essay, discuss how Melville is poking fun at his friend Ralph Waldo Emerson and other Romantics.

I and My Chimney

    I and my chimney, two grey-headed old smokers, reside in the country. We are, I may say, old settlers here; particularly my old chimney, which settles more and more every day.
Though I always say, *I and My Chimney*, as Cardinal Wolsey used to say, "*I and My King*," yet this egotistic way of speaking, wherein I take precedence of my chimney, is hereby borne out by the facts; in everything, except the above phrase, my chimney taking precedence of me.
Within thirty feet of the turf-sided road, my chimney--a huge, corpulent old Harry VIII of a chimney--rises full in front of me and all my possessions. Standing well up a hillside, my chimney, like Lord Rosse's monster telescope, swung vertical to hit the meridian

moon, is the first object to greet the approaching traveler's eye, nor is it the last which the sun salutes. My chimney, too, is before me in receiving the first-fruits of the seasons. The snow is on its head ere on my hat; and every spring, as in a hollow beech tree, the first swallows build their nests in it.

But it is within doors that the pre-eminence of my chimney is most manifest. When in the rear room, set apart for that object, I stand to receive my guests (who, by the way call more, I suspect, to see my chimney than me) I then stand, not so much before, as, strictly speaking, behind my chimney, which is, indeed, the true host. Not that I demur. In the presence of my betters, I hope I know my place.

 From this habitual precedence of my chimney over me, some even think that I have got into a sad rearward way altogether; in short, from standing behind my old-fashioned chimney so much, I have got to be quite behind the age too, as well as running behindhand in everything else. But to tell the truth, I never was a very forward old fellow, nor what my farming neighbors call a forehanded one. Indeed, those rumors about my behindhandedness are so far correct, that I have an odd sauntering way with me sometimes of going about with my hands behind my back. As for my belonging to the rear-guard in general, certain it is, I bring up the rear of my chimney--which, by the way, is this moment before me--and that, too, both in fancy and fact. In brief, my chimney is my superior; my superior, too, in that humbly bowing over with shovel and tongs, I much minister to it; yet never does it minister, or incline over to me; but, if anything, in its settlings, rather leans the other way.

 My chimney is grand seignior here--the one great domineering object, not more of the landscape, than of the house; all the rest of which house, in each architectural arrangement, as may shortly appear, is, in the most marked manner, accommodated, not to my wants, but to my chimney's, which, among other things, has the center of the house to himself, leaving but the odd holes and corners to me.

 But I and my chimney must explain; and as we are both rather obese, we may have to expatiate.

In those houses which are strictly double houses--that is, where the hall is in the middle--the fireplaces usually are on opposite sides; so that while one member of the household is warming himself at a fire built into a recess of the north wall, say another member, the former's own brother, perhaps, may be holding his feet to the blaze before a hearth in the south wall--the two thus fairly sitting back to back. Is this well? Be it put to any man who has a proper fraternal feeling. Has it not a sort of sulky appearance? But very probably this style of chimney building originated with some architect afflicted with a quarrelsome family.

Then again, almost every modem fireplace has its separate flue--separate throughout, from hearth to chimney-top. At least such an arrangement is deemed desirable. Does not this look egotistical, selfish? But still more, all these separate flues, instead of having independent masonry establishments of their own, or instead of being grouped together in one federal stock in the middle of the house--instead of this, I say, each flue is surreptitiously honey-combed into the walls; so that these last are here and there, or indeed almost anywhere, treacherously hollow, and, in consequence, more or less weak. Of course, the main reason of this style of chimney building is to economize room. In cities, where lots are sold by the inch, small space is to spare for a chimney constructed on magnanimous principles; and, as with most thin men, who are generally tall, so with such houses, what is lacking in breadth, must be made up in height. This remark holds true even with regard to many very stylish abodes, built by the most stylish of gentlemen. And yet, when that stylish gentleman, Louis le Grand of France, would build a palace for his lady, friend, Madame de Maintenon, he built it but one story high--in fact in the cottage style. But then, how uncommonly quadrangular, spacious, and broad--horizontal acres, not vertical ones. Such is the palace, which, in all its one-storied magnificence of Languedoc marble, in the garden of Versailles, still remains to this day. Any man can buy a square foot of land and plant a liberty-pole on it; but it takes a king to set apart whole acres for a grand triannon.

But nowadays it is different; and furthermore, what originated in a necessity has been mounted into a vaunt. In towns there is large rivalry in building tall houses. If one gentleman builds his house four stories high, and another gentleman comes next door and builds five stories high, then the former, not to be looked down upon that way, immediately sends for his architect and claps a fifth and a sixth story on top of his previous four. And, not till the gentleman has achieved his aspiration, not till he has stolen over the way by twilight and observed how his sixth story soars beyond his neighbor's fifth--not till then does he retire to his rest with satisfaction.
Such folks, it seems to me, need mountains for neighbors, to take this emulous conceit of soaring out of them.

If, considering that mine is a very wide house, and by no means lofty, aught in the above may appear like interested pleading, as if I did but fold myself about in the cloak of a general proposition, cunningly to tickle my individual vanity beneath it, such misconception must vanish upon my frankly conceding, that land adjoining my alder swamp was sold last month for ten dollars an acre, and thought a rash purchase at that; so that for wide houses hereabouts there is plenty of room, and cheap. Indeed so cheap--dirt cheap--is the soil, that our elms thrust out their roots in it, and hang their great boughs over it, in the most lavish and reckless way. Almost all our crops, too, are sown broadcast, even peas and turnips. A farmer among us, who should go about his twenty-acre field, poking his finger into it here and there, and dropping down a mustard seed, would be thought a penurious, narrow-minded husbandman. The dandelions in the river-meadows, and the forget-me-nots along the mountain roads, you see at once they are put to no economy in space. Some seasons, too, our rye comes up here and there a spear, sole and single like a church-spire. It doesn't care to crowd itself where it knows there is such a deal of room. The world is wide, the world is all before us, says the rye. Weeds, too, it is amazing how they spread. No such thing as arresting them--some of our pastures being a sort of Alsatia for the weeds. As for the grass, every spring it is like Kossuth's rising of what he calls the peoples. Mountains, too, a regular camp-meeting of them. For the same reason, the same all-sufficiency of room, our shadows march and countermarch, going through their various drills and masterly evolutions, like the old imperial guard on the Champs de Mars. As for the hills, especially where the roads cross them the supervisors of our various towns have given notice to all concerned, that they can come and dig them down and cart them off, and never a cent to pay, no more than for the privilege of picking

blackberries. The stranger who is buried here, what liberal-hearted landed proprietor among us grudges him six feet of rocky pasture?
Nevertheless, cheap, after all, as our land is, and much as it is trodden under foot, I, for one, am proud of it for what it bears; and chiefly for its three great lions--the Great Oak, Ogg Mountain, and my chimney.

Most houses, here, are but one and a half stories high; few exceed two. That in which I and my chimney dwell, is in width nearly twice its height, from sill to eaves-- which accounts for the magnitude of its main content--besides showing that in this house, as in this country at large, there is abundance of space, and to spare, for both of us. The frame of the old house is of wood--which but the more sets forth the solidity of the chimney, which is of brick. And as the great wrought nails, binding the clapboards, are unknown in these degenerate days, so are the huge bricks in the chimney walls. The architect of the chimney must have had the pyramid of Cheops before him; for, after that famous structure, it seems modeled, only its rate of decrease towards the summit is considerably less, and it is truncated. From the exact middle of the mansion it soars from the cellar, right up through each successive floor, till, four feet square, it breaks water from the ridge-pole of the roof, like an anvil-headed whale, through the crest of a billow. Most people, though, liken it, in that part, to a razed observatory, masoned up.

The reason for its peculiar appearance above the roof touches upon rather delicate ground. How shall I reveal that, forasmuch as many years ago the original gable roof of the old house had become very leaky, a temporary proprietor hired a band of woodmen, with their huge, cross-cut saws, and went to sawing the old gable roof clean off. Off it went, with all its birds' nests, and dormer windows. It was replaced with a modern roof, more fit for a railway wood-house than an old country gentleman's abode. This operation- -razeeing the structure some fifteen feet--was, in effect upon the chimney, something like the falling of the great spring tides. It left uncommon low water all about the chimney--to abate which appearance, the same person now proceeds to slice fifteen feet off the chimney itself, actually beheading my royal old chimney--a regicidal act, which, were it not for the palliating fact that he was a poulterer by trade, and, therefore, hardened to such neck-wringings, should send that former proprietor down to posterity in the same cart with Cromwell.

Owing to its pyramidal shape, the reduction of the chimney inordinately widened its razed summit. Inordinately, I say, but only in the estimation of such as have no eye to the picturesque. What care I, if, unaware that my chimney, as a free citizen of this free land, stands upon an independent basis of its own, people passing it, wonder how such a brick-kiln, as they call it, is supported upon mere joists and rafters? What care I? I will give a traveler a cup of switchel, if he want it; but am I bound to supply him with a sweet taste? Men of cultivated minds see, in my old house and chimney, a goodly old elephant-and-castle.

All feeling hearts will sympathize with me in what I am now about to add. The surgical operation, above referred to, necessarily brought into the open air a part of the chimney previously under cover, and intended to remain so, and, therefore, not built of what are called weather-bricks. In consequence, the chimney, though of a vigorous constitution, suffered not a little, from so naked an exposure; and, unable to acclimate itself, ere long began to fail--showing blotchy symptoms akin to those in measles. Whereupon travelers, passing my way, would wag their heads, laughing; "See that wax nose--how it melts off!" But what cared I? The same travelers would travel across the sea to view Kenilworth peeling away, and for a very good reason: that of all artists of the picturesque, decay wears the palm--I would say, the ivy. In fact, I've often thought that the proper place for my old chimney is ivied old England.

    In vain my wife--with what probable ulterior intent will, ere long, appear--solemnly warned me, that unless something were done, and speedily, we should be burnt to the ground, owing to the holes crumbling through the aforesaid blotchy parts, where the chimney joined the roof. "Wife," said I, "far better that my house should bum down, than that my chimney should be pulled down, though but a few feet. They call it a wax nose; very good; not for me to tweak the nose of my superior." But at last the man who has a mortgage on the house dropped me a note, reminding me that, if my chimney was allowed to stand in that invalid condition, my policy of insurance would be void. This was a sort of hint not to be neglected. All the world over, the picturesque yields to the pocketesque. The mortgagor cared not, but the mortgagee did.

So another operation was performed. The wax nose was taken off, and a new one fitted on. Unfortunately for the expression--being put up by a squint-eyed mason, who, at the time, had a bad stitch in the same side--the new nose stands a little awry, in the same direction.

Of one thing, however, I am proud. The horizontal dimensions of the new part are unreduced.

Large as the chimney appears upon the roof, that is nothing to its spaciousness below. At its base in the cellar, it is precisely twelve feet square; and hence covers precisely one hundred and forty-four superficial feet. What an appropriation of terra firma for a chimney, and what a huge load for this earth! In fact, it was only because I and my chimney formed no part of his ancient burden, that that stout peddler, Atlas of old, was enabled to stand up so bravely under his pack. The dimensions given may, perhaps, seem fabulous. But, like those stones at Gilgal, which Joshua set up for a memorial of having passed over Jordan, does not my chimney remain, even unto this day?

    Very often I go down into my cellar, and attentively survey that vast square of masonry. I stand long, and ponder over, and wonder at it. It has a druidical look, away down in the umbrageous cellar there whose numerous vaulted passages, and far glens of gloom, resemble the dark, damp depths of primeval woods. So strongly did this conceit steal over me, so deeply was I penetrated with wonder at the chimney, that one day--when I was a little out of my mind, I now think--getting a spade from the garden, I set to work, digging round the foundation, especially at the corners thereof, obscurely prompted by dreams of striking upon some old, earthen-worn memorial of that by-gone day, when, into all this gloom, the light of heaven entered, as the masons laid the foundation-stones, peradventure sweltering under an August sun, or pelted by a March storm. Plying my blunted spade, how vexed was I by that ungracious interruption of a neighbor who, calling to see me upon some business, and being informed that I was below said I need not be troubled to come up, but he would go down to me; and so, without ceremony, and without my having been forewarned, suddenly discovered me, digging in my cellar.

"Gold digging, sir?"

"Nay, sir," answered I, starting, "I was merely--ahem!--merely--I say I was merely digging-round my chimney."

"Ah, loosening the soil, to make it grow. Your chimney, sir, you regard as too small, I suppose; needing further development, especially at the top?"

"Sir!" said I, throwing down the spade, "do not be personal. I and my chimney--"
"Personal?"

"Sir, I look upon this chimney less as a pile of masonry than as a personage. It is the king of the house. I am but a suffered and inferior subject."

In fact, I would permit no gibes to be cast at either myself or my chimney; and never again did my visitor refer to it in my hearing, without coupling some compliment with the mention. It well deserves a respectful consideration. There it stands, solitary and alone--not a council--of ten flues, but, like his sacred majesty of Russia, a unit of an autocrat.

Even to me, its dimensions, at times, seem incredible. It does not look so big--no, not even in the cellar. By the mere eye, its magnitude can be but imperfectly comprehended, because only one side can be received at one time; and said side can only present twelve feet, linear measure. But then, each other side also is twelve feet long; and the whole obviously forms a square and twelve times twelve is one hundred and forty-four. And so, an adequate conception of the magnitude of this chimney is only to be got at by a sort of process in the higher mathematics by a method somewhat akin to those whereby the surprising distances of fixed stars are computed.

It need hardly be said, that the walls of my house are entirely free from fireplaces. These all congregate in the middle--in the one grand central chimney, upon all four sides of which are hearths--two tiers of hearths--so that when, in the various chambers, my family and guests are warming themselves of a cold winter's night, just before retiring, then, though at the time they may not be thinking so, all their faces mutually look towards each other, yea, all their feet point to one center; and, when they go to sleep in their beds, they all sleep round one warm chimney, like so many Iroquois Indians, in the woods, round their one heap of embers. And just as the Indians' fire serves, not only to keep them comfortable, but also to keep off wolves, and other savage monsters, so my chimney, by its obvious smoke at top, keeps off prowling burglars from the towns--for what burglar or murderer would dare break into an abode from whose chimney issues such a continual smoke--betokening that if the inmates are not stirring, at least fires are, and in case of an alarm, candles may readily be lighted, to say nothing of muskets.

But stately as is the chimney--yea, grand high altar as it is, right worthy for the celebration of high mass before the Pope of Rome, and all his cardinals--yet what is there perfect in this world? Caius Julius Caesar, had he not been so inordinately great, they say that Brutus, Cassius, Antony, and the rest, had been greater. My chimney, were it not so mighty in its magnitude, my chambers had been larger. How often has my wife ruefully told me, that my chimney, like the English aristocracy, casts a contracting shade all round it. She avers that endless domestic inconveniences arise--more particularly from the chimney's stubborn central locality. The grand objection with her is, that it stands midway in the place where a fine entrance-hall ought to be. In truth, there is no hall whatever to the house--nothing but a sort of square landing-place, as you enter from the wide front door. A roomy enough landing-place, I admit, but not attaining to the dignity of a hall. Now, as the front door is precisely in the middle of the front of the house, inwards it faces the chimney. In fact, the opposite wall of the landing-place is formed solely by the chimney; and hence-owing to the gradual tapering of the chimney--is a little less than twelve feet in width. Climbing the chimney in this part, is the principal staircase--which, by three abrupt turns, and three minor landing-places, mounts to the second floor, where, over the front door, runs a sort of narrow gallery, something less than twelve feet long, leading to chambers on either hand. This gallery, of course, is railed; and so, looking down upon the stairs, and all those landing-places together, with the main one at bottom, resembles not a little a balcony for musicians, in some jolly old abode, in times Elizabethan. Shall I tell a weakness? I cherish the cobwebs there, and many a time arrest Biddy in the act of brushing them with her broom, and have many a quarrel with my wife and daughters about it.

Now the ceiling, so to speak, of the place where you enter the house, that ceiling is, in fact, the ceiling of the second floor, not the first. The two floors are made one here; so that ascending this turning stairs, you seem going up into a kind of soaring tower, or lighthouse. At the second landing, midway up the chimney, is a mysterious door, entering to a mysterious closet; and here I keep mysterious cordials, of a choice, mysterious flavor, made so by the constant nurturing and subtle ripening of the chimney's gentle heat, distilled through that warm mass of masonry. Better for wines is it than voyages to the Indias; my chimney itself a tropic. A chair by my chimney in a November day is as good for an invalid as a long season spent in Cuba. Often I think how grapes might ripen against my chimney. How my wife's geraniums bud there! Bud in December. Her eggs, too--can't keep them near the chimney, an account of the hatching. Ah, a warm heart has my chimney.

How often my wife was at me about that projected grand entrance-hall of hers, which was to be knocked clean through the chimney, from one end of the house to the other, and astonish all guests by its generous amplitude. "But, wife," said I, "the chimney--consider the chimney: if you demolish the foundation, what is to support the superstructure?" "Oh, that will rest on the second floor." The truth is, women know next to nothing about the realities of architecture. However, my wife still talked of running her entries and partitions. She spent many long nights elaborating her plans; in imagination building her boasted hall through the chimney, as though its high mightiness were a mere spear of sorrel-top. At last, I gently reminded her that, little as she might fancy it, the chimney was a fact--a sober, substantial fact, which, in all her plannings, it would be well to take into full consideration. But this was not of much avail.
And here, respectfully craving her permission, I must say a few words about this enterprising wife of mine. Though in years nearly old as myself, in spirit she is young as my little sorrel mare, Trigger, that threw me last fall. What is extraordinary, though she comes of a rheumatic family, she is straight as a pine, never has any aches; while for me with the sciatica, I am sometimes as crippled up as any old apple-tree. But she has not so much as a toothache. As for her hearing--let me enter the house in my dusty boots, and she away up in the attic. And for her sight--Biddy, the housemaid, tells other people's housemaids, that her mistress will spy a spot on the dresser straight through the pewter

platter, put up on purpose to hide it. Her faculties are alert as her limbs and her senses. No danger of my spouse dying of torpor. The longest night in the year I've known her lie awake, planning her campaign for the morrow. She is a natural projector. The maxim, "Whatever is, is right," is not hers. Her maxim is, Whatever is, is wrong; and what is more, must be altered; and what is still more, must be altered right away. Dreadful maxim for the wife of a dozy old dreamer like me, who dote on seventh days as days of rest, and out of a sabbatical horror of industry, will, on a week day, go out of my road a quarter of a mile, to avoid the sight of a man at work.

That matches are made in heaven, may be, but my wife would have been just the wife for Peter the Great, or Peter the Piper. How she would have set in order that huge littered empire of the one, and with indefatigable painstaking picked the peck of pickled peppers for the other.

But the most wonderful thing is, my wife never thinks of her end. Her youthful incredulity, as to the plain theory, and still plainer fact of death, hardly seems Christian. Advanced in years, as she knows she must be, my wife seems to think that she is to teem on, and be inexhaustible forever. She doesn't believe in old age. At that strange promise in the plain of Mamre, my old wife, unlike old Abraham's, would not have jeeringly laughed within herself.

Judge how to me, who, sitting in the comfortable shadow of my chimney, smoking my comfortable pipe, with ashes not unwelcome at my feet, and ashes not unwelcome all but in my mouth; and who am thus in a comfortable sort of not unwelcome, though, indeed, ashy enough way, reminded of the ultimate exhaustion even of the most fiery life; judge how to me this unwarrantable vitality in my wife must come, sometimes, it is true, with a moral and a calm, but oftener with a breeze and a ruffle.

If the doctrine be true, that in wedlock contraries attract, by how cogent a fatality must I have been drawn to my wife! While spicily impatient of present and past, like a glass of ginger-beer she overflows with her schemes; and, with like energy as she puts down her foot, puts down her preserves and her pickles, and lives with them in a continual future; or ever full of expectations both from time and space, is ever restless for newspapers, and ravenous for letters. Content with the years that are gone, taking no thought for the morrow, and looking for no new thing from any person or quarter whatever, I have not a single scheme or expectation on earth, save in unequal resistance of the undue encroachment of hers.

Old myself, I take to oldness in things; for that cause mainly loving old Montague, and old cheese, and old wine; and eschewing young people, hot rolls, new books, and early potatoes and very fond of my old claw-footed chair, and old club-footed Deacon White, my neighbor, and that still nigher old neighbor, my betwisted old grape-vine, that of a summer evening leans in his elbow for cosy company at my window-sill, while I, within doors, lean over mine to meet his; and above all, high above all, am fond of my high-mantled old chimney. But she, out of the infatuate juvenility of hers, takes to nothing but newness; for that cause mainly, loving new cider in autumn, and in spring, as if she were own daughter of Nebuchadnezzar, fairly raving after all sorts of salads and spinages, and more particularly green cucumbers (though all the time nature rebukes such unsuitable young hankerings in so elderly a person, by never permitting such things to agree with her), and has an itch after recently- discovered fine prospects (so no graveyard be in the background), and also after Sweden-borganism, and the Spirit Rapping philosophy, with other new views, alike in things natural and unnatural; and immortally hopeful, is forever making new flower-beds even on the north side of the house where the bleak mountain wind would scarce allow the wiry weed called hard-hack to gain a thorough footing; and on the road-side sets out mere pipe-stems of young elms; though there is no hope of any shade from them, except over the ruins of her great granddaughter's gravestones; and won't wear caps, but plaits her gray hair; and takes the Ladies' Magazine for the fashions; and always buys her new almanac a month before the new year; and rises at dawn; and to the warmest sunset turns a cold shoulder; and still goes on at odd hours with her new course of history, and her French, and her music; and likes a young company; and offers to ride young colts; and sets out young suckers in the orchard; and has a spite against my elbowed old grape-vine, and my club-footed old neighbor, and my claw-footed old chair, and above all, high above all, would fain persecute, until death, my high-mantled old chimney. By what perverse magic, I a thousand times think, does such a very autumnal old lady have such a very vernal young soul? When I would remonstrate at times, she spins round on me with, "Oh, don't you grumble, old man (she always calls me old man), it's I, young I, that keep you from stagnating." Well, I suppose it is so. Yea, after all, these things are well ordered. My wife, as one of her poor relations, good soul, intimates, is the salt of the earth, and none the less the salt of my sea, which otherwise were unwholesome. She is its monsoon, too, blowing a brisk gale over it, in the one steady direction of my chimney.

 Not insensible of her superior energies, my wife has frequently made me propositions to take upon herself all the responsibilities of my affairs. She is desirous that, domestically, I should abdicate; that, renouncing further rule, like the venerable Charles V, I should retire into some sort of monastery. But indeed, the chimney excepted, I have little authority to lay down. By my wife's ingenious application of the principle that certain things belong of right to female jurisdiction, I find myself, through my easy compliances, insensibly stripped by degrees of one masculine prerogative after another. In a dream I go about my fields, a sort of lazy, happy-go-lucky, good-for-nothing, loafing old Lear. Only by some sudden revelation am I reminded who is over me; as year before last, one day seeing in one corner of the premises fresh deposits of mysterious boards and timbers, the oddity of the incident at length begat serious meditation. "Wife," said I, "whose boards and timbers are those I see near the orchard there? Do you know anything about them, wife? Who put them there? You know I do not like the neighbors to use my land that way, they should ask permission first."

 She regarded me with a pitying smile.

 "Why, old man, don't you know I am building a new barn? Didn't you know that, old man?"

 This is the poor old lady who was accusing me of tyrannizing over her.

 To return now to the chimney. Upon being assured of the futility of her proposed hall, so long as the obstacle remained, for a time my wife was for a modified project. But I could never exactly comprehend it. As far as I could see through it, it seemed to involve the general idea of a sort of irregular archway, or elbowed tunnel, which was to penetrate the chimney at some convenient point under the staircase, and carefully avoiding dangerous contact with the fireplaces, and particularly steering clear of the great interior flue, was to conduct the enterprising traveler from the front door all the way into the dining-room in the remote rear of the mansion. Doubtless it was a bold stroke of genius, that plan of hers, and so was Nero's when he schemed his grand canal through the Isthmus of Corinth. Nor will I take oath, that, had her project been accomplished, then, by help of lights hung at judicious intervals through the tunnel, some Belzoni or other might have succeeded in future ages in penetrating through the masonry, and actually emerging into the dining-room, and once there, it would have been inhospitable treatment of such a traveler to have denied him a recruiting meal.

But my bustling wife did not restrict her objections, nor in the end confine her proposed alterations to the first floor. Her ambition was of the mounting order. She ascended with her schemes to the second floor, and so to the attic. Perhaps there was some small ground for her discontent with things as they were. The truth is, there was no regular passage-way up-stairs or down, unless we again except that little orchestra-gallery before mentioned. And all this was owing to the chimney, which my gamesome spouse seemed despitefully to regard as the bully of the house. On all its four sides, nearly all the chambers sidled up to the chimney for the benefit of a fireplace. The chimney would not go to them; they must needs go to it. The consequence was, almost every room, like a philosophical system, was in itself an entry, or passage-way to other rooms, and systems of rooms--a whole suite of entries, in fact. Going through the house, you seem to be forever going somewhere, and getting nowhere. It is like losing one's self in the woods; round and round the chimney you go, and if you arrive at all, it is just where you started, and so you begin again, and again get nowhere. Indeed--though I say it not in the way of faultfinding at all--never was there so labyrinthine an abode. Guests will tarry with me several weeks and every now and then, be anew astonished at some unforseen apartment.

The puzzling nature of the mansion, resulting from the chimney, is peculiarly noticeable in the dining-room, which has no less than nine doors, opening in all directions, and into all sorts of places. A stranger for the first time entering this dining-room, and naturally taking no special heed at which door he entered, will, upon rising to depart, commit the strangest blunders. Such, for instance, as opening the first door that comes handy, and finding himself stealing up-stairs by the back passage. Shutting that he will proceed to another, and be aghast at the cellar yawning at his feet. Trying a third, he surprises the housemaid at her work. In the end, no more relying on his own unaided efforts, he procures a trusty guide in some passing person, and in good time successfully emerges. Perhaps as curious a blunder as any, was that of a certain stylish young gentleman, a great exquisite, in whose judicious eyes my daughter Anna had found especial favor. He called upon the young lady one evening, and found her alone in the dining-room at her needlework. He stayed rather late; and after abundance of superfine discourse, all the while retaining his hat and cane, made his profuse adieus, and with repeated graceful bows proceeded to depart, after fashion of courtiers from the Queen, and by so doing, opening a door at random, with one hand placed behind, very effectually succeeded in backing himself into a dark pantry, where be carefully shut himself up, wondering there was no light in the entry. After several strange noises as of a cat among the crockery, he reappeared through the same door, looking uncommonly crestfallen, and, with a deeply embarrassed air, requested my daughter to designate at which of the nine he should find exit. When the mischievous Anna told me the story, she said it was surprising how unaffected and matter-of-fact the young gentleman's manner was after his reappearance. He was more candid than ever, to be sure; having inadvertently thrust his white kids into an open drawer of Havana sugar, under the impression, probably, that being what they call "a sweet fellow," his route might possibly lie in that direction.

Another inconvenience resulting from the chimney is, the bewilderment of a guest in gaining his chamber, many strange doors lying between him and it. To direct him by finger-posts would look rather queer; and just as queer in him to be knocking at every door on his route, like London's city guest, the king, at Temple-Bar.

Now, of all these things and many, many more, my family continually complained. At last my wife came out with her sweeping proposition--in toto to abolish the chimney.

"What!" said I, "abolish the chimney? To take out the backbone of anything, wife, is a hazardous affair. Spines out of backs, and chimneys out of houses, are not to be taken like frosted lead pipes from the ground. Besides," added I, "the chimney is the one grand permanence of this abode. If undisturbed by innovators, then in future ages, when all the house shall have crumbled from it, this chimney will still survive--a Bunker Hill monument. No, no, wife, I can't abolish my backbone."

So said I then. But who is sure of himself, especially an old man, with both wife and daughters ever at his elbow and ear? In time, I was persuaded to think a little better of it; in short, to take the matter into preliminary consideration. At length it came to pass that a master-mason--a rough sort of architect--one Mr. Scribe, was summoned to a conference. I formally introduced him to my chimney. A previous introduction from my wife had introduced him to myself. He had been not a little employed by that lady, in preparing plans and estimates for some of her extensive operations in drainage. Having, with much ado, exhorted from my spouse the promise that she would leave us to an unmolested survey, I began by leading Mr. Scribe down to the root of the matter, in the cellar. Lamp in hand, I descended; for though up-stairs it was noon, below it was night.

We seemed in the pyramids; and I, with one hand holding my lamp over head, and with the other pointing out, in the obscurity, the hoar mass of the chimney, seemed some Arab guide, showing the cobwebbed mausoleum of the great god Apis.

"This is a most remarkable structure, sir," said the master-mason, after long contemplating it in silence, "a most remarkable structure, sir."

"Yes," said I complacently, "every one says so."

"But large as it appears above the roof, I would not have inferred the magnitude of this foundation, sir," eyeing it critically.

Then taking out his rule, he measured it.

"Twelve feet square; one hundred and forty-four square feet! Sir, this house would appear to have been built simply for the accommodation of your chimney."

"Yes, my chimney and me. Tell me candidly, now," I added, "would you have such a famous chimney abolished?"

"I wouldn't have it in a house of mine, sir, for a gift," was the reply. "It's a losing affair altogether, sir. Do you know, sir, that in retaining this chimney, you are losing, not only one hundred and forty-four square feet of good ground, but likewise a considerable interest upon a considerable principal?"

"How?"

Look, sir!" said he, taking a bit of red chalk from his pocket, and figuring against a whitewashed wall, "twenty times eight is so and so; then forty-two times thirty--nine is so and so--ain't it, sir? Well, add those together, and subtract this here, then that makes so and so, " still chalking away.

To be brief, after no small ciphering, Mr. Scribe informed me that my chimney contained, I am ashamed to say how many thousand and odd valuable bricks.

"No more," said I fidgeting. "Pray now, let us have a look above."

In that upper zone we made two more circumnavigations for the first and second floors. That done, we stood together at the foot of the stairway by the front door; my hand upon the knob, and Mr. Scribe hat in hand.

"Well, sir," said he, a sort of feeling his way, and, to help himself, fumbling with his hat, "well, sir, I think it can be done."

"What, pray, Mr. Scribe; *what* can be done?"

"Your chimney, sir; it can without rashness be removed, I think."

"I will think of it, too, Mr. Scribe" said I, turning the knob and bowing him towards the open space without, "I will *think* of it, sir; it demands consideration; much obliged to ye; good morning, Mr. Scribe."

"It is all arranged, then," cried my wife with great glee, bursting from the nighest room.

"When will they begin?" demanded my daughter Julia.

"To-morrow?" asked Anna.

"Patience, patience, my dears," said I, "such a big chimney is not to be abolished in a minute."

Next morning it began again.

"You remember the chimney," said my wife. "Wife," said I, "it is never out of my house and never out of my mind."

"But when is Mr. Scribe to begin to pull it down?" asked Anna.

"Not to-day, Anna," said I.

"*When*, then?" demanded Julia, in alarm.

Now, if this chimney of mine was, for size, a sort of belfry, for ding-donging at me about it, my wife and daughters were a sort of bells, always chiming together, or taking up each other's melodies at every pause, my wife the key-clapper of all. A very sweet ringing, and pealing, and chiming, I confess; but then, the most silvery of bells may, sometimes, dismally toll, as well as merrily play. And as touching the subject in question, it became so now. Perceiving a strange relapse of opposition in me, wife and daughters began a soft and dirge-like, melancholy tolling over it.

At length my wife, getting much excited, declared to me, with pointed finger, that so long as that chimney stood, she should regard it as the monument of what she called my broken pledge. But finding this did not answer, the next day, she gave me to understand that either she or the chimney must quit the house.

Finding matters coming to such a pass, I and my pipe philosophized over them awhile, and finally concluded between us, that little as our hearts went with the plan, yet for peace' sake, I might write out the chimney's death-warrant, and, while my hand was in, scratch a note to Mr. Scribe.

Considering that I, and my chimney, and my pipe, from having been so much together, were three great cronies, the facility with which my pipe consented to a project so fatal to the goodliest of our trio; or rather, the way in which I and my pipe, in secret, conspired together, as it were, against our unsuspicious old comrade--this may seem rather strange, if not suggestive of sad reflections upon us two. But, indeed, we, sons of clay, that is my pipe and I, are no better than the rest. Far from us, indeed, to have volunteered the betrayal of our crony. We are of a peaceable nature, too. But that love of peace it was which made us false to a mutual friend, as soon as his cause demanded a vigorous vindication. But, I rejoice to add, that better and braver thoughts soon returned, as will now briefly be set forth.

To my note, Mr. Scribe replied in person.

Once more we made a survey, mainly now with a view to a pecuniary estimate.

"I will do it for five hundred dollars," said Mr. Scribe at last, again hat in hand.

"Very well, Mr. Scribe, I will think of it," replied I, again bowing him to the door.

Not unvexed by this, for the second time, unexpected response, again he withdrew, and from my wife, and daughters again burst the old exclamations.
The truth is, resolved how I would, at the last pinch I and my chimney could not be parted.

So Holofernes will have his way, never mind whose heart breaks for it" said my wife next morning, at breakfast, in that half-didactic, half-reproachful way of hers, which is harder to bear than her most energetic assault. Holofernes, too, is with her a pet name for any fell domestic despot. So, whenever, against her most ambitious innovations, those which saw me quite across the grain, I, as in the present instance, stand with however little steadfastness on the defense, she is sure to call me Holofernes, and ten to one takes the first opportunity to read aloud, with a suppressed emphasis, of an evening, the first newspaper paragraph about some tyrannic day-laborer, who, after being for many years the Caligula of his family, ends by beating his long-suffering spouse to death, with a garret door wrenched off its hinges, and then, pitching his little innocents out of the window, suicidally turns inward towards the broken wall scored with the butcher's and baker's bills, and so rushes headlong to his dreadful account.
Nevertheless, for a few days, not a little to my surprise, I heard no further reproaches. An intense calm pervaded my wife, but beneath which, as in the sea, there was no knowing what portentous movements might be going on. She frequently went abroad, and in a direction which I thought not unsuspicious; namely, in the direction of New Petra, a griffin-like house of wood and stucco, in the highest style of ornamental art, graced with four chimneys in the form of erect dragons spouting smoke from their nostrils; the elegant modern residence of Mr. Scribe, which he had built for the purpose of a standing advertisement, not more of his taste as an architect, than his solidity as a master-mason.

At last, smoking my pipe one morning, I heard a rap at the door, and my wife, with an air unusually quiet for her brought me a note. As I have no correspondents except

Solomon, with whom in his sentiments, at least, I entirely correspond, the note occasioned me some little surprise, which was not dismissed upon reading the following:-

>NEW PETRA, April 1st.
>Sir--During my last examination of your chimney, possibly you may have noted that I frequently applied my rule to it in a manner apparently unnecessary. Possibly, also, at the same time, you might have observed in me more or less of perplexity, to which, however, I refrained from giving any verbal expression. I now feel it obligatory upon me to inform you of what was then but a dim suspicion, and as such would have been unwise to give utterance to, but which now, from various subsequent calculations assuming no little probability, it may be important that you should not remain in further ignorance of. It is my solemn duty to warn you, sir, that there is architectural cause to conjecture that somewhere concealed in your chimney is a reserved space, hermetically closed, in short, a secret chamber, or rather closet. How long it has been there, it is for me impossible to say. What it contains is hid, with itself, in darkness. But probably a secret closet would not have been contrived except for some extraordinary object, whether for the concealment of treasure, or for what other purpose, may be left to those better acquainted with the history of the house to guess. But enough: in making this disclosure, sir, my conscience is eased. Whatever step you choose to take upon it, is of course a matter of indifference to me; though, I confess, as respects the character of the closet, I cannot but share in a natural curiosity. Trusting that you may be guided aright, in determining whether it is Christian-like knowingly to reside in a house, hidden in which is a secret closet, I remain, with much respect, Yours very humbly,
>HIRAM SCRIBE.

My first thought upon reading this note was, not of the alleged mystery of manner to which, at the outset, it alluded-for none such had I at all observed in the master-mason during his surveys--but of my late kinsman, Captain Julian Dacres, long a ship-master and merchant in the Indian trade, who, about thirty years ago, and at the ripe age of ninety, died a bachelor, and in this very house, which he had built. He was supposed to have retired into this country with a large fortune. But to the general surprise, after being at great cost in building himself this mansion, he settled down into a sedate, reserved and inexpensive old age, which by the neighbors was thought all the better for his heirs: but lo! upon opening the will, his property was found to consist but of the house and grounds, and some ten thousand dollars in stocks; but the place, being found heavily mortgaged, was in consequence sold. Gossip had its day, and left the grass quietly to creep over the captain's grave, where he still slumbers in a privacy as unmolested as if the billows of the Indian Ocean, instead of the billows of inland verdure, rolled over him. Still, I remembered long ago, hearing strange solutions whispered by the country people for the mystery involving his will, and, by reflex, himself; and that, too, as well in conscience as purse. But people who could circulate the report (which they did), that Captain Julian Dacres had, in his day, been a Borneo pirate, surely were not worthy of credence in their collateral notions. It is queer what wild whimsies of rumors will, like toadstools, spring up about any eccentric stranger, who settling down among a rustic population, keeps quietly to himself. With some, inoffensiveness would seem a prime cause of offense. But what chiefly had led me to scout at these rumors, particularly as referring to concealed treasure, was the circumstance, that the stranger (the same who razed the roof and the chimney) into whose hands the estate had passed on my kinsman's death, was of that sort of character, that had there been the least ground for those reports, he would speedily have tested them, by tearing down and rummaging the walls.

Nevertheless, the note of Mr. Scribe, so strangely recalling the memory of my kinsman, very naturally chimed in with what had been mysterious, or at least unexplained, about him; vague flashings of ingots united in my mind with vague gleamings of skulls. But the first cool thought soon dismissed such chimeras; and, with a calm smile, I turned towards my wife, who, meantime, had been sitting nearby, impatient enough, I dare say, to know who could have taken it into his head to write me a letter.

"Well, old man," said she, "who is it from, and what is it about?"

"Read it, wife," said I, handing it.

Read it she did, and then--such an explosion! I will not pretend to describe her emotions, or repeat her expressions. Enough that my daughters were quickly called in to share the excitement. Although they had never dreamed of such a revelation as Mr. Scribe's; yet upon the first suggestion they instinctively saw the extreme likelihood of it. In corroboration, they cited first my kinsman, and second, my chimney; alleging that the profound mystery involving the former, and the equally profound masonry involving the latter, though both acknowledged facts, were alike preposterous on any other supposition than the secret closet.

But all this time I was quietly thinking to myself: Could it be hidden from me that my credulity in this instance would operate very favorably to a certain plan of theirs? How to get to the secret closet, or how to have any certainty about it at all, without making such fell work with my chimney as to render its set destruction superfluous? That my wife wished to get rid of the chimney, it needed no reflection to show; and that Mr. Scribe, for all his pretended disinterestedness, was not opposed to pocketing five hundred dollars by the operation, seemed equally evident. That my wife had, in secret, laid heads together with Mr. Scribe, I at present refrain from affirming. But when I consider her enmity against my chimney, and the steadiness with which at the last she is wont to carry out her schemes, if by hook or crook she can, especially after having been once baffled, why, I scarcely knew at what step of hers to be surprised.

Of one thing only was I resolved, that I and my chimney should not budge. In vain all protests. Next morning I went out into the road, where I had noticed a diabolical-looking old gander, that, for its doughty exploits in the way of scratching into forbidden enclosures, had been rewarded by its master with a portentous, four-pronged, wooden decoration, in the shape of a collar of the Order of the Garotte. This gander I cornered and rummaging out its stiffest quill, plucked it, took it home, and making a stiff pen, inscribed the following stiff note:

>CHIMNEY SIDE, April 2.
>MR. SCRIBE
>Sir:-For your conjecture, we return you our joint thanks and compliments, and beg leave to assure you, that we shall remain,
>Very faithfully,
>The same,
>I AND MY CHIMNEY.

Of course, for this epistle we had to endure some pretty sharp raps. But having at last explicitly understood from me that Mr. Scribe's note had not altered my mind one jot, my wife, to move me, among other things said, that if she remembered aright, there was a statute placing the keeping in private of secret closets on the same unlawful footing with the keeping of gunpowder. But it had no effect.

A few days after, my spouse changed her key.

It was nearly midnight, and all were in bed but ourselves, who sat up, one in each chimney-corner; she, needles in hand, indefatigably knitting a sock; I, pipe in mouth, indolently weaving my vapors.

It was one of the first of the chill nights in autumn. There was a fire on the hearth, burning low. The air without was torpid and heavy; the wood, by an oversight, of the sort called soggy.

"Do look at the chimney," she began; "can't you see that something must be in it?"

"Yes, wife. Truly there is smoke in the chimney, as in Mr. Scribe's note."

"Smoke? Yes, indeed, and in my eyes, too. How you two wicked old sinners do smoke!--this wicked old chimney and you."

"Wife," said I, "I and my chimney like to have a quiet smoke together, it is true, but we don't like to be called names."

"Now, dear old man," said she, softening down, and a little shifting the subject, "when you think of that old kinsman of yours, you *know* there must be a secret closet in this chimney."

"Secret ash-hole, wife, why don't you have it? Yes, I dare say there is a secret ash-hole in the chimney; for where do all the ashes go to that drop down the queer hole yonder?"

"I know where they go to; I've been there almost as many times as the cat."

"What devil, wife, prompted you to crawl into the ash-hole? Don't you know that St. Dunstan's devil emerged from the ash-hole? You will get your death one of these days, exploring all about as you do. But supposing there be a secret closet, what then?"

"What then? why what should be in a secret closet but--"

"Dry bones, wife," broke in I with a puff, while the sociable old chimney broke in with another.

"There again! Oh, how this wretched old chimney smokes," wiping her eyes with her handkerchief. "I've no doubt the reason it smokes so is, because that secret closet interferes with the flue. Do see, too, how the jambs here keep settling; and it's down hill all the way from the door to this hearth. This horrid old chimney will fall on our heads yet; depend upon it, old man."

"Yes, wife, I do depend on it; yes indeed, I place every dependence on my chimney. As for its settling, I like it. I, too, am settling, you know, in my gait. I and my chimney are settling together, and shall keep settling, too, till, as in a great feather-bed, we shall both have settled away clean out of sight. But this secret oven; I mean, secret closet of yours, wife; where exactly do you suppose that secret closet is?"

"That is for Mr. Scribe to say."

"But suppose he cannot say exactly; what, then?"

"Why then he can prove, I am sure, that it must be somewhere or other in this horrid old chimney."

"And if he can't prove that; what, then?"

"Why then, old man," with a stately air, "I shall say little more about it."

"Agreed, wife," returned I, knocking my pipe-bowl against the jamb, "and now, to-morrow, I will for a third time send for Mr. Scribe. Wife, the sciatica takes me; be so good as to put this pipe on the mantel."

"If you get the step-ladder for me, I will. This shocking old chimney, this abominable old-fashioned old chimney's mantels are so high, I can't reach them."
No opportunity, however trivial, was overlooked for a subordinate fling at the pile. Here, by way of introduction, it should be mentioned, that besides the fireplaces all round it, the chimney was, in the most haphazard way, excavated on each floor for certain curious out-of-the-way cupboards and closets, of all sorts and sizes, clinging here and there, like nests in the crotches of some old oak. On the second floor these closets were by far the most irregular and numerous. And yet this should hardly have been so, since the theory of the chimney was, that it pyramidically diminished as it ascended. The abridgment of its square on the roof was obvious enough; and it was supposed that the reduction must be methodically graduated from bottom to top.

"Mr. Scribe," said I when, the next day, with an eager aspect, that individual again came, "my object in sending for you this morning is, not to arrange for the demolition of my chimney, nor to have any particular conversation about it, but simply to allow you every reasonable facility for verifying, if you can, the conjecture communicated in your note."

Though in secret not a little crestfallen, it may be, by my phlegmatic reception, so different from what he had looked for; with much apparent alacrity he commenced the survey; throwing open the cupboards on the first floor, and peering into the closets on the second; measuring one within, and then comparing that measurement with the measurement without. Removing the fireboards, he would gaze up the flues. But no sign of the hidden work yet.
Now, on the second floor the rooms were the most rambling conceivable. They, as it were, dovetailed into each other. They were of all shapes; not one mathematically square room among them all--a peculiarity which by the master-mason had not been unobserved. With a significant, not to say portentous expression, he took a circuit of the chimney, measuring the area of each room around it; then going down stairs, and out of doors, he measured the entire ground area; then compared the sum total of the areas of all the rooms on the second floor with the ground area; then, returning to me in no small

excitement, announced that there was a difference of no less than two hundred and odd square feet--room enough, in all conscience, for a secret closet.

"But, Mr. Scribe," said I, stroking my chin, "have you allowed for the walls, both main and sectional? They take up some space, you know."

"Ah, I had forgotten that," tapping his forehead; "but," still ciphering on his paper, "that will not make up the deficiency."

"But, Mr. Scribe, have you allowed for the recesses of so many fireplaces on a floor, and for the fire-walls, and the flues; in short, Mr. Scribe, have you allowed for the legitimate chimney itself--some one hundred and forty-four square feet or thereabouts, Mr. Scribe?"

"How unaccountable. That slipped my mind, too."

"Did it, indeed, Mr. Scribe?"

He faltered a little, and burst forth with, "But we must now allow one hundred and forty-four square feet for the legitimate chimney. My position is, that within those undue limits the secret closet is contained."

I eyed him in silence a moment; then spoke:

"Your survey is concluded, Mr. Scribe; be so good now as to lay your finger upon the exact part of the chimney wall where you believe this secret closet to be; or would a witch-hazel wand assist you, Mr. Scribe?"

"No, Sir, but a crowbar would," he, with temper, rejoined.

Here, now, thought I to myself, the cat leaps out of the bag. I looked at him with a calm glance, under which he seemed somewhat uneasy. More than ever now I suspected a plot. I remembered what my wife had said about abiding by the decision of Mr. Scribe. In a bland way, I resolved to buy up the decision of Mr. Scribe.

"Sir," said I, "really, I am much obliged to you for this survey. It has quite set my mind at rest. And no doubt you, too, Mr. Scribe, must feel much relieved. Sir," I added, "you have made three visits to the chimney. With a business man, time is money. Here are fifty dollars, Mr. Scribe. Nay, take it. You have earned it. Your opinion is worth it. And by the way,"--as he modestly received the money-"have you any objections to give me a--a--little certificate--something, say, like a steamboat certificate, certifying that you, a competent surveyor, have surveyed my chimney, and found no reason to believe any unsoundness; in short, any--any secret closet in it. Would you be so kind, Mr. Scribe?"

"But, but, sir," stammered he with honest hesitation.

"Here, here are pen and paper," said I, with entire assurance.

Enough.

That evening I had the certificate framed and hung over the dining-room fireplace, trusting that the continual sight of it would forever put at rest at once the dreams and stratagems of my household.

But, no. Inveterately bent upon the extirpation of that noble old chimney, still to this day my wife goes about it, with my daughter Anna's geological hammer, tapping the wall all over, and then holding her ear against it, as I have seen the physicians of life insurance companies tap a man's chest, and then incline over for the echo. Sometimes of nights she almost frightens one, going about on this phantom errand, and still following the sepulchral response of the chimney, round and round, as if it were leading her to the threshold of the secret closet.

"How hollow it sounds," she will hollowly cry. "Yes, I declare," with an emphatic tap, "there is a secret closet here. Here, in this very spot. Hark! How hollow!"

"Psha! wife, of course it is hollow. Who ever heard of a solid chimney?" But nothing avails. And my daughters take after, not me, but their mother. Sometimes all three abandon the theory of the secret closet and return to the genuine ground of attack--the unsightliness of so cumbrous a pile, with comments upon the great addition of room to be gained by its demolition, and the fine effect of the projected grand hall, and the convenience resulting from the collateral running in one direction and another of their various partitions. Not more ruthlessly did the Three Powers partition away poor Poland, than my wife and daughters would fain partition away my chimney. But seeing that, despite all, I and my chimney still smoke our pipes, my wife reoccupies the ground of the secret closet, enlarging upon what wonders are there, and what a shame it is, not to seek it out and explore it.

"Wife," said I, upon one of these occasions, "why speak more of that secret closet, when there before you hangs contrary testimony of a master mason, elected by yourself to decide. Besides, even if there were a secret closet, secret it should remain, and secret it shall. Yes, wife, here for once I must say my say. Infinite sad mischief has resulted from the profane bursting open of secret recesses. Though standing in the heart of this house, though hitherto we have all nestled about it, unsuspicious of aught hidden within, this chimney may or may not have a secret closet. But if it have, it is my kinsman's. To break into that wall, would be to break into his breast. And that wall-breaking wish of Momus I account the wish of a churchrobbing gossip and knave. Yes, wife, a vile eavesdropping varlet was Momus."

"Moses? Mumps? Stuff with your mumps and Moses?"

The truth is, my wife, like all the rest of the world, cares not a fig for philosophical jabber. In dearth of other philosophical companionship, I and my chimney have to smoke and philosophize together. And sitting up so late as we do at it, a mighty smoke it is that we two smoky old philosophers make.

But my spouse, who likes the smoke of my tobacco as little as she does that of the soot, carries on her war against both. I live in continual dread lest, like the golden bowl, the pipes of me and my chimney shall yet be broken. To stay that mad project of my wife's, naught answers. Or, rather, she herself is incessantly answering, incessantly besetting me with her terrible alacrity for improvement, which is a softer name for destruction. Scarce a day I do not find her with her tape-measure, measuring for her grand hall, while Anna holds a yardstick on one side, and Julia looks approvingly on from the other. Mysterious intimations appear in the nearest village paper, signed "Claude," to the effect that a certain structure, standing on a certain hill, is a sad blemish to an otherwise lovely landscape. Anonymous letters arrive, threatening me with I know not what, unless I remove my chimney. Is it my wife, too, or who, that sets up the neighbors to badgering me on the same subject, and hinting to me that my chimney, like a huge elm, absorbs all moisture from my garden? At night, also, my wife will start as from sleep, professing to hear ghostly noises from the secret closet. Assailed on all sides, and in all ways, small peace have I and my chimney.

Were it not for the baggage, we would together pack up and remove from the country.

What narrow escapes have been ours! Once I found in a drawer a whole portfolio of plans and estimates. Another time, upon returning after a day's absence, I discovered my wife standing before the chimney in earnest conversation with a person whom I at once recognized as a meddlesome architectural reformer, who, because he had no gift for putting up anything was ever intent upon pulling them down; in various parts of the country having prevailed upon half-witted old folks to destroy their old-fashioned houses, particularly the chimneys.

But worst of all was, that time I unexpectedly returned at early morning from a visit to the city, and upon approaching the house, narrowly escaped three brickbats which fell, from high aloft, at my feet. Glancing up, what was my horror to see three savages, in blue jean overalls in the very act of commencing the long-threatened attack. Aye, indeed, thinking of those three brickbats, I and my chimney have had narrow escapes.

It is now some seven years since I have stirred from my home. My city friends all wonder why I don't come to see them, as in former times. They think I am getting sour and unsocial. Some say that I have become a sort of mossy old misanthrope, while all the time the fact is, I am simply standing guard over my mossy old chimney; for it is resolved between me and my chimney, that I and my chimney will never surrender.

Answer: *Melville is comparing the chimney to nature. He shows how absurd Romantics can be. While the chimney is necessary to a house, it is not necessarily beautiful. Likewise a snowstorm. He also pokes fun at the Romantics who intersect human relationship (i.e., the protagonist and his wife) with the chimney. The chimney, like nature, is an inanimate object.*

Supplemental Resources:

W. H. Auden, "The Christian Tragic Hero." In *New York Times Book Review*, December 16, 1945.

    Auden is an incredible poet and not half-bad critic. This article is seminal in studies on Romanticism.

Consider the Sea (VHS Tape)

    This is another very fine video on Melville, et al.

Famous Authors: Herman Melville (VHS Tape)

    This is an exhaustive video presentation of Melville's life.

Field Trip Possibility: The New Bedford Whaling Museum (New Bedford, MA)

    This museum is located across from the famous chapel in *Moby Dick*.

Leslie Fiedler, *Love and Death in the American Novel*

    This book is only tangentially connected to Melville but I really like Fiedler's criticisms of literary works.

Harry Levin, *The Power of Blackness: Hawthorne, Poe, Melville*

    The use of darkness in Romantic writers. Interesting.

Perry Miller,"Melville and Transcendentalism." In *Virginia Quarterly Review*, 29 (Autumn 1953)

    Perhaps no one is better able to speak to the tension in Melville's transition from Romanticism to Realism.

Carl Van Doren, *The American Novel*

    A great, general overview of the rise of the American novel (of which *Billy Budd* help prominence).

Nathalia Wright, *Melville's Use of the Bible*
    Hard to find resource that discusses Melville's biblical motifs.

Notes:

Lesson Sixteen Test

Discussion Question: (100 Points)

Compare Ch. 28 of *Moby Dick* with *Billy Budd*–both are written by Herman Melville. In your answer, compare tone, style, characterization, symbolism, and theme.

    For several days after leaving Nantucket, nothing above hatches was seen of Captain Ahab. The mates regularly relieved each other at the watches, and for aught that could be seen to the contrary, they seemed to be the only commanders of the ship; only they sometimes issued from the cabin with orders so sudden and peremptory, that after all it was plain they but commanded vicariously. Yet, their supreme lord and dictator was there, though hitherto unseen by any eyes not permitted to penetrate into the now sacred retreat of the cabin.

    Every time I ascended to the deck from my watches below, I instantly gazed aft to mark if any strange face was visible; for my first vague disquietude touching the unknown captain, now in the seclusion of the sea became almost a perturbation. This was strangely heightened at times by the ragged Elijah's diabolical incoherences uninvitedly recurring to me, with a subtle energy I could not have before conceived of. But poorly could I withstand them, much as in other moods I was almost ready to smile at the solemn whimsicalities of that outlandish prophet of the wharves. But whatever it was of apprehensiveness or uneasiness- to call it so- which I felt, yet whenever I came to look about me in the ship, it seemed against all warranty to cherish such emotions. For though the harpooneers, with the great body of the crew, were a far more barbaric, heathenish, and motley set than any of the tame merchant-ship companies which my previous experiences had made me acquainted with, still I ascribed this- and rightly ascribed it- to the fierce uniqueness of the very nature of that wild Scandinavian vocation in which I had so abandonedly embarked. But it was especially the aspect of the three chief officers of the ship, the mates, which was most forcibly calculated to allay these colorless misgivings, and induce confidence and cheerfulness in every presentment of the voyage. Three better, more likely sea-officers and men, each in his own different way, could not readily be found, and they were every one of them Americans; a Nantucketer, a Vineyarder, a Cape man. Now, it being Christmas when the ship shot from out her harbor, for a space we had biting Polar weather, though all the time running away from it to the southward; and by every degree and minute of latitude which we sailed, gradually leaving that merciless winter, and all its intolerable weather behind us. It was one of those less lowering, but still grey and gloomy enough mornings of the transition, when with a fair wind the ship was rushing through the water with a vindictive sort of leaping and melancholy rapidity, that as I mounted to the deck at the call of the forenoon watch, so soon as I levelled my glance towards the taffrail, foreboding shivers ran over me. Reality outran apprehension; Captain Ahab stood upon his quarter-deck.

There seemed no sign of common bodily illness about him, nor of the recovery from any. He looked like a man cut away from the stake, when the fire has overrunningly wasted all the limbs without consuming them, or taking away one particle from their compacted aged robustness. His whole high, broad form, seemed made of solid bronze, and shaped in an unalterable mould, like Cellini's cast Perseus. Threading its way out from among his grey hairs, and continuing right down one side of his tawny scorched face and neck, till it disappeared in his clothing, you saw a slender rod-like mark, lividly whitish. It resembled that perpendicular seam sometimes made in the straight, lofty trunk of a great tree, when the upper lightning tearingly darts down it, and without wrenching a single twig, peels and grooves out the bark from top to bottom ere running off into the soil, leaving the tree still greenly alive, but branded. Whether that mark was born with him, or whether it was the scar left by some desperate wound, no one could certainly say. By some tacit consent, throughout the voyage little or no allusion was made to it, especially by the mates. But once Tashtego's senior, an old Gay-Head Indian among the crew, superstitiously asserted that not till he was full forty years old did Ahab become that way branded, and then it came upon him, not in the fury of any mortal fray, but in an elemental strife at sea. Yet, this wild hint seemed inferentially negatived, by what a grey Manxman insinuated, an old sepulchral man, who, having never before sailed out of Nantucket, had never ere this laid eye upon wild Ahab. Nevertheless, the old sea-traditions, the immemorial credulities, popularly invested this old Manxman with preternatural powers of discernment. So that no white sailor seriously contradicted him when he said that if ever Captain Ahab should be tranquilly laid out- which might hardly come to pass, so he muttered- then, whoever should do that last office for the dead, would find a birth-mark on him from crown to sole.

So powerfully did the whole grim aspect of Ahab affect me, and the livid brand which streaked it, that for the first few moments I hardly noted that not a little of this overbearing grimness was owing to the barbaric white leg upon which he partly stood. It had previously come to me that this ivory leg had at sea been fashioned from the polished bone of the sperm whale's jaw. "Aye, he was dismasted off Japan," said the old Gay-Head Indian once; "but like his dismasted craft, he shipped another mast without coming home for it. He has a quiver of 'em."

I was struck with the singular posture he maintained. Upon each side of the Pequod's quarter deck, and pretty close to the mizzen shrouds, there was an auger hole, bored about half an inch or so, into the plank. His bone leg steadied in that hole; one arm elevated, and holding by a shroud; Captain Ahab stood erect, looking straight out beyond the ship's ever-pitching prow. There was an infinity of firmest fortitude, a determinate, unsurrenderable wilfulness, in the fixed and fearless, forward dedication of that glance. Not a word he spoke; nor did his officers say aught to him; though by all their minutest gestures and expressions, they plainly showed the uneasy, if not painful, consciousness of being under a troubled master-eye. And not only that, but moody stricken Ahab stood before them with a crucifixion in his face; in all the nameless regal overbearing dignity of some mighty woe.

Ere long, from his first visit in the air, he withdrew into his cabin. But after that morning, he was every day visible to the crew; either standing in his pivot-hole, or seated upon an ivory stool he had; or heavily walking the deck. As the sky grew less gloomy; indeed, began to grow a little genial, he became still less and less a recluse; as if, when the ship had sailed from home, nothing but the dead wintry bleakness of the sea had then kept him so secluded. And, by and by, it came to pass, that he was almost continually in the air; but, as yet, for all that he said, or perceptibly did, on the at last sunny deck, he seemed as unnecessary there as another mast. But the Pequod was only making a passage now; not regularly cruising; nearly all whaling preparatives needing supervision the mates were fully competent to, so that there was little or nothing, out of himself, to employ or excite Ahab, now; and thus chase away, for that one interval, the clouds that layer upon layer were piled upon his brow, as ever all clouds choose the loftiest peaks to pile themselves upon.

Nevertheless, ere long, the warm, warbling persuasiveness of the pleasant, holiday weather we came to, seemed gradually to charm him from his mood. For, as when the red-cheeked, dancing girls, April and May, trip home to the wintry, misanthropic woods; even the barest, ruggedest, most thunder-cloven old oak will at least send forth some few green sprouts, to welcome such gladhearted visitants; so Ahab did, in the end, a little respond to the playful allurings of that girlish air. More than once did he put forth the faint blossom of a look, which, in any other man, would have soon flowered out in a smile.

Lesson Sixteen Test Answers

Discussion Question: (100 Points)

Compare Ch. 28 of *Moby Dick* with *Billy Budd*–both are written by Herman Melville. In your answer, compare tone, style, characterization, symbolism, and theme.

Melville's uses long, developed sentences that are full of metaphor and symbols. Ahab is a Romantic epic hero–fighting against fate. He is a biblical figure–Saul– like who is doomed but does not know it. There is the theme of journey and revenge–both popular Melville themes that are intimated in both works. Both novels also occur at sea. In fact, there are remarkable similarities in both novels.

Lesson Seventeen

Readings Due For This Lesson
Students should have read *Billy Budd*, Herman Melville.

Reading Ahead
Students should read *The Red Badge of Courage*, Stephen Crane (Lesson Eighteen)

Suggested Weekly Implementation

Day One	Day Two	Day Three	Day Four	Day Five
1. Students will rewrite graded essays from last week and review Lesson Sixteen test. 2. Students should have read the required reading(s) *before* the assigned lesson begins. 3. Teacher may want to discuss assigned reading(s) with student. 4. Teacher shall assign the required essays. Choose two or three. The rest of the essays can be outlined, answered with shorter answers, or skipped.	1. Student should begin reading(s) from next lesson. 2. Student should outline essays due at the end of the week. 3. Students should answer one or two of the essays that are not assigned as formal essays.	1. Students should write rough drafts of assigned essays. 2. The teacher should correct rough drafts.	Student will write final copy of essays due tomorrow.	1. Essays are due. 2. Students should take Lesson Seventeen test. 3. Student should read *The Red Badge of Courage*, Stephen Crane.

Melville...

Challenge Question

Perhaps the best characterization of Melville is found in the writings of his good friend Nathaniel Hawthorne. Hawthorne describes Melville in this way:

> *We took a pretty long walk together, and sat down in a hollow among the sand hills... Melville, as he always does, began to reason of Providence and futurity, and of everything that lies beyond human ken, and informed me that he had 'pretty much made up his mind to be annihilated'; but still he does not seem to rest in that anticipation; and, I think, will never rest until he gets hold of a definite belief... He can neither believe, nor be comfortable in his unbelief; and he is too honest and courageous not to try to do one or the other...*

He can neither believe, nor be comfortable in his unbelief. What a marvelous description of modern man. David F. Wells in his book *God in the Wasteland: The Reality of Truth in a World of Fading Dreams*, is convinced that since the middle of the last century human society has embraced "an ironic recapitulation of the first dislocation in which God's creatures replaced their Creator and exiled Him from His own world" (p. 14). Find examples of this development in *Billy Budd*. Agree or disagree with Wells' statement and find examples both in this book and contemporary life that support or refute this statement. *The free and flawed biblical analogies, the divorce of morality from its Judeo-Christian roots, and the primacy of human experience over biblical truth foreshadows much trouble for the American soul.*

For Further Enrichment

Over the next few weeks become a character who is born in 1820 and dies in 1920. Keep a personal diary. Reflect on historical events as they unfold in your pretend life.

Obviously each historical event will have different degrees of relevance to your situation; however, have an opinion about every event that reflects a correct historical understanding of the event and its significance to American history. This will require some historical research on your part.

REBECCA HAWTHORNE. You are a white, Boston born resident. Your father is a whaler. While delivering your little brother, your mother will die from tuberculosis when you are ten.

PRISCILLA DINWIDDIE. You are a black slave living in Virginia. You have assumed the name of your master, Dinwiddie. Your master is a wealthy plantation owner who owns hundreds of slaves. When you are twelve your mother and father will be sold to a plantation in South Carolina. Your grandmother will raise you.

ROBERT STRONG. You are a white person living in Tennessee. Your father owns three slaves. You have fourteen brothers and sisters.

DAVID ARMSTRONG. You are born into a white Pennsylvania farm family. When you are six your father will be killed in a farming accident.

WHITEWATER RAPIDS. You are a Sioux warrior. You were born in Illinois. But before long the white men come and drive you off your land... Before you are twenty years old, four family members die from Smallpox.

You should begin each entry with "Dear diary..." and you should write about one-page (or more) for each entry. Each entry should be in essay form.

--It is 1828. President Jackson has just been elected president. How did your parents react?

--It is 1832. the Cherokees have been relocated to Oklahoma in the "trail of tears." What is this?

--Two things happen this year: Your relatives are part of or you hear of the Underground Railroad. What is it? How does it effect you? And, you hear about the Alamo. What year is this? You are married to an immigrant from Germany who does not know how to speak English (or your language).

--Your parents obtain a copy of William Lloyd Garrison's newspaper *The Liberator*. What is their reaction? Why?

--It is 1845. The Mexican War has started. Your older brother joins up. Several members of your hometown think that it is a bad war. In fact, your closet friend was arrested for civil disobedience. How do your parents react?

--Nat Turner is a name that terrorizes your household. Why?

--The Fugitive Slave Act is passed. What is it? Does it bother your wife?

--You fight in the Civil War and are wounded at Cold Harbor. Create a diary with entries about the way the whole war affected you. Have at least ten entries.

--You join the Klu Klux Klan, your husband joins the Klan, or you have been hurt by the Klan.

Answer: *Answers will vary.*

> Two quintessential questions our culture raises by its nature and development are *what is truth?* and *what can we believe?* Our culture doesn't know the answer. It never did. The Puritans knew that. They looked beyond themselves. They looked to God. But from this point in American literature we will be entering a wasteland . . . after the humorist Mark Twain wrote his satire and early Realism, American writers lost confidence in a single truth and came to the conclusion that truth is unattainable. Today we hold to a plurality of truths and the tolerance of them is now a virtue. Truth, to our secular world, is discovered in this struggle. Watch this cultural warfare unfold in the next lessons.

Supplemental Resources:

W. H. Auden, "The Christian Tragic Hero." In *New York Times Book Review*, December 16, 1945
    Auden is an incredible poet and not half-bad critic. This article is seminal in studies on Romanticism.

Consider the Sea (VHS Tape)
> This is another very fine video on Melville, et al.

Famous Authors: Herman Melville (VHS Tape)
> This is an exhaustive video presentation of Melville's life.

Field Trip Possibility: The New Bedford Whaling Museum (New Bedford, MA)
> This museum is located across from the famous chapel in *Moby Dick*.

Leslie Fiedler, *Love and Death in the American Novel*
> This book is only tangentially connected to Melville but I really like Fiedler's criticisms of literary works.

Harry Levin, *The Power of Blackness: Hawthorne, Poe, Melville*
> The use of darkness in Romantic writers. Interesting.

Perry Miller, "Melville and Transcendentalism." In *Virginia Quarterly Review*, 29 (Autumn 1953)
> Perhaps no one is better able to speak to the tension in Melville's transition from Romanticism to Realism.

Carl Van Doren, *The American Novel*
> A great, general overview of the rise of the American novel (of which *Billy Budd* help prominence).

Nathalia Wright, *Melville's Use of the Bible*
> Hard to find resource that discusses Melville's biblical motifs.

Notes:

Lesson Seventeen Test

Discussion Questions: (100 Points)

A. Melville begins his small novel with a reference to the "Handsome Sailor." Who is he?

B. Why would the "Handsome Sailor" be an African native?

C. What are the historical contexts of the story? Why is this important?

D. Why does Billy willingly except his impressment?

E. Why does Lieutenant Radcliffe seem to be more important than Captain Graveling

F. How do you interpret Melville's definition of "Natural Depravity"?

G. What is Billy's one flaw?

H. To what mythical figure is Billy compared?

I. Billy is an unusual hero. Why?

J. Discuss how Vere's condemnation of Billy is like Abraham's sacrifice of Isaac.

Lesson Seventeen Test Answers

Discussion Questions (100 Points):

A. Melville begins his small novel with a reference to the "Handsome Sailor." Who is he? *An archetype, good, moral man.*

B. Why would the "Handsome Sailor" be an African native? *To the Romantic author, Melville, an uncivilized individual is the perfect paradigm of virtue.*

C. What are the historical contexts of the story? Why is this important? *Several mutinies have occurred in this war between the French and the English.*

D. Why does Billy willingly except his impressment? *Billy is the stoic, the man of no guile. He is the contented man.*

E. Why does Lieutenant Radcliffe seem to be more important than Captain Graveling *Radclliffe is an English officer and Graveling is a privateer.*

F. How do you interpret Melville's definition of "Natural Depravity"? *Someone who does not embrace the "naturalness of human good" so amply portrayed by Billy Budd.*

G. What is Billy's one flaw? *He stutters.*

H. To what mythical figure is Billy compared? *Hercules.*

I. Billy is an unusual hero. Why? *He is without guile, has no authority or power, nor does he want any. He controls nothing; serves everyone.*

J. Discuss how Vere's condemnation of Billy is like Abraham's sacrifice of Isaac. *Vere reluctantly sacrifices innocent Billy as an impediment to further mutinies.*

LESSON EIGHTEEN

Readings Due For This Lesson

Students should have read *The Red Badge of Courage*, Stephen Crane.

Reading Ahead

Students should read *Ethan Frome*, Edith Wharton (Lesson Twenty)

Suggested Weekly Implementation

Day One	Day Two	Day Three	Day Four	Day Five
1. Students will rewrite graded essays from last week and review Lesson Seventeen test. 2. Students should have read the required reading(s) *before* the assigned lesson begins. 3. Teacher may want to discuss assigned reading(s) with student. 4. Teacher shall assign the required essays. Choose two or three. The rest of the essays can be outlined, answered with shorter answers, or skipped.	1. Student should begin reading(s) from next lesson. 2. Student should outline essays due at the end of the week. 3. Students should answer one or two of the essays that are not assigned as formal essays.	1. Students should write rough drafts of assigned essays. 2. The teacher should correct rough drafts.	Student will write final copy of essays due tomorrow.	1. Essays are due. 2. Students should take Lesson Eighteen test. 3. Students should begin to read *Ethan Frome*, Edith Wharton.

The Red Badge of Courage
By Stephen Crane
(Published in 1895)

Book Checkup

__a___ 1.

__b___ 2.

__a___ 3.

__d___ 4.

__d___ 5.

Suggested Vocabulary Words
    Word
- hilarious *(comical)*
- impregnable *(invincible)*
- impetus *(force)*
- perambulating *(strolling)*
- imprecations *(curses)*
- querulous *(irritable)*
- trepidation *(fear)*
- perfunctory *(cursory)*
- petulantly *(angry)*
- deprecating *(condemning)*
- temerity *(shyness)*
- imperious *(overbearing)*
- expletive *(exclamation)*
- stentorian *(very loud)*

Biblical Application

Compare and contrast Stephen Crane's view of death with Jack London's view of death in this short story.

To Build a Fire

Day had broken cold and grey, exceedingly cold and grey, when the man turned aside from the main Yukon trail and climbed the high earth- bank, where a dim and little-travelled trail led eastward through the fat spruce timberland. It was a steep bank, and he paused for breath at the top, excusing the act to himself by looking at his watch. It was nine o'clock. There was no sun nor hint of sun, though there was not a cloud in the sky. It was a clear day, and yet there seemed an intangible pall over the face of things, a subtle gloom that made the day dark, and that was due to the absence of sun. This fact did not worry the man. He was used to the lack of sun. It had been days since he had seen the sun, and he knew that a few more days must pass before that cheerful orb, due south, would just peep above the sky- line and dip immediately from view.

The man flung a look back along the way he had come. The Yukon lay a mile wide and hidden under three feet of ice. On top of this ice were as many feet of snow. It was

> In both literary pieces, nature is ubiquitous and malevolent.

all pure white, rolling in gentle undulations where the ice-jams of the freeze-up had formed. North and south, as far as his eye could see, it was unbroken white, save for a dark hair-line that curved and twisted from around the spruce- covered island to the south, and that curved and twisted away into the north, where it disappeared behind another spruce-covered island. This dark hair-line was the trail--the main trail--that led south five hundred miles to the Chilcoot Pass, Dyea, and salt water; and that led north seventy miles to Dawson, and still on to the north a thousand miles to Nulato, and finally to St. Michael on Bering Sea, a thousand miles and half a thousand more.

But all this--the mysterious, far-reaching hairline trail, the absence of sun from the sky, the tremendous cold, and the strangeness and weirdness of it all--made no impression on the man. It was not because he was long used to it. He was a new-comer in the land, a chechaquo, and this was his first winter. The trouble with him was that he was without imagination. He was quick and alert in the things of life, but only in the things, and not in the significances. Fifty degrees below zero meant eighty odd degrees of frost. Such fact impressed him as being cold and uncomfortable, and that was all. It did not lead him to meditate upon his frailty as a creature of temperature, and upon man's frailty in general, able only to live within certain narrow limits of heat and cold; and from there on it did not lead him to the conjectural field of immortality and man's place in the universe. Fifty degrees below zero stood for a bite of frost that hurt and that must be guarded against by the use of mittens, ear-flaps, warm moccasins, and thick socks. Fifty degrees below zero was to him just precisely fifty degrees below zero. That there should be anything more to it than that was a thought that never entered his head.

As he turned to go on, he spat speculatively. There was a sharp, explosive crackle that startled him. He spat again. And again, in the air, before it could fall to the snow, the spittle crackled. He knew that at fifty below spittle crackled on the snow, but this spittle had crackled in the air. Undoubtedly it was colder than fifty below--how much colder he did not know. But the temperature did not matter. He was bound for the old claim on the left fork of Henderson Creek, where the boys were already. They had come over across the divide from the Indian Creek country, while he had come the roundabout way to take a look at the possibilities of getting out logs in the spring from the islands in the Yukon. He would be in to camp by six o'clock; a bit after dark, it was true, but the boys would be there, a fire would be going, and a hot supper would be ready. As for lunch, he pressed his hand against the protruding bundle under his jacket. It was also under his shirt, wrapped up in a handkerchief and lying against the naked skin. It was the only way to keep the biscuits from freezing. He smiled agreeably to himself as he thought of those biscuits, each cut open and sopped in bacon grease, and each enclosing a generous slice of fried bacon.

He plunged in among the big spruce trees. The trail was faint. A foot of snow had fallen since the last sled had passed over, and he was glad he was without a sled, travelling light. In fact, he carried nothing but the lunch wrapped in the handkerchief. He was surprised, however, at the cold. It certainly was cold, he concluded, as he rubbed his numbed nose and cheek-bones with his mittened hand. He was a warm-whiskered man, but the hair on his face did not protect the high cheek-bones and the eager nose that thrust itself aggressively into the frosty air.

At the man's heels trotted a dog, a big native husky, the proper wolf-dog, grey-coated and without any visible or temperamental difference from its brother, the wild wolf. The animal was depressed by the tremendous cold. It knew that it was no time for travelling. Its instinct told it a truer tale than was told to the man by the man's judgment. In reality, it was not merely colder than fifty below zero; it was colder than sixty below, than seventy below. It was seventy-five below zero. Since the freezing-point is thirty-two above zero, it meant that one hundred and seven degrees of frost obtained. The dog did not know anything about thermometers. Possibly in its brain there was no sharp consciousness of a condition of very cold such as was in the man's brain. But the brute had its instinct. It experienced a vague but menacing apprehension that subdued it and made it slink along at the man's heels, and that made it question eagerly every unwonted movement of the man as if expecting him to go into camp or to seek shelter somewhere and build a fire. The dog had learned fire, and it wanted fire, or else to burrow under the snow and cuddle its warmth away from the air.

The frozen moisture of its breathing had settled on its fur in a fine powder of frost, and especially were its jowls, muzzle, and eyelashes whitened by its crystalled breath. The man's red beard and moustache were likewise frosted, but more solidly, the deposit taking the form of ice and increasing with every warm, moist breath he exhaled. Also, the man was chewing tobacco, and the muzzle of ice held his lips so rigidly that he was unable to clear his chin when he expelled the juice. The result was that a crystal beard of the colour and solidity of amber was increasing its length on his chin. If he fell down it would shatter itself, like glass, into brittle fragments. But he did not mind the appendage. It was the penalty all tobacco- chewers paid in that country, and he had been out before in two cold snaps. They had not been so cold as this, he knew, but by the spirit thermometer at Sixty Mile he knew they had been registered at fifty below and at fifty-five.

He held on through the level stretch of woods for several miles, crossed a wide flat of nigger-heads, and dropped down a bank to the frozen bed of a small stream. This was Henderson Creek, and he knew he was ten miles from the forks. He looked at his watch. It was ten o'clock. He was making four miles an hour, and he calculated that he would arrive at the forks at half-past twelve. He decided to celebrate that event by eating his lunch there.

The dog dropped in again at his heels, with a tail drooping discouragement, as the man swung along the creek-bed. The furrow of the old sled-trail was plainly visible, but a dozen inches of snow covered the marks of the last runners. In a month no man had come up or down that silent creek. The man held steadily on. He was not much given to thinking, and just then particularly he had nothing to think about save that he would eat lunch at the forks and that

> There is very little difference between the man and the dog. In fact, they are both creatures trying to survive in the wild. The wilderness is the great equalizer and, ironically, the dog is better equip to survive than the so-called "more intelligent" man. This is a supreme irony endemic to Nauturalism.

at six o'clock he would be in camp with the boys. There was nobody to talk to and, had there been, speech would have been impossible because of the ice-muzzle on his mouth. So he continued monotonously to chew tobacco and to increase the length of his amber beard.

Once in a while the thought reiterated itself that it was very cold and that he had never experienced such cold. As he walked along he rubbed his cheek-bones and nose with the back of his mittened hand. He did this automatically, now and again changing hands. But rub as he would, the instant he stopped his cheek-bones went numb, and the following instant the end of his nose went numb. He was sure to frost his cheeks; he knew that, and experienced a pang of regret that he had not devised a nose-strap of the sort Bud wore in cold snaps. Such a strap passed across the cheeks, as well, and saved them. But it didn't matter much, after all. What were frosted cheeks? A bit painful, that was all; they were never serious.

Empty as the man's mind was of thoughts, he was keenly observant, and he noticed the changes in the creek, the curves and bends and timber- jams, and always he sharply noted where he placed his feet. Once, coming around a bend, he shied abruptly, like a startled horse, curved away from the place where he had been walking, and retreated several paces back along the trail. The creek he knew was frozen clear to the bottom--no creek could contain water in that arctic winter--but he knew also that there were springs that bubbled out from the hillsides and ran along under the snow and on top the ice of the creek. He knew that the coldest snaps never froze these springs, and he knew likewise their danger. They were traps. They hid pools of water under the snow that might be three inches deep, or three feet. Sometimes a skin of ice half an inch thick covered them, and in turn was covered by the snow. Sometimes there were alternate layers of water and ice-skin, so that when one broke through he kept on breaking through for a while, sometimes wetting himself to the waist.

That was why he had shied in such panic. He had felt the give under his feet and heard the crackle of a snow-hidden ice-skin. And to get his feet wet in such a temperature meant trouble and danger. At the very least it meant delay, for he would be forced to stop and build a fire, and under its protection to bare his feet while he dried his socks and moccasins. He stood and studied the creek-bed and its banks, and decided that the flow of water came from the right. He reflected awhile, rubbing his nose and cheeks, then skirted to the left, stepping gingerly and testing the footing for each step. Once clear of the danger, he took a fresh chew of tobacco and swung along at his four-mile gait.

In the course of the next two hours he came upon several similar traps. Usually the snow above the hidden pools had a sunken, candied appearance that advertised the danger. Once again, however, he had a close call; and once, suspecting danger, he compelled the dog to go on in front. The dog did not want to go. It hung back until the man shoved it forward, and then it went quickly across the white, unbroken surface. Suddenly it broke through, floundered to one side, and got away to firmer footing. It had wet its forefeet and legs, and almost immediately the water that clung to it turned to ice. It made quick efforts to lick the ice off its legs, then dropped down in the snow and began to bite out the ice that had formed between the toes. This was a matter of instinct. To permit the ice to remain would mean sore feet. It did not know this. It merely obeyed the mysterious prompting that arose from the deep crypts of its being. But the man knew, having achieved a judgment on the subject, and he removed the mitten from his right hand and helped tear out the ice- particles. He did not expose his fingers more than a minute, and was astonished at the swift numbness that smote them. It certainly was cold. He pulled on the mitten hastily, and beat the hand savagely across his chest.

At twelve o'clock the day was at its brightest. Yet the sun was too far south on its winter journey to clear the horizon. The bulge of the earth intervened between it and Henderson Creek, where the man walked under a

> In both books God is impersonal and uninterested in the plight of human beings.

clear sky at noon and cast no shadow. At half-past twelve, to the minute, he arrived at the forks of the creek. He was pleased at the speed he had made. If he kept it up, he would certainly be with the boys by six. He unbuttoned his jacket and shirt and drew forth his lunch. The action consumed no more than a quarter of a minute, yet in that brief moment the numbness laid hold of the exposed fingers. He did not put the mitten on, but, instead, struck the fingers a dozen sharp smashes against his leg. Then he sat down on a snow-covered log to eat. The sting that followed upon the striking of his fingers against his leg ceased so quickly that he was startled, he had had no chance to take a bite of biscuit. He struck the fingers repeatedly and returned them to the mitten, baring the other hand for the purpose of eating. He tried to take a mouthful, but the ice-muzzle prevented. He had forgotten to build a fire and thaw out. He chuckled at his foolishness, and as he chuckled he noted the numbness creeping into the exposed fingers. Also, he noted that the stinging which had first come to his toes when he sat down was already passing away. He wondered whether the toes were warm or numbed. He moved them inside the moccasins and decided that they were numbed.

He pulled the mitten on hurriedly and stood up. He was a bit frightened. He stamped up and down until the stinging returned into the feet. It certainly was cold, was his thought. That man from Sulphur Creek had spoken the truth when telling how cold it sometimes got in the country. And he had laughed at him at the time! That showed one must not be too sure of things. There was no mistake about it, it was cold. He strode up and down, stamping his feet and threshing his arms, until reassured by the returning warmth.

> *He was a bit frightened* is a statement of weakness in both novels. In fact, this statement presages the demise of both characters. This statement is not given to evoke sympathy from the reader. It should evoke scorn from the reader, for only the naive, the romantic, and the weak express fear. London and Crane argue that "fear" and other abstract emotions are superfluous.

Then he got out matches and proceeded to make a fire. From the undergrowth, where high water of the previous spring had lodged a supply of seasoned twigs, he got his firewood. Working carefully from a small beginning, he soon had a roaring fire, over which he thawed the ice from his face and in the protection of which he ate his biscuits. For the moment the cold of space was outwitted. The dog took satisfaction in the fire, stretching out close enough for warmth and far enough away to escape being singed.

When the man had finished, he filled his pipe and took his comfortable time over a smoke. Then he pulled on his mittens, settled the ear-flaps of his cap firmly about his ears, and took the creek trail up the left fork. The dog was disappointed and yearned back toward the fire. This man did not know cold. Possibly all the generations of his ancestry had been ignorant of cold, of real cold, of cold one hundred and seven degrees below freezing-point. But the dog knew; all its ancestry knew, and it had inherited the knowledge. And it knew that it was not good to walk abroad in such fearful cold. It was the time to lie snug in a hole in the snow and wait for a curtain of cloud to be drawn across the face of outer space whence this cold came. On the other hand, there was keen intimacy between the dog and the man. The one was the toil-slave of the other, and the only caresses it had ever received were the caresses of the whip- lash and of harsh and menacing throat-sounds that threatened the whip-lash. So the dog made no effort to communicate its apprehension to the man. It was not concerned in the welfare of the man; it was for its own sake that it yearned back toward the fire. But the man whistled, and spoke to it with the sound of whip-lashes, and the dog swung in at the man's heels and followed after.

The man took a chew of tobacco and proceeded to start a new amber beard. Also, his moist breath quickly powdered with white his moustache, eyebrows, and lashes. There did not seem to be so many springs on the left fork of the Henderson, and for half an hour the man saw no signs of any. And then it happened. At a place where there were no signs, where the soft, unbroken snow seemed to advertise solidity beneath, the man broke through. It was not deep. He wetted himself half-way to the knees before he floundered out to the firm crust.

    He was angry, and cursed his luck aloud. He had hoped to get into camp with the boys at six o'clock, and this would delay him an hour, for he would have to build a fire and dry out his foot-gear. This was imperative at that low temperature--he knew that much; and he turned aside to the bank, which he climbed. On top, tangled in the underbrush about the trunks of several small spruce trees, was a high-water deposit of dry firewood--sticks and twigs principally, but also larger portions of seasoned branches and fine, dry, last-year's grasses. He threw down several large pieces on top of the snow. This served for a foundation and prevented the young flame from drowning itself in the snow it otherwise would melt. The flame he got by touching a match to a small shred of birch-bark that he took from his pocket. This burned even more readily than paper. Placing it on the foundation, he fed the young flame with wisps of dry grass and with the tiniest dry twigs.

    He worked slowly and carefully, keenly aware of his danger. Gradually, as the flame grew stronger, he increased the size of the twigs with which he fed it. He squatted in the snow, pulling the twigs out from their entanglement in the brush and feeding directly to the flame. He knew there must be no failure. When it is seventy-five below zero, a man must not fail in his first attempt to build a fire--that is, if his feet are wet. If his feet are dry, and he fails, he can run along the trail for half a mile and restore his circulation. But the circulation of wet and freezing feet cannot be restored by running when it is seventy-five below. No matter how fast he runs, the wet feet will freeze the harder.

    All this the man knew. The old-timer on Sulphur Creek had told him about it the previous fall, and now he was appreciating the advice. Already all sensation had gone out of his feet. To build the fire he had been forced to remove his mittens, and the fingers had quickly gone numb. His pace of four miles an hour had kept his heart pumping blood to the surface of his body and to all the extremities. But the instant he stopped, the action of the pump eased down. The cold of space smote the unprotected tip of the planet, and he, being on that unprotected tip, received the full force of the blow. The blood of his body recoiled before it. The blood was alive, like the dog, and like the dog it wanted to hide away and cover itself up from the fearful cold. So long as he walked four miles an hour, he pumped that blood, willy-nilly, to the surface; but now it ebbed away and sank down into the recesses of his body. The extremities were the first to feel its absence. His wet feet froze the faster, and his exposed fingers numbed the faster, though they had not yet begun to freeze. Nose and cheeks were already freezing, while the skin of all his body chilled as it lost its blood.

    But he was safe. Toes and nose and cheeks would be only touched by the frost, for the fire was beginning to burn with strength. He was feeding it with twigs the size of his finger. In another minute he would be able to feed it with branches the size of his wrist, and then he could remove his wet foot-gear, and, while it dried, he could keep his naked feet warm by the fire, rubbing them at first, of course, with snow. The fire was a success. He was safe. He remembered the advice of the old-timer on Sulphur Creek, and smiled. The old-timer had been very serious in laying down the law that no man must travel alone in the Klondike after fifty below. Well, here he was; he had had the accident; he was alone; and he had saved himself. Those old-timers were rather womanish, some of them, he thought. All a man had to do was to keep his head, and he was all right. Any man who was a man could travel alone. But it was surprising, the rapidity with which his cheeks and nose were freezing. And he had not thought his fingers could go lifeless in so short a time. Lifeless they were, for he could scarcely make them move together to grip a twig, and they seemed remote from his body and from him. When he touched a twig, he had to look and see whether or not he had hold of it. The wires were pretty well down between him and his finger-ends.

All of which counted for little. There was the fire, snapping and crackling and promising life with every dancing flame. He started to untie his moccasins. They were coated with ice; the thick German socks were like sheaths of iron half-way to the knees; and the moccasin strings were like rods of steel all twisted and knotted as by some conflagration. For a moment he tugged with his numbed fingers, then, realizing the folly of it, he drew his sheath-knife.

But before he could cut the strings, it happened. It was his own fault or, rather, his mistake. He should not have built the fire under the spruce tree. He should have built it in the open. But it had been easier to pull the twigs from the brush and drop them directly on the fire. Now the tree under which he had done this carried a weight of snow on its boughs. No wind had blown for weeks, and each bough was fully freighted. Each time he had pulled a twig he had communicated a slight agitation to the tree--an imperceptible agitation, so far as he was concerned, but an agitation sufficient to bring about the disaster. High up in the tree one bough capsized its load of snow. This fell on the boughs beneath, capsizing them. This process continued, spreading out and involving the whole tree. It grew like an avalanche, and it descended without warning upon the man and the fire, and the fire was blotted out! Where it had burned was a mantle of fresh and disordered snow.

The man was shocked. It was as though he had just heard his own sentence of death. For a moment he sat and stared at the spot where the fire had been. Then he grew very calm. Perhaps the old-timer on Sulphur Creek was right. If he had only had a trail-mate he would have been in no danger now.

> *Then he grew very calm.* In Naturalistic prose, this moment of "calm" is a moment when the character (in both literary pieces) stoically accepts his fate.

The trail-mate could have built the fire. Well, it was up to him to build the fire over again, and this second time there must be no failure. Even if he succeeded, he would most likely lose some toes. His feet must be badly frozen by now, and there would be some time before the second fire was ready.

Such were his thoughts, but he did not sit and think them. He was busy all the time they were passing through his mind, he made a new foundation for a fire, this time in the open; where no treacherous tree could blot it out. Next, he gathered dry grasses and tiny twigs from the high-water flotsam. He could not bring his fingers together to pull them out, but he was able to gather them by the handful. In this way he got many rotten twigs and bits of green moss that were undesirable, but it was the best he could do. He worked methodically, even collecting an armful of the larger branches to be used later when the fire gathered strength. And all the while the dog sat and watched him, a certain yearning wistfulness in its eyes, for it looked upon him as the fire-provider, and the fire was slow in coming.

When all was ready, the man reached in his pocket for a second piece of birch-bark. He knew the bark was there, and, though he could not feel it with his fingers, he could hear its crisp rustling as he fumbled for it. Try as he would, he could not clutch hold of it. And all the time, in his consciousness, was the knowledge that each instant his feet were freezing. This thought tended to put him in a panic, but he fought against it and kept calm. He pulled on his mittens with his teeth, and threshed his arms back and forth, beating his hands with all his might against his sides. He did this sitting down, and he stood up to do it; and all the while the dog sat in the snow, its wolf-brush of a tail curled around warmly over its forefeet, its sharp wolf-ears pricked forward intently as it watched the man. And the man as he beat and threshed with his arms and hands, felt a great surge of envy as he regarded the creature that was warm and secure in its natural covering.

After a time he was aware of the first far-away signals of sensation in his beaten fingers. The faint tingling grew stronger till it evolved into a stinging ache that was excruciating, but which the man hailed with satisfaction. He stripped the mitten from his right hand and fetched forth the birch-bark. The exposed fingers were quickly going numb again. Next he brought out his bunch of sulphur matches. But the tremendous cold had already driven the life out of his fingers. In his effort to separate one match from the others, the whole bunch fell in the snow. He tried to pick it out of the snow, but failed. The dead fingers could neither touch nor clutch. He was very careful. He drove the thought of his freezing feet; and nose, and cheeks, out of his mind, devoting his whole soul to the matches. He watched, using the sense of vision in place of that of touch, and when he saw his fingers on each side the bunch, he closed them--that is, he willed to close them, for the wires were drawn, and the fingers did not obey. He pulled the mitten on the right hand, and beat it fiercely against his knee. Then, with both mittened hands, he scooped the bunch of matches, along with much snow, into his lap. Yet he was no better off.

After some manipulation he managed to get the bunch between the heels of his mittened hands. In this fashion he carried it to his mouth. The ice crackled and snapped when by a violent effort he opened his mouth. He drew the lower jaw in, curled the upper lip out of the way, and scraped the bunch with his upper teeth in order to separate a match. He succeeded in getting one, which he dropped on his lap. He was no better off. He could not pick it up. Then he devised a way. He picked it up in his teeth and scratched it on his leg. Twenty times he scratched before he succeeded in lighting it. As it flamed he held it with his teeth to the birch-bark. But the burning brimstone went up his nostrils and into his lungs, causing him to cough spasmodically. The match fell into the snow and went out.

The old-timer on Sulphur Creek was right, he thought in the moment of controlled despair that ensued: after fifty below, a man should travel with a partner. He beat his hands, but failed in exciting any sensation. Suddenly he bared both hands, removing the mittens with his teeth. He caught the whole bunch between the heels of his hands. His arm-muscles not being frozen enabled him to press the hand-heels tightly against the matches. Then he scratched the bunch along his leg. It flared into flame, seventy sulphur matches at once! There was no wind to blow them out. He kept his head to one side to escape the strangling fumes, and held the blazing bunch to the birch-bark. As he so held it, he became aware of sensation in his hand. His flesh was burning. He could smell it. Deep down below the surface he could feel it. The sensation developed into pain that grew acute. And still he endured it, holding the flame of the matches clumsily to the bark that would not light readily because his own burning hands were in the way, absorbing most of the flame.

At last, when he could endure no more, he jerked his hands apart. The blazing matches fell sizzling into the snow, but the birch-bark was alight. He began laying dry grasses and the tiniest twigs on the flame. He could not pick and choose, for he had to lift the fuel between the heels of his hands. Small pieces of rotten wood and green moss clung to the twigs, and he bit them off as well as he could with his teeth. He cherished the flame carefully and awkwardly. It meant life, and it must not perish. The withdrawal of blood from the surface of his body now made him begin to shiver, and he grew more awkward. A large piece of green moss fell squarely on the little fire. He tried to poke it out with his fingers, but his shivering frame made him poke too far, and he disrupted the nucleus of the little fire, the burning grasses and tiny twigs separating and scattering. He tried to poke them together again, but in spite of the tenseness of the effort, his shivering got away with him, and the twigs were hopelessly scattered. Each twig gushed a puff of smoke and went out. The fire-provider had failed. As he looked apathetically about him, his eyes chanced on the dog, sitting across the ruins of the fire from him, in the snow, making restless, hunching movements, slightly lifting one forefoot and then the other, shifting its weight back and forth on them with wistful eagerness.

The sight of the dog put a wild idea into his head. He remembered the tale of the man, caught in a blizzard, who killed a steer and crawled inside the carcass, and so was saved. He would kill the dog and bury his hands in the warm body until the numbness went out of them. Then he could build another fire. He spoke to the dog, calling it to him; but in his voice was a strange note of fear that frightened the animal, who had never known the man to speak in such way before. Something was the matter, and its suspicious nature sensed danger--it knew not what danger but somewhere, somehow, in its brain arose an apprehension of the man. It flattened its ears down at the sound of the man's voice, and its restless, hunching movements and the liftings and shiftings of its forefeet became more pronounced but it would not come to the man. He got on his hands and knees and crawled toward the dog. This unusual posture again excited suspicion, and the animal sidled mincingly away.

The man sat up in the snow for a moment and struggled for calmness. Then he pulled on his mittens, by means of his teeth, and got upon his feet. He glanced down at first in order to assure himself that he was really standing up, for the absence of sensation in his feet left him unrelated to the earth. His erect position in itself started to drive the webs of suspicion from the dog's mind; and when he spoke peremptorily, with the sound of whip-lashes in his voice, the dog rendered its customary allegiance and came to him. As it came within reaching distance, the man lost his control. His arms flashed out to the dog, and he experienced genuine surprise when he discovered that his hands could not clutch, that there was neither bend nor feeling in the lingers. He had forgotten for the moment that they were frozen and that they were freezing more and more. All this happened quickly, and before the animal could get away, he encircled its body with his arms. He sat down in the snow, and in this fashion held the dog, while it snarled and whined and struggled.

But it was all he could do, hold its body encircled in his arms and sit there. He realized that he could not kill the dog. There was no way to do it. With his helpless hands he could neither draw nor hold his sheath-knife nor throttle the animal. He released it, and it plunged wildly away, with tail between its legs, and still snarling. It halted forty feet away and surveyed him curiously, with ears sharply pricked forward. The man looked down at his hands in order to locate them, and found them hanging on the ends of his arms. It struck him as curious that one should have to use his eyes in order to find out where his hands were. He began threshing his arms back and forth, beating the mittened hands against his sides. He did this for five minutes, violently, and his heart pumped enough blood up to the surface to put a stop to his shivering. But no sensation was aroused in the hands. He had an impression that they hung like weights on the ends of his arms, but when he tried to run the impression down, he could not find it.

A certain fear of death, dull and oppressive, came to him. This fear quickly became poignant as he realized that it was no longer a mere matter of freezing his fingers and toes, or of losing his hands and feet, but that it was a matter of life and death with the chances against him. This threw him into a panic, and he turned and ran up the creek-bed along the old, dim trail. The dog joined in behind and kept up with him. He ran blindly, without intention, in fear such as he had never known in his life.

> The dog, like all animals, has one purpose in life: to provide for the survival of the stronger species. In this case the man could not kill the dog and warm his hands. Thus, he dies. The dog lives. London and Crane both accept these eventualities with no apologies and with scant comment. There is very little room for hyperbole in the Naturalistic world view.

Slowly, as he ploughed and floundered through the snow, he began to see things again-- the banks of the creek, the old timber-jams, the leafless aspens, and the sky. The running made him feel better. He did not shiver. Maybe, if he ran on, his feet would thaw out; and, anyway, if he ran far enough, he would reach camp and the boys. Without doubt he would lose some fingers and toes and some of his face; but the boys would take care of him, and save the rest of him when he got there. And at the same time there was another thought in his mind that said he would never get to the camp and the boys; that it was too many miles away, that the freezing had too great a start on him, and that he would soon be stiff and dead. This thought he kept in the background and refused to consider. Sometimes it pushed itself forward and demanded to be heard, but he thrust it back and strove to think of other things.

It struck him as curious that he could run at all on feet so frozen that he could not feel them when they struck the earth and took the weight of his body. He seemed to himself to skim along above the surface and to have no connection with the earth. Somewhere he had once seen a winged Mercury, and he wondered if Mercury felt as he felt when skimming over the earth.

His theory of running until he reached camp and the boys had one flaw in it: he lacked the endurance. Several times he stumbled, and finally he tottered, crumpled up, and fell. When he tried to rise, he failed. He must sit and rest, he decided, and next time he would merely walk and keep on going. As he sat and regained his breath, he noted that he was feeling quite warm and comfortable. He was not shivering, and it even seemed that a warm glow had come to his chest and trunk. And yet, when he touched his nose or cheeks, there was no sensation. Running would not thaw them out. Nor would it thaw out his hands and feet. Then the thought came to him that the frozen portions of his body must be extending. He tried to keep this thought down, to forget it, to think of something else; he was aware of the panicky feeling that it caused, and he was afraid of the panic. But the thought asserted itself, and persisted, until it produced a vision of his body totally frozen. This was too much, and he made another wild run along the trail. Once he slowed down to a walk, but the thought of the freezing extending itself made him run again.

And all the time the dog ran with him, at his heels. When he fell down a second time, it curled its tail over its forefeet and sat in front of him facing him curiously eager and intent. The warmth and security of the animal angered him, and he cursed it till it flattened down its ears appeasingly. This time the shivering came more quickly upon the man. He was losing in his battle with the frost. It was creeping into his body from all sides. The thought of it drove him on, but he ran no more than a hundred feet, when

> There is a moment in most Naturalistic novels and short stories where the protagonist accepts the inevitability of death. He does so with no fanfare or philosophical reflection. This happens to the man in this short story and in *The Red Badge of Courage*. It is theme we will see developed even more in the writings of Ernest Hemingway.

he staggered and pitched headlong. It was his last panic. When he had recovered his breath and control, he sat up and entertained in his mind the conception of meeting death with dignity. However, the conception did not come to him in such terms. His idea of it was that he had been making a fool of himself, running around like a chicken with its head cut off--such was the simile that occurred to him. Well, he was bound to freeze anyway, and he might as well take it decently. With this new-found peace of mind came the first glimmerings of drowsiness. A good idea, he thought, to sleep off to death. It was like taking an anaesthetic. Freezing was not so bad as people thought. There were lots worse ways to die.

He pictured the boys finding his body next day. Suddenly he found himself with them, coming along the trail and looking for himself. And, still with them, he came around a turn in the trail and found himself lying in the snow. He did not belong with himself any more, for even then he was out of himself, standing with the boys and looking at himself in the snow. It certainly was cold, was his thought. When he got back to the States he could tell the folks what real cold was. He drifted on from this to a vision of the old-timer on Sulphur Creek. He could see him quite clearly, warm and comfortable, and smoking a pipe.

"You were right, old hoss; you were right," the man mumbled to the old-timer of Sulphur Creek.

Then the man drowsed off into what seemed to him the most comfortable and satisfying sleep he had ever known. The dog sat facing him and waiting. The brief day drew to a close in a long, slow twilight. There were no signs of a fire to be made, and, besides, never in the dog's experience had it known a man to sit like that in the snow and make no fire. As the twilight drew on, its eager yearning for the fire mastered it, and with a great lifting and shifting of forefeet, it whined softly, then flattened its ears down in anticipation of being chidden by the man. But the man remained silent. Later, the dog whined loudly. And still later it crept close to the man and caught the scent of death. This made the animal bristle and back away. A little longer it delayed, howling under the stars that leaped and danced and shone brightly in the cold sky. Then it turned and trotted up the trail in the direction of the camp it knew, where were the other food-providers and fire-providers.

Supplemental Resources:

Lars Ahnebrink, *The Beginnings of Naturalism in American fiction*
    I haven't read this yet but it appears to be an excellent resource.

Maurice Bassan, *Stephen Crane: A Collection of Critical Essays*
    Somewhat pedantic, but insightful essays on Crane's *major works*.

Stephen Crane, *Great Short Works of Stephen Crane: Red Badge of Courage, Monster, Maggie, Open Boat, Blue Hotel, Bride Comes to Yellow Sky and Other Works*
    An excellent, unedited version of Crane's works.

Joseph Katz (Editor), *The Complete Poems of Stephen Crane*
    While Crane is a less accomplished poet, his works are worth examining.

The Red Badge of Courage (1951) movie
    This epic version of Crane's novel, starring Audie Murphy, is a fairly accurate version of the book.

Notes:

Lesson Eighteen Test

Discussion Questions: (100 Points)
Find ten examples of Naturalism in the following short story, state the paragraph number, and defend your answer.

The Open Boat
By Stephen Crane

1 None of them knew the color of the sky. Their eyes glanced level, and were fastened upon the waves that swept toward them. These waves were of the hue of slate, save for the tops, which were of foaming white, and all of the men knew the colors of the sea. The horizon narrowed and widened, and dipped and rose, and at all times its edge was jagged with waves that seemed thrust up in points like rocks.

2 Many a man ought to have a bath-tub larger than the boat which here rode upon the sea. These waves were most wrongfully and barbarously abrupt and tall, and each froth-top was a problem in small boat navigation.

3 The cook squatted in the bottom and looked with both eyes at the six inches of gunwale which separated him from the ocean. His sleeves were rolled over his fat forearms, and the two flaps of his unbuttoned vest dangled as he bent to bail out the boat. Often he said: "Gawd! That was a narrow clip." As he remarked it he invariably gazed eastward over the broken sea.

4 The oiler, steering with one of the two oars in the boat, sometimes raised himself suddenly to keep clear of water that swirled in over the stern. It was a thin little oar and it seemed often ready to snap.

5 The correspondent, pulling at the other oar, watched the waves and wondered why he was there.

6 The injured captain, lying in the bow, was at this time buried in that profound dejection and indifference which comes, temporarily at least, to even the bravest and most enduring when, willy nilly, the firm fails, the army loses, the ship goes down. The mind of the master of a vessel is rooted deep in the timbers of her, though he command for a day or a decade, and this captain had on him the stern impression of a scene in the grays of dawn of seven turned faces, and later a stump of a top-mast with a white ball on it that slashed to and fro at the waves, went low and lower, and down. Thereafter there was something strange in his voice. Although steady, it was deep with mourning, and of a quality beyond oration or tears.

7 "Keep'er a little more south, Billie," said he.

8 "'A little more south,' sir," said the oiler in the stern.

9 A seat in this boat was not unlike a seat upon a bucking broncho, and, by the same token, a broncho is not much smaller. The craft pranced and reared, and plunged like an animal. As each wave came, and she rose for it, she seemed like a horse making at a fence outrageously high. The manner of her scramble over these walls of water is a mystic thing, and, moreover, at the top of them were ordinarily these problems in white water, the foam racing down from the summit of each wave, requiring a new leap, and a

leap from the air. Then, after scornfully bumping a crest, she would slide, and race, and splash down a long incline and arrive bobbing and nodding in front of the next menace.

10 A singular disadvantage of the sea lies in the fact that after successfully surmounting one wave you discover that there is another behind it just as important and just as nervously anxious to do something effective in the way of swamping boats. In a ten-foot dingey one can get an idea of the resources of the sea in the line of waves that is not probable to the average experience, which is never at sea in a dingey. As each slaty wall of water approached, it shut all else from the view of the men in the boat, and it was not difficult to imagine that this particular wave was the final outburst of the ocean, the last effort of the grim water. There was a terrible grace in the move of the waves, and they came in silence, save for the snarling of the crests.

11 In the wan light, the faces of the men must have been gray. Their eyes must have glinted in strange ways as they gazed steadily astern. Viewed from a balcony, the whole thing would doubtlessly have been weirdly picturesque. But the men in the boat had no time to see it, and if they had had leisure there were other things to occupy their minds. The sun swung steadily up the sky, and they knew it was broad day because the color of the sea changed from slate to emerald-green, streaked with amber lights, and the foam was like tumbling snow. The process of the breaking day was unknown to them. They were aware only of this effect upon the color of the waves that rolled toward them.

12 In disjointed sentences the cook and the correspondent argued as to the difference between a life-saving station and a house of refuge. The cook had said: "There's a house of refuge just north of the Mosquito Inlet Light, and as soon as they see us, they'll come off in their boat and pick us up."

13 "As soon as who see us?" said the correspondent.

14 "The crew," said the cook.

15 "Houses of refuge don't have crews," said the correspondent. "As I understand them, they are only places where clothes and grub are stored for the benefit of shipwrecked people. They don't carry crews."

16 "Oh, yes, they do," said the cook.

17 "No, they don't," said the correspondent.

18 "Well, we're not there yet, anyhow," said the oiler, in the stern.

19 "Well," said the cook, "perhaps it's not a house of refuge that I'm thinking of as being near Mosquito Inlet Light. Perhaps it's a life-saving station."

20 "We're not there yet," said the oiler, in the stern.

II.

21 As the boat bounced from the top of each wave, the wind tore through the hair of the hatless men, and as the craft plopped her stern down again the spray slashed past them. The crest of each of these waves was a hill, from the top of which the men surveyed, for a moment, a broad tumultuous expanse; shining and wind-riven. It was probably splendid. It was probably glorious, this play of the free sea, wild with lights of emerald and white and amber.

22 "Bully good thing it's an on-shore wind," said the cook. "If not, where would we be? Wouldn't have a show."

23 "That's right," said the correspondent.

24 The busy oiler nodded his assent.

25 Then the captain, in the bow, chuckled in a way that expressed humor, contempt, tragedy, all in one. "Do you think we've got much of a show, now, boys?" said he.

26 Whereupon the three were silent, save for a trifle of hemming and hawing. To express any particular optimism at this time they felt to be childish and stupid, but they all doubtless possessed this sense of the situation in their mind. A young man thinks doggedly at such times. On the other hand, the ethics of their condition was decidedly against any open suggestion of hopelessness. So they were silent.

27 "Oh, well," said the captain, soothing his children, "we'll get ashore all right."

28 But there was that in his tone which made them think, so the oiler quoth: "Yes! If this wind holds!"

29 The cook was bailing: "Yes! If we don't catch hell in the surf."

30 Canton flannel gulls flew near and far. Sometimes they sat down on the sea, near patches of brown sea-weed that rolled over the waves with a movement like carpets on line in a gale. The birds sat comfortably in groups, and they were envied by some in the dingey, for the wrath of the sea was no more to them than it was to a covey of prairie chickens a thousand miles inland. Often they came very close and stared at the men with black bead-like eyes. At these times they were uncanny and sinister in their unblinking scrutiny, and the men hooted angrily at them, telling them to be gone. One came, and evidently decided to alight on the top of the captain's head. The bird flew parallel to the boat and did not circle, but made short sidelong jumps in the air in chicken-fashion. His black eyes were wistfully fixed upon the captain's head. "Ugly brute," said the oiler to the bird. "You look as if you were made with a jack-knife." The cook and the correspondent swore darkly at the creature. The captain naturally wished to knock it away with the end of the heavy painter, but he did not dare do it, because anything resembling an emphatic gesture would have capsized this freighted boat, and so with his open hand, the captain gently and carefully waved the gull away. After it had been discouraged from the pursuit the captain breathed easier on account of his hair, and others breathed easier because the bird struck their minds at this time as being somehow gruesome and ominous.

31 In the meantime the oiler and the correspondent rowed. And also they rowed.

32 They sat together in the same seat, and each rowed an oar. Then the oiler took both oars; then the correspondent took both oars; then the oiler; then the correspondent. They rowed and they rowed. The very ticklish part of the business was when the time came for the reclining one in the stern to take his turn at the oars. By the very last star of truth, it is easier to steal eggs from under a hen than it was to change seats in the dingey. First the man in the stern slid his hand along the thwart and moved with care, as if he were of Sevres. Then the man in the rowing seat slid his hand along the other thwart. It was all done with the most extraordinary care. As the two sidled past each other, the whole party kept watchful eyes on the coming wave, and the captain cried: "Look out now! Steady there!"

33 The brown mats of sea-weed that appeared from time to time were like islands, bits of earth. They were traveling, apparently, neither one way nor the other. They were, to all intents stationary. They informed the men in the boat that it was making progress slowly toward the land.

34 The captain, rearing cautiously in the bow, after the dingey soared on a great swell, said that he had seen the lighthouse at Mosquito Inlet. Presently the cook remarked that he had seen it. The correspondent was at the oars, then, and for some reason he too wished to look at the lighthouse, but his back was toward the far shore and the waves were important, and for some time he could not seize an opportunity to turn his head. But at last there came a wave more gentle than the others, and when at the crest of it he swiftly scoured the western horizon.

35 "See it?" said the captain.

36 "No," said the correspondent, slowly, "I didn't see anything."

37 "Look again," said the captain. He pointed. "It's exactly in that direction."

38 At the top of another wave, the correspondent did as he was bid, and this time his eyes chanced on a small still thing on the edge of the swaying horizon. It was precisely like the point of a pin. It took an anxious eye to find a lighthouse so tiny.

39 "Think we'll make it, captain?"

40 "If this wind holds and the boat don't swamp, we can't do much else," said the captain.

41 The little boat, lifted by each towering sea, and splashed viciously by the crests, made progress that in the absence of sea-weed was not apparent to those in her. She seemed just a wee thing wallowing, miraculously, top-up, at the mercy of five oceans. Occasionally, a great spread of water, like white flames, swarmed into her.

42 "Bail her, cook," said the captain, serenely.

43 "All right, captain," said the cheerful cook.

III

44 IT would be difficult to describe the subtle brotherhood of men that was here established on the seas. No one said that it was so. No one mentioned it. But it dwelt in the boat, and each man felt it warm him. They were a captain, an oiler, a cook, and a correspondent, and they were friends, friends in a more curiously iron-bound degree than may be common. The hurt captain, lying against the water-jar in the bow, spoke always in a low voice and calmly, but he could never command a more ready and swiftly obedient crew than the motley three of the dingey. It was more than a mere recognition of what was best for the common safety. There was surely in it a quality that was personal and heartfelt. And after this devotion to the commander of the boat there was this comradeship that the correspondent, for instance, who had been taught to be cynical of men, knew even at the time was the best experience of his life. But no one said that it was so. No one mentioned it.

45 "I wish we had a sail," remarked the captain. "We might try my overcoat on the end of an oar and give you two boys a chance to rest." So the cook and the correspondent held the mast and spread wide the overcoat. The oiler steered, and the little boat made good way with her new rig. Sometimes the oiler had to scull sharply to keep a sea from breaking into the boat, but otherwise sailing was a success.

46 Meanwhile the light-house had been growing slowly larger. It had now almost assumed color, and appeared like a little gray shadow on the sky. The man at the oars could not be prevented from turning his head rather often to try for a glimpse of this little gray shadow.

47 At last, from the top of each wave the men in the tossing boat could see land. Even as the light-house was an upright shadow on the sky, this land seemed but a long black shadow on the sea. It certainly was thinner than paper. "We must be about opposite New Smyrna," said the cook, who had coasted this shore often in schooners. "Captain, by the way, I believe they abandoned that life-saving station there about a year ago."

48 "Did they?" said the captain.

49 The wind slowly died away. The cook and the correspondent were not now obliged to slave in order to hold high the oar. But the waves continued their old impetuous swooping at the dingey, and the little craft, no longer under way, struggled woundily over them. The oiler or the correspondent took the oars again.

50 Shipwrecks are apropos of nothing. If men could only train for them and have them occur when the men had reached pink condition, there would be less drowning at sea. Of the four in the dingey none had slept any time worth mentioning for two days and two nights previous to embarking in the dingey, and in the excitement of clambering about the deck of a foundering ship they had also forgotten to eat heartily.

51 For these reasons, and for others, neither the oiler nor the correspondent was fond of rowing at this time. The correspondent wondered ingenuously how in the name of all that was sane could there be people who thought it amusing to row a boat. It was not an amusement; it was a diabolical punishment, and even a genius of mental aberrations could never conclude that it was anything but a horror to the muscles and a crime against the back. He mentioned to the boat in general how the amusement of rowing struck him, and the weary-faced oiler smiled in full sympathy. Previously to the foundering, by the way, the oiler had worked double-watch in the engine-room of the ship.

52 "Take her easy, now, boys," said the captain. "Don't spend yourselves. If we have to run a surf you'll need all your strength, because we'll sure have to swim for it. Take your time."

53 Slowly the land arose from the sea. From a black line it became a line of black and a line of white, trees, and sand. Finally, the captain said that he could make out a house on the shore. "That's the house of refuge, sure," said the cook. "They'll see us before long, and come out after us."

54 The distant light-house reared high. "The keeper ought to be able to make us out now, if he's looking through a glass," said the captain. "He'll notify the life-saving people."

55 "None of those other boats could have got ashore to give word of the wreck," said the oiler, in a low voice. "Else the life-boat would be out hunting us."

56 Slowly and beautifully the land loomed out of the sea. The wind came again. It had veered from the northeast to the southeast. Finally, a new sound struck the ears of the men in the boat. It was the low thunder of the surf on the shore. "We'll never be able to make the light-house now," said the captain. "Swing her head a little more north, Billie," said the captain.

57 "'A little more north,' sir," said the oiler.

58 Whereupon the little boat turned her nose once more down the wind, and all but the oarsman watched the shore grow. Under the influence of this expansion doubt and direful apprehension was leaving the minds of the men. The management of the boat was still most absorbing, but it could not prevent a quiet cheerfulness. In an hour, perhaps, they

would be ashore.

59 Their back-bones had become thoroughly used to balancing in the boat and they now rode this wild colt of a dingey like circus men. The correspondent thought that he had been drenched to the skin, but happening to feel in the top pocket of his coat, he found therein eight cigars. Four of them were soaked with sea-water; four were perfectly scatheless. After a search, somebody produced three dry matches, and thereupon the four waifs rode in their little boat, and with an assurance of an impending rescue shining in their eyes, puffed at the big cigars and judged well and ill of all men. Everybody took a drink of water.

IV

60 "COOK," remarked the captain, "there don't seem to be any signs of life about your house of refuge."

61 "No," replied the cook. "Funny they don't see us!"

62 A broad stretch of lowly coast lay before the eyes of the men. It was of low dunes topped with dark vegetation. The roar of the surf was plain, and sometimes they could see the white lip of a wave as it spun up the beach. A tiny house was blocked out black upon the sky. Southward, the slim light-house lifted its little gray length.

63 Tide, wind, and waves were swinging the dingey northward. "Funny they don't see us," said the men.

64 The surf's roar was here dulled, but its tone was, nevertheless, thunderous and mighty. As the boat swam over the great rollers, the men sat listening to this roar. "We'll swamp sure," said everybody.

65 It is fair to say here that there was not a life-saving station within twenty miles in either direction, but the men did not know this fact and in consequence they made dark and opprobrious remarks concerning the eyesight of the nation's life-savers. Four scowling men sat in the dingey and surpassed records in the invention of epithets.

66 "Funny they don't see us."

67 The light-heartedness of a former time had completely faded. To their sharpened minds it was easy to conjure pictures of all kinds of incompetency and blindness and indeed, cowardice. There was the shore of the populous land, and it was bitter and bitter to them that from it came no sign.

68 "Well," said the captain, ultimately, "I suppose we'll have to make a try for ourselves. If we stay out here too long, we'll none of us have strength left to swim after the boat swamps."

69 And so the oiler, who was at the oars, turned the boat straight for the shore. There was a sudden tightening of muscles. There was some thinking.

70 "If we don't all get ashore -- " said the captain. "If we don't all get ashore, I suppose you fellows know where to send news of my finish?"

71 They then briefly exchanged some addresses and admonitions. As for the reflections of the men, there was a great deal of rage in them. Perchance they might be formulated thus: "If I am going to be drowned -- if I am going to be drowned -- if I am going to be drowned, why, in the name of the seven mad gods who rule the sea, was I allowed to come thus far and contemplate sand and trees? Was I brought here merely to have my nose dragged away as I was about to nibble the sacred cheese of life? It is preposterous.

If this old ninny-woman, Fate, cannot do better than this, she should be deprived of the management of men's fortunes. She is an old hen who knows not her intention. If she has decided to drown me, why did she not do it in the beginning and save me all this trouble. The whole affair is absurd. . . . But, no, she cannot mean to drown me. She dare not drown me. She cannot drown me. Not after all this work." Afterward the man might have had an impulse to shake his fist at the clouds: "Just you drown me, now, and then hear what I call you!"

72 The billows that came at this time were more formidable. They seemed always just about to break and roll over the little boat in a turmoil of foam. There was a preparatory and long growl in the speech of them. No mind unused to the sea would have concluded that the dingey could ascend these sheer heights in time. The shore was still afar. The oiler was a wily surfman. "Boys," he said, swiftly, "she won't live three minutes more and we're too far out to swim. Shall I take her to sea again, captain?"

73 "Yes! Go ahead!" said the captain.

74 This oiler, by a series of quick miracles, and fast and steady oarsmanship, turned the boat in the middle of the surf and took her safely to sea again.

75 There was a considerable silence as the boat bumped over the furrowed sea to deeper water. Then somebody in gloom spoke. "Well, anyhow, they must have seen us from the shore by now."

76 The gulls went in slanting flight up the wind toward the gray desolate east. A squall, marked by dingy clouds, and clouds brick-red, like smoke from a burning building, appeared from the southeast.

77 "What do you think of those life-saving people? Ain't they peaches?"

78 "Funny they haven't seen us."

79 "Maybe they think we're out here for sport! Maybe they think we're fishin'. Maybe they think we're damned fools."

80 It was a long afternoon. A changed tide tried to force them southward, but wind and wave said northward. Far ahead, where coast-line, sea, and sky formed their mighty angle, there were little dots which seemed to indicate a city on the shore.

81 "St. Augustine?"

82 The captain shook his head. "Too near Mosquito Inlet."

82 And the oiler rowed, and then the correspondent rowed. Then the oiler rowed. It was a weary business. The human back can become the seat of more aches and pains than are registered in books for the composite anatomy of a regiment. It is a limited area, but it can become the theater of innumerable muscular conflicts, tangles, wrenches, knots, and other comforts.

84 "Did you ever like to row, Billie?" asked the correspondent.

85 "No," said the oiler. "Hang it."

86 When one exchanged the rowing-seat for a place in the bottom of the boat, he suffered a bodily depression that caused him to be careless of everything save an obligation to wiggle one finger. There was cold sea-water swashing to and fro in the boat, and he lay in it. His head, pillowed on a thwart, was within an inch of the swirl of a wave crest, and sometimes a particularly obstreperous sea came in-board and drenched him once more. But these matters did not annoy him. It is almost certain that if the boat had capsized he

would have tumbled comfortably out upon the ocean as if he felt sure it was a great soft mattress.
87 "Look! There's a man on the shore!"
88 "Where?"
89 "There! See 'im? See 'im?"
90 "Yes, sure! He's walking along."
91 "Now he's stopped. Look! He's facing us!"
92 "He's waving at us!"
93 "So he is! By thunder!"
94 "Ah, now, we're all right! Now we're all right! There'll be a boat out here for us in half an hour."
95 "He's going on. He's running. He's going up to that house there."
96 The remote beach seemed lower than the sea, and it required a searching glance to discern the little black figure. The captain saw a floating stick and they rowed to it. A bath-towel was by some weird chance in the boat, and, tying this on the stick, the captain waved it. The oarsman did not dare turn his head, so he was obliged to ask questions.
97 "What's he doing now?"
98 "He's standing still again. He's looking, I think. . . . There he goes again. Toward the house. . . . Now he's stopped again."
99 "Is he waving at us?"
100 "No, not now! he was, though."
101 "Look! There comes another man!"
102 "He's running."
103 "Look at him go, would you."
104 "Why, he's on a bicycle. Now he's met the other man. They're both waving at us. Look!"
105 "There comes something up the beach."
106 "What the devil is that thing?"
107 "Why, it looks like a boat."
108 "Why, certainly it's a boat."
109 "No, it's on wheels."
110 "Yes, so it is. Well, that must be the life-boat. They drag them along shore on a wagon."
111 "That's the life-boat, sure."
112 "No, by -- -- , it's -- it's an omnibus."
113 "I tell you it's a life-boat."
114 "It is not! It's an omnibus. I can see it plain. See? One of these big hotel omnibuses."
115 "By thunder, you're right. It's an omnibus, sure as fate. What do you suppose they are doing with an omnibus? Maybe they are going around collecting the life-crew, hey?"
116 "That's it, likely. Look! There's a fellow waving a little black flag. He's standing on the steps of the omnibus. There come those other two fellows. Now they're all talking together. Look at the fellow with the flag. Maybe he ain't waving it."
117 "That ain't a flag, is it? That's his coat. Why, certainly, that's his coat."
118 "So it is. It's his coat. He's taken it off and is waving it around his head. But would

you look at him swing it."

119 "Oh, say, there isn't any life-saving station there. That's just a winter resort hotel omnibus that has brought over some of the boarders to see us drown."

120 "What's that idiot with the coat mean? What's he signaling, anyhow?"

121 "It looks as if he were trying to tell us to go north. There must be a life-saving station up there."

122 "No! He thinks we're fishing. Just giving us a merry hand. See? Ah, there, Willie."

123 "Well, I wish I could make something out of those signals. What do you suppose he means?"

124 "He don't mean anything. He's just playing."

125 "Well, if he'd just signal us to try the surf again, or to go to sea and wait, or go north, or go south, or go to hell -- there would be some reason in it. But look at him. He just stands there and keeps his coat revolving like a wheel. The ass!"

126 "There come more people."

127 "Now there's quite a mob. Look! Isn't that a boat?"

128 "Where? Oh, I see where you mean. No, that's no boat."

129 "That fellow is still waving his coat."

130 "He must think we like to see him do that. Why don't he quit it. It don't mean anything."

131 "I don't know. I think he is trying to make us go north. It must be that there's a life-saving station there somewhere."

132 "Say, he ain't tired yet. Look at 'im wave."

133 "Wonder how long he can keep that up. He's been revolving his coat ever since he caught sight of us. He's an idiot. Why aren't they getting men to bring a boat out. A fishing boat -- one of those big yawls -- could come out here all right. Why don't he do something?"

134 "Oh, it's all right, now."

135 "They'll have a boat out here for us in less than no time, now that they've seen us."

136 A faint yellow tone came into the sky over the low land. The shadows on the sea slowly deepened. The wind bore coldness with it, and the men began to shiver.

137 "Holy smoke!" said one, allowing his voice to express his impious mood, "if we keep on monkeying out here! If we've got to flounder out here all night!"

138 "Oh, we'll never have to stay here all night! Don't you worry. They've seen us now, and it won't be long before they'll come chasing out after us."

139 The shore grew dusky. The man waving a coat blended gradually into this gloom, and it swallowed in the same manner the omnibus and the group of people. The spray, when it dashed uproariously over the side, made the voyagers shrink and swear like men who were being branded.

140 "I'd like to catch the chump who waved the coat. I feel like soaking him one, just for luck."

141 "Why? What did he do?"

142 "Oh, nothing, but then he seemed so damned cheerful."

143 In the meantime the oiler rowed, and then the correspondent rowed, and then the oiler rowed. Gray-faced and bowed forward, they mechanically, turn by turn, plied the

leaden oars. The form of the light-house had vanished from the southern horizon, but finally a pale star appeared, just lifting from the sea. The streaked saffron in the west passed before the all-merging darkness, and the sea to the east was black. The land had vanished, and was expressed only by the low and drear thunder of the surf.

144 "If I am going to be drowned -- if I am going to be drowned -- if I am going to be drowned, why, in the name of the seven mad gods, who rule the sea, was I allowed to come thus far and contemplate sand and trees? Was I brought here merely to have my nose dragged away as I was about to nibble the sacred cheese of life?"

145 The patient captain, drooped over the water-jar, was sometimes obliged to speak to the oarsman.

146 "Keep her head up! Keep her head up!"

147 "'Keep her head up,' sir." The voices were weary and low.

148 This was surely a quiet evening. All save the oarsman lay heavily and listlessly in the boat's bottom. As for him, his eyes were just capable of noting the tall black waves that swept forward in a most sinister silence, save for an occasional subdued growl of a crest.

149 The cook's head was on a thwart, and he looked without interest at the water under his nose. He was deep in other scenes. Finally he spoke. "Billie," he murmured, dreamfully, "what kind of pie do you like best?"

V

150 "PIE," said the oiler and the correspondent, agitatedly. "Don't talk about those things, blast you!"

151 "Well," said the cook, "I was just thinking about ham sandwiches, and -- "

152 A night on the sea in an open boat is a long night. As darkness settled finally, the shine of the light, lifting from the sea in the south, changed to full gold. On the northern horizon a new light appeared, a small bluish gleam on the edge of the waters. These two lights were the furniture of the world. Otherwise there was nothing but waves.

153 Two men huddled in the stern, and distances were so magnificent in the dingey that the rower was enabled to keep his feet partly warmed by thrusting them under his companions. Their legs indeed extended far under the rowing-seat until they touched the feet of the captain forward. Sometimes, despite the efforts of the tired oarsman, a wave came piling into the boat, an icy wave of the night, and the chilling water soaked them anew. They would twist their bodies for a moment and groan, and sleep the dead sleep once more, while the water in the boat gurgled about them as the craft rocked.

154 The plan of the oiler and the correspondent was for one to row until he lost the ability, and then arouse the other from his sea-water couch in the bottom of the boat.

155 The oiler plied the oars until his head drooped forward, and the overpowering sleep blinded him. And he rowed yet afterward. Then he touched a man in the bottom of the boat, and called his name. "Will you spell me for a little while?" he said, meekly.

156 "Sure, Billie," said the correspondent, awakening and dragging himself to a sitting position. They exchanged places carefully, and the oiler, cuddling down to the sea-water at the cook's side, seemed to go to sleep instantly.

157 The particular violence of the sea had ceased. The waves came without snarling. The obligation of the man at the oars was to keep the boat headed so that the tilt of the rollers would not capsize her, and to preserve her from filling when the crests rushed past. The

black waves were silent and hard to be seen in the darkness. Often one was almost upon the boat before the oarsman was aware.

158 In a low voice the correspondent addressed the captain. He was not sure that the captain was awake, although this iron man seemed to be always awake. "Captain, shall I keep her making for that light north, sir?"

159 The same steady voice answered him. "Yes. Keep it about two points off the port bow."

160 The cook had tied a life-belt around himself in order to get even the warmth which this clumsy cork contrivance could donate, and he seemed almost stove-like when a rower, whose teeth invariably chattered wildly as soon as he ceased his labor, dropped down to sleep.

161 The correspondent, as he rowed, looked down at the two men sleeping under foot. The cook's arm was around the oiler's shoulders, and, with their fragmentary clothing and haggard faces, they were the babes of the sea, a grotesque rendering of the old babes in the wood.

162 Later he must have grown stupid at his work, for suddenly there was a growling of water, and a crest came with a roar and a swash into the boat, and it was a wonder that it did not set the cook afloat in his life-belt. The cook continued to sleep, but the oiler sat up, blinking his eyes and shaking with the new cold.

163 "Oh, I'm awful sorry, Billie," said the correspondent, contritely.

164 "That's all right, old boy," said the oiler, and lay down again and was asleep.

165 Presently it seemed that even the captain dozed, and the correspondent thought that he was the one man afloat on all the oceans. The wind had a voice as it came over the waves, and it was sadder than the end.

166 There was a long, loud swishing astern of the boat, and a gleaming trail of phosphorescence, like blue flame, was furrowed on the black waters. It might have been made by a monstrous knife.

167 Then there came a stillness, while the correspondent breathed with the open mouth and looked at the sea.

168 Suddenly there was another swish and another long flash of bluish light, and this time it was alongside the boat, and might almost have been reached with an oar. The correspondent saw an enormous fin speed like a shadow through the water, hurling the crystalline spray and leaving the long glowing trail.

169 The correspondent looked over his shoulder at the captain. His face was hidden, and he seemed to be asleep. He looked at the babes of the sea. They certainly were asleep. So, being bereft of sympathy, he leaned a little way to one side and swore softly into the sea.

170 But the thing did not then leave the vicinity of the boat. Ahead or astern, on one side or the other, at intervals long or short, fled the long sparkling streak, and there was to be heard the whiroo of the dark fin. The speed and power of the thing was greatly to be admired. It cut the water like a gigantic and keen projectile.

171 The presence of this biding thing did not affect the man with the same horror that it would if he had been a picnicker. He simply looked at the sea dully and swore in an undertone.

172 Nevertheless, it is true that he did not wish to be alone with the thing. He wished one

of his companions to awaken by chance and keep him company with it. But the captain hung motionless over the water-jar and the oiler and the cook in the bottom of the boat were plunged in slumber.

VI

173 "IF I am going to be drowned -- if I am going to be drowned -- if I am going to be drowned, why, in the name of the seven mad gods, who rule the sea, was I allowed to come thus far and contemplate sand and trees?"

174 During this dismal night, it may be remarked that a man would conclude that it was really the intention of the seven mad gods to drown him, despite the abominable injustice of it. For it was certainly an abominable injustice to drown a man who had worked so hard, so hard. The man felt it would be a crime most unnatural. Other people had drowned at sea since galleys swarmed with painted sails, but still --

175 When it occurs to a man that nature does not regard him as important, and that she feels she would not maim the universe by disposing of him, he at first wishes to throw bricks at the temple, and he hates deeply the fact that there are no bricks and no temples. Any visible expression of nature would surely be pelleted with his jeers.

176 Then, if there be no tangible thing to hoot he feels, perhaps, the desire to confront a personification and indulge in pleas, bowed to one knee, and with hands supplicant, saying: "Yes, but I love myself."

177 A high cold star on a winter's night is the word he feels that she says to him. Thereafter he knows the pathos of his situation.

178 The men in the dingey had not discussed these matters, but each had, no doubt, reflected upon them in silence and according to his mind. There was seldom any expression upon their faces save the general one of complete weariness. Speech was devoted to the business of the boat.

179 To chime the notes of his emotion, a verse mysteriously entered the correspondent's head. He had even forgotten that he had forgotten this verse, but it suddenly was in his mind.

180 A soldier of the Legion lay dying in Algiers,
181 There was lack of woman's nursing, there was dearth of woman's tears;
182 But a comrade stood beside him, and he took that comrade's hand
183 And he said: "I shall never see my own, my native land."

184 In his childhood, the correspondent had been made acquainted with the fact that a soldier of the Legion lay dying in Algiers, but he had never regarded the fact as important. Myriads of his school-fellows had informed him of the soldier's plight, but the dinning had naturally ended by making him perfectly indifferent. He had never considered it his affair that a soldier of the Legion lay dying in Algiers, nor had it appeared to him as a matter for sorrow. It was less to him than breaking of a pencil's point.

185 Now, however, it quaintly came to him as a human, living thing. It was no longer merely a picture of a few throes in the breast of a poet, meanwhile drinking tea and warming his feet at the grate; it was an actuality -- stern, mournful, and fine.

186 The correspondent plainly saw the soldier. He lay on the sand with his feet out

straight and still. While his pale left hand was upon his chest in an attempt to thwart the going of his life, the blood came between his fingers. In the far Algerian distance, a city of low square forms was set against a sky that was faint with the last sunset hues. The correspondent, plying the oars and dreaming of the slow and slower movements of the lips of the soldier, was moved by a profound and perfectly impersonal comprehension. He was sorry for the soldier of the Legion who lay dying in Algiers.
187 The thing which had followed the boat and waited had evidently grown bored at the delay. There was no longer to be heard the slash of the cut-water, and there was no longer the flame of the long trail. The light in the north still glimmered, but it was apparently no nearer to the boat. Sometimes the boom of the surf rang in the correspondent's ears, and he turned the craft seaward then and rowed harder. Southward, someone had evidently built a watch-fire on the beach. It was too low and too far to be seen, but it made a shimmering, roseate reflection upon the bluff back of it, and this could be discerned from the boat. The wind came stronger, and sometimes a wave suddenly raged out like a mountain-cat and there was to be seen the sheen and sparkle of a broken crest.
188 The captain, in the bow, moved on his water-jar and sat erect. "Pretty long night," he observed to the correspondent. He looked at the shore. "Those life-saving people take their time." 189 "Did you see that shark playing around?"
190 "Yes, I saw him. He was a big fellow, all right."
191 "Wish I had known you were awake."
192 Later the correspondent spoke into the bottom of the boat.
193 "Billie!" There was a slow and gradual disentanglement. "Billie, will you spell me?"
194 "Sure," said the oiler.
195 As soon as the correspondent touched the cold comfortable sea-water in the bottom of the boat, and had huddled close to the cook's life-belt he was deep in sleep, despite the fact that his teeth played all the popular airs. This sleep was so good to him that it was but a moment before he heard a voice call his name in a tone that demonstrated the last stages of exhaustion. "Will you spell me?"
196 "Sure, Billie."
197 The light in the north had mysteriously vanished, but the correspondent took his course from the wide-awake captain.
198 Later in the night they took the boat farther out to sea, and the captain directed the cook to take one oar at the stern and keep the boat facing the seas. He was to call out if he should hear the thunder of the surf. This plan enabled the oiler and the correspondent to get respite together. "We'll give those boys a chance to get into shape again," said the captain. They curled down and, after a few preliminary chatterings and trembles, slept once more the dead sleep. Neither knew they had bequeathed to the cook the company of another shark, or perhaps the same shark.
199 As the boat caroused on the waves, spray occasionally bumped over the side and gave them a fresh soaking, but this had no power to break their repose. The ominous slash of the wind and the water affected them as it would have affected mummies.
200 "Boys," said the cook, with the notes of every reluctance in his voice, "she's drifted in pretty close. I guess one of you had better take her to sea again." The correspondent, aroused, heard the crash of the toppled crests.

201 As he was rowing, the captain gave him some whiskey and water, and this steadied the chills out of him. "If I ever get ashore and anybody shows me even a photograph of an oar -- "

202 At last there was a short conversation.

203 "Billie. . . . Billie, will you spell me?"

204 "Sure," said the oiler.

VII

205 WHEN the correspondent again opened his eyes, the sea and the sky were each of the gray hue of the dawning. Later, carmine and gold was painted upon the waters. The morning appeared finally, in its splendor with a sky of pure blue, and the sunlight flamed on the tips of the waves.

206 On the distant dunes were set many little black cottages, and a tall white wind-mill reared above them. No man, nor dog, nor bicycle appeared on the beach. The cottages might have formed a deserted village.

207 The voyagers scanned the shore. A conference was held in the boat. "Well," said the captain, "if no help is coming, we might better try a run through the surf right away. If we stay out here much longer we will be too weak to do anything for ourselves at all." The others silently acquiesced in this reasoning. The boat was headed for the beach. The correspondent wondered if none ever ascended the tall wind-tower, and if then they never looked seaward. This tower was a giant, standing with its back to the plight of the ants. It represented in a degree, to the correspondent, the serenity of nature amid the struggles of the individual -- nature in the wind, and nature in the vision of men. She did not seem cruel to him, nor beneficent, nor treacherous, nor wise. But she was indifferent, flatly indifferent. It is, perhaps, plausible that a man in this situation, impressed with the unconcern of the universe, should see the innumerable flaws of his life and have them taste wickedly in his mind and wish for another chance. A distinction between right and wrong seems absurdly clear to him, then, in this new ignorance of the grave-edge, and he understands that if he were given another opportunity he would mend his conduct and his words, and be better and brighter during an introduction, or at a tea.

208 "Now, boys," said the captain, "she is going to swamp sure. All we can do is to work her in as far as possible, and then when she swamps, pile out and scramble for the beach. Keep cool now and don't jump until she swamps sure."

209 The oiler took the oars. Over his shoulders he scanned the surf. "Captain," he said, "I think I'd better bring her about, and keep her head-on to the seas and back her in."

210 "All right, Billie," said the captain. "Back her in." The oiler swung the boat then and, seated in the stern, the cook and the correspondent were obliged to look over their shoulders to contemplate the lonely and indifferent shore.

211 The monstrous inshore rollers heaved the boat high until the men were again enabled to see the white sheets of water scudding up the slanted beach. "We won't get in very close," said the captain. Each time a man could wrest his attention from the rollers, he turned his glance toward the shore, and in the expression of the eyes during this contemplation there was a singular quality. The correspondent, observing the others, knew that they were not afraid, but the full meaning of their glances was shrouded.

212 As for himself, he was too tired to grapple fundamentally with the fact. He tried to

coerce his mind into thinking of it, but the mind was dominated at this time by the muscles, and the muscles said they did not care. It merely occurred to him that if he should drown it would be a shame.

213 There were no hurried words, no pallor, no plain agitation. The men simply looked at the shore. "Now, remember to get well clear of the boat when you jump," said the captain.

214 Seaward the crest of a roller suddenly fell with a thunderous crash, and the long white comber came roaring down upon the boat.

215 "Steady now," said the captain. The men were silent. They turned their eyes from the shore to the comber and waited. The boat slid up the incline, leaped at the furious top, bounced over it, and swung down the long back of the waves. Some water had been shipped and the cook bailed it out.

216 But the next crest crashed also. The tumbling boiling flood of white water caught the boat and whirled it almost perpendicular. Water swarmed in from all sides. The correspondent had his hands on the gunwale at this time, and when the water entered at that place he swiftly withdrew his fingers, as if he objected to wetting them.

217 The little boat, drunken with this weight of water, reeled and snuggled deeper into the sea.

218 "Bail her out, cook! Bail her out," said the captain.

219 "All right, captain," said the cook.

220 "Now, boys, the next one will do for us, sure," said the oiler. "Mind to jump clear of the boat."

221 The third wave moved forward, huge, furious, implacable. It fairly swallowed the dingey, and almost simultaneously the men tumbled into the sea. A piece of life-belt had lain in the bottom of the boat, and as the correspondent went overboard he held this to his chest with his left hand.

222 The January water was icy, and he reflected immediately that it was colder than he had expected to find it off the coast of Florida. This appeared to his dazed mind as a fact important enough to be noted at the time. The coldness of the water was sad; it was tragic. This fact was somehow mixed and confused with his opinion of his own situation that it seemed almost a proper reason for tears. The water was cold.

223 When he came to the surface he was conscious of little but the noisy water. Afterward he saw his companions in the sea. The oiler was ahead in the race. He was swimming strongly and rapidly. Off to the correspondent's left, the cook's great white and corked back bulged out of the water, and in the rear the captain was hanging with his one good hand to the keel of the overturned dingey.

224 There is a certain immovable quality to a shore, and the correspondent wondered at it amid the confusion of the sea.

225 It seemed also very attractive, but the correspondent knew that it was a long journey, and he paddled leisurely. The piece of life-preserver lay under him, and sometimes he whirled down the incline of a wave as if he were on a hand-sled.

226 But finally he arrived at a place in the sea where travel was beset with difficulty. He did not pause swimming to inquire what manner of current had caught him, but there his progress ceased. The shore was set before him like a bit of scenery on a stage, and he

looked at it and understood with his eyes each detail of it.

227 As the cook passed, much farther to the left, the captain was calling to him, "Turn over on your back, cook! Turn over on your back and use the oar."

228 "All right, sir!" The cook turned on his back, and, paddling with an oar, went ahead as if he were a canoe.

229 Presently the boat also passed to the left of the correspondent with the captain clinging with one hand to the keel. He would have appeared like a man raising himself to look over a board fence, if it were not for the extraordinary gymnastics of the boat. The correspondent marveled that the captain could still hold to it.

230 They passed on, nearer to shore -- the oiler, the cook, the captain -- and following them went the water-jar, bouncing gayly over the seas.

231 The correspondent remained in the grip of this strange new enemy -- a current. The shore, with its white slope of sand and its green bluff, topped with little silent cottages, was spread like a picture before him. It was very near to him then, but he was impressed as one who in a gallery looks at a scene from Brittany or Algiers.

232 He thought: "I am going to drown? Can it be possible? Can it be possible? Can it be possible?" Perhaps an individual must consider his own death to be the final phenomenon of nature.

233 But later a wave perhaps whirled him out of this small deadly current, for he found suddenly that he could again make progress toward the shore. Later still, he was aware that the captain, clinging with one hand to the keel of the dingey, had his face turned away from the shore and toward him, and was calling his name. "Come to the boat! Come to the boat!"

234 In his struggle to reach the captain and the boat, he reflected that when one gets properly wearied, drowning must really be a comfortable arrangement, a cessation of hostilities accompanied by a large degree of relief, and he was glad of it, for the main thing in his mind for some moments had been horror of the temporary agony. He did not wish to be hurt.

235 Presently he saw a man running along the shore. He was undressing with most remarkable speed. Coat, trousers, shirt, everything flew magically off him.

236 "Come to the boat," called the captain.

237 "All right, captain." As the correspondent paddled, he saw the captain let himself down to bottom and leave the boat. Then the correspondent performed his one little marvel of the voyage. A large wave caught him and flung him with ease and supreme speed completely over the boat and far beyond it. It struck him even then as an event in gymnastics, and a true miracle of the sea. An overturned boat in the surf is not a plaything to a swimming man.

238 The correspondent arrived in water that reached only to his waist, but his condition did not enable him to stand for more than a moment. Each wave knocked him into a heap, and the under-tow pulled at him.

239 Then he saw the man who had been running and undressing, and undressing and running, come bounding into the water. He dragged ashore the cook, and then waded toward the captain, but the captain waved him away, and sent him to the correspondent. He was naked, naked as a tree in winter, but a halo was about his head, and he shone like

a saint. He gave a strong pull, and a long drag, and a bully heave at the correspondent's hand. The correspondent, schooled in the minor formulae, said: "Thanks, old man." But suddenly the man cried: "What's that?" He pointed a swift finger. The correspondent said: "Go."

240 In the shallows, face downward, lay the oiler. His forehead touched sand that was periodically, between each wave, clear of the sea.

241 The correspondent did not know all that transpired afterward. When he achieved safe ground he fell, striking the sand with each particular part of his body. It was as if he had dropped from a roof, but the thud was grateful to him.

242 It seems that instantly the beach was populated with men with blankets, clothes, and flasks, and women with coffee-pots and all the remedies sacred to their minds. The welcome of the land to the men from the sea was warm and generous, but a still and dripping shape was carried slowly up the beach, and the land's welcome for it could only be the different and sinister hospitality of the grave.

243 When it came night, the white waves paced to and fro in the moonlight, and the wind brought the sound of the great sea's voice to the men on shore, and they felt that they could then be interpreters.

Lesson Eighteen Test Answers

Discussion Questions: (100 Points)

Find ten examples of Naturalism in the following short story, state the paragraph number, and defend your answer.

The Open Boat
By Stephen Crane

1 None of them knew the color of the sky. Their eyes glanced level, and were fastened upon the waves that swept toward them. These waves were of the hue of slate, save for the tops, which were of foaming white, and all of the men knew the colors of the sea.

> The men are introduced without names. They are nameless, animals facing the unknown and fate. They are together, but separate–both at the same time.

The horizon narrowed and widened, and dipped and rose, and at all times its edge was jagged with waves that seemed thrust up in points like rocks.

2 Many a man ought to have a bath-tub larger than the boat which here rode upon the sea. These waves were most wrongfully and barbarously abrupt and tall, and each froth-top was a problem in small boat navigation.

3 The cook squatted in the bottom and looked with both eyes at the six inches of gunwale which separated him from the ocean. His sleeves were rolled over his fat forearms, and the two flaps of his unbuttoned vest dangled as he bent to bail out the boat. Often he said: "Gawd! That was a narrow clip." As he remarked it he invariably gazed eastward over the broken sea.

4 The oiler, steering with one of the two oars in the boat, sometimes raised himself suddenly to keep clear of water that swirled in over the stern. It was a thin little oar and it seemed often ready to snap.

5 The correspondent, pulling at the other oar, watched the waves and wondered why he was there.

6 The injured captain, lying in the bow, was at this time buried in that profound dejection and indifference which comes, temporarily at least, to even the bravest and most enduring when, willy nilly, the firm fails, the army loses, the ship goes down. The mind of the master of a vessel is rooted deep in the timbers of her, though he command for a day or a decade, and this captain had on him the stern impression of a scene in the grays of dawn of seven turned faces, and later a stump of a top-mast with a white ball on it that slashed to and fro at the waves, went low and lower, and down. Thereafter there was something strange in his voice. Although steady, it was deep with mourning, and of a quality beyond oration or tears.

7 "Keep'er a little more south, Billie," said he.

8 "'A little more south,' sir," said the oiler in the stern.

9 A seat in this boat was not unlike a seat upon a bucking broncho, and, by the same token, a broncho is not much smaller. The craft pranced and reared, and plunged like an animal. As each wave came, and she rose for it, she seemed like a horse making at a fence outrageously high. The manner of her scramble over these walls of water is a mystic thing, and, moreover, at the top of them were ordinarily these problems in white water, the foam racing down from the summit of each wave, requiring a new leap, and a leap from the air. Then, after scornfully bumping a crest, she would slide, and race, and splash down a long incline and arrive bobbing and nodding in front of the next menace.

> Men are confused and disoriented by the exigencies of life.

10 A singular disadvantage of the sea lies in the fact that after successfully surmounting one wave you discover that there is another behind it just as important and just as nervously anxious to do something effective in the way of swamping boats. In a ten-foot dingey one can get an idea of the resources of the sea in the line of waves that is not probable to the average experience, which is never at sea in a dingey. As each slaty wall of water approached, it shut all else from the view of the men in the boat, and it was not difficult to imagine that this particular wave was the final outburst of the ocean, the last effort of the grim water. There was a terrible grace in the move of the waves, and they came in silence, save for the snarling of the crests.

11 In the wan light, the faces of the men must have been gray. Their eyes must have glinted in strange ways as they gazed steadily astern. Viewed from a balcony, the whole thing would doubtlessly have been weirdly picturesque. But the men in the boat had no time to see it, and if they had had leisure there were other things to occupy their minds. The sun swung steadily up the sky, and they knew it was broad day because the color of the sea changed from slate to emerald-green, streaked with amber lights, and the foam was like tumbling snow. The process of the breaking day was unknown to them. They were aware only of this effect upon the color of the waves that rolled toward them.

> Nature is unfriendly and indifferent.

12 In disjointed sentences the cook and the correspondent argued as to the difference between a life-saving station and a house of refuge. The cook had said: "There's a house of refuge just north of the Mosquito Inlet Light, and as soon as they see us, they'll come off in their boat and pick us up."

13 "As soon as who see us?" said the correspondent.

14 "The crew," said the cook.

15 "Houses of refuge don't have crews," said the correspondent. "As I understand them, they are only places where clothes and grub are stored for the benefit of shipwrecked people.

> Naturalism is full of irony. There is a life saving station but no crew to man it!

They don't carry crews."

16 "Oh, yes, they do," said the cook.

17 "No, they don't," said the correspondent.

18 "Well, we're not there yet, anyhow," said the oiler, in the stern.

19 "Well," said the cook, "perhaps it's not a house of refuge that I'm thinking of as being near Mosquito Inlet Light. Perhaps it's a life-saving station."

20 "We're not there yet," said the oiler, in the stern.

II.

21 As the boat bounced from the top of each wave, the wind tore through the hair of the hatless men, and as the craft plopped her stern down again the spray slashed past them. The crest of each of these waves was a hill, from the top of which the men surveyed, for a moment, a broad tumultuous expanse; shining and wind-riven. It was probably splendid. It was probably glorious, this play of the free sea, wild with lights of emerald and white and amber.

22 "Bully good thing it's an on-shore wind," said the cook. "If not, where would we be? Wouldn't have a show."

23 "That's right," said the correspondent.

24 The busy oiler nodded his assent.

25 Then the captain, in the bow, chuckled in a way that expressed humor, contempt, tragedy, all in one. "Do you think we've got much of a show, now, boys?" said he.

26 Whereupon the three were silent, save for a trifle of hemming and hawing. To express any particular optimism at this time they felt to be childish and stupid, but they all doubtless possessed this sense of the situation in their mind. A young man thinks doggedly at such times. On the other hand, the ethics of their condition was decidedly against any open suggestion of hopelessness. So they were silent.

27 "Oh, well," said the captain, soothing his children, "we'll get ashore all right."

28 But there was that in his tone which made them think, so the oiler quoth: "Yes! If this wind holds!"

29 The cook was bailing: "Yes! If we don't catch hell in the surf."

Again, there future is contingent upon the unfriendly elements.

30 Canton flannel gulls flew near and far. Sometimes they sat down on the sea, near patches of brown sea-weed that rolled over the waves with a movement like carpets on line in a gale. The birds sat comfortably in groups, and they were envied by some in the dingey, for the wrath of the sea was no more to them than it was to a covey of prairie chickens a thousand miles inland. Often they came very close and stared at the men with black bead-like eyes. At these times they were uncanny and sinister in their unblinking scrutiny, and the men hooted angrily at them, telling them to be gone. One came, and evidently decided to

Nature is unfriendly and uncaring–just as God is (to Crane).

alight on the top of the captain's head. The bird flew parallel to the boat and did not circle, but made short sidelong jumps in the air in chicken-fashion. His black eyes were wistfully fixed upon the captain's head. "Ugly brute," said the oiler to the bird. "You look as if you were made with a jack-knife." The cook and the correspondent swore darkly at the creature. The captain naturally wished to knock it away with the end of the heavy painter, but he did not dare do it, because anything resembling an emphatic gesture would have capsized this freighted boat, and so with his open hand, the captain gently and carefully waved the gull away. After it had been discouraged from the pursuit the captain breathed easier on account of his hair, and others breathed easier because the bird struck their minds at this time as being somehow gruesome and ominous.

31 In the meantime the oiler and the correspondent rowed. And also they rowed.

32 They sat together in the same seat, and each rowed an oar. Then the oiler took both oars; then the correspondent took both oars; then the oiler; then the correspondent. They rowed and they rowed. The very ticklish part of the business was when the time came for the reclining one in the stern to take his turn at the oars. By the very last star of truth, it is easier to steal eggs from under a hen than it was to change seats in the dingey. First the man in the stern slid his hand along the thwart and moved with care, as if he were of Sevres. Then the man in the rowing seat slid his hand along the other thwart. It was all done with the most extraordinary care. As the two sidled past each other, the whole party kept watchful eyes on the coming wave, and the captain cried: "Look out now! Steady there!"

33 The brown mats of sea-weed that appeared from time to time were like islands, bits of earth. They were traveling, apparently, neither one way nor the other. They were, to all intents stationary. They informed the men in the boat that it was making progress slowly toward the land.

34 The captain, rearing cautiously in the bow, after the dingey soared on a great swell, said that he had seen the lighthouse at Mosquito Inlet. Presently the cook remarked that he had seen it. The correspondent was at the oars, then, and for some reason he too wished to look at the lighthouse, but his back was toward the far shore and the waves were important, and for some time he could not seize an opportunity to turn his head. But at last there came a wave more gentle than the others, and when at the crest of it he swiftly scoured the western horizon.

35 "See it?" said the captain.

36 "No," said the correspondent, slowly, "I didn't see anything."

37 "Look again," said the captain. He pointed. "It's exactly in that direction."

38 At the top of another wave, the correspondent did as he was bid, and this time his eyes chanced on a small still thing on the edge of the swaying horizon. It was precisely like the point of a pin. It took an anxious eye to find a lighthouse so tiny.

39 "Think we'll make it, captain?"

40 "If this wind holds and the boat don't swamp, we can't do much else," said the captain.

41 The little boat, lifted by each towering sea, and splashed viciously by the crests, made progress that in the absence of sea-weed was not apparent to those in her. She seemed just a wee thing wallowing, miraculously, top-up, at the mercy of five oceans. Occasionally, a great spread of water, like white flames, swarmed into her.

42 "Bail her, cook," said the captain, serenely.

43 "All right, captain," said the cheerful cook.

III

44 IT would be difficult to describe the subtle brotherhood of men that was here established on the seas. No one said that it was so. No one mentioned it. But it dwelt in the boat, and each man felt it warm him. They were a captain, an oiler, a cook, and a correspondent, and they were friends, friends in a more curiously iron-bound degree than may be common. The hurt captain, lying against the water-jar in the bow, spoke always in a low voice and calmly, but he could never command a more ready and swiftly obedient crew than the motley three of the dingey. It was more than a mere recognition of what was best for the common safety. There was surely in it a quality that was personal and heartfelt. And after this devotion to the commander of the boat there was this comradeship that the correspondent, for instance, who had been taught to be cynical of men, knew even at the time was the best experience of his life. But no one said that it was so. No one mentioned it.

> If there is brotherhood there is a sense that they are all doomed together. Or they are in the same game together with the same advantages and disadvantages.

45 "I wish we had a sail," remarked the captain. "We might try my overcoat on the end of an oar and give you two boys a chance to rest." So the cook and the correspondent held the mast and spread wide the overcoat. The oiler steered, and the little boat made good way with her new rig. Sometimes the oiler had to scull sharply to keep a sea from breaking into the boat, but otherwise sailing was a success.

46 Meanwhile the light-house had been growing slowly larger. It had now almost assumed color, and appeared like a little gray shadow on the sky. The man at the oars could not be prevented from turning his head rather often to try for a glimpse of this little gray shadow.

47 At last, from the top of each wave the men in the tossing boat could see land. Even as the light-house was an upright shadow on the sky, this land seemed but a long black shadow on the sea. It certainly was thinner than paper. "We must be about opposite New Smyrna," said the cook, who had coasted this shore often in schooners. "Captain, by the way, I believe they abandoned that life-saving station there about a year ago."

48 "Did they?" said the captain.

49 The wind slowly died away. The cook and the correspondent were not now obliged to slave in order to hold high the oar. But the waves continued their old impetuous swooping at the dingey, and the little craft, no longer under way, struggled woundily over them. The oiler or the correspondent took the oars again.

50 Shipwrecks are apropos of nothing. If men could only train for them and have them occur when the men had reached pink condition, there would be less drowning at sea. Of the four in the dingey none had slept any time worth mentioning for two days and two nights previous to embarking in the dingey, and in the excitement of clambering about the deck of a foundering ship they had also forgotten to eat heartily.

51 For these reasons, and for others, neither the oiler nor the correspondent was fond of rowing at this time. The correspondent wondered ingenuously how in the name of all that

was sane could there be people who thought it amusing to row a boat. It was not an amusement; it was a diabolical punishment, and even a genius of mental aberrations could never conclude that it was anything but a horror to the muscles and a crime against the back. He mentioned to the boat in general how the amusement of rowing struck him, and the weary-faced oiler smiled in full sympathy. Previously to the foundering, by the way, the oiler had worked double-watch in the engine-room of the ship.

52 "Take her easy, now, boys," said the captain. "Don't spend yourselves. If we have to run a surf you'll need all your strength, because we'll sure have to swim for it. Take your time."

53 Slowly the land arose from the sea. From a black line it became a line of black and a line of white, trees, and sand. Finally, the captain said that he could make out a house on the shore. "That's the house of refuge, sure," said the cook. "They'll see us before long, and come out after us."

54 The distant light-house reared high. "The keeper ought to be able to make us out now, if he's looking through a glass," said the captain. "He'll notify the life-saving people."

55 "None of those other boats could have got ashore to give word of the wreck," said the oiler, in a low voice. "Else the life-boat would be out hunting us."

56 Slowly and beautifully the land loomed out of the sea. The wind came again. It had veered from the northeast to the southeast. Finally, a new sound struck the ears of the men in the boat. It was the low thunder of the surf on the shore. "We'll never be able to make the light-house now," said the captain. "Swing her head a little more north, Billie," said the captain.

57 "'A little more north,' sir," said the oiler.

58 Whereupon the little boat turned her nose once more down the wind, and all but the oarsman watched the shore grow. Under the influence of this expansion doubt and direful apprehension was leaving the minds of the men. The management of the boat was still most absorbing, but it could not prevent a quiet cheerfulness. In an hour, perhaps, they would be ashore.

59 Their back-bones had become thoroughly used to balancing in the boat and they now rode this wild colt of a dingey like circus men. The correspondent thought that he had been drenched to the skin, but happening to feel in the top pocket of his coat, he found therein eight cigars. Four of them were soaked with sea-water; four were perfectly scatheless. After a search, somebody produced three dry matches, and thereupon the four waifs rode in their little boat, and with an assurance of an impending rescue shining in their eyes, puffed at the big cigars and judged well and ill of all men. Everybody took a drink of water.

IV

60 "COOK," remarked the captain, "there don't seem to be any signs of life about your house of refuge."

61 "No," replied the cook. "Funny they don't see us!"

62 A broad stretch of lowly coast lay before the eyes of the men. It was of low dunes topped with dark vegetation. The roar of the surf was plain, and sometimes they could see the white lip of a wave as it spun up the beach. A tiny house was blocked out black upon the sky. Southward, the slim light-house lifted its little gray length.

63 Tide, wind, and waves were swinging the dingey northward. "Funny they don't see us," said the men.

64 The surf's roar was here dulled, but its tone was, nevertheless, thunderous and mighty. As the boat swam over the great rollers, the men sat listening to this roar. "We'll swamp sure," said everybody.

65 It is fair to say here that there was not a life-saving station within twenty miles in either direction, but the men did not know this fact and in consequence they made dark and opprobrious remarks concerning the eyesight of the nation's life-savers.

> People are without hope but they do not know it. There is no sense of a Providence and hope. Contrast this with William Bradford in Lesson One.

Four scowling men sat in the dingey and surpassed records in the invention of epithets.

66 "Funny they don't see us."

67 The light-heartedness of a former time had completely faded. To their sharpened minds it was easy to conjure pictures of all kinds of incompetency and blindness and indeed, cowardice. There was the shore of the populous land, and it was bitter and bitter to them that from it came no sign.

68 "Well," said the captain, ultimately, "I suppose we'll have to make a try for ourselves. If we stay out here too long, we'll none of us have strength left to swim after the boat swamps."

69 And so the oiler, who was at the oars, turned the boat straight for the shore. There was a sudden tightening of muscles. There was some thinking.

70 "If we don't all get ashore -- " said the captain. "If we don't all get ashore, I suppose you fellows know where to send news of my finish?"

71 They then briefly exchanged some addresses and admonitions. As for the reflections of the men, there was a great deal of rage in them. Perchance they might be formulated thus: "If I am going to be drowned -- if I am going to be drowned -- if I am going to be drowned, why, in the name of the seven mad gods who rule the sea, was I allowed to come thus far and contemplate sand and trees? Was I brought here merely to have my nose dragged away as I was about to nibble the sacred cheese of life? It is preposterous. If this old ninny-woman, Fate, cannot do better

> This is the cry of all Naturalists.

than this, she should be deprived of the management of men's fortunes. She is an old hen who knows not her intention. If she has decided to drown me, why did she not do it in the beginning and save me all this trouble. The whole affair is absurd. . . . But, no, she cannot mean to drown me. She dare not drown me. She cannot drown me. Not after all this work." Afterward the man might have had an impulse to shake his fist at the clouds: "Just you drown me, now, and then hear what I call you!"

72 The billows that came at this time were more formidable. They seemed always just about to break and roll over the little boat in a turmoil of foam. There was a preparatory and long growl in the speech of them. No mind unused to the sea would have concluded

that the dingey could ascend these sheer heights in time. The shore was still afar. The oiler was a wily surfman. "Boys," he said, swiftly, "she won't live three minutes more and we're too far out to swim. Shall I take her to sea again, captain?"

73 "Yes! Go ahead!" said the captain.

74 This oiler, by a series of quick miracles, and fast and steady oarsmanship, turned the boat in the middle of the surf and took her safely to sea again.

75 There was a considerable silence as the boat bumped over the furrowed sea to deeper water. Then somebody in gloom spoke. "Well, anyhow, they must have seen us from the shore by now."

76 The gulls went in slanting flight up the wind toward the gray desolate east. A squall, marked by dingy clouds, and clouds brick-red, like smoke from a burning building, appeared from the southeast.

77 "What do you think of those life-saving people? Ain't they peaches?"

78 "Funny they haven't seen us."

79 "Maybe they think we're out here for sport! Maybe they think we're fishin'. Maybe they think we're damned fools."

80 It was a long afternoon. A changed tide tried to force them southward, but wind and wave said northward. Far ahead, where coast-line, sea, and sky formed their mighty angle, there were little dots which seemed to indicate a city on the shore.

81 "St. Augustine?"

82 The captain shook his head. "Too near Mosquito Inlet."

82 And the oiler rowed, and then the correspondent rowed. Then the oiler rowed. It was a weary business. The human back can become the seat of more aches and pains than are registered in books for the composite anatomy of a regiment. It is a limited area, but it can become the theater of innumerable muscular conflicts, tangles, wrenches, knots, and other comforts.

84 "Did you ever like to row, Billie?" asked the correspondent.

85 "No," said the oiler. "Hang it."

86 When one exchanged the rowing-seat for a place in the bottom of the boat, he suffered a bodily depression that caused him to be careless of everything save an obligation to wiggle one finger. There was cold sea-water swashing to and fro in the boat, and he lay in it. His head, pillowed on a thwart, was within an inch of the swirl of a wave crest, and sometimes a particularly obstreperous sea came in-board and drenched him once more. But these matters did not annoy him. It is almost certain that if the boat had capsized he would have tumbled comfortably out upon the ocean as if he felt sure it was a great soft mattress.

87 "Look! There's a man on the shore!"

88 "Where?"

89 "There! See 'im? See 'im?"

90 "Yes, sure! He's walking along."

91 "Now he's stopped. Look! He's facing us!"

92 "He's waving at us!"

93 "So he is! By thunder!"

94 "Ah, now, we're all right! Now we're all right! There'll be a boat out here for us in half

an hour."

95 "He's going on. He's running. He's going up to that house there."

96 The remote beach seemed lower than the sea, and it required a searching glance to discern the little black figure. The captain saw a floating stick and they rowed to it. A bath-towel was by some weird chance in the boat, and, tying this on the stick, the captain waved it. The oarsman did not dare turn his head, so he was obliged to ask questions.

97 "What's he doing now?"

98 "He's standing still again. He's looking, I think. . . . There he goes again. Toward the house. . . . Now he's stopped again."

99 "Is he waving at us?"

100 "No, not now! he was, though."

101 "Look! There comes another man!"

102 "He's running."

103 "Look at him go, would you."

104 "Why, he's on a bicycle. Now he's met the other man. They're both waving at us. Look!"

105 "There comes something up the beach."

106 "What the devil is that thing?"

107 "Why, it looks like a boat."

108 "Why, certainly it's a boat."

109 "No, it's on wheels."

110 "Yes, so it is. Well, that must be the life-boat. They drag them along shore on a wagon."

111 "That's the life-boat, sure."

112 "No, by -- -- , it's -- it's an omnibus."

113 "I tell you it's a life-boat."

114 "It is not! It's an omnibus. I can see it plain. See? One of these big hotel omnibuses."

115 "By thunder, you're right. It's an omnibus, sure as fate. What do you suppose they are doing with an omnibus? Maybe they are going around collecting the life-crew, hey?"

116 "That's it, likely. Look! There's a fellow waving a little black flag. He's standing on the steps of the omnibus. There come those other two fellows. Now they're all talking together. Look at the fellow with the flag. Maybe he ain't waving it."

117 "That ain't a flag, is it? That's his coat. Why, certainly, that's his coat."

118 "So it is. It's his coat. He's taken it off and is waving it around his head. But would you look at him swing it."

119 "Oh, say, there isn't any life-saving station there. That's just a winter resort hotel omnibus that has brought over some of the boarders to see us drown."

120 "What's that idiot with the coat mean? What's he signaling, anyhow?"

121 "It looks as if he were trying to tell us to go north. There must be a life-saving station up there."

122 "No! He thinks we're fishing. Just giving us a merry hand. See? Ah, there, Willie."

123 "Well, I wish I could make something out of those signals. What do you suppose he means?"

124 "He don't mean anything. He's just playing."

125 "Well, if he'd just signal us to try the surf again, or to go to sea and wait, or go north, or go south, or go to hell -- there would be some reason in it. But look at him. He just stands there and keeps his coat revolving like a wheel. The ass!"
126 "There come more people."
127 "Now there's quite a mob. Look! Isn't that a boat?"
128 "Where? Oh, I see where you mean. No, that's no boat."
129 "That fellow is still waving his coat."
130 "He must think we like to see him do that. Why don't he quit it. It don't mean anything."
131 "I don't know. I think he is trying to make us go north. It must be that there's a life-saving station there somewhere."
132 "Say, he ain't tired yet. Look at 'im wave."
133 "Wonder how long he can keep that up. He's been revolving his coat ever since he caught sight of us. He's an idiot. Why aren't they getting men to bring a boat out. A fishing boat -- one of those big yawls -- could come out here all right. Why don't he do something?"
134 "Oh, it's all right, now."
135 "They'll have a boat out here for us in less than no time, now that they've seen us."
136 A faint yellow tone came into the sky over the low land. The shadows on the sea slowly deepened. The wind bore coldness with it, and the men began to shiver.
137 "Holy smoke!" said one, allowing his voice to express his impious mood, "if we keep on monkeying out here! If we've got to flounder out here all night!"
138 "Oh, we'll never have to stay here all night! Don't you worry. They've seen us now, and it won't be long before they'll come chasing out after us."
139 The shore grew dusky. The man waving a coat blended gradually into this gloom, and it swallowed in the same manner the omnibus and the group of people. The spray, when it dashed uproariously over the side, made the voyagers shrink and swear like men who were being branded.

> In the midst of hope, there is hopelessness again. Life is futile, the struggle to live is futile.

140 "I'd like to catch the chump who waved the coat. I feel like soaking him one, just for luck."
141 "Why? What did he do?"
142 "Oh, nothing, but then he seemed so damned cheerful."
143 In the meantime the oiler rowed, and then the correspondent rowed, and then the oiler rowed. Gray-faced and bowed forward, they mechanically, turn by turn, plied the leaden oars. The form of the light-house had vanished from the southern horizon, but finally a pale star appeared, just lifting from the sea. The streaked saffron in the west passed before the all-merging darkness, and the sea to the east was black. The land had vanished, and was expressed only by the low and drear thunder of the surf.
144 "If I am going to be drowned -- if I am going to be drowned -- if I am going to be drowned, why, in the name of the seven mad gods, who rule the sea, was I allowed to come thus far and contemplate sand and trees? Was I brought here merely to have my

nose dragged away as I was about to nibble the sacred cheese of life?"

145 The patient captain, drooped over the water-jar, was sometimes obliged to speak to the oarsman.

146 "Keep her head up! Keep her head up!"

147 "'Keep her head up,' sir." The voices were weary and low.

148 This was surely a quiet evening. All save the oarsman lay heavily and listlessly in the boat's bottom. As for him, his eyes were just capable of noting the tall black waves that swept forward in a most sinister silence, save for an occasional subdued growl of a crest.

149 The cook's head was on a thwart, and he looked without interest at the water under his nose. He was deep in other scenes. Finally he spoke. "Billie," he murmured, dreamfully, "what kind of pie do you like best?"

V

150 "PIE," said the oiler and the correspondent, agitatedly. "Don't talk about those things, blast you!"

151 "Well," said the cook, "I was just thinking about ham sandwiches, and -- "

152 A night on the sea in an open boat is a long night. As darkness settled finally, the shine of the light, lifting from the sea in the south, changed to full gold. On the northern horizon a new light appeared, a small bluish gleam on the edge of the waters. These two lights were the furniture of the world. Otherwise there was nothing but waves.

153 Two men huddled in the stern, and distances were so magnificent in the dingey that the rower was enabled to keep his feet partly warmed by thrusting them under his companions. Their legs indeed extended far under the rowing-seat until they touched the feet of the captain forward. Sometimes, despite the efforts of the tired oarsman, a wave came piling into the boat, an icy wave of the night, and the chilling water soaked them anew. They would twist their bodies for a moment and groan, and sleep the dead sleep once more, while the water in the boat gurgled about them as the craft rocked.

154 The plan of the oiler and the correspondent was for one to row until he lost the ability, and then arouse the other from his sea-water couch in the bottom of the boat.

155 The oiler plied the oars until his head drooped forward, and the overpowering sleep blinded him. And he rowed yet afterward. Then he touched a man in the bottom of the boat, and called his name. "Will you spell me for a little while?" he said, meekly.

156 "Sure, Billie," said the correspondent, awakening and dragging himself to a sitting position. They exchanged places carefully, and the oiler, cuddling down to the sea-water at the cook's side, seemed to go to sleep instantly.

157 The particular violence of the sea had ceased. The waves came without snarling. The obligation of the man at the oars was to keep the boat headed so that the tilt of the rollers would not capsize her, and to preserve her from filling when the crests rushed past. The black waves were silent and hard to be seen in the darkness. Often one was almost upon the boat before the oarsman was aware. 158 In a low voice the correspondent addressed the captain. He was not sure that the captain was awake, although this iron man seemed to be always awake. "Captain, shall I keep her making for that light north, sir?"

159 The same steady voice answered him. "Yes. Keep it about two points off the port bow."

160 The cook had tied a life-belt around himself in order to get even the warmth which

this clumsy cork contrivance could donate, and he seemed almost stove-like when a rower, whose teeth invariably chattered wildly as soon as he ceased his labor, dropped down to sleep.

161 The correspondent, as he rowed, looked down at the two men sleeping under foot. The cook's arm was around the oiler's shoulders, and, with their fragmentary clothing and haggard faces, they were the babes of the sea, a grotesque rendering of the old babes in the wood.

162 Later he must have grown stupid at his work, for suddenly there was a growling of water, and a crest came with a roar and a swash into the boat, and it was a wonder that it did not set the cook afloat in his life-belt. The cook continued to sleep, but the oiler sat up, blinking his eyes and shaking with the new cold.

163 "Oh, I'm awful sorry, Billie," said the correspondent, contritely.

164 "That's all right, old boy," said the oiler, and lay down again and was asleep.

165 Presently it seemed that even the captain dozed, and the correspondent thought that he was the one man afloat on all the oceans. The wind had a voice as it came over the waves, and it was sadder than the end.

166 There was a long, loud swishing astern of the boat, and a gleaming trail of phosphorescence, like blue flame, was furrowed on the black waters. It might have been made by a monstrous knife.

167 Then there came a stillness, while the correspondent breathed with the open mouth and looked at the sea.

168 Suddenly there was another swish and another long flash of bluish light, and this time it was alongside the boat, and might almost have been reached with an oar. The correspondent saw an enormous fin speed like a shadow through the water, hurling the crystalline spray and leaving the long glowing trail.

169 The correspondent looked over his shoulder at the captain. His face was hidden, and he seemed to be asleep. He looked at the babes of the sea. They certainly were asleep. So, being bereft of sympathy, he leaned a little way to one side and swore softly into the sea.

170 But the thing did not then leave the vicinity of the boat. Ahead or astern, on one side or the other, at intervals long or short, fled the long sparkling streak, and there was to be heard the whiroo of the dark fin. The speed and power of the thing was greatly to be admired. It cut the water like a gigantic and keen projectile.

171 The presence of this biding thing did not affect the man with the same horror that it would if he had been a picnicker. He simply looked at the sea dully and swore in an undertone.

172 Nevertheless, it is true that he did not wish to be alone with the thing. He wished one of his companions to awaken by chance and keep him company with it. But the captain hung motionless over the water-jar and the oiler and the cook in the bottom of the boat were plunged in slumber.

> Nature is malevolent and beautiful–both at the same time.

VI

173 "IF I am going to be drowned -- if I am going to be drowned -- if I am going to be drowned, why, in the name of the seven mad gods, who rule the sea, was I allowed to come thus far and contemplate sand and trees?"

174 During this dismal night, it may be remarked that a man would conclude that it was really the intention of the seven mad gods to drown him, despite the abominable injustice of it. For it was certainly an abominable injustice to drown a man who had worked so hard, so hard. The man felt it would be a crime most unnatural. Other people had drowned at sea since galleys swarmed with painted sails, but still --

175 When it occurs to a man that nature does not regard him as important, and that she feels she would not maim the universe by disposing of him, he at first wishes to throw bricks at the temple, and he hates deeply the fact that there are no bricks and no temples. Any visible expression of nature would surely be pelleted with his jeers.

176 Then, if there be no tangible thing to hoot he feels, perhaps, the desire to confront a personification and indulge in pleas, bowed to one knee, and with hands supplicant, saying: "Yes, but I love myself."

177 A high cold star on a winter's night is the word he feels that she says to him. Thereafter he knows the pathos of his situation.

178 The men in the dingey had not discussed these matters, but each had, no doubt, reflected upon them in silence and according to his mind. There was seldom any expression upon their faces save the general one of complete weariness. Speech was devoted to the business of the boat.

179 To chime the notes of his emotion, a verse mysteriously entered the correspondent's head. He had even forgotten that he had forgotten this verse, but it suddenly was in his mind.

180 A soldier of the Legion lay dying in Algiers,

181 There was lack of woman's nursing, there was dearth of woman's tears;

182 But a comrade stood beside him, and he took that comrade's hand

183 And he said: "I shall never see my own, my native land."

184 In his childhood, the correspondent had been made acquainted with the fact that a soldier of the Legion lay dying in Algiers, but he had never regarded the fact as important. Myriads of his school-fellows had informed him of the soldier's plight, but the dinning had naturally ended by making him perfectly indifferent. He had never considered it his affair that a soldier of the Legion lay dying in Algiers, nor had it appeared to him as a matter for sorrow. It was less to him than breaking of a pencil's point.

> Death was part of life. It was something over which none had control.

185 Now, however, it quaintly came to him as a human, living thing. It was no longer merely a picture of a few throes in the breast of a poet, meanwhile drinking tea and warming his feet at the grate; it was an actuality -- stern, mournful, and fine.

186 The correspondent plainly saw the soldier. He lay on the sand with his feet out straight and still. While his pale left hand was upon his chest in an attempt to thwart the going of his life, the blood came between his fingers. In the far Algerian distance, a city

of low square forms was set against a sky that was faint with the last sunset hues. The correspondent, plying the oars and dreaming of the slow and slower movements of the lips of the soldier, was moved by a profound and perfectly impersonal comprehension. He was sorry for the soldier of the Legion who lay dying in Algiers.

187 The thing which had followed the boat and waited had evidently grown bored at the delay. There was no longer to be heard the slash of the cut-water, and there was no longer the flame of the long trail. The light in the north still glimmered, but it was apparently no nearer to the boat. Sometimes the boom of the surf rang in the correspondent's ears, and he turned the craft seaward then and rowed harder. Southward, someone had evidently built a watch-fire on the beach. It was too low and too far to be seen, but it made a shimmering, roseate reflection upon the bluff back of it, and this could be discerned from the boat. The wind came stronger, and sometimes a wave suddenly raged out like a mountain-cat and there was to be seen the sheen and sparkle of a broken crest.

188 The captain, in the bow, moved on his water-jar and sat erect. "Pretty long night," he observed to the correspondent. He looked at the shore. "Those life-saving people take their time."

189 "Did you see that shark playing around?"

190 "Yes, I saw him. He was a big fellow, all right."

191 "Wish I had known you were awake."

192 Later the correspondent spoke into the bottom of the boat.

193 "Billie!" There was a slow and gradual disentanglement. "Billie, will you spell me?"

194 "Sure," said the oiler.

195 As soon as the correspondent touched the cold comfortable sea-water in the bottom of the boat, and had huddled close to the cook's life-belt he was deep in sleep, despite the fact that his teeth played all the popular airs. This sleep was so good to him that it was but a moment before he heard a voice call his name in a tone that demonstrated the last stages of exhaustion. "Will you spell me?"

196 "Sure, Billie."

197 The light in the north had mysteriously vanished, but the correspondent took his course from the wide-awake captain.

198 Later in the night they took the boat farther out to sea, and the captain directed the cook to take one oar at the stern and keep the boat facing the seas. He was to call out if he should hear the thunder of the surf. This plan enabled the oiler and the correspondent to get respite together. "We'll give those boys a chance to get into shape again," said the captain. They curled down and, after a few preliminary chatterings and trembles, slept once more the dead sleep. Neither knew they had bequeathed to the cook the company of another shark, or perhaps the same shark.

199 As the boat caroused on the waves, spray occasionally bumped over the side and gave them a fresh soaking, but this had no power to break their repose. The ominous slash of the wind and the water affected them as it would have affected mummies.

200 "Boys," said the cook, with the notes of every reluctance in his voice, "she's drifted in pretty close. I guess one of you had better take her to sea again." The correspondent, aroused, heard the crash of the toppled crests.

201 As he was rowing, the captain gave him some whiskey and water, and this steadied

the chills out of him. "If I ever get ashore and anybody shows me even a photograph of an oar -- "

202 At last there was a short conversation.

203 "Billie. . . . Billie, will you spell me?"

204 "Sure," said the oiler.

VII

205 WHEN the correspondent again opened his eyes, the sea and the sky were each of the gray hue of the dawning. Later, carmine and gold was painted upon the waters. The morning appeared finally, in its splendor with a sky of pure blue, and the sunlight flamed on the tips of the waves.

206 On the distant dunes were set many little black cottages, and a tall white wind-mill reared above them. No man, nor dog, nor bicycle appeared on the beach. The cottages might have formed a deserted village.

207 The voyagers scanned the shore. A conference was held in the boat. "Well," said the captain, "if no help is coming, we might better try a run through the surf right away. If we stay out here much longer we will be too weak to do anything for ourselves at all." The others silently acquiesced in this reasoning. The boat was headed for the beach. The correspondent wondered if none ever ascended the tall wind-tower, and if then they never looked seaward. This tower was a giant, standing with its back to the plight of the ants. It represented in a degree, to the correspondent, the serenity of nature amid the struggles of the individual -- nature in the wind, and nature in the vision of men. She did not seem cruel to him, nor beneficent, nor treacherous, nor wise.

But she was indifferent, flatly indifferent. It is, perhaps, plausible that a man in this situation, impressed with the unconcern of the universe, should see the innumerable flaws of his life and have them taste wickedly in his mind and wish for another chance. A distinction between right and wrong seems absurdly clear to him, then, in this new ignorance of the grave-edge, and he understands that if he were given another opportunity he would mend his conduct and his words, and be better and brighter during an introduction, or at a tea.

Nature is indifferent.

208 "Now, boys," said the captain, "she is going to swamp sure. All we can do is to work her in as far as possible, and then when she swamps, pile out and scramble for the beach. Keep cool now and don't jump until she swamps sure."

209 The oiler took the oars. Over his shoulders he scanned the surf. "Captain," he said, "I think I'd better bring her about, and keep her head-on to the seas and back her in."

210 "All right, Billie," said the captain. "Back her in." The oiler swung the boat then and, seated in the stern, the cook and the correspondent were obliged to look over their shoulders to contemplate the lonely and indifferent shore.

211 The monstrous inshore rollers heaved the boat high until the men were again enabled to see the white sheets of water scudding up the slanted beach. "We won't get in very close," said the captain. Each time a man could wrest his attention from the rollers, he turned his glance toward the shore, and in the expression of the eyes during this contemplation there was a singular quality. The correspondent, observing the others, knew that they were not afraid, but the full meaning of their glances was shrouded.

212 As for himself, he was too tired to grapple fundamentally with the fact. He tried to coerce his mind into thinking of it, but the mind was dominated at this time by the muscles, and the muscles said they did not care. It merely occurred to him that if he should drown it would be a shame.

213 There were no hurried words, no pallor, no plain agitation. The men simply looked at the shore. "Now, remember to get well clear of the boat when you jump," said the captain.

214 Seaward the crest of a roller suddenly fell with a thunderous crash, and the long white comber came roaring down upon the boat.

215 "Steady now," said the captain. The men were silent. They turned their eyes from the shore to the comber and waited. The boat slid up the incline, leaped at the furious top, bounced over it, and swung down the long back of the waves. Some water had been shipped and the cook bailed it out.

216 But the next crest crashed also. The tumbling boiling flood of white water caught the boat and whirled it almost perpendicular. Water swarmed in from all sides. The correspondent had his hands on the gunwale at this time, and when the water entered at that place he swiftly withdrew his fingers, as if he objected to wetting them.

217 The little boat, drunken with this weight of water, reeled and snuggled deeper into the sea.

218 "Bail her out, cook! Bail her out," said the captain.

219 "All right, captain," said the cook.

220 "Now, boys, the next one will do for us, sure," said the oiler. "Mind to jump clear of the boat."

221 The third wave moved forward, huge, furious, implacable. It fairly swallowed the dingey, and almost simultaneously the men tumbled into the sea. A piece of life-belt had lain in the bottom of the boat, and as the correspondent went overboard he held this to his chest with his left hand.

222 The January water was icy, and he reflected immediately that it was colder than he had expected to find it off the coast of Florida. This appeared to his dazed mind as a fact important enough to be noted at the time. The coldness of the water was sad; it was tragic. This fact was somehow mixed and confused with his opinion of his own situation that it seemed almost a proper reason for tears. The water was cold.

223 When he came to the surface he was conscious of little but the noisy water. Afterward he saw his companions in the sea. The oiler was ahead in the race. He was swimming strongly and rapidly. Off to the correspondent's left, the cook's great white and corked back bulged out of the water, and in the rear the captain was hanging with his one good hand to the keel of the overturned dingey.

224 There is a certain immovable quality to a shore, and the correspondent wondered at it amid the confusion of the sea.

225 It seemed also very attractive, but the correspondent knew that it was a long journey, and he paddled leisurely. The piece of life-preserver lay under him, and sometimes he whirled down the incline of a wave as if he were on a hand-sled.

226 But finally he arrived at a place in the sea where travel was beset with difficulty. He did not pause swimming to inquire what manner of current had caught him, but there his

progress ceased. The shore was set before him like a bit of scenery on a stage, and he looked at it and understood with his eyes each detail of it.

227 As the cook passed, much farther to the left, the captain was calling to him, "Turn over on your back, cook! Turn over on your back and use the oar."

228 "All right, sir!" The cook turned on his back, and, paddling with an oar, went ahead as if he were a canoe.

229 Presently the boat also passed to the left of the correspondent with the captain clinging with one hand to the keel. He would have appeared like a man raising himself to look over a board fence, if it were not for the extraordinary gymnastics of the boat. The correspondent marveled that the captain could still hold to it.

230 They passed on, nearer to shore -- the oiler, the cook, the captain -- and following them went the water-jar, bouncing gayly over the seas.

231 The correspondent remained in the grip of this strange new enemy -- a current. The shore, with its white slope of sand and its green bluff, topped with little silent cottages, was spread like a picture before him. It was very near to him then, but he was impressed as one who in a gallery looks at a scene from Brittany or Algiers.

232 He thought: "I am going to drown? Can it be possible? Can it be possible? Can it be possible?" Perhaps an individual must consider his own death to be the final phenomenon of nature.

> Death to a human, like it is to any animal, is inevitable and natural.

233 But later a wave perhaps whirled him out of this small deadly current, for he found suddenly that he could again make progress toward the shore. Later still, he was aware that the captain, clinging with one hand to the keel of the dingey, had his face turned away from the shore and toward him, and was calling his name. "Come to the boat! Come to the boat!"

234 In his struggle to reach the captain and the boat, he reflected that when one gets properly wearied, drowning must really be a comfortable arrangement, a cessation of hostilities accompanied by a large degree of relief, and he was glad of it, for the main thing in his mind for some moments had been horror of the temporary agony. He did not wish to be hurt.

235 Presently he saw a man running along the shore. He was undressing with most remarkable speed. Coat, trousers, shirt, everything flew magically off him.

236 "Come to the boat," called the captain.

237 "All right, captain." As the correspondent paddled, he saw the captain let himself down to bottom and leave the boat. Then the correspondent performed his one little marvel of the voyage. A large wave caught him and flung him with ease and supreme speed completely over the boat and far beyond it. It struck him even then as an event in gymnastics, and a true miracle of the sea. An overturned boat in the surf is not a plaything to a swimming man.

238 The correspondent arrived in water that reached only to his waist, but his condition did not enable him to stand for more than a moment. Each wave knocked him into a heap, and the under-tow pulled at him.

239 Then he saw the man who had been running and undressing, and undressing and running, come bounding into the water. He dragged ashore the cook, and then waded toward the captain, but the captain waved him away, and sent him to the correspondent. He was naked, naked as a tree in winter, but a halo was about his head, and he shone like a saint. He gave a strong pull, and a long drag, and a bully heave at the correspondent's hand. The correspondent, schooled in the minor formulae, said: "Thanks, old man." But suddenly the man cried: "What's that?" He pointed a swift finger. The correspondent said: "Go."

240 In the shallows, face downward, lay the oiler. His forehead touched sand that was periodically, between each wave, clear of the sea.

241 The correspondent did not know all that transpired afterward. When he achieved safe ground he fell, striking the sand with each particular part of his body. It was as if he had dropped from a roof, but the thud was grateful to him.

242 It seems that instantly the beach was populated with men with blankets, clothes, and flasks, and women with coffee-pots and all the remedies sacred to their minds. The welcome of the land to the men from the sea was warm and generous, but a still and dripping shape was carried slowly up the beach, and the land's welcome for it could only be the different and sinister hospitality of the grave.

> Nature is indifferent. The only thing mankind learns in tragedy is that there is no predictability or reason in the cosmos.

243 When it came night, the white waves paced to and fro in the moonlight, and the wind brought the sound of the great sea's voice to the men on shore, and they felt that they could then be interpreters.

LESSON NINETEEN

Readings Due For This Lesson
Students should have read *The Red Badge of Courage*, Stephen Crane.

Reading Ahead

Students should read *Ethan Frome*, Edith Wharton (Lesson Twenty)

Suggested Weekly *Implementation*

Day One	Day Two	Day Three	Day Four	Day Five
1. Students will rewrite graded essays from last week and review Lesson Eighteen test. 2. Students should have read the required reading(s) *before* the assigned lesson begins. 3. Teacher may want to discuss assigned reading(s) with student. 4. Teacher shall assign the required essays. Choose two or three. The rest of the essays can be outlined, answered with shorter answers, or skipped.	1. Student should begin reading(s) from next lesson. 2. Student should outline essays due at the end of the week. 3. Students should answer one or two of the essays that are not assigned as formal essays.	1. Students should write rough drafts of assigned essays. 2. The teacher should correct rough drafts.	Student will write final copy of essays due tomorrow.	1. Essays are due. 2. Students should take Lesson Nineteen test. 3. Student should read *Ethan Frome*, Edith Wharton.

Biblical Application (cont.)

Naturalism stresses the discoverable, deterministic laws of nature. If God exists in the Naturalistic word, He is, like nature, cold and indifferent. What Scripture verses can you find that contradicts this view? *Psalm 139:1-15, "O LORD, You have searched me and known me. You know when I sit down and when I rise up; You understand my thought from afar. You scrutinize my path and my lying down, And are intimately acquainted with all my ways. Even before there is a word on my tongue, Behold, O LORD, You know it all. You have enclosed me behind and before, And laid Your hand upon me. Such knowledge is too wonderful for me; It is too high, I cannot attain to it. Where can I go from Your Spirit? Or where can I flee from Your presence? If I ascend to heaven, You are there; If I make my bed in Sheol, behold, You are there. If I take the wings of the dawn, If I dwell in the remotest part of the sea, Even there Your hand will lead me, And Your right hand will lay hold of me. If I say, "Surely the darkness will overwhelm me, And the light around me will be night," Even the darkness is not dark to You, And the night is as bright as the day. Darkness and light are alike to You. For You formed my inward parts;*
You wove me in my mother's womb". John 3: 16:" For God so loved the world, that He gave His only begotten Son, that whoever believes in Him shall not perish, but have eternal life. Our God is literally very interested in all of us!"

Literary Criticism

A. Describe the way Crane develops his plot. *There is a certain episodic feature in his organization. At the same time, we watch Henry come alive--that is discarding his idealism for realism. So there are two levels in the plot: the metaphysical realm and the actual plot. Most readers confusingly see this novel as a Civil War novel. In fact, when one examines the world view war that is occurring, one sees that this is a novel about Naturalism vs. Romanticism–in other words, a world view conflict.*

B. The plot, to some critics, has major flaws. For instance, after running farther and faster than anyone else, Henry Fleming proves to be one of the bravest soldiers in the regiment. Some critics feel that this is unbelievable. Do you agree? If you feel that the transformation is believable, explain with reasons from the book why you do. *I find the transformation to be completely believable in Crane's Naturalistic world; however, Henry is a late nineteenth century man--not a true Civil War man. In that sense it is not a credible plot. Remember: in 1861-65 there was no extant Naturalistic view. I once saw a movie about medieval knights set to urban rap music! What an anachronism! That is the way I feel when I read Stephen Crane. Fleming seems like a late 19th century man in a middle 19th century war. It is an anachronism.*

C. Describe Crane's tone and writing style. *Crane writes in a terse, powerful style. His images are powerful and striking. While his metaphors are rich, they are cogent and precise. He wastes no words. He is no James Fenimore Cooper! This style is later imitated by other Nturalistic writers (e.g., Ernest Hemingway).*

Critical Thinking

A. "Let a thing become a tradition and it becomes half a lie," Crane said. He never created a Hester Prynne who gave her life to absolute truth or to a Huck Finn who had affectionate tolerance toward differing opinions. Crane's world was cynical and very dangerous. His world was full of opportunistic "demons" who sought to do him in. He was "A man adrift on a slim spar/A horizon smaller than the rim of a bottle/Tented waves rearing lashy dark points/The near whine of froth in circles./God is cold." (from the poem "Adrift on a Spar") In a short story entitled "The Open Boat" Crane hauntingly described the frustration of being in an open boat near enough to see the shore but unable to reach the shore and safety:

> *If I am going to be drowned--if I am going to be drowned--if I am going to be drowned, why, in the name of the seven mad gods who rule the sea, was I allowed to come thus far and contemplate sand and trees? Was I brought here merely to have my nose dragged away as I was about to nibble the sacred cheese of life?*

The moribundity expressed by Crane becomes a recurring theme in American literature. Gone is the God of the Puritans and even the God whom Hester Prynne so faithfully served. The great-great-grandchildren of Anne Bradstreet doubted God really loved them at all. "Fate" was the true power that determined their future.

Find examples of this hopelessness in modern movies, television programs, and music. Why, as Christian believers, should we reject this pessimism? *Answers will vary. Most television heroes(oines) are unmarried, divorced, or unhappy in general. We are sure that our God can do all things. We know, too, that God is very much in control (Romans 8).*

B. Crane had never seen a battle when he wrote this book. Can you tell? *Yes. As I said, Crane's cynicism in some ways reflects a Spanish American or World War I story more than a Civil War story. The truth is most Civil War soldiers were very idealist and brave. The metaphysical struggles with which Fleming struggled were mostly foreign to Civil War Americans. Not for a moment can I imagine an American in 1861 wondering if there was a God.*

C. Define maturity. How was Henry more mature at the end of the novel than he was at the beginning? *I define maturity partly as "delaying pleasure." I find Henry to be more mature or, is he just a modern, unfeeling American. I am not sure. I find Hester Prynne to be a far more mature character.*

D. Pretend that Henry was court marshaled for desertion. Should he be convicted? Why or why not? *Crane would say no. He only followed his instincts--one could expect nothing else. I might agree but I would argue for mercy–he did show cowardice. To*

Crane, who has no absolute moral paradigm with which to run his life, Fleming is free to act in his best interests. To a Theist, Fleming sinned–but can be shown mercy.

E. To Crane, nature has lost all contact with humanity. "It was surprising that Nature had gone tranquilly on with her golden process in the midst of so much devilment." Contrast this view with some of the earlier Romantic writers (e.g., Hawthorne). *Hawthorne's Nature is merely a reflection of God. It is not a separate entity. To Crane, a Naturalist, nature is neither omniscient nor omnipotent, but it is malevolent. To Hawthorne, Emerson, and Cooper Nature is benevolent. To the Puritans, God is benevolent, personal, and omnipotent.*

Challenge Question

King Ahab in 1 Kings 16 is an example of a modern man. He is everything to everyone. What bothers Ahab is that Elijah is so parochial. That is, Elijah believes in God--as Ahab does--but Elijah claims there is one and only one God. We Christians rarely get into trouble for standing up for Christ until we suggest that Christ is the one and the only Christ. Then the modern world punishes us.

Find evidences in your own life where you have taken a stand for absolute truth and experienced rejection or persecution.

Answers will vary.

For Further Enrichment

A. How was Crane affected by social Darwinism? *The strongest survive. The weak do not. Charles Darwin published in 1859* <u>On The Origin of Species by Means of Natural Selection, or the Preservation of Favoured Races in the Struggle for Life</u>. *Darwin in 1858 had co-authored (with Alfred Russel Wallace) the theory of natural selection, which says that superior biological variations tend to be preserved. In the struggle for existence, the fit are not those who survive but those who reproduce. Natural selection also leads to diversification as different organisms adapt to particular ecological circumstances. Darwin said all biological similarities and differences are caused by descent with modification. He concluded that all organisms are descended from only one ancestor. Evolution is the name for this biological process that goes back to one common ancestor 3-1/2 billion years ago. Charles Darwin, then, was the father of the theory of evolution.*

"We have reason to believe, as stated in the first chapter, that a change in the conditions of life, by specially acting on the reproductive system, causes or increases variability; and in the foregoing case the conditions of life are supposed to have undergone a change, and this would manifestly be favourable to natural selection, by giving a better chance of profitable variations occurring; and unless profitable variations do occur, natural *selection can do nothing. Not that, as I believe, any extreme amount of variability is necessary; as man can certainly produce great results by adding up in any given direction mere individual differences, so could Nature, but far more easily, from having incomparably longer time at her disposal. Nor do I believe that any great physical change, as of climate, or any unusual degree of isolation to check immigration, is actually necessary to produce new and unoccupied places for natural selection to fill up by modifying and improving some of the varying inhabitants. For as all the inhabitants of each country are struggling together with nicely balanced forces, extremely slight modifications in the structure or habits of one inhabitant would often give it an advantage over others; and still further modifications of the same kind would often still further increase the advantage".– <u>The Origin of Species</u>*

B. Read Upton Sinclair, *The Jungle*, or Frank Norris' *MacTeague* and tell why these are naturalistic novels. *Sinclair's The Jungle and Norris' MacTeague are stories of immigrants whose experiences in America were less than desirable.*

C. In *Principles of Psychology* (1855) Herbert Spencer, a British philosopher, took Darwin's theory into the social realm. He influenced a generation of sociologists and authors like Stephen Crane. He wrote that all organic matter originated in a unified state and that individual characteristics gradually developed through evolution. The evolutionary progression from simple to more complex and diverse states was an important theme in most of Spencer's later works. In summary, Spencer argued that the strongest individuals and social systems survived. The weakest did not. This was an example of a scientific theory being transposed on human society and experience. The same thing happened with Einstein's theory of relativity. "Who would imagine that this simple law (constancy of the velocity of light) has plunged the conscientiously thoughtful physicist into the greatest intellectual difficulties?" Einstein wrote. He was horrified that social scientists took his theory about the quantum nature of light, a description of molecular motion, and the special theory of relativity and created a social theory called Relativism. Relativism argued that persons should make decisions based upon the "relative worth" of that decision based on circumstances. In other words, persons were free to do what was relatively beneficial to his situation regardless of the consequences to others. Why do social scientist indulge themselves in such contrived chicanery and what is its ramifications? *Both scientific theory and social science theory is cheapened.*

D. Read the following short story by Crane entitled *Blue Hotel* (1898) and write an essay highlighting Naturalistic themes. *See text boxes below.*

I

The Palace Hotel at Fort Romper was painted a light blue, a shade that is on the legs of a kind of heron, causing the bird to declare its position against any background. The Palace Hotel, then, was always screaming and howling in a way that made the dazzling winter landscape of Nebraska seem only a gray swampish hush. It stood alone on the prairie, and when the snow was falling the town two hundred yards away was not visible. But when the traveler alighted at the railway station he was obliged to pass the Palace Hotel before he could come upon the company of low clapboard houses which composed Fort Romper,

> Notice the way Crane uses the setting. In Naturalistic writings the setting is almost always dreary and incidental.

and it was not to be thought that any traveler could pass the Palace Hotel without looking at it. Pat Scully, the proprietor, had proved himself a master of strategy when he chose his paints. It is true that on clear days, when the great trans-continental expresses, long lines of swaying Pullmans, swept through Fort Romper, passengers were overcome at the sight, and the cult that knows the brown-reds and the subdivisions of the dark greens of the East expressed shame, pity, horror, in a laugh. But to the citizens of this prairie town, and to the people who would naturally stop there, Pat`Scully had performed a feat. With this opulence and splendor, these creeds, classes, egotisms, that streamed through Romper on the rails day after day, they had no color in common.

As if the displayed delights of such a blue hotel were not sufficiently enticing, it was Scully's habit to go every morning and evening to meet the leisurely trains that stopped at Romper and work his seductions upon any man that he might see wavering, gripsack in hand.

One morning, when a snow-crusted engine dragged its long string of freight cars and its one passenger coach to the station, Scully performed the marvel of catching three men. One was a shaky and quick-eyed Swede, with a great shining cheap valise; one was a tall bronzed cowboy, who was on his

> Naturalistic and Realistic characters are ordinary--like the person who lives next door.

way to a ranch near the Dakota line; one was a little silent man from the East, who didn't look it, and didn't announce it. Scully practically made them prisoners. He was so nimble and merry and kindly that each probably felt it would be the height of brutality to try to escape. They trudged off over the creaking board sidewalks in the wake of the eager little Irishman.

He wore a heavy fur cap squeezed tightly down on his head. It caused his two red ears to stick out stiffly, as if they were made of tin. At last, Scully, elaborately, with boisterous hospitality, conducted them through the portals of the blue hotel. The room which they entered was small. It seemed to be merely a proper temple for an enormous stove, which, in the center, was humming with godlike violence. At various points on its surface the iron had become luminous and glowed yellow from the heat. Beside the stove Scully's son Johnnie was playing High-Five with an old farmer who had whiskers both gray and sandy. They were quarreling. Frequently the old farmer turned his face toward a box of sawdust- colored brown from tobacco juice- that was behind the stove, and spat with an air of great impatience and irritation. With a loud flourish of words Scully destroyed the game of cards, and bustled his son upstairs with part of the baggage of the new guests. He himself conducted them to three basins of the coldest water in the world. The cowboy and the Easterner burnished themselves fiery red with this water, until it seemed to be some kind of a metal polish. The Swede, however, merely dipped his fingers gingerly and with trepidation. It was notable that throughout this series of small ceremonies the three travelers were made to feel that Scully was very benevolent. He was conferring great favors upon them. He handed the towel from one to the other with an air of philanthropic impulse.

Afterward they went to the first room, and, sitting about the stove, listened to Scully's officious clamor at his daughters, who were preparing the midday meal. They reflected in the silence of experienced men who tread carefully amid new people. Nevertheless, the old farmer, stationary, invincible in his chair near the warmest part of the stove, turned his face from the sawdust box frequently and addressed a glowing commonplace to the strangers. Usually he was answered in short but adequate sentences by either the cowboy or the Easterner. The Swede said nothing. He seemed to be occupied in making furtive estimates of each man in the room. One might have thought that he had the sense of silly suspicion which comes to guilt. He resembled a badly frightened man.

Later, at dinner, he spoke a little, addressing his conversation entirely to Scully. He volunteered that he had come from New York, where for ten years he had worked as a tailor. These facts seem to strike Scull as fascinating, and afterward he volunteered that he had lived at Romper for fourteen years. The Swede asked about the crops and the price of labor. He seemed barely to listen to Scales extended replies. His eyes continued to rove from man to man.

Finally, with a laugh and a wink, he said that some of these Western Communities were very dangerous; and after his statement he straightened his legs under the table, tilted his head, and laughed again, loudly. It was plain that the demonstration had no meaning to the others. They looked at him wondering and in silence.

II

As the men trooped heavily back into the front room, the two little windows presented views of a turmoiling sea of snow. The huge arms of the wind were making attempts- mighty, circular, futile- to embrace the flakes as they sped. A gate-post like a still man with a blanched face stood aghast amid this profligate fury. In a hearty voice Scully announced the presence of a blizzard. The guests of the blue hotel, lighting their pipes, assented with grunts of lazy masculine contentment. No island of the sea could be exempt in the degree of this little room with its humming stove. Johnnie, son of Scully, in a tone which defined his opinion of his ability as a card-player, challenged the old farmer of both gray and sandy whiskers to a game of High-Five. The farmer agreed with a contemptuous and bitter scoff. They sat close to the stove, and squared their knees under a wide board. The cowboy and the Easterner watched the game with interest. The Swede remained near the window, aloof, but with a countenance that showed signs of an inexplicable excitement.

The play of Johnnie and the gray-beard was suddenly ended by another quarrel. The old man arose while casting a look of heated scorn at his adversary. He slowly buttoned his coat, and then stalked with fabulous dignity from the room. In the discreet silence of all other men the Swede laughed. His laughter rang somehow childishly. Men by this time had begun to look at him askance, as if they wished to inquire what ailed him.

A new game was formed jocosely. The cowboy volunteered to become the partner of Johnnie, and them all then turned to ask the Swede to throw in his lot with the little Easterner. He asked some questions about the game, and learning that it wore many names, and that he had played it when it was under an alias, he accepted the invitation. He strode toward the men nervously, as if he expected to be assaulted. Finally, seated, he gazed from face to face and laughed shrilly. This laugh was so strange that the Easterner looked up quickly, the cowboy sat intent and with his mouth open, and Johnnie paused, holding the cards with still fingers. Afterward there was a short silence. Then Johnnie said: "Well, let's get at it. Come on now!" They pulled their chairs forward until their knees were bunched under the board. They began to play, and their interest in the game caused the others to forget the manner of the Swede.

The cowboy was a board-whacker. Each time that he held superior cards he whanged them, one by one, with exceeding force, down upon the improvised table, and took the tricks with a glowing air of prowess and pride that sent thrills of indignation into the hearts of his opponents. A game with a board-whacker in it is sure to become intense. The countenances of the Easterner and the Swede were miserable whenever the cowboy thundered down his aces and kings, while Johnnie, his eyes gleaming with joy, chuckled and chuckled. Because of the absorbing play none considered the strange ways of the Swede. They paid strict heed to the game. Finally, during a lull caused by a new deal, the Swede suddenly addressed Johnnie: "I suppose there have been a good many men killed in this room." The jaws of the others dropped and they looked at him. "What in hell are you talking about?" said Johnnie. The Swede laughed again his blatant laugh, full of a kind of false courage and defiance. "Oh, you know what I mean all right," he answered.

"I'm a liar if I do!" Johnnie protested. The card was halted, and the men stared at the Swede. Johnnie evidently felt that as the son of the proprietor he should make a direct inquiry. "Now, what might you be drivin' at, mister?" he asked. The Swede winked at him. It was a wink full of cunning. His fingers shook on the edge of the board. "Oh, maybe you think I have been to nowheres. Maybe you think I'm a tenderfoot?"

"I don't know nothin' about you," answered Johnnie, "and I don't give a damn where you've been. All I got to say is that I don't know what you're driving at. There hain't never been nobody killed in this room." The cowboy, who had been steadily gazing at the Swede, then spoke. "What's wrong with you, mister?"

Apparently it seemed to the Swede that he was formidably menaced. He shivered and turned white near the corners of his mouth. He sent an appealing glance in the direction of the little Easterner. During these moments he did not forget to wear his air of advanced pot-valor. "They say they don't know what I mean," he remarked mockingly to the Easterner.

The latter answered after prolonged and cautious reflection. "I don't understand you," he

269

said, impassively.

The Swede made a movement then which announced that he thought he had encountered treachery from the only quarter where he had expected sympathy if not help. "Oh, I see you are all against me. I see-" The cowboy was in a state of deep stupefaction. "Say," he cried, as he tumbled the deck violently down upon the board. "Say, what are you gittin' at, hey?"

The Swede sprang up with the celerity of a man escaping from a snake on the floor. "I don't want to fight!" he shouted. "I don't want to fight!"

The cowboy stretched his long legs indolently and deliberately. His hands were in his pockets. He spat into the sawdust box. "Well, who the hell thought you did?" he inquired.

The Swede backed rapidly toward a corner of the room. His hands were out protectingly in front of his chest, but he was making an obvious struggle to control his fright. "Gentlemen," he quavered, "I suppose I am going to be killed before I can leave this house! I suppose I am going to be killed before I can leave this house." In his eyes was the dying swan look. Through the windows could be seen the snow turning blue in the shadow of dusk. The wind tore at the house and some loose thing beat regularly against the clapboard like a spirit tapping.

A door opened, and Scully himself entered. He paused in surprise as he noted the tragic attitude of the Swede. Then he said: "What's the matter here?"

The Swede answered him swiftly and eagerly: "These men are going to kill me." "Kill you!" ejaculated Scully. "Kill you! What are you talkin'?"

The Swede made the gesture of a martyr.

Scully wheeled sternly upon his son. "What is this, Johnnie?"

The lad had grown sullen. "Damned if I know," he answered. "I can't make no sense to it." He began to shuffle the cards, fluttering them together with an angry snap. "He says a good many men have been killed in this room, or something like that. And he says he's goin' to be killed here too. I don't know what ails him. He's crazy, I shouldn't wonder."

Scully then looked for explanation to the cowboy, but the cowboy simply shrugged his shoulders.

"Kill you?" said Scully again to the Swede. "Kill you? Man, you're off your nut."

"Oh, I know," burst out the Swede. "I know what will happen. Yes, I'm crazy- yes. Yes, of course, I'm crazy- yes. But I know one thing-" There was a sort of sweat of misery and terror upon his face. "I know I won't get out of here alive."

The cowboy drew a deep breath, as if his mind was passing into the last stages of dissolution. "Well, I'm dog-goned," he whispered to himself. Scully wheeled suddenly and faced his son. "You've been troublin' this man!"

Johnnie's voice was loud with its burden of grievance. "Why, good Gawd, I ain't done nothin' to 'im."

The Swede broke in. "Gentlemen, do not disturb yourselves. I will leave this house. I will go 'way because-" He accused them dramatically with his glance. "Because I do not want to be killed."

Scully was furious with his son. "Will you tell me what is the matter, you young divil? What's the matter, anyhow? Speak out!"

"Blame it," cried Johnnie in despair, "don't I tell you I don't know. He- he says we want to kill him, and that's all I know. I can't tell what ails him."

The Swede continued to repeat: "Never mind, Mr. Scully, never mind. I will leave this house. I will go away, because I do not wish to be killed. Yes, of course, I am crazy- yes. But I know one thing! I will go away. I will leave this house. Never mind, Mr. Scully, never mind. I will go away."

"You will not go 'way," said Scully. "You will not go 'way until I hear the reason of this business. If anybody has troubled you I will take care of him. This is my house. You are under my roof, and I will not allow any peaceable man to be troubled here." He cast a terrible eye upon Johnnie, the cowboy, and the Easterner.

"Never mind, Mr. Scully; never mind. I will go 'way. I do not wish to be killed." The Swede moved toward the door, which opened upon the stairs. It was evidently his intention to go at once for his baggage.

"No, no," shouted Scully peremptorily; but the whitefaced man slid by him and disappeared. "Now," said Scully severely, "what does this mane?"

Johnnie and the cowboy cried together: "Why, we didn't do nothin' to 'im!"

Scully's eyes were cold. "No," he said, "you didn't?"

Johnnie swore a deep oath. "Why, this is the wildest loon I ever see. We didn't do nothin' at all. We were jest sittin' here playin' cards and he-" The father suddenly spoke to the Easterner. "Mr. Blanc," he asked, "what has these boys been doin'?"

The Easterner reflected again. "I didn't see anything wrong at all," he said at last slowly.

Scully began to howl. "But what does it mane?" He stared ferociously at his son. "I have a mind to lather you for this, me boy."

Johnnie was frantic. "Well, what have I done?" he bawled at his father.

III

"I think you are tongue-tied," said Scully finally to his son, the cowboy and the Easterner, and at the end of this scornful sentence he left the room.

Upstairs the Swede was swiftly fastening the straps of his great valise. Once his back happened to be half-turned toward the door, and hearing a noise there, he wheeled and sprang up, uttering a loud cry. Scully's wrinkled visage showed grimly in the light of the small lamp he carried. This yellow effulgence, streaming upward, colored only his prominent features, and left his eyes, for instance, in mysterious shadow. He resembled a murderer.

"Man, man!" he exclaimed, "have you gone daffy?"

"Oh, no! Oh, no!" rejoined the other. "There are people in this world who know pretty nearly as much as you do- understand?" For a moment they stood gazing at each other. Upon the Swede's deathly pale cheeks were two spots brightly crimson and sharply edged, as if they had been carefully painted. Scully placed the light on the table and sat himself on the edge of the bed. He spoke ruminatively. "By cracky, I never heard of such a thing in my life. It's a complete muddle. I can't for the soul of me think how you ever got this idea into your head." Presently he lifted his eyes and asked: "And did you sure think they were going to kill you?" The Swede scanned the old man as if he wished to see into his mind. "I did," he said at last. He obviously suspected that this answer might precipitate an outbreak. As he pulled on a strap his whole arm shook, the elbow wavering like a bit of paper.

Scully banged his hand impressively on the foot-board of the bed. "Why, man, we're goin' to have a line of ilictric street-cars in this town next spring."

"'A line of electric street-cars,'" repeated the Swede stupidly.

"And," said Scully, "there's a new railroad goin' to be built down from Broken Arm to here. Not to mention the four churches and the smashin' big brick schoolhouse. Then there's the big factory, too. Why, in two years Romper'll be a met-tro-pol-is."

Having finished the preparation of his baggage, the Swede straightened himself. "Mr. Scully," he said with sudden hardihood, "how much do I owe you?"

"You don't owe me anythin'," said the old man angrily. "Yes, I do," retorted the Swede. He took seventy-five cents from his pocket and tendered it to Scully; but the latter snapped his fingers in disdainful refusal. However, it happened that they both stood gazing in a strange fashion at three silver pieces in the Swede's open palm.

"I'll not take your money," said Scully at last. "Not after what's been goin' on here." Then a plan seemed to strike him. "Here," he cried, picking up his lamp and moving toward the door. "Here! Come with me a minute."

"No," said the Swede in overwhelming alarm.

"Yes," urged the old man. "Come on! I want you to come and see a picter- just across the hall- in my room."

The Swede must have concluded that his hour was come. His jaw dropped and his teeth showed like a dead man's. He ultimately followed Scully across the corridor, but he had the step of one hung in chains.

Scully flashed the light high on the wall of his own chamber. There was revealed a ridiculous photograph of a little girl. She was leaning against a balustrade of gorgeous decoration, and the formidable bang to her hair was prominent. The figure was as graceful as an upright sled-stake, and, withal, it was of the hue of lead. "There," said Scully tenderly. "That's the picter of my little girl that died. Her name was Carrie. She had the purtiest hair you ever saw! I was that fond of her, she-" Turning then he saw that the Swede was not contemplating the picture at all, but, instead, was keeping keen watch on the gloom in the rear.

"Look, man!" shouted Scully heartily. "That's the picter of my little gal that died. Her name was Carrie. And then here's the picter of my oldest boy, Michael. He's a lawyer in Lincoln an' doin' well. I gave that boy a grand eddycation, and I'm glad for it now. He's a fine boy. Look at 'im now. Ain't he bold as blazes, him there in Lincoln, an honored an' respicted gintleman. An honored an' respicted gintleman," concluded Scully with a flourish. And so saying, he smote the Swede jovially on the back.

The Swede faintly smiled.

"Now," said the old man, "there's only one more thing." He dropped suddenly to the floor and thrust his head beneath the bed. The Swede could hear his muffled voice. "I'd keep it under me piller if it wasn't for that boy Johnnie. Then there's the old woman- Where is it now? I never put it twice in the same place. Ah, now come out with you!" Presently he backed clumsily from under the bed, dragging with him an old coat rolled into a bundle. "I've fetched him" he muttered. Kneeling on the floor he unrolled the coat and extracted from its heart a large yellow-brown whisky bottle.

His first maneuver was to hold the bottle up to the light. Reassured, apparently, that nobody had been tampering with it, he thrust it with a generous movement toward the Swede.

The weak-kneed Swede was about to eagerly clutch this element of strength, but he suddenly jerked his hand away and cast a look of horror upon Scully.

"Drink," said the old man affectionately. He had arisen to his feet, and now stood facing the Swede.

There was a silence. Then again Scully said: "Drink!"

The Swede laughed wildly. He grabbed the bottle, put it to his mouth, and as his lips curled absurdly around the opening and his throat worked, he kept his glance burning with hatred upon the old man's face.

IV

After the departure of Scully the three men, with the card-board still upon their knees, preserved for a long time an astounded silence. Then Johnnie said: "That's the dod-dangest Swede I ever see." "He ain't no Swede," said the cowboy scornfully.

"Well, what is he then?" cried Johnnie. "What is he then?"

"It's my opinion," replied the cowboy deliberately, "he's some kind of a Dutchman." It was a venerable custom of the country to entitle as Swedes all light-haired men who spoke with a heavy tongue. In consequence the idea of the cowboy was not without its daring. "Yes, sir," he repeated. "It's my opinion this feller is some kind of a Dutchman."

"Well, he says he's a Swede, anyhow," muttered Johnnie sulkily. He turned to the Easterner: "What do you think, Mr. Blanc?"

"Oh, I don't know," replied the Easterner.

"Well, what do you think makes him act that way?" asked the cowboy.

"Why, he's frightened!" The Easterner knocked his pipe against a rim of the stove. "He's clear frightened out of his boots."

"What at?" cried Johnnie and cowboy together.

The Easterner reflected over his answer.

"What at?" cried the others again.

"Oh, I don't know, but it seems to me this man has been reading dime-novels, and he thinks he's right out in the middle of it- the shootin' and stabbin' and all."

"But," said the cowboy, deeply scandalized, "this ain't Wyoming, ner none of them places. This is Nebrasker."

"Yes," added Johnnie, "an' why don't he wait till he gits out West?"

The traveled Easterner laughed. "It isn't different there even- not in these days. But he thinks he's right in the middle of hell."

Johnnie and the cowboy mused long.

"It's awful funny," remarked Johnnie at last.

"Yes," said the cowboy. "This is a queer game. I hope we don't git snowed in, because then we'd have to stand this here man bein' around with us all the time. That wouldn't be no good."

"I wish pop would throw him out," said Johnnie.

Presently they heard a loud stamping on the stairs, accompanied by ringing jokes in the voice of old Scully, and laughter, evidently from the Swede. The men around the stove stared vacantly at each other. "Gosh," said the cowboy. The door flew open, and old Scully, flushed and anecdotal, came into the room. He was jabbering at the Swede, who followed him, laughing bravely. It was the entry of two roysterers from a banquet hall.

"Come now," said Scully sharply to the three seated men, "move up and give us a chance at the stove." The cowboy and the Easterner obediently sidled their chairs to make room for the newcomers. Johnnie, however, simply arranged himself in a more indolent attitude, and then remained motionless.

"Come! Git over, there," said Scully.

"Plenty of room on the other side of the stove," said Johnnie.

"Do you think we want to sit in the draught?" roared the father.

But the Swede here interposed with a grandeur of confidence. "No, no. Let the boy sit where he likes," he cried in a bullying voice to the father. "All right! All right!" said Scully deferentially. The cowboy and the Easterner exchanged glances of wonder.

The five chairs were formed in a crescent about one side of the stove. The Swede began to talk; he talked arrogantly, profanely, angrily. Johnnie, the cowboy and the Easterner maintained a morose silence, while old Scully appeared to be receptive and eager, breaking in constantly with sympathetic ejaculations.

Finally the Swede announced that he was thirsty. He moved in his chair, and said that he would go for a drink of water.

"I'll git it for you," cried Scully at once.

"No," said the Swede contemptuously. "I'll get it for myself." He arose and stalked with the air of an owner off into the executive parts of the hotel.

As soon as the Swede was out of hearing Scully sprang to his feet and whispered intensely to the others. "Upstairs he thought I was tryin' to poison 'im."

"Say," said Johnnie, "this makes me sick. Why don't you throw 'im out in the snow?"

"Why, he's all right now," declared Scully. "It was only that he was
from the East and he thought this was a tough place. That's all.
He's all right now."

The cowboy looked with admiration upon the Easterner. "You were
straight," he said, "You were on to that there Dutchman."

"Well," said Johnnie to his father, "he may be all right now, but
I don't see it. Other time he was scared, and now he's too fresh."

Scully's speech was always a combination of Irish brogue and idiom, Western twang and idiom, and scraps of curiously formal diction taken from the story-books and newspapers. He now hurled a strange mass of language at the head of his son. "What do I keep? What do I keep? What do I keep?" he demanded in a voice of thunder. He slapped his knee impressively, to indicate that he himself was going to make reply, and that all should heed. "I keep a hotel," he shouted. "A hotel, do you mind? A guest under my roof has sacred privileges. He is to be intimidated by none. Not one word shall he hear that would prijudice him in favor of goin' away. I'll not have it. There's no place in this here town where they can say they iver took in a guest of mine because he was afraid to stay here." He wheeled suddenly upon the cowboy and the Easterner. "Am I right?" "Yes, Mr. Scully," said the cowboy, "I think you're right." "Yes, Mr. Scully," said the

Easterner, "I think you're right."
                    V

   At six-o'clock supper, the Swede fizzed like a firewheel. He sometimes seemed on the point of bursting into riotous song, and in all his madness he was encouraged by old Scully. The Easterner was incased in reserve; the cowboy sat in wide-mouthed amazement, forgetting to eat, while Johnnie wrathily demolished great plates of food. The daughters of the house when they were obliged to replenish the biscuits approached as warily as Indians, and, having succeeded in their purposes, fled with ill-concealed trepidation. The Swede domineered the whole feast, and he gave it the appearance of a cruel bacchanal. He seemed to have grown suddenly taller; he gazed, brutally disdainful, into every face. His voice rang through the room. Once when he jabbed out harpoon-fashion with his fork to pinion a biscuit the weapon nearly impaled the hand of the Easterner which had been stretched quietly out for the same biscuit.   After supper, as the men filed toward the other room, the Swede smote Scully ruthlessly on the shoulder. "Well, old boy, that was a good square meal." Johnnie looked hopefully at his father; he knew that shoulder was tender from an old fall; and indeed it appeared for a moment as if Scully was going to flame out over the matter, but in the end he smiled a sickly smile and remained silent. The others understood from his manner that he was admitting his responsibility for the Swede's new viewpoint.
   Johnnie, however, addressed his parent in an aside. "Why don't you license somebody to kick you downstairs?" Scully scowled darkly by way of reply.
   When they were gathered about the stove, the Swede insisted on another game of High-Five. Scully gently deprecated the plan at first, but the Swede turned a wolfish glare upon him. The old man subsided, and the Swede canvassed the others. In his tone there was always a great threat. The cowboy and the Easterner both remarked indifferently that they would play. Scully said that he would presently have to go to meet the 6.58 train, and so the Swede turned menacingly upon Johnnie. For a moment their glances crossed like blades, and then Johnnie smiled and said: "Yes, I'll play." They formed a square with the little board on their knees. The Easterner and the Swede were again partners. As the play went on, it was noticeable that the cowboy was not board-whacking as usual. Meanwhile, Scully, near the lamp, had put on his spectacles and, with an appearance curiously like an old priest, was reading a newspaper. In time he went out to meet the 6.58 train, and, despite his precautions, a gust of polar wind whirled into the room as he opened the door. Besides scattering the cards, it chilled the players to the marrow. The Swede cursed frightfully. When Scully returned, his entrance disturbed a cozy and friendly scene. The Swede again cursed. But presently they were once more intent, their heads bent forward and their hands moving swiftly. The Swede had adopted the fashion of board-whacking.   Scully took up his paper and for a long time remained immersed in matters which were extraordinarily remote from him. The lamp burned badly, and once he stopped to adjust the wick. The newspaper as he turned from page to page rustled with a slow and comfortable sound. Then suddenly he heard three terrible words: "You are cheatin'!" Such scenes often prove that there can be little of dramatic import in environment. Any room can present a tragic front; any room can be comic. This little den

was now hideous as a torture-chamber. The new faces of the men themselves had changed it upon the instant. The Swede held a huge fist in front of Johnnie's face, while the latter looked steadily over it into the blazing orbs of his accuser. The Easterner had grown pallid; the cowboy's jaw had dropped in that expression of bovine amazement which was one of his important mannerisms. After the three words, the first sound in the room was made by Scully's paper as it floated forgotten to his feet. His spectacles had also fallen from his nose, but by a clutch he had saved them in air. His hand, grasping the spectacles, now remained poised awkwardly and near his shoulder. He stared at the card-players.

Probably the silence was while a second elapsed. Then, if the floor had been suddenly twitched out from under the men they could not have moved quicker. The five had projected themselves headlong toward a common point. It happened that Johnnie in rising to hurl himself upon the Swede had stumbled slightly because of his curiously instinctive care for the cards and the board. The loss of the moment allowed time for the arrival of Scully, and also allowed the cowboy time to give the Swede a great push which sent him staggering back. The men found tongue together, and hoarse shouts or rage, appeal or fear burst from every throat. The cowboy pushed and jostled feverishly at the Swede, and the Easterner and Scully clung wildly to Johnnie; but, through the smoky air, above the swaying bodies of the peace-compellers, the eyes of the two warriors ever sought each other in glances of challenge that were at once hot and steely.

Of course the board had been overturned, and now the whole company of cards was scattered over the floor, where the boots of the men trampled the fat and painted kings and queens as they gazed with their silly eyes at the war that was waging above them.

Scully's voice was dominating the yells. "Stop now! Stop, I say! Stop, now-"

Johnnie, as he struggled to burst through the rank formed by Scully and the Easterner, was crying: "Well, he says I cheated! He says I cheated! I won't allow no man to say I cheated! If he says I cheated, he's a-!"

The cowboy was telling the Swede: "Quit, now! Quit, d'ye hear-" The screams of the Swede never ceased. "He did cheat! I saw him! I saw him-" As for the Easterner, he was importuning in a voice that was not heeded. "Wait a moment, can't you? Oh, wait a moment. What's the good of a fight over a game of cards? Wait a moment-" In this tumult no complete sentences were clear. "Cheat"- "Quit"- "He says"- These fragments pierced the uproar and rang out sharply. It was remarkable that whereas Scully undoubtedly made the most noise, he was the least heard of any of the riotous band.

Then suddenly there was a great cessation. It was as if each man had paused for breath, and although the room was still lighted with the anger of men, it could be seen that there was no danger of immediate conflict, and at once Johnnie, shouldering his ways forward, almost succeeded in confronting the Swede. "What did you say I cheated for? What did you say I cheated for? I don't cheat and I won't let no man say I do!"

The Swede said: "I saw you! I saw you!"

"Well," cried Johnnie, "I'll fight any man what says I cheat!"

"No, you won't," said the cowboy. "Not here."

"Ah, be still, can't you?" said Scully, coming between them.

The quiet was sufficient to allow the Easterner's voice to be heard. He was repeating: "Oh, wait a moment, can't you? What's the good of a fight over a game of cards? Wait a moment."

Johnnie, his red face appearing above his father's shoulder, hailed the Swede again. "Did you say I cheated?"

The Swede showed his teeth. "Yes."

"Then," said Johnnie, "we must fight."

"Yes, fight," roared the Swede. He was like a demoniac. "Yes, fight! I'll show you what kind of a man I am! I'll show you who you want to fight! Maybe you think I can't fight! Maybe you think I can't! I'll show you, you skin, you card-sharp! Yes, you cheated! You cheated! You cheated!"

"Well, let's git at it, then, mister," said Johnnie coolly.

The cowboy's brow was beaded with sweat from his efforts in intercepting all sorts of raids. He turned in despair to Scully. "What are you goin' to do now?"

A change had come over the Celtic visage of the old man. He now seemed all eagerness; his eyes glowed.

"We'll let them fight," he answered stalwartly. "I can't put up with it any longer. I've stood this damned Swede till I'm sick. We'll let them fight."

VI

The men prepared to go out of doors. The Easterner was so nervous that he had great difficulty in getting his arms into the sleeves of his new leather-coat. As the cowboy drew his fur-cap down over his ears his hands trembled. In fact, Johnnie and old Scully were the only ones who displayed no agitation. These preliminaries were conducted without words.

Scully threw open the door. "Well, come on," he said. Instantly a terrific wind caused the flame of the lamp to struggle at its wick, while a puff of black smoke sprang from the chimney-top. The stove was in midcurrent of the blast, and its voice swelled to equal the roar of the storm. Some of the scarred and bedabbled cards were caught up from the floor and dashed helplessly against the further wall. The men lowered their heads and plunged into the tempest as into a sea.

No snow was falling, but great whirls and clouds of flakes, swept up from the ground by the frantic winds, were streaming southward with the speed of bullets. The covered land was blue with the sheen of an unearthly satin, and there was no other hue save where at the low black railway station- which seemed incredibly distant- one light gleamed like a tiny jewel. As the men floundered into a thigh-deep drift, it was known that the Swede was bawling out something. Scully went to him, put a hand on his shoulder and projected an ear.

"What's that you say?" he shouted.

"I say," bawled the Swede again, "I won't stand much show against this gang. I know you'll all pitch on me."

Scully smote him reproachfully on the arm. "Tut, man," he yelled. The wind tore the words from Scully's lips and scattered them far a-lee. "You are all a gang of-" boomed the Swede, but the storm also seized the remainder of this sentence. Immediately turning their backs upon the wind, the men had swung around a corner to the sheltered side of the hotel. It was the function of the little house to preserve here, amid this great devastation of snow, an irregular V-shape of heavily-incrusted grass, which crackled beneath the feet. One could imagine the great drifts piled against the windward side. When the party reached the comparative peace of this spot it was found that the Swede was still bellowing.

"Oh, I know what kind of a thing this is! I know you'll all pitch on me. I can't lick you all!"

Scully turned upon him panther-fashion. "You'll not have to whip all of us. You'll have to whip my son Johnnie. An' the man what troubles you durin' that time will have me to dale with."

The arrangements were swiftly made. The two men faced each other, obedient to the harsh commands of Scully, whose face, in the subtly luminous gloom, could be seen set in the austere impersonal lines that are pictured on the countenances of the Roman veterans. The Easterner's teeth were chattering, and he was hopping up and down like a mechanical toy. The cowboy stood rock-like.

The contestants had not stripped off any clothing. Each was in his ordinary attire. Their fists were up, and they eyed each other in a calm that had the elements of leonine cruelty in it.

During this pause, the Easterner's mind, like a film, took lasting impressions of three men- the iron-nerved master of the ceremony; the Swede, pale, motionless, terrible; and Johnnie, serene yet ferocious, brutish yet heroic. The entire prelude had in it a tragedy greater than the tragedy of action, and this aspect was accentuated by the long mellow cry of the blizzard, as it sped the tumbling and wailing flakes into the black abyss of the south.

"Now!" said Scully.

The two combatants leaped forward and crashed together like bullocks. There was heard the cushioned sound of blows, and of a curse squeezing out from between the tight teeth of one.

As for the spectators, the Easterner's pent-up breath exploded from him with a pop of relief, absolute relief from the tension of the preliminaries. The cowboy bounded into the air with a yowl. Scully was immovable as from supreme amazement and fear at the fury of the fight which he himself had permitted and arranged.

For a time the encounter in the darkness was such a perplexity of flying arms that it presented no more detail than would a swiftly-revolving wheel. Occasionally a face, as if illumined by a flash of light, would shine out, ghastly and marked with pink spots. A moment later, the men might have been known as shadows, if it were not for the involuntary utterance of oaths that came from them in whispers.

Suddenly a holocaust of warlike desire caught the cowboy, and he bolted forward with the speed of a broncho. "Go it, Johnnie; go it! Kill him! Kill him!"

Scully confronted him. "Kape back," he said; and by his glance the cowboy could tell that this man was Johnnie's father.

To the Easterner there was a monotony of unchangeable fighting that was an

abomination. This confused mingling was eternal to his sense, which was concentrated in a longing for the end, the priceless end. Once the fighters lurched near him, and as he scrambled
hastily backward, he heard them breathe like men on the rack.

"Kill him, Johnnie! Kill him! Kill him! Kill him!" The cowboy's face was contorted like one of those agony masks in museums.

"Keep still," said Scully icily.

Then there was a sudden loud grunt, incomplete, cut short, and Johnnie's body swung away from the Swede and fell with sickening heaviness to the grass. The cowboy was barely in time to prevent the mad Swede from flinging himself upon his prone adversary. "No, you don't," said the cowboy, interposing an arm. "Wait a second."

Scully was at his son's side. "Johnnie! Johnnie, me boy?" His voice had a quality of melancholy tenderness. "Johnnie? Can you go on with it?" He looked anxiously down into the bloody pulpy face of his son.

There was a moment of silence, and then Johnnie answered in his ordinary voice: "Yes, I- it- yes."

Assisted by his father he struggled to his feet. "Wait a bit now till you git your wind," said the old man.

A few paces away the cowboy was lecturing the Swede. "No, you don't! Wait a second!"

The Easterner was plucking at Scully's sleeve. "Oh, this is enough," he pleaded. "This is enough! Let it go as it stands. This is enough!"

"Bill," said Scully, "git out of the road." The cowboy stepped aside. "Now." The combatants were actuated by a new caution as they advanced toward collision. They glared at each other, and then the Swede aimed a lightning blow that carried with it his entire weight. Johnnie was evidently half-stupid from weakness, but he miraculously dodged, and his fist sent the over-balanced Swede sprawling.

The cowboy, Scully and the Easterner burst into a cheer that was like a chorus of triumphant soldiery, but before its conclusion the Swede had scuffled agilely to his feet and come in berserk abandon at his foe. There was another perplexity of flying arms, and Johnnie's body again swung away and fell, even as a bundle might fall from a roof. The Swede instantly staggered to a little wind-waved tree and leaned upon it, breathing like an engine, while his savage and flame-lit eyes roamed from face to face as the men bent over Johnnie. There was a splendor of isolation in his situation at this time which the Easterner felt once when, lifting his eyes from the man on the ground, he beheld that mysterious and lonely figure, waiting. "Are you any good yet, Johnnie?" asked Scully in a broken voice. The son gasped and opened his eyes languidly. After a moment he answered: "No- I ain't- any good- any- more." Then, from shame and bodily ill, he began to weep, the tears furrowing down through the bloodstains on his face. "He was too- too- too heavy for me." Scully straightened and addressed the waiting figure. "Stranger," he said, evenly, "it's all up with our side." Then his voice changed into that vibrant huskiness which is commonly the tone of the most simple
and deadly announcements. "Johnnie is whipped."

Without replying, the victor moved off on the route to the front door of the hotel.

The cowboy was formulating new and unspellable blasphemies. The Easterner was startled to find that they were out in a wind that seemed to come direct from the shadowed arctic floes. He heard again the wail of the snow as it was flung to its grave in the south. He knew now that all this time the cold had been sinking into him deeper and deeper, and he wondered that he had not perished. He felt indifferent to the condition of the vanquished man.

"Johnnie, can you walk?" asked Scully.

"Did I hurt- hurt him any?" asked the son.

"Can you walk, boy? Can you walk?"

Johnnie's voice was suddenly strong. There was a robust impatience in it. "I asked you whether I hurt him any!"

"Yes, yes, Johnnie," answered the cowboy consolingly; "he's hurt a good deal."

They raised him from the ground, and as soon as he was on his feet he went tottering off, rebuffing all attempts at assistance. When the party rounded the corner they were fairly blinded by the pelting of the snow. It burned their faces like fire. The cowboy carried Johnnie through the drift to the door. As they entered some cards again rose from the floor and beat against the wall.

The Easterner rushed to the stove. He was so profoundly chilled that he almost dared to embrace the glowing iron. The Swede was not in the room. Johnnie sank into a chair, and folding his arms on his knees, buried his face in them. Scully, warming one foot and then the other at the rim of the stove, muttered to himself with Celtic mournfulness. The cowboy had removed his fur-cap, and with a dazed and rueful air he was now running one hand through his tousled locks. From overhead they could hear the creaking of boards, as the Swede tramped here and there in his room. The sad quiet was broken by the sudden flinging open of a door that led toward the kitchen. It was instantly followed by an inrush of women. They precipitated themselves upon Johnnie amid a chorus of lamentation. Before they carried their prey off to the kitchen, there to be bathed and harangued with a mixture of sympathy and abuse which is a feat of their sex, the mother straightened herself and fixed old Scully with an eye of stern reproach. "Shame be upon you, Patrick Scully!" she cried, "Your own son, too. Shame be upon you!"

"There, now! Be quiet, now!" said the old man weakly.

"Shame be upon you, Patrick Scully!" The girls rallying to this slogan, sniffed disdainfully in the direction of those trembling accomplices, the cowboy and the Easterner. Presently they bore Johnnie away, and left the three men to dismal reflection.

VII

"I'd like to fight this here Dutchman myself," said the cowboy, breaking a long silence.

Scully wagged his head sadly. "No, that wouldn't do. It wouldn't be right. It wouldn't be right."

"Well, why wouldn't it?" argued the cowboy. "I don't see no harm in it."

"No," answered Scully with mournful heroism. "It wouldn't be right. It was Johnnie's fight, and now we mustn't whip the man just because he whipped Johnnie."

"Yes, that's true enough," said the cowboy; "but- he better not get fresh with me, because I couldn't stand no more of it."

"You'll not say a word to him," commanded Scully, and even then they heard the tread of the Swede on the stairs. His entrance was made theatric. He swept the door back with a bang and swaggered to the middle of the room. No one looked at him. "Well," he cried, insolently, at Scully, "I s'pose you'll tell me now how much I owe you?"

The old man remained stolid. "You don't owe me nothin'."

"Huh!" said the Swede, "huh! Don't owe 'im nothin'."

The cowboy addressed the Swede. "Stranger, I don't see how you come to be so gay around here."

Old Scully was instantly alert. "Stop!" he shouted, holding his hand forth, fingers upward. "Bill, you shut up!"

The cowboy spat carelessly into the sawdust box. "I didn't say a word, did I?" he asked.

"Mr. Scully," called the Swede, "how much do I owe you?" It was seen that he was attired for departure, and that he had his valise in his hand.

"You don't owe me nothin'," repeated Scully in his same imperturbable way.

"Huh!" said the Swede. "I guess you're right. I guess if it was any way at all, you'd owe me somethin'. That's what I guess." He turned to the cowboy, "'Kill him! Kill him! Kill him!'" he mimicked, and then guffawed victoriously. "'Kill him!'" He was convulsed with ironical humor.

But he might have been jeering the dead. The three men were immovable and silent, staring with glassy eyes at the stove. The Swede opened the door and passed into the storm, giving one derisive glance backward at the still group. As soon as the door was closed, Scully and the cowboy leaped to their feet and began to curse. They trampled to and fro, waving their arms and smashing into the air with their fists. "Oh, but that was a hard minute! Him there leerin' and scoffin'! One bang at his nose was worth forty dollars to me that minute! How did you stand it, Bill?" "How did I stand it?" cried the cowboy in a quivering voice. "How did I stand it? Oh!"

The old man burst into sudden brogue. "I'd loike to take that Swade," he wailed, " and hould 'im down on a shtone flure and bate 'im to a jelly wid a shtick!" The cowboy groaned in sympathy. "I'd like to git him by the neck and ha-ammer him"- he brought his hand down on a chair with a noise like a pistol-shot- "hammer that there Dutchman until he couldn't tell himself from a dead coyote!"

"I'd bate 'im until he-"

"I'd show him some things-"

And then together they raised a yearning fanatic cry. "Oh-o-oh! if we only could-"

"Yes!"

"Yes!"

"And then I'd-" "O-o-oh!"

VIII

The Swede, tightly gripping his valise, tacked across the face of the storm as if he carried sails. He was following a line of little naked gasping trees, which he knew must mark the way of the road. His face, fresh from the pounding of Johnnie's fists, felt more

281

pleasure than pain in the wind and the driving snow. A number of square shapes loomed upon him finally, and he knew them as the houses of the main body of the town. He found a street and made travel along it, leaning heavily upon the wind whenever, at a corner, a terrific blast caught him. He might have been in a deserted village. We picture the world as thick with conquering and elate humanity, but here, with the bugles of the tempest pealing, it was hard to imagine a peopled earth. One viewed the existence of man then as a marvel, and conceded a glamour of wonder to these lice which were caused to cling to a whirling, fire-smote, ice-locked, disease-stricken, space-lost bulb. The conceit of man was explained by this storm to be the very engine of life. One was a coxcomb not to die in it. However, the Swede found a saloon. In front of it an indomitable red light was burning, and the snowflakes were made blood-color as they flew through the circumscribed territory of the lamp's shining. The Swede pushed open the door of the saloon and entered. A sanded expanse was before him, and at the end of it four men sat about a table drinking. Down one side of the room extended a radiant bar, and its guardian was leaning upon his elbows listening to the talk of the men at the table. The Swede dropped his valise upon the floor, and, smiling fraternally upon the barkeeper, said: "Gimme some whisky, will you?" The man placed a bottle, a whisky-glass, and glass of ice-thick water upon the bar. The Swede poured himself an abnormal portion of whisky and drank it in three gulps. "Pretty bad night," remarked the bartender indifferently. He was making the pretension of blindness, which is usually a distinction of his class; but it could have been seen that he was furtively studying the half-erased blood-stains on the face of the Swede. "Bad night," he said again.

"Oh, it's good enough for me," replied the Swede, hardily, as he poured himself some more whisky. The barkeeper took his coin and maneuvered it through its reception by the highly-nickeled cash-machine. A bell rang; a card labeled "20 cts." had appeared.

"No," continued the Swede, "this isn't too bad weather. It's good enough for me."

"So?" murmured the barkeeper languidly.

The copious drams made the Swede's eyes swim, and he breathed a trifle heavier. "Yes, I like this weather. I like it. It suits me." It was apparently his design to impart a deep significance to these words.

"So?" murmured the bartender again. He turned to gaze dreamily at the scroll-like birds and bird-like scrolls which had been drawn with soap upon the mirrors back of the bar.

"Well, I guess I'll take another drink," said the Swede presently. "Have something?"

"No, thanks; I'm not drinkin'," answered the bartender. Afterward he asked: "How did you hurt your face?"

The Swede immediately began to boast loudly. "Why, in a fight. I thumped the soul out of a man down here at Scully's hotel."

The interest of the four men at the table was at last aroused.

"Who was it?" said one.

"Johnnie Scully," blustered the Swede. "Son of the man what runs it. He will be pretty near dead for some weeks, I can tell you. I made a nice thing of him, I did. He couldn't get up. They carried him in the house. Have a drink?"

Instantly the men in some subtle way incased themselves in reserve. "No, thanks," said one. The group was of curious formation. Two were prominent local business men; one was the district-attorney; and one was a professional gambler of the kind known as "square." But a scrutiny of the group would not have enabled an observer to pick the gambler from the men of more reputable pursuits. He was, in fact, a man so delicate in manner, when among people of fair class, and so judicious in his choice of victims, that in the strictly masculine part of the town's life he had come to be explicitly trusted and admired. People called him a thoroughbred. The fear and contempt with which his craft was regarded was undoubtedly the reason that his quiet dignity shone conspicuous above the quiet dignity of men who might be merely hatters, billiard-markers or grocery clerks. Beyond an occasional unwary traveler, who came by rail, this gambler was supposed to prey solely upon reckless and senile farmers, who, when flush with good crops, drove into town in all the pride and confidence of an absolutely invulnerable stupidity. Hearing at times in circuitous fashion of the despoilment of such a farmer, the important men of Romper invariably laughed in contempt of the victim, and if they thought of the wolf at all, it was with a kind of pride at the knowledge that he would never dare think of attacking their wisdom and courage. Besides, it was popular that this gambler had a real wife, and two real children in a neat cottage in a suburb, where he led an exemplary home life, and when any one even suggested a discrepancy in his character, the crowd immediately vociferated descriptions of this virtuous family circle. Then men who led exemplary home lives, and men who did not lead exemplary home lives, all subsided in a bunch, remarking that there was nothing more to be said. However, when a restriction was placed upon him- as, for instance, when a strong clique of members of the new Pollywog Club refused to permit him, even as a spectator, to appear in the rooms of the organization- the candor and gentleness with which he accepted the judgment disarmed many of his foes and made his friends more desperately partisan. He invariably distinguished between himself and a respectable Romper man so quickly and frankly that his manner actually appeared to be a continual broadcast compliment. And one must not forget to declare the fundamental fact of his entire position in Romper. It is irrefutable that in all affairs outside of his business, in all matters that occur eternally and commonly between man and man, this thieving card-player was so generous, so just, so moral, that, in a contest, he could have put to flight the consciences of nine-tenths of the citizens of Romper. And so it happened that he was seated in this saloon with the two prominent local merchants and the district-attorney.

The Swede continued to drink raw whisky, meanwhile babbling at the barkeeper and trying to induce him to indulge in potations. "Come on. Have a drink. Come on. What- no? Well, have a little one then. By gawd, I've whipped a man to-night, and I want to celebrate. I whipped him good, too. Gentlemen," the Swede cried to the men at the table, "have a drink?"

"Ssh!" said the barkeeper.

The group at the table, although furtively attentive, had been pretending to be deep in talk, but now a man lifted his eyes toward the Swede and said shortly: "Thanks. We don't want any more." At this reply the Swede ruffled out his chest like a rooster. "Well," he exploded, "it seems I can't get anybody to drink with me in this town. Seems so, don't it?

Well!" "Ssh!" said the barkeeper. "Say," snarled the Swede, "don't you try to shut me up. I won't have it. I'm a gentleman, and I want people to drink with me. And I want 'em to drink with me now. Now- do you understand?" He rapped the bar with his knuckles.

Years of experience had calloused the bartender. He merely grew sulky. "I hear you," he answered. "Well," cried the Swede, "listen hard then. See those men over there? Well, they're going to drink with me, and don't you forget it. Now you watch." "Hi!" yelled the barkeeper, "this won't do!" "Why won't it?" demanded the Swede. He stalked over to the table, and by chance laid his hand upon the shoulder of the gambler. "How about this?" he asked, wrathfully. "I asked you to drink with me." The gambler simply twisted his head and spoke over his shoulder. "My friend, I don't know you."

"Oh, hell!" answered the Swede, "come and have a drink."

"Now, my boy," advised the gambler kindly, "take your hand off my shoulder and go 'way and mind your own business." He was a little slim man, and it seemed strange to hear him use this tone of heroic patronage to the burly Swede. The other men at the table said nothing. "What? You won't drink with me, you little dude! I'll make you then! I'll make you!" The Swede had grasped the gambler frenziedly at the throat, and was dragging him from his chair. The other men sprang up. The barkeeper dashed around the corner of his bar. There was a great tumult, and then was seen a long blade in the hand of the gambler. It shot forward, and a human body, this citadel of virtue, wisdom, power, was pierced as easily as if it had been a melon. The Swede fell with a cry of supreme astonishment. The prominent merchants and the district-attorney must have at once tumbled out of the place backward. The bartender found himself hanging limply to the arm of a chair and gazing into the eyes of a murderer. "Henry," said the latter, as he wiped his knife on one of the towels that hung beneath the bar-rail, "you tell 'em where to find me. I'll be home, waiting for 'em." Then he vanished. A moment afterward the barkeeper was in the street dinning through the storm for help, and, moreover, companionship.

The corpse of the Swede, alone in the saloon, had its eyes fixed upon a dreadful legend that dwelt a-top of the cash-machine. "This registers the amount of your purchase."

IX

Months later, the cowboy was frying pork over the stove of a little ranch near the Dakota line, when there was a quick thud of hoofs outside, and, presently, the Easterner entered with the letters and the papers. "Well," said the Easterner at once, "the chap that killed the Swede has got three years. Wasn't much, was it?" "He has? Three years?" The cowboy poised his pan of pork, while he ruminated upon the news. "Three years. That ain't much." "No. It was a light sentence," replied the Easterner as he unbuckled his spurs. "Seems there was a good deal of sympathy for him in Romper."

"If the bartender had been any good," observed the cowboy thoughtfully, "he would have gone in and cracked that there Dutchman on the head with a bottle in the beginnin' of it and stopped all this here murderin'."

"Yes, a thousand things might have happened," said the Easterner tartly.

The cowboy returned his pan of pork to the fire, but his philosophy continued. "It's funny, ain't it? If he hadn't said Johnnie was cheatin' he'd be alive this minute. He was an awful fool. Game played for fun, too. Not for money. I believe he was crazy."

"I feel sorry for that gambler," said the Easterner.

"Oh, so do I," said the cowboy. "He don't deserve none of it for killin' who he did."

"The Swede might not have been killed if everything had been square."

"Might not have been killed?" exclaimed the cowboy. "Everythin' square? Why, when he said that Johnnie was cheatin' and acted like such a jackass? And then in the saloon he fairly walked up to git hurt?" With these arguments the cowboy browbeat the Easterner and reduced him to rage. "You're a fool!" cried the Easterner viciously. "You're a bigger jackass than the Swede by a million majority. Now let me tell you one thing. Let me tell you something. Listen! Johnnie was cheating!" "'Johnnie,'" said the cowboy blankly. There was a minute of silence, and then he said robustly: "Why, no. The game was only for fun."

> The Romantic is killed by the cold Realist. Notice the way irony is used in this story.

"Fun or not," said the Easterner, "Johnnie was cheating. I saw him. I know it. I saw him. And I refused to stand up and be a man. I let the Swede fight it out alone. And you- you were simply puffing around the place and wanting to fight. And then old Scully himself! We are all in it! This poor gambler isn't even a noun. He is kind of an adverb. Every sin is the result of a collaboration. We, five of us, have collaborated in the murder of this Swede. Usually there are from a dozen to forty women really involved in every murder, but in this case it seems to be only five men- you, I, Johnnie, old Scully, and that fool of an unfortunate gambler came merely as a culmination, the apex of a human movement, and gets all the punishment."

The cowboy, injured and rebellious, cried out blindly into this fog of mysterious theory. "Well, I didn't do anythin', did I?"

Supplemental Resources:

Lars Ahnebrink, *The Beginnings of Naturalism in American fiction*
    I haven't read this yet but it appears to be an excellent resource.

Maurice Bassan, *Stephen Crane: A Collection of Critical Essays*
    Somewhat pedantic, but insightful essays on Crane's major works.

Stephen Crane, *Great Short Works of Stephen Crane: Red Badge of Courage, Monster, Maggie, Open Boat, Blue Hotel, Bride Comes to Yellow Sky and Other Works*

An excellent, unedited version of Crane's works.

Joseph Katz (Editor), *The Complete Poems of Stephen Crane*
While Crane is a less accomplished poet, his works are worth examining.

The Red Badge of Courage (1951) movie
This epic version of Crane's novel, starring Audie Murphy, is a fairly accurate version of the book.

Notes:

Lesson Nineteen Test

Essay (100 Points)

While participating in an American literature community college course discussion, you courageously mentioned that *The Red Badge of Courage* is not about the Civil War. The instructor, and his students are shocked. To reward you for your insightful comments, the instructors asks you to write a 150 word essay defending your argument. In the space below, and on the back of this paper, argue that *The Red Badge of Courage* is really not about the Civil War.

Lesson Nineteen Test Answers

Essay (100 Points)

While participating in an American literature community college course discussion, you courageously mentioned that *The Red Badge of Courage* is not about the Civil War. The instructor, and his students are shocked. To reward you for your insightful comments, the instructors asks you to write a 150 word essay defending your argument. In the space below, and on the back of this paper, argue that *The Red Badge of Courage* is really not about the Civil War. *First Crane was not old enough to participate in the American Civil War; however, he was a correspondence in Cuba during the Spanish American War. Secondly, Henry Fleming is too "modern" to be a real Civil War hero. His speculation about the cosmos, about God and His sovereignty, imply a world view far beyond 1865. Red Badge exhibits a world view–Naturalism–that belongs in the late 19th century.*

LESSON TWENTY

Readings Due For This Lesson

Students should have read *Ethan Frome*, Edith Wharton.

Reading Ahead

Read selections from 20th century poetry (Lesson Twenty-Three).

Suggested Weekly Implementation

Day One	Day Two	Day Three	Day Four	Day Five
1. Students will rewrite graded essays from last week and review Lesson Nineteen test. 2. Students should have read the required reading(s) *before* the assigned lesson begins. 3. Teacher may want to discuss assigned reading(s) with student. 4. Teacher shall assign the required essays. Choose two or three. The rest of the essays can be outlined, answered with shorter answers, or skipped.	1. Student should begin reading(s) from next lesson. 2. Student should outline essays due at the end of the week. 3. Students should answer one or two of the essays that are not assigned as formal essays.	1. Students should write rough drafts of assigned essays. 2. The teacher should correct rough drafts.	Student will write final copy of essays due tomorrow.	1. Essays are due. 2. Students should take Lesson Twenty test. 3. Read selections from 20th century poetry (Lesson Twenty-Three)

Ethan Frome
By Edith Wharton
(Published in 1911)

Book Checkup

___d___ 1.

___c___ 2.

___a___ 3.

___b___ 4.

___b___ 5.

Vocabulary Words

        taciturnity *(reserved)*
        exanimate *(lifeless)*
        sardonically *(mockingly)*
        oblique *(indirect)*
        scintillating *(sparkling)*
        querulous *(fretful)*
        languidly *(listlessly)*
        ominous *(threatening)*

Supplementary Readings:

Millicent Bell, ed. *The Cambridge Companion to Edith Wharton*
    Bell offers a wonderful, insightful companion to the Wharton corpus.

Harold Bloom, ed. *Edith Wharton: New Essays in Criticism*
    Bloom is one of the best literary critics of the 20th century.

Ethan Frome (VHS)
    A very fine, true to the book video. However, ask your parents before you rent it (I do not know how it is rated but I saw it and did not find anything objectionable).

Richard Hofstadter, *Social Darwinisn in American Thought*

Hofstadter is a brilliant Revisionist historian who presents an accurate picture of social Darwinism (a world view popular among Naturalists).

Paul Johnson, *Modern Times*
This is a very helpful history of the time period in which Wharton lived. A sample is found on page 48, "Among the advanced races, the decline and ultimately the collapse of the religious impulse would leave a huge vacuum. The history of modern times is in great part the history of how that vacuum is filled. Nietzsche (whom Davis calls post-modern) rightly perceived that the most likely candidate would be what he called the 'Will to Power,' which offered a far more comprehensive and in the end more plausible explanation of human behavior than either Marx or Freud. In place of religious belief, there would be secular ideology. Those who once filled the ranks of the totalitarian clergy would become totalitarian politicians. And, above all, the Will to Power would produce a new kind of messiah, uninhibited by any religious sanctions whatever, and with an unappeasable appetite for controlling mankind. The end of the old order, with an unguided world adrift in a relativistic universe, was a summons to such gangster-statesmen to emerge. They were not slow to make their appearance."

David O. Moberg. *The Great Reversal: Evangelism and Social Concern*
Moberg offers a foil to Naturalist criticisms of Evangelical Christianity (see Stephen Crane, *Maggie*). He says "The question of how to deal with poverty and the numerous other interrelated problems of our day has divided Christians into two camps One of them builds a strong case for evangelism as the basic solution, while the other emphasizes direct social involvement. Each accuses the other of being untrue to the essential nature of Christianity." (p. 13)

Alan Price, *.he End of the Age of Innocence: Edith Wharton and the First World War*
Price places Wharton and her writings in her time period.

George Gaylord Simpson, *The Meaning of Evolution*
Simpson elucidates the dangers of evolution (a bedrock tenant of Naturalism). He states "Man is the result of a purposeless and materialistic process that did not have him in mind. He was snot planned ... Discovery that the universe . . . Lacked any purpose or plan has the inevitable corollary that the workings of the universe cannot provide any automatic, universal, eternal, or absolute criteria of Right and wrong.."

Notes:

Lesson Twenty Test

Discussion Questions: (100 Points)

A. The nameless narrator only appears in the prologue and in the epilogue of the novel. Some critics argue that he is a young engineer with time to kill in Starkfield. With the instinct of a scientist, he investigates Ethan, and with the skill of an experienced writer he tells Ethan's story. Why does Wharton choose this particular narrator and why doesn't she have him be a part of the story?

B. It is interesting that the scientist or engineer is scorned by Hawthorne (e.g., Chillingsworth and Alymer) but extolled by Wharton. Why?

C. What are two possible themes of *Ethan Frome*?

D. How does Wharton use the setting to advance her themes?

E. Why, in Wharton's world, are Ethan and Maggie doomed?

F. What role does Mrs. Andrew Hale play in this novel?

G. The use of darkness and light is an important motif for Romantic writers. Likewise, Wharton uses darkness and light to make a point. The contrast between the brilliant light inside the church and the darkness outside is drawn vividly. She does it several other times too. Why? What is her point?

H. Several of the novels we have read this year have characters who are isolated. Hester Prynne is isolated from her community; Huck Finn is isolated and living alone; Henry Fleming is isolated and alone when he flees from the battlefield; now Ethan is isolated from all others by his shyness and social inadequacies. Yet, there is a considerable difference between Hester's isolation and all the rest. Why?

I. Mattie has virtually no personality at all. She is critical to the plot but remains completely undeveloped. Why?

J. Because Edith Wharton came from high society some scholars doubted that Wharton had the insight to write about ordinary country people. On scholar wrote that *Ethan Frome* "was not a New England story and certainly not the granite "folk tale" of New England its admirers have claimed it to be. (Mrs. Wharton) knew little of the New England common world and perhaps cared even less. The world of the Frome tragedy is abstract. She never knew how the poor lived in Paris or London; she knew even less of how they lived in the New England villages where she spent an occasional summer." Agree or disagree with this critic and defend your answer.

Lesson Twenty Test Answers

Discussion Questions: (100 Points)

A. The nameless narrator only appears in the prologue and in the epilogue of the novel. Some critics argue that he is a young engineer with time to kill in Starkfield. With the instinct of a scientist, he investigates Ethan, and with the skill of an experienced writer he tells Ethan's story. Why does Wharton choose this particular narrator and why doesn't she have him be a part of the story? *The Naturalistic Wharton values a neutral, uninterested, uninvolved narrator. Contrast this with the narrator in Poe's short story "The Fall of the House of Usher." He likewise is a reliable narrator but he is not an engineer..*

B. It is interesting that the scientist or engineer is scorned by Hawthorne (e.g., Chillingsworth and Alymer) but extolled by Wharton. Why? *Continuing the previous discussion, Chillingsworth and Alymer would be useful to the empiricist/Naturalist Wharton. Romanticist Hawthorne prefers the poet (see "Old Stone Face") to the scientist.*

C. What are two possible themes of *Ethan Frome*? *Alienation and loneliness or moribundity (i.e., death).*

D. How does Wharton use the setting to advance her themes? *When Ethan is gloomy the weather is gloomy; when he is happy there is sunshine. The harsh New England winters suit Wharton just fine.*

E. Why, in Wharton's world, are Ethan and Maggie doomed? *They harbor Romantic hopes in a Naturalistic world. They actually think that they can be happy! Just as Henry Fleming must lose his Romantic world view in Red Badge or be killed, likewise Ethan and Maggie need to discord morality and do the "Naturalistic thing"–which presumably is to do what is right in their own eyes.*

F. What role does Mrs. Andrew Hale play in this novel? *She is Ethan's conscience–he can't possibly pressure or cheat Mr. Hale when Mrs. Hale is obviously so fine a woman. This forces Ethan to stay the course with his moral position.*

G. The use of darkness and light is an important motif for Romantic writers. Likewise, Wharton uses darkness and light to make a point. The contrast between the brilliant light inside the church and the darkness outside is drawn vividly. She does it several other times too. Why? What is her point? *To Hawthorne, darkness is evil and light is openness and goodness. To Wharton dark ness is ignorance and secrecy–both anathema to the empiricist/Naturalist. Likewise, to Wharton, light implies beauty and to her false hope. Maggie, for instance, lights up Ethan's face.*

H. Several of the novels we have read this year have characters who are isolated. Hester Prynne is isolated from her community; Huck Finn is isolated and living alone; Henry Fleming is isolated and alone when he flees from the battlefield; now Ethan is isolated from all others by his shyness and social inadequacies. Yet, there is a considerable difference between Hester's isolation and all the rest. Why? *Within her isolated repentance Hester finds new life and hope. Ethan's isolation ultimately leads to disaster.*

I. Mattie has virtually no personality at all. She is critical to the plot but remains completely undeveloped. Why? *Her only purpose is to develop Ethan and to help Wharton make a Naturalistic statement about the cosmos.*

J. Because Edith Wharton came from high society some scholars doubted that Wharton had the insight to write about ordinary country people. On scholar wrote that *Ethan Frome* "was not a New England story and certainly not the granite "folk tale" of New England its admirers have claimed it to be. (Mrs. Wharton) knew little of the New England common world and perhaps cared even less. The world of the Frome tragedy is abstract. She never knew how the poor lived in Paris or London; she knew even less of how they lived in the NewEngland villages where she spent an occasional summer." Agree or disagree with this critic and defend your answer. *Wharton's novel is far more than a social statement about New England–it is a statement about the cosmos–it advances the Naturalist world view.*

LESSON TWENTY-ONE

Readings Due For This Lesson
Students should have read *Ethan Frome*, Edith Wharton.

Reading Ahead

Read selections from 20th century poetry (Lesson Twenty-Three).

Suggested Weekly Implementation

Day One	Day Two	Day Three	Day Four	Day Five
1. Students will rewrite graded essays from last week and review Lesson Twenty test. 2. Students should have read the required reading(s) *before* the assigned lesson begins. 3. Teacher may want to discuss assigned reading(s) with student. 4. Teacher shall assign the required essays. Choose two or three. The rest of the essays can be outlined, answered with shorter answers, or skipped.	1. Student should begin reading(s) from next lesson. 2. Student should outline essays due at the end of the week. 3. Students should answer one or two of the essays that are not assigned as formal essays.	1. Students should write rough drafts of assigned essays. 2. The teacher should correct rough drafts.	Student will write final copy of essays due tomorrow.	1. Essays are due. 2. Students should take Lesson Twenty-One test. 3. Read selections from 20th century poetry (Lesson Twenty-Three)

Wharton. . .

Biblical Application

At the end of the novel we observe three people captured by unforgivingness. They are, in effect, in a "living hell." What does the Bible say about unforgivingness? *If we do not forgive others, God will not forgive us.* How can you forgive someone who has grievously wronged you? *By purposing to do so and asking God to help you.*

Literary Criticism

A. The man telling the story is never real. Why? *Wharton does not want us to be distracted. The story is not about an outsider/visitor.*

B. Time and time again the reader is invited to interpret the story through Ethan's eyes... *We begin to see things from Ethan's perspective. This builds empathy between the reader and Ethan. Most readers willingly identify with Ethan. He is trapped.. Ethan is a likeable person and one is tempted to see him as a victim. But to do so would buy into a morality structure that presumes that adultery is acceptable under certain conditions. Of course Ethan never committed adultery and the reader is sorry that Ethan and Mattie were injured, but at the same time we Christians must be careful not to condone his actions.*

C. The life span of a story--or the number of years that it will be read--is determined to a large degree by its deeper meaning, or *theme...Love, human effort, even hard work ultimately fail in the face of fate. That is Wharton's theme–but it is not true. God is in control and gives meaning to life.*

D. This tragic book is marked by *irony...Ethan, who was so afraid of silence, is now in silence all the time. Zeena, once the weakest, is ironically called to be the strongest member of the family.* What other instances of irony do you find in Mrs. Hale's conversation? *The fading New England woman is an unlikely interpreter of the Ethan Frome narrative to her visitor.*

Critical Thinking

B. Find examples of *imagery* in this book. *There are many examples. The village lay under two feet of snow, with drifts at the windy corners. In a sky of iron the points of the Dipper hung like icicles and Orion flashed his cold fires. The moon had set, but the night was so transparent that the white house-fronts between the elms looked gray against the snow, clumps of bushes made black stains on it, and the basement windows of the church sent shafts of yellow light far across the endless undulations. (Ch. 1)*

C. How does the narrator draw the reader into this story? *We are given information in small increments as we are drawn into the tragedy.*

D. How is interest increased by the conversation between Mattie and Denis Eady? *Ethan is jealous–an uncharacteristic personality trait. The reader observes that Ethan is more complicated than he first appeared.*

E. Retell the story from Zeena's perspective. Do the same thing with Mattie. *Zeena would be less generous with Mattie and Ethan. I think Zeena is the real victim of this story. She is the victim of bad choices by other people. Ethan and Mattie, too, are victims in a way. Poor Mattie. They made the mistake of being idealistic in a Naturalistic novel.*

Supplementary Readings:

Millicent Bell, ed. *The Cambridge Companion to Edith Wharton*
　　Bell offers a wonderful, insightful companion to the Wharton corpus.

Harold Bloom, ed. *Edith Wharton: New Essays in Criticism*
　　Bloom is one of the best literary critics of the 20th century.

Ethan Frome (VHS)
　　A very fine, true to the book video. However, ask your parents before you rent it (I do not know how it is rated but I saw it and did not find anything objectionable).

Richard Hofstadter, *Social Darwinisn in American Thought*
　　Hofstadter is a brilliant Revisionist historian who presents an accurate picture of social Darwinism (a world view popular among Naturalists).

Paul Johnson, *Modern Times*
　　This is a very helpful history of the time period in which Wharton lived. A sample is found on page 48, "Among the advanced races, the decline and ultimately the collapse of the religious impulse would leave a huge vacuum. The history of modern times is in great part the history of how that vacuum is filled. Nietzsche (whom Davis calls post-modern) rightly perceived that the most likely candidate would be what he called the 'Will to Power,' which offered a far more comprehensive and in the end more plausible explanation of human behavior than either Marx or Freud. In place of religious belief, there would be secular ideology. Those who once filled the ranks of the totalitarian clergy would become totalitarian politicians. And, above all, the Will to Power would

produce a new kind of messiah, uninhibited by any religious sanctions whatever, and with an unappeasable appetite for controlling mankind. The end of the old order, with an unguided world adrift in a relativistic universe, was a summons to such gangster-statesmen to emerge. They were not slow to make their appearance."

David O. Moberg. *The Great Reversal: Evangelism and Social Concern*
    Moberg offers a foil to Naturalist criticisms of Evangelical Christianity (see Stephen Crane, *Maggie*). He says "The question of how to deal with poverty and the numerous other interrelated problems of our day has divided Christians into two camps One of them builds a strong case for evangelism as the basic solution, while the other emphasizes direct social involvement. Each accuses the other of being untrue to the essential nature of Christianity." (p. 13)

Alan Price, *.he End of the Age of Innocence: Edith Wharton and the First World War*
    Price places Wharton and her writings in her time period.

George Gaylord Simpson, *The Meaning of Evolution*
    Simpson elucidates the dangers of evolution (a bedrock tenant of Naturalism). He states "Man is the result of a purposeless and materialistic process that did not have him in mind. He was snot planned ... Discovery that the universe . . . Lacked any purpose or plan has the inevitable corollary that the workings of the universe cannot provide any automatic, universal, eternal, or absolute criteria of Right and wrong.."

Notes:

Lesson Twenty-One Test

Identification: (100 Points)

Identify the author of the following passages and explain why you made your choice. Choose from Ralph Waldo Emerson, Nathaniel Hawthorne, William Bradford, Mark Twain, Stephen Crane, Edgar Allan Poe, and Edith Wharton.

A. It was many and many a year ago,
In a kingdom by the sea,
That a maiden there lived whom you may know
By the name of Annabel Lee;
And this maiden she lived with no other thought
Than to love and be loved by me.

I was a child and she was a child,
In this kingdom by the sea;
But we loved with a love that was more than love-
I and my Annabel Lee;
With a love that the winged seraphs of heaven
Coveted her and me.

B. There is a time in every man's education when he arrives at the conviction that envy is ignorance; that imitation is suicide; that he must take himself for better, for worse, as his portion; that though the wide universe is full of good, no kernel of nourishing corn can come to him but through his toil bestowed on that plot of ground which is given to him to till. The power which resides in him is new in nature, and none but he knows what that is which he can do, nor does he know until he has tried. Not for nothing one face, one character, one fact, makes much impression on him, and another none. This sculpture in the memory is not without preestablished harmony. The eye was placed where one ray should fall, that it might testify of that particular ray. We but half express ourselves, and are ashamed of that divine idea which each of us represents. It may be safely trusted as proportionate and of good issues, so it be faithfully imparted, but God will not have his work made manifest by cowards. A man is relieved and gay when he has put his heart into his work and done his best; but what he has said or done otherwise, shall give him no peace. It is a deliverance which does not deliver. In the attempt his genius deserts him; no muse befriends; no invention, no hope.

C. Being thus arrived in a good harbor and brought safe to land, they fell upon their knees and blessed the God of heaven, who had brought them over the vast and furious ocean, and delivered them from all the perils and miseries thereof, again to set their feet on the firm and stable earth, their proper element. And no marvel if they were thus joyful, seeing wise Seneca was so affected with sailing a few miles on the coast of his own Italy;

299

as he affirmed, that he had rather remain twenty years on his way by land, then pass by sea to any place in a short time; so tedious and dreadful was the same unto him..

D. No expense had been spared on the setting, which was acknowledged to be very beautiful even by people who shared his acquaintance with the Opera houses of Paris and Vienna. The foreground, to the footlights, was covered with emerald green cloth. In the middle distance symmetrical mounds of woolly green moss bounded by croquet hoops formed the base of shrubs shaped like orange-trees but studded with large pink and red roses. Gigantic pansies, considerably larger than the roses, and closely resembling the floral pen-wipers made by female parishioners for fashionable clergymen, sprang from the moss beneath the rose-trees; and here and there a daisy grafted on a rose-branch flowered with a luxuriance prophetic of Mr. Luther Burbank's far-off prodigies. In the centre of this enchanted garden Madame Nilsson, in white cashmere slashed with pale blue satin, a reticule dangling from a blue girdle, and large yellow braids carefully disposed on each side of her muslin chemisette, listened with downcast eyes to M. Capoul's impassioned wooing, and affected a guileless incomprehension of his designs whenever, by word or glance, he persuasively indicated the ground floor window of the neat brick villa projecting obliquely from the right wing.

E. For the most wild, yet most homely narrative which I am about to pen, I neither expect nor solicit belief. Mad indeed would I be to expect it, in a case where my very senses reject their own evidence. Yet, mad am I not ——and very surely do I not dream. But to-morrow I die, and to-day I would unburthen my soul. My immediate purpose is to place before the world, plainly, succinctly, and without comment, a series of mere household events. In their consequences, these events have terrified ——have tortured ——have destroyed me. Yet I will not attempt to expound them. To me, they have presented little but Horror ——to many they will seem less terrible than *barroques*. Hereafter, perhaps, some intellect may be found which will reduce my phantasm to the common-place ——some intellect more calm, more logical, and far less excitable than my own, which will perceive, in the circumstances I detail with awe, nothing more than an ordinary succession of very natural causes and effects.

F. The House of the Seven Gables, antique as it now looks, was not the first habitation erected by civilized man on precisely the same spot of ground. Pyncheon-street formerly bore the humbler appellation of Maule's-lane, from the name of the original occupant of the soil, before whose cottage-door it was a cow-path. A natural spring of soft and pleasant water -- a rare treasure on the sea-girt peninsula, where the Puritan settlement was made -- had early induced Matthew Maule to build a hut, shaggy with thatch, at this point, although somewhat too remote from what was then the centre of the village. In the growth of the town, however, after some thirty or forty years, the site covered by this rude hovel had become exceedingly desirable in the eyes of a prominent and powerful personage, who asserted plausible claims to the proprietorship of this, and a large adjacent tract of land, on the strength of a grant from the legislature. Colonel Pyncheon, the claimant, as we gather from whatever traits of him are preserved, was characterized by an iron energy of purpose. Matthew Maule, on the other hand, though an obscure man, was stubborn in the defence of what he considered his right; and, for several years, he succeeded in protecting the acre or two of earth, which, with his own toil, he had hewn out of the primeval forest, to be his garden-ground and homestead.

G. There was a feller here once by the name of *Jim* Smiley, in the winter of '49 -- or maybe it was the spring of '50 -- I don't recollect exactly, somehow, though what makes me think it was one or the other is because I remember the big flume wasn't finished when he first came to the camp; but any way, he was the curiosest man about always betting on any thing that turned up you ever see, if he could get any body to bet on the other side, and if he couldn't he'd change sides -- any way that suited the other man would suit *him* -- any way just so's he got a bet, *he* was satisfied. But still, he was lucky -- uncommon lucky; he most always come out winner. He was always ready and laying for a chance; there couldn't be no solitry thing mentioned but that feller'd offer to bet on it -- and take any side you please, as I was just telling you. If there was a horse-race, you'd find him flush, or you'd find him busted at the end of it; if there was a dog-fight, he'd bet on it; if there was a cat-fight, he'd bet on it; if there was a chicken-fight, he'd bet on it; why, if there was two birds setting on a fence, he would bet you which one would fly first -- or if there was a camp-meeting, he would be there reglar, to bet on Parson Walker, which he judged to be the best exhorter about here, and so he was, too, and a good man. If he even seen a straddle-bug start to go any wheres, he would bet you how long it would take him to get wherever he was going to, and if you took him up, he would foller that straddle-bug to Mexico but what he would find out where he was bound for and how long he was on the road. Lots of the boys here has seen that Smiley, and can tell you about him. Why, it never made no difference to *him* -- he would bet on *anything* -- the dangdest feller. Parson Walker's wife laid very sick, once, for a good while, and it seemed as if they warn't going to save her; but one morning he come in, and Smiley asked him how she was, and he said she was considerable better -- thank the Lord for his inf'nit mercy -- and coming on so smart that, with the blessing of Providence, she'd get well yet -- and Smiley, before he thought, says, "Well, I'll resk two-and-a-half that she don't, anyway."

H. During the afternoon of the storm, the whirling snows acted as drivers, as men with whips, and at half-past three, the walk before the closed doors of the house was covered with wanderers of the street, waiting. For some distance on either side of the place they could be seen lurking in doorways and behind projecting parts of buildings, gathering in close bunches in an effort to get warm. A covered wagon drawn up near the curb sheltered a dozen of them. Under the stairs that led to the elevated railway station, there were six or eight, their hands stuffed deep in their pockets, their shoulders stooped, jiggling their feet. Others always could be seen coming, a strange procession, some slouching along with the characteristic hopeless gait of professional strays, some coming with hesitating steps wearing the air of men to whom this sort of thing was new. It was an afternoon of incredible length. The snow, blowing in twisting clouds, sought out the men in their meagre hiding-places and skilfully beat in among them, drenching their persons with showers of fine, stinging flakes. They crowded together, muttering, and fumbling in their pockets to get their red, inflamed wrists covered by the cloth.

I. The cause of so much amazement may appear sufficiently slight. Mr. Hooper, a gentlemanly person, of about thirty, though still a bachelor, was dressed with due clerical neatness, as if a careful wife had starched his band, and brushed the weekly dust from his Sunday's garb. There was but one thing remarkable in his appearance. Swathed about his forehead, and hanging down over his face, so low as to be shaken by his breath, Mr. Hooper had on a black veil. On a nearer view it seemed to consist of two folds of crape, which entirely concealed his features, except the mouth and chin, but probably did not intercept his sight, further than to give a darkened aspect to all living and inanimate things. With this gloomy shade before him, good Mr. Hooper walked onward, at a slow and quiet pace, stooping somewhat, and looking on the ground, as is customary with abstracted men, yet nodding kindly to those of his parishioners who still waited on the meeting-house steps. But so wonder-struck were they that his greeting hardly met with a return.

J. His aunt Polly stood surprised a moment, and then broke into a gentle laugh.
"Hang the boy, can't I never learn anything? Ain't he played me tricks enough like that for me to be looking out for him by this time? But old fools is the biggest fools there is. Can't learn an old dog new tricks, as the saying is. But my goodness, he never plays them alike, two days, and how is a body to know what's coming? He 'pears to know just how long he can torment me before I get my dander up, and he knows if he can make out to put me off for a minute or make me laugh, it's all down again and I can't hit him a lick. I ain't doing my duty by that boy, and that's the Lord's truth, goodness knows. Spare the rod and spile the child, as the Good Book says. I'm a laying up sin and suffering for us both, *I* know. He's full of the Old Scratch, but laws-a-me! he's my own dead sister's boy, poor thing, and I ain't got the heart to lash him, somehow. Every time I let him off, my conscience does hurt me so, and every time I hit him my old heart most breaks. Well-a-well, man that is born of woman is of few days and full of trouble, as the Scripture says, and I reckon it's so. He'll play hookey this evening, and I'll just be obleeged to make him work, to-morrow, to punish him. It's mighty hard to make him work Saturdays, when all the boys is having holiday, but he hates work more than he hates anything else, and I've *got* to do some of my duty by him, or I'll be the ruination of the child."

Lesson Twenty-One Test Answers

Identification: (100 Points)

Identify the author of the following passages and explain why you made your choice. Choose from Ralph Waldo Emerson, Nathaniel Hawthorne, William Bradford, Mark Twain, Stephen Crane, Edgar Allan Poe, and Edith Wharton.

A. It was many and many a year ago,
In a kingdom by the sea,
That a maiden there lived whom you may know
By the name of Annabel Lee;
And this maiden she lived with no other thought
Than to love and be loved by me.

I was a child and she was a child,
In this kingdom by the sea;
But we loved with a love that was more than love-
I and my Annabel Lee;
With a love that the winged seraphs of heaven
Coveted her and me.

"Anabel Lee" by E. A. Poe. Notice the rime and style of this poem and the Romantic images (i.e., immutability and death).

B. There is a time in every man's education when he arrives at the conviction that envy is ignorance; that imitation is suicide; that he must take himself for better, for worse, as his portion; that though the wide universe is full of good, no kernel of nourishing corn can come to him but through his toil bestowed on that plot of ground which is given to him to till. The power which resides in him is new in nature, and none but he knows what that is which he can do, nor does he know until he has tried. Not for nothing one face, one character, one fact, makes much impression on him, and another none. This sculpture in the memory is not without preestablished harmony. The eye was placed where one ray should fall, that it might testify of that particular ray. We but half express ourselves, and are ashamed of that divine idea which each of us represents. It may be safely trusted as proportionate and of good issues, so it be faithfully imparted, but God will not have his work made manifest by cowards. A man is relieved and gay when he has put his heart into his work and done his best; but what he has said or done otherwise, shall give him no peace. It is a deliverance which does not deliver. In the attempt his genius deserts him; no muse befriends; no invention, no hope. *In "Self-Reliance" Ralph Waldo Emerson invites the reader to a subjective understanding of reality in line with Transcendentalism.*

C. Being thus arrived in a good harbor and brought safe to land, they fell upon their knees and blessed the God of heaven, who had brought them over the vast and furious ocean, and delivered them from all the perils and miseries thereof, again to set their feet on the firm and stable earth, their proper element. And no marvel if they were thus joyful, seeing wise Seneca was so affected with sailing a few miles on the coast of his own Italy; as he affirmed, that he had rather remain twenty years on his way by land, then pass by sea to any place in a short time; so tedious and dreadful was the same unto him.
In Of Plimoth Plantation, William Bradford speaks as a Christian Theist.

D. No expense had been spared on the setting, which was acknowledged to be very beautiful even by people who shared his acquaintance with the Opera houses of Paris and Vienna. The foreground, to the footlights, was covered with emerald green cloth. In the middle distance symmetrical mounds of woolly green moss bounded by croquet hoops formed the base of shrubs shaped like orange-trees but studded with large pink and red roses. Gigantic pansies, considerably larger than the roses, and closely resembling the floral pen-wipers made by female parishioners for fashionable clergymen, sprang from the moss beneath the rose-trees; and here and there a daisy grafted on a rose-branch flowered with a luxuriance prophetic of Mr. Luther Burbank's far-off prodigies. In the centre of this enchanted garden Madame Nilsson, in white cashmere slashed with pale blue satin, a reticule dangling from a blue girdle, and large yellow braids carefully disposed on each side of her muslin chemisette, listened with downcast eyes to M. Capoul's impassioned wooing, and affected a guileless incomprehension of his designs whenever, by word or glance, he persuasively indicated the ground floor window of the neat brick villa projecting obliquely from the right wing. *In Age of Innocence, Edith Wharton exhibits her penchant to aristocratic images that exhibit presumption and superficiality.*

E. For the most wild, yet most homely narrative which I am about to pen, I neither expect nor solicit belief. Mad indeed would I be to expect it, in a case where my very senses reject their own evidence. Yet, mad am I not ——and very surely do I not dream. But to-morrow I die, and to-day I would unburthen my soul. My immediate purpose is to place before the world, plainly, succinctly, and without comment, a series of mere household events. In their consequences, these events have terrified ——have tortured ——have destroyed me. Yet I will not attempt to expound them. To me, they have presented little but Horror ——to many they will seem less terrible than *barroques*. Hereafter, perhaps, some intellect may be found which will reduce my phantasm to the common-place ——some intellect more calm, more logical, and far less excitable than my own, which will perceive, in the circumstances I detail with awe, nothing more than an ordinary succession of very natural causes and effects.
Typically "The Black Cat," by E. A. Poe, uses first person narration and images of horror to advance a Romantic agenda.

F. The House of the Seven Gables, antique as it now looks, was not the first habitation erected by civilized man on precisely the same spot of ground. Pyncheon-street formerly bore the humbler appellation of Maule's-lane, from the name of the original occupant of the soil, before whose cottage-door it was a cow-path. A natural spring of soft and pleasant water -- a rare treasure on the sea-girt peninsula, where the Puritan settlement was made -- had early induced Matthew Maule to build a hut, shaggy with thatch, at this point, although somewhat too remote from what was then the centre of the village. In the growth of the town, however, after some thirty or forty years, the site covered by this rude hovel had become exceedingly desirable in the eyes of a prominent and powerful personage, who asserted plausible claims to the proprietorship of this, and a large adjacent tract of land, on the strength of a grant from the legislature. Colonel Pyncheon, the claimant, as we gather from whatever traits of him are preserved, was characterized by an iron energy of purpose. Matthew Maule, on the other hand, though an obscure man, was stubborn in the defence of what he considered his right; and, for several years, he succeeded in protecting the acre or two of earth, which, with his own toil, he had hewn out of the primeval forest, to be his garden-ground and homestead. *In The House of Seven Gables, Nathaniel Hawthorne, continues to explore his Puritan, Christian Theistic past.*

G. There was a feller here once by the name of *Jim* Smiley, in the winter of '49 -- or maybe it was the spring of '50 -- I don't recollect exactly, somehow, though what makes me think it was one or the other is because I remember the big flume wasn't finished when he first came to the camp; but any way, he was the curiosest man about always betting on any thing that turned up you ever see, if he could get any body to bet on the other side, and if he couldn't he'd change sides -- any way that suited the other man would suit *him* -- any way just so's he got a bet, *he* was satisfied. But still, he was lucky -- uncommon lucky; he most always come out winner. He was always ready and laying for a chance; there couldn't be no solitry thing mentioned but that feller'd offer to bet on it -- and take any side you please, as I was just telling you. If there was a horse-race, you'd find him flush, or you'd find him busted at the end of it; if there was a dog-fight, he'd bet on it; if there was a cat-fight, he'd bet on it; if there was a chicken-fight, he'd bet on it; why, if there was two birds setting on a fence, he would bet you which one would fly first -- or if there was a camp-meeting, he would be there reglar, to bet on Parson Walker, which he judged to be the best exhorter about here, and so he was, too, and a good man. If he even seen a straddle-bug start to go any wheres, he would bet you how long it would take him to get wherever he was going to, and if you took him up, he would foller that straddle-bug to Mexico but what he would find out where he was bound for and how long he was on the road. Lots of the boys here has seen that Smiley, and can tell you about him. Why, it never made no difference to *him* -- he would bet on *anything* -- the dangdest feller. Parson Walker's wife laid very sick, once, for a good while, and it seemed as if they warn't going to save her; but one morning he come in, and Smiley asked him how she was, and he said she was considerable better -- thank the Lord for his inf'nit mercy -- and coming on so smart that, with the blessing of Providence, she'd get well yet -- and Smiley, before he thought, says, "Well, I'll resk two-and-a-half that she don't, anyway." *Typically "The Celebrated Jumping Frog of Calaveras County," exhibits Mark Twain's colloquialism and humor.*

H. During the afternoon of the storm, the whirling snows acted as drivers, as men with whips, and at half-past three, the walk before the closed doors of the house was covered with wanderers of the street, waiting. For some distance on either side of the place they could be seen lurking in doorways and behind projecting parts of buildings, gathering in close bunches in an effort to get warm. A covered wagon drawn up near the curb sheltered a dozen of them. Under the stairs that led to the elevated railway station, there were six or eight, their hands stuffed deep in their pockets, their shoulders stooped, jiggling their feet. Others always could be seen coming, a strange procession, some slouching along with the characteristic hopeless gait of professional strays, some coming with hesitating steps wearing the air of men to whom this sort of thing was new. It was an afternoon of incredible length. The snow, blowing in twisting clouds, sought out the men in their meagre hiding-places and skilfully beat in among them, drenching their persons with showers of fine, stinging flakes. They crowded together, muttering, and fumbling in their pockets to get their red, inflamed wrists covered by the cloth. *In "Men in the Storm," Stephen Crane describes nature in malevolent terms.*

I. The cause of so much amazement may appear sufficiently slight. Mr. Hooper, a gentlemanly person, of about thirty, though still a bachelor, was dressed with due clerical neatness, as if a careful wife had starched his band, and brushed the weekly dust from his Sunday's garb. There was but one thing remarkable in his appearance. Swathed about his forehead, and hanging down over his face, so low as to be shaken by his breath, Mr. Hooper had on a black veil. On a nearer view it seemed to consist of two folds of crape, which entirely concealed his features, except the mouth and chin, but probably did not intercept his sight, further than to give a darkened aspect to all living and inanimate things. With this gloomy shade before him, good Mr. Hooper walked onward, at a slow and quiet pace, stooping somewhat, and looking on the ground, as is customary with abstracted men, yet nodding kindly to those of his parishioners who still waited on the meeting-house steps. But so wonder-struck were they that his greeting hardly met with a return. *"The Minister in the Black Veil," Nathaniel Hawthorne*

J. His aunt Polly stood surprised a moment, and then broke into a gentle laugh.
"Hang the boy, can't I never learn anything? Ain't he played me tricks enough like that for me to be looking out for him by this time? But old fools is the biggest fools there is. Can't learn an old dog new tricks, as the saying is. But my goodness, he never plays them alike, two days, and how is a body to know what's coming? He 'pears to know just how long he can torment me before I get my dander up, and he knows if he can make out to put me off for a minute or make me laugh, it's all down again and I can't hit him a lick. I ain't doing my duty by that boy, and that's the Lord's truth, goodness knows. Spare the rod and spile the child, as the Good Book says. I'm a laying up sin and suffering for us both, *I* know. He's full of the Old Scratch, but laws-a-me! he's my own dead sister's boy, poor thing, and I ain't got the heart to lash him, somehow. Every time I let him off, my conscience does hurt me so, and every time I hit him my old heart most breaks. Well-a-well, man that is born of woman is of few days and full of trouble, as the Scripture says, and I reckon it's so. He'll play hookey this evening, and I'll just be obleeged to make him

work, to-morrow, to punish him. It's mighty hard to make him work Saturdays, when all the boys is having holiday, but he hates work more than he hates anything else, and I've *got* to do some of my duty by him, or I'll be the ruination of the child."
The Adventures of Tom Sawyer, Mark Twain

LESSON TWENTY-TWO

Readings Due For This Lesson

Students should have read *Ethan Frome*, Edith Wharton.

Reading Ahead

Read selections from 20th century poetry (Lesson Twenty-Three).

Suggested Weekly Implementation

Day One	Day Two	Day Three	Day Four	Day Five
1. Students will rewrite graded essays from last week and review Lesson Twenty-One test. 2. Students should have read the required reading(s) *before* the assigned lesson begins. 3. Teacher may want to discuss assigned reading(s) with student. 4. Teacher shall assign the required essays. Choose two or three. The rest of the essays can be outlined, answered with shorter answers, or skipped.	1. Student should begin reading(s) from next lesson. 2. Student should outline essays due at the end of the week. 3. Students should answer one or two of the essays that are not assigned as formal essays.	1. Students should write rough drafts of assigned essays. 2. The teacher should correct rough drafts.	Student will write final copy of essays due tomorrow.	1. Essays are due. 2. Students should take Lesson Twenty-Two test. 3. Read selections from 20th century poetry (Lesson Twenty-Three)

Wharton...

Challenge Question

Producing interest in the plot is called creating *suspense*. How does Wharton create suspense? *She controls the information that is given. Using foreshadowing, the reader wonders what will happen next. We know that Ethan and Mattie are debilitated. It is a skilled writer who tells his/her readers the ending the first chapter in the book!*

For Further Enrichment

A. As an example of the way an author builds suspense, read *A Tale of Two Cities* by Charles Dickens. How does Dickens create suspense? *Dickens gives the reader insights into the plot that characters do not see. Charles Darnay and Sydney Charlton exchange places at the end of the novel.*

Historical Background

In what ways is this novel present a pessimistic view of life? *Fate is in control. There is no loving God present.* In what ways, though, does Wharton retain some moral vision? *Ethan and Mattie do suffer for their bad choice.*

Supplementary Resources:

Millicent Bell, ed. *The Cambridge Companion to Edith Wharton*
    Bell offers a wonderful, insightful companion to the Wharton corpus.

Harold Bloom, ed. *Edith Wharton: New Essays in Criticism*
    Bloom is one of the best literary critics of the 20th century.

Ethan Frome (VHS)
    A very fine, true to the book video. However, ask your parents before you rent it (I do not know how it is rated but I saw it and did not find anything objectionable).

Richard Hofstadter, *Social Darwinisn in American Thought*
    Hofstadter is a brilliant Revisionist historian who presents an accurate picture of

social Darwinism (a world view popular among Naturalists).

Paul Johnson, *Modern Times*
  This is a very helpful history of the time period in which Wharton lived. A sample is found on page 48, "Among the advanced races, the decline and ultimately the collapse of the religious impulse would leave a huge vacuum. The history of modern times is in great part the history of how that vacuum is filled. Nietzsche (whom Davis calls post-modern) rightly perceived that the most likely candidate would be what he called the 'Will to Power,' which offered a far more comprehensive and in the end more plausible explanation of human behavior than either Marx or Freud. In place of religious belief, there would be secular ideology. Those who once filled the ranks of the totalitarian clergy would become totalitarian politicians. And, above all, the Will to Power would produce a new kind of messiah, uninhibited by any religious sanctions whatever, and with an unappeasable appetite for controlling mankind. The end of the old order, with an unguided world adrift in a relativistic universe, was a summons to such gangster-statesmen to emerge. They were not slow to make their appearance."

David O. Moberg. *The Great Reversal: Evangelism and Social Concern*
  Moberg offers a foil to Naturalist criticisms of Evangelical Christianity (see Stephen Crane, *Maggie*). He says "The question of how to deal with poverty and the numerous other interrelated problems of our day has divided Christians into two camps One of them builds a strong case for evangelism as the basic solution, while the other emphasizes direct social involvement. Each accuses the other of being untrue to the essential nature of Christianity." (p. 13)

Alan Price, *.he End of the Age of Innocence: Edith Wharton and the First World War*
  Price places Wharton and her writings in her time period.

George Gaylord Simpson, *The Meaning of Evolution*
  Simpson elucidates the dangers of evolution (a bedrock tenant of Naturalism). He states "Man is the result of a purposeless and materialistic process that did not have him in mind. He was snot planned ... Discovery that the universe . . . Lacked any purpose or plan has the inevitable corollary that the workings of the universe cannot provide any automatic, universal, eternal, or absolute criteria of Right and wrong.."

Notes:

Lesson Twenty-Two Test

Essay: (100 Points)

Because of your reputation as a literary analysis, and a keen sense of how to cast actors and actresses in the right roles, you have been retained by a prestigious movie company to find actors and actresses to play the following characters for a G rated movie based on *Ethan Frome*. More than that, though, you are required to give reasons for your decisions. Write a 150 word essay identifying each character and casting him/her appropriately.

ETHAN FROME
ZEENA
MATTIE
NARRATOR
DENIS EADY
JOTHAM POWELL
MR. ANDREW HALE
MRS. ANDREW HALE
MRS. RUTH VARNUM HALE
HARMON GOW

Lesson Twenty-Two Test Answers

Essay: (100 Points)

Because of your reputation as a literary analysis, and a keen sense of how to cast actors and actresses in the right roles, you have been retained by a prestigious movie company to find actors and actresses to play the following characters for a G rated movie based on *Ethan Frome*. More than that, though, you are required to give reasons for your decisions. Write a 150 word essay identifying each character and casting him/her appropriately. *I have no idea how to cast each character.*

ETHAN FROME
The protagonist of the novel.

ZEENA
Ethan's shrewish wife.

MATTIE
Zeena's house companion in whom Ethan falls in love.

NARRATOR
The young nameless narrator tells the story.

DENIS EADY
Ethan's rival for Mattie's affections.

JOTHAM POWELL
Jotham, Ethan's hired hand, helps take care of the farm and mill.

MR. ANDREW HALE
Mr. Hale buys lumber from Ethan for building houses. A somewhat shady character, he doesn't pay on delivery but waits three months.

MRS. ANDREW HALE
Mrs. Hale is probably the friendliest person in Starkfield.

MRS. RUTH VARNUM HALE
Ruth is the landlady of the Varnum house, where the novel's narrator stays during his time in Starkfield.

HARMON GOW
Starkfield's stage driver.

Lesson Twenty-Three

Readings Due For This Lesson
Students should have read selections from 20th century poetry.

Reading Ahead
Students should read *A Farewell To Arms*, Ernest Hemingway

Suggested Weekly Implementation

Day One	Day Two	Day Three	Day Four	Day Five
1. Students will rewrite graded essays from last week and review Lesson Twenty-Two test. 2. Students should have read the required reading(s) *before* the assigned lesson begins. 3. Teacher may want to discuss assigned reading(s) with student. 4. Teacher shall assign the required essays. Choose two or three. The rest of the essays can be outlined, answered with shorter answers, or skipped.	1. Student should begin reading(s) from next lesson. 2. Student should outline essays due at the end of the week. 3. Students should answer one or two of the essays that are not assigned as formal essays.	1. Students should write rough drafts of assigned essays. 2. The teacher should correct rough drafts.	Student will write final copy of essays due tomorrow.	1. Essays are due. 2. Students should take Lesson Twenty-Three test. 3. Read selections from 20th century poetry (Lesson Twenty-Three)

Twentieth Century Poetry

A. Read as many poems as possible by Edwin Arlington Robinson, Stephen Crane, Robert Frost, Vachel Lindsay, John Crowe Ransom, and other poets not listed above.

B. Here are statements on the poetry of Robert Frost by two well-known critics. Agree or disagree with each critic:

> *At his best, of course, Frost does not philosophize. The anecdote is absorbed into symbol. The method of indirection operates fully: the senses of realistic detail, the air of casual comment, are employed to build up and intensify a serious effect. (Cleanth Brooks, Modern Poetry, p. 113)*

> *Despite his great virtues, you cannot read a great deal of Frost without this effect of the deja vu. Sententiousness and a relative absence of formal daring are his main defects. Even in his finest work, the conventionality of rhythm and rhyme contributes a certain tedium, temporarily relegated to a dim corner of the reader's consciousness. (M.L. Rosenthal, The Modern Poets, pp. 112-113)*

Answers will vary but Cleanth Brooks correctly highlights Frost's powerful Realism and Naturalism. One needs to remember this when one reads Frost on the surface. Below the surface, Frost is an angry man.

Rosenthal makes some good points. He argues that Frost's images are predictable and bland. I do not necessarily agree.

C. Read poems by Cummings, Crane, and Stevens.

D. In the poem "The Unknown Citizen," by Auden, what is the poet's attitude toward the unknown citizen? How far have we come in American poetry? Compare to the poetry of Anne Bradstreet and Edward Taylor. *Auden, who is a Christian poet, laments the dehumanizing potential of American society. W. H. Auden's poem, "The Unknown Citizen" is headed with "To JS/07 M 378/ This Marble Monument/ Is Erected by the State." The citizen to whom the monument is dedicated does not even have a name. As the poem progresses, the reader sees that "The Unknown Citizen" is nameless. He is by definition nameless, simply an example of the perfect cog in the social machine. There are similarities between "The Unknown Citizen" and the science fiction novel Brave New World, in which the focus is also on society and the community at the expense of the individual. Both works exhibit a view that is in stark contrast to the Christian emphasis on eternity and the individual soul, on heaven and what an individual has there. The Theistic poet Anne Bradstreet in "Upon The Burning of Our House" expresses this view.*

The Unknown citizen has had this monument erected to him because "in everything he did he served the Greater Community." Note the way "Greater Community" is capitalized. The state is supreme above the individual, who is regarded simply a component cell of the greater organism. As we continue with the poem, we see that "The Unknown Citizen" seems to be the man who fits into society perfectly and manages to please everybody. He "satisfied his employers, Fudge Motors Inc/Yet he wasn't a scab or odd in his views/ For his Union reports that he paid his dues/(Our report on his Union shows it was sound)." We also learn that "He was fully sensible to the advantages of the installment plan" that "The press are convinced he bought a paper every day/And his reactions to advertisements were normal in every way" and "Our researchers into Public Opinion are content/That he held the proper opinions for that time of year/When there was peace, he was for peace, when there was war, he went." This citizen boosts the economy, agrees with public opinion, serves his country and in general is the all around good little, well conditioned citizen. It is possible at this point to make comparisons between "The Unknown Citizen" and the people of the "Utopia" of Brave New World.

In Brave New World people are not born, but created in little bottles, where they are engineered to fulfill certain functions in society. They are raised in child conditioning centers, where they are a given a moral education through the means of lessons given to them while they are asleep ("His reactions to advertisements were normal in every way"). In these lessons, they are taught to be glad that they are a member of their caste, and not some other social class, as well as to consume the right amount of materials to support the economy ("He bought a paper every day"). There are indeed definite similarities between the two different works. In both, the people are well-conditioned citizens who boost the economy by the proper amount of consumption, agree with public opinion, and in general are good little, round pegs in round holes. The focus is on material possessions and the here-and-now.

In both works, too, the individual is essentially defined by his material possessions and his service to the community. The inner soul is lost, as W. H. Auden makes clear in the last two lines, "Was he free? Was he happy? The question is absurd:/Had anything been wrong, we surely would have heard." The pressures of social conformity and duty to the state overwhelm the concern about individual persons. This actually makes sense, given an atheistic worldview, since man rarely lives longer than a hundred years, while civilizations can last for centuries. This is in stark contrast to the Christian world view, which ultimately is more concerned with individual salvation than the overall social structure, since, in the Christian world view, a man's soul lasts forever, while a civilization may last for, at most, perhaps a few thousand years.

In Bradstreet's poem, "On the Burning of Our House", which shows the Christian emphasis on eternity, and not the present community, she speaks of fire consuming all her possessions, "I starting up, the light did spy,/ And to my God my heart did cry/To strengthen me in my distress,/Then coming out beheld a space/The flame consume my dwelling place." She says it was after all Gods anyway ("It was his own: it was not mine/Far be it that I should repine"), but this does not seem very consoling, for after that she continues "He might of all justly bereft/But yet sufficient for us left/When by the ruins oft I passed,/My sorrowing eyes aside did cast,/And here and there the places spy/Where oft I sat and long did lie." The emphasis seems to again be on material possessions, the here-and-now. However, she chides herself saying "Then straight I gin my heart to chide/Did they wealth on earth abide?/.../Though has an house on high erect/Framed by that mighty architect." Earthly possessions are dust (Unlike the man "Who was fully sensible to the advantages of the installment plan") Bradstreet does not conform to society, for she is without a house, without earthly possessions. As a member of the social body she is a useless hindrance, for all she does is take up welfare money. She does work and "benefit the Greater Community", at least not in a material sense. This poem states that there is more to the universe, and hence more to person than what can be physically seen ("Thy has a house on high erect/Framed by that mighty architect")here-and-now   Unlike Brave New World and "The Unknown Citizen" which deal with the loss of the individual in the tumult and pressure of the here-and-now, of focusing on this world and living in only it, this poem ends with looking forward, past today and the here-and-now, to what matters far most, to heaven and eternity, and what an individual has there. (Aaron)

E. Compare the poem "The Unknown Citizen" by W. H. Auden with "Where Have all The Flowers Gone?" by Pete Seeger. *Both poems commiserate with modern Americans. Both celebrate transcendental values--although one hopes that Auden is pointing toward God even if in a subtle way.*

F. Another modern poem by the Beatles, entitled "Lucy in the Sky With Diamonds," approaches surrealism and absurdism. Explain what I mean and give evidence from the poem.

"Lucy in the Sky With Diamonds" is a poem by the Beatles, which borders on surrealism and absurdism. It focuses on various trivial, rather meaningless impressions and details.

The thread running through the poem is "The girl with kaleidoscope eyes" a.k.a. "Lucy in the Sky With Diamonds." She appears at the beginning and at the end of the poem, and in the chorus in between. The poem opens with "Picture yourself on a boat in a river/With tangerine trees and marmalade skies/Somebody calls you, you answer quite slowly/A girl with kaleidoscope eyes." You can see the absurdist imagery from the beginning "tangerine trees and marmalade skies."

Throughout the poem the persona (person) of the poem seems to pursues this girl with the hope that she may hold the answer to life. However, she seems to constantly to elude hhim. "Look for the girl with the sun in her eyes and she's gone." This girl is unreachable, as is signified by the chorus of "Lucy in the sky with diamonds/Lucy in the sky with diamonds/Lucy in the sky with diamonds, ah/" She is in the sky with diamonds (the answer to it all) unattainable and unreachable.

As the persona moves on with his quest for meaning, he is constantly surrounded by the absurdity of life. "Rocking horse people eat marshmallow pies" and "plasticine porters with looking glass ties" as well as *"Cellophane flowers of yellow and green/Towering over your head." The "Cellophane flowers...towering over your head" express the personas feeling of smallness and insignificance. He is a speck of dust, who matters to no one. The "Rocking horse people" who "eat marshmallow pies, as well as the "plasticine porters with looking glass ties" are intended to convey a sort of crazy "Alice in Wonderland" feel (a despairing version of it no less), which after all, is the heart of absurdism.*

In the end, the persona has one final glimpse of "The girl with kaleidoscope eyes". However, again she eludes him, and the poem ends with a despairing final chorus of "Lucy in the Sky With Diamonds." (Aaron)

Absurdism is a world view arising in the sixties that says there simply is no meaning in life at all. Period. It is both a frightening and hilarious. It is frightening because, as Oz Guinness says, American societies is really coming unglued. On the other hand, to say the central truth of American life is that there is no truth is to invite hilarity.

G. Read "Home Burial" and "Death of a Hired Hand" by Robert Frost--another New England writer--and compare the themes of these poems with *Ethan Frome*. Identify elements of Naturalism and realism in these literary works. How does nature function in these two writer's prose/poetry? How does each author use irony? Why is irony a particularly effective literary device for naturalistic writers to use? *Frost and Wharton use nature to emphasize the absence of God and neutrality or malevolence of nature.*

Robert Frost's The poems "Home Burial" and "Death of a Hired Hand" have similar themes to Edith Wharton's Ethan Frome. These themes are conflict, loneliness, and isolation. Both works focus on rocky, painful, relations, and the inability of the individuals involved to be friends. They display a naturalistic world view, which is evidenced by the use of irony, which is particularly suited to expressing the naturalistic world view. These poems can be taken as warnings to try and get along with each other before it is too late.

"Death of a Hired Hand" is simply about , quite simply, the death of a hired hand (Silas). The poem opens with the return of a New England the farmer, Warren, from his field. He is met by his wife, Mary, who tells him "Silas is back/...Be kind." Warren responds rather bitterly "When was I ever anything but kind to him? /But I'll not have the fellow back.../I told him so last haying, didn't I? /If he left then,' I said, 'that ended it'" We learn that Silas seems to be an old, drifting man. "Who else will harbor him/At his age for the little he can do? /What help he is there's no depending on." Notable is the section about how Silas fought with Harold Wilson, a college student. "On education you know how they fought/All through July under the blazing sun/..."Yes, I took care to keep well out of earshot"/...After so many years, he still keeps finding arguments he might have used." Silas has trouble getting along with anybody. However, when Mary tried talking to Silas, she says he talked about him and Harold were a good team. As the poem continues we learn that he has a brother, who however, wants nothing to do with him. "Silas is what he is-we wouldn't mind him /But just the kind that kinfolks can't abide./He never did a so thing so very bad/He don't know why he isn't quite as good as anyone."

Silas is alone, unloved and unwanted. Mary says Silas "Has nothing to look backward to with pride/And nothing to look forward to with hope" The poem ends when Warren goes to talk to Silas. The final lines are "Warren returned-too soon it seemed to her,/Slipped to her side, caught up her hand and waited/ "Warren?" she questioned/"Dead" was all he answered." See the irony present in the poem. Warren and Mary are discussing Silas, with Warren rather critical, and Mary sticking up for Silas.

Meanwhile, Silas is dying or dead. Irony is also present when Warren, the one who had the most problems with Silas goes to talk to him, and finds him. Warren's troubles with Silas are over. Irony is a particularly effective instrument for Naturalists because, for Naturalists, the world is painful and senseless. Therefore, bitter irony of the kind found in "Death of a Hired Hand" is particularly effective for them, because it portrays the pain and lack of meaning in life. Irony can be found in the section about Silas' argument with Harold Wilson. They fought long and bitterly "on Education," yet after the fact, Silas sees that he and Harold made a good team. This irony could be taken as a warning to us to repair broken or damaged relationships before it is too late.

"Home Burial" focuses on the burial of a child, and the subsequent burial of a marriage. It opens with a wife trying to leave the house, and her husband trying to stop her, to repair their marriage, to find out what is wrong. The man realizes that what she is upset about is the death of her child. He says "Can't a man speak of his own child he's lost." His wife says simply "Don't, don't, don't," She says that she always goes to other peoples homes because there she can share her feelings with other people, while he is only a callous statue. He says "We could have some arrangement/By which I'd bind myself to keep hands off anything you're a-mind to name/Though I don't like such things twixt those that love/Two that don't cant live together without em/But those that do can't live with em" eventually coming back to his indignation that "A man cant speak of his own child that's dead. She says "You could if you had a heart.../(Speaking of him digging the grave) "I saw from that very window there,/making the gravel leap and leap in air,/I thought, who is that man, I don't know you." She continues "I can repeat the very words you were saying, "Three foggy mornings and one rainy day/ Will rot the best birch fence a man can build." Think of it, talk like that at such time." The poem ends with her leaving while he shouts "Where do you mean to go? First tell me that./I'll follow and bring you back by force. I will!--"

The comparisons to Ethan Frome are immediately obvious. Ethan Frome shares the same themes. Likewise, they are two people living together who cannot stand each other. The husband says of their agreement to leave certain things alone says "Those that do (love) can't live together with em." The problem is that they don't love. Their love has all dried up do to the death of the child. Their child's death has set of a chain reaction, with "grave" results.

Together, these two poems focus on the way in which some people fight and cannot stand each other, as in Ethan Frome. Warren cannot stand Silas, or perhaps, rather, Silas cannot stand Harold Wilson. The mother of the buried child cannot stand her husband, and her husband cannot stand her. All of these portray a despairing, naturalistic world view, which has no end but death or madness, due to the painful relationships and the lack of connection with others. They are also warnings to mend broken relationships before it is too late. (Aaron)

H. Compare and contrast "Cassandra", "Richard Cory," and "Mr. Flood's Party," by Edwin Arlington Robinson. *Inevitably a Robinson poem portrays a naturalistic vision of hopelessness and loss of control. "Cassandra" laments the fast passage of hopeless time (akin to Emerson's "Day"). Ditto "Richard Cory" and "Mr. Flood's Party." Often the characters in a Robinson poem are full of hopelessness.*

I. In Robert Frost's poem *Fire and Ice*, what's the speaker's tone of voice in the first two lines? Is it surprising? How does his tone suit or contrast with the content of what he's saying? It hardly sounds "like poetry" at all, just like casual speech. What gives it power? *Frost is evoking common images–fire and ice–to express an apocalyptic vision that is the heart of all Naturalism.*

J. My favorite contemporary poet is Theodore Roethke. Theodore Roethke (1908-1963) was son of a greenhouse owner. Roethke evolved a special language evoking the "greenhouse world" of tiny insects and unseen roots: "Worm, be with me. / This is my hard time." His love poems in *Words for the Wind* (1958) celebrate beauty and desire with innocent passion: One poem begins "I knew a woman, lovely in her bones, / When small birds sighed, she would sigh back at them." Sometimes his poems seem like nature's shorthand or ancient riddles: "Who stunned the dirt into noise? / Ask the mole, he knows." I discovered Roethke while I was an undergraduate English major. His gentle simplicity spoke to my heart. Read several poems by Roethke.

Challenge Question

In my sermons in the last 25 years I have quoted Edwin Arlington Robinson more than any other poet. Why? What makes his poetry so relevant to contemporary American life? *Robinson's poetry captures the hopelessness of American life without any sentimental comment. It therefore invites the listener to examine his own life and hopefully to embrace the reality that faith in Christ can bring into a person's life.*

Supplementary Resources

Thomas R. Arp (Editor), *Perrine's Literature: Structure, Sound and Sense*
    An excellent resource on poetry.

Norman Friedman, *E. E. Cummings: The Art of His Poetry*

Laurence Perrine, *Perrine's Sound and Sense: An Introduction to Poetry*
    Perrine set the standard for poetry interpretation.

Sanford Schwartz, *The Matrix of Modernism: Pound, Eliot, and Early Twentieth-Century Thought*

Notes:

Lesson Twenty-Three Test

Discussion Question: (75 Points)

A. Analyze the following poem in a 75-150 word essay. In your essay discuss the theme, setting, rime scheme, literary techniques (e.g., alliteration, metaphor), and other literary elements (e.g.., symbolism).

The Pity of the Leaves
Edwin Arlington Robinson

Vengeful across the cold November moors,
Loud with ancestral shame there came the bleak
Sad wind that shrieked, and answered with a shriek,
Reverberant through lonely corridors.
The old man heard it; and he heard, perforce,
Words out of lips that were no more to speak --
Words of the past that shook the old man's cheek
Like dead, remembered footsteps on old floors.

And then there were the leaves that plagued him so!
The brown, thin leaves that on the stones outside
Skipped with a freezing whisper. Now and then
They stopped, and stayed there -- just to let him know
How dead they were; but if the old man cried,
They fluttered off like withered souls of men.

B. Compare with Ralph Waldo Emerson's *The Snow Storm*.

The Snow Storm
R. W. Emerson

Announced by all the trumpets of the sky,
Arrives the snow, and, driving o'er the fields,
Seems nowhere to alight: the whited air
Hides hills and woods, the river, and the heaven,
And veils the farm-house at the garden's end.
The sled and traveller stopped, the courier's feet
Delayed, all friends shut out, the housemates sit
Around the radiant fireplace, enclosed

In a tumultuous privacy of storm.

Come see the north wind's masonry.
Out of an unseen quarry evermore
Furnished with tile, the fierce artificer
Curves his white bastions with projected roof
Round every windware stake, or tree, or door.
Speeding, the myriad-handed, his wild work
So fanciful, so savage, nought cares he
For number or proportion. Mockingly,
On coop or kennel he hangs Parian wreaths;

A swan-like form invests the hidden thorn;
Fills up the farmer's lane from wall to wall,
Maugre the farmer's sighs; and at the gate
A tapering turret overtops the work.
And when his hours are numbered, and the world
Is all his own, retiring, as he were not,
Leaves, when the sun appears, astonished Art
To mimic in slow structures, stone by stone,
Built in an age, the mad wind's night-work,
The frolic architecture of the snow.

B. Write your own poem. Write your name down the page. Use adjectives or nouns that describe you that also begin with each of the letters. For example: (25 Points)

Jolly
Athlete
Maudlin
Encounter
Simple

Lesson Twenty-Three Test Answers

Discussion Question: (75 Points)

A. Analyze the following poem in a 75-150 word essay. In your essay discuss the theme, setting, rime scheme, literary techniques (e.g., alliteration, metaphor), and other literary elements (e.g.., symbolism).

The Pity of the Leaves
Edwin Arlington Robinson

Vengeful across the cold November moors,   *a*
Loud with ancestral shame there came the bleak   *b*
Sad wind that shrieked, and answered with a shriek,   *a*
Reverberant through lonely corridors.   *a*
The old man heard it; and he heard, perforce,   *c*
Words out of lips that were no more to speak –   *d*
Words of the past that shook the old man's cheek   *d*
Like dead, remembered footsteps on old floors.   *a*

And then there were the leaves that plagued him so!   *e*
The brown, thin leaves that on the stones outside   *f*
Skipped with a freezing whisper. Now and then   *g*
They stopped, and stayed there -- just to let him know   *h*
How dead they were; but if the old man cried,   *i*
They fluttered off like withered souls of men.   *g*

On the surface this poem offers the reader an image leaves falling and blowing in the wind. It is both beautiful and sad. The image reminds the old man that his life is ending too. The poem has an underlying current of death–the life dies and the narrators. There is also an agnostic conclusion–the speaker does not know what is in store for him after death.

B. Compare with Ralph Waldo Emerson's *The Snow Storm*.

The Snow Storm
R. W. Emerson

Announced by all the trumpets of the sky,
Arrives the snow, and, driving o'er the fields,
Seems nowhere to alight: the whited air
Hides hills and woods, the river, and the heaven,

And veils the farm-house at the garden's end.
The sled and traveller stopped, the courier's feet
Delayed, all friends shut out, the housemates sit
Around the radiant fireplace, enclosed
In a tumultuous privacy of storm.

Come see the north wind's masonry.
Out of an unseen quarry evermore
Furnished with tile, the fierce artificer
Curves his white bastions with projected roof
Round every windware stake, or tree, or door.
Speeding, the myriad-handed, his wild work
So fanciful, so savage, nought cares he
For number or proportion. Mockingly,
On coop or kennel he hangs Parian wreaths;

A swan-like form invests the hidden thorn;
Fills up the farmer's lane from wall to wall,
Maugre the farmer's sighs; and at the gate
A tapering turret overtops the work.
And when his hours are numbered, and the world
Is all his own, retiring, as he were not,
Leaves, when the sun appears, astonished Art
To mimic in slow structures, stone by stone,
Built in an age, the mad wind's night-work,
The frolic architecture of the snow.

The Romantic Emerson expresses nothing but positive things about nature. The Naturalist Robinson is less generous with nature.

B. Write your own poem. Write your name down the page. Use adjectives or nouns that describe you that also begin with each of the letters. For example: (25 Points)

Jolly
Athlete
Maudlin
Encounter
Simple

LESSON TWENTY-FOUR

Readings Due For This Lesson
Students should have read *A Farewell To Arms*, Ernest Hemingway

Reading Ahead

Students should read *The Unvanquished*, William Faulkner (Lesson Twenty-Six)

Suggested Weekly Implementation

Day One	Day Two	Day Three	Day Four	Day Five
1. Students will rewrite graded essays from last week and review Lesson Twenty-Three test. 2. Students should have read the required reading(s) *before* the assigned lesson begins. 3. Teacher may want to discuss assigned reading(s) with student. 4. Teacher shall assign the required essays. Choose two or three. The rest of the essays can be outlined, answered with shorter answers, or skipped.	1. Student should begin reading(s) from next lesson. 2. Student should outline essays due at the end of the week. 3. Students should answer one or two of the essays that are not assigned as formal essays.	1. Students should write rough drafts of assigned essays. 2. The teacher should correct rough drafts.	Student will write final copy of essays due tomorrow.	1. Essays are due. 2. Students should take Lesson Twenty-Four test. 3. Read *The Unvanquished* by William Faulkner.

A Farewell To Arms
By Ernest Hemingway
(Published in 1929)

Book Checkup

__b__ 1.

__a__ 2.

__d__ 3.

__a__ 4.

__b__ 5.

Suggested Vocabulary Words

    feigned *(imitate)*
    felicitations *(congratulations)*

Supplemental Resources:

E.R. Dodds, *Pagan and Christian in an Age of Anxiety*
    4th century way of dealing with hostile environment. Christianity triumphed over paganism because Christianity rejected all gods but accepted all people. They promised eternal life in heaven yet they showed love to all persons. In the face of Hemingway's Naturalism, Dodd argued that many Christians experienced a loss of nerve.

Kenneth J. Gergen, *The Saturated Self: Dilemmas of Identity in Contemporary Life*
    The whole concept of identity began with Freud, but Hemingway and other modernist writers explored the concept of self and invited the reader to unprecedented levels of self-centeredness.

Nathan O. Hatch, *Taking the Measure of the Evangelical Resurgence: 1942-1992*
If there is such a huge resurgence of evangelicalism, why is there a disconnection problem? Hatch examines a time much like the time in which Hemingway lived–when culture was re-examining all presumptions.

John Keegan, *An Illustrated History of World War I*
Keegan, a British historian, writes the best overall survey of World War I that is on the market today.

George Marsden, *The Soul of the American University*
Marsden explains why American academic life excludes religion, and argues that since the reasons for this exclusion are not valid, there should be more room for the free exercise of religion in higher learning. Initially, the relegation of region to the periphery of American universities was justified on Enlightenment grounds. Today, however, few believe in pure scientific objectivity and understand that all intellectual inquiry takes place in a framework of presuppositions and moral commitments. We find today the university in a moral crisis. Tolerance and diversity are the preview values, but there is no longer any standard by which limits can be placed on tolerance. This movement gained momentum when Hemingway was alive.

Mark Noll, *The Scandal of the Evangelical Mind*
Given the "intellectual disaster" of some Christian groups, Noll aims to reconnect evangelicals to their pre-fundamentalist heritage. Noll is bold in asking evangelicals to soften their distinctive themes for the sake of intellectual engagement.

Thomas C. Oden, *Agenda For Theology: After Modernity...What?*
Oden issues a call to students and others to return to tradition and orthodoxy. Modernity is defined as "A Time, A Mentality, and a Malaise." Major revealing features of modern consciousness are an unrestrained, individual freedom, the goal of which is to liberate one from all restrictions, constraints, traditions, and all social patenting--all of which are self-evidently presumed to be humanizing. (p.47). Modernity has a contempt for other viewpoints. Modernity is reductionistic Naturalism.

Neil Postman, *Amusing Ourselves to Death*
Television is transforming our culture into one vast arena for show business (p. 80). TV is the highest order of abstract thinking that television consistently undermines (p.41). The early church was low tech but high commitment. Clear boundaries. Today we are high-tech and low commitment.

Quentin Schultze, *Televangelism and American Culture*
To examine how and why televanglists are helping to transform American Christianity from a church into a business, from a historic faith into a popular religion based at least in part on superstition. An examination of these trends indicates that marketing and ministry are now close partners. Each influences the other, and not usually for the good

(p.11).

Leonard I. Sweet, *The Modernization of Protestant Religion in America*

Hemingway and his expatriate community in Paris turned their back on mainline religion and embraced a hedonistic Naturalism. Factors that contributed to the decline of the mainline churches are: the growth of individualism, high criticism professionalization of the clergy, unwise and unpopular decisions made by denominational bureaucrats, ecumenism, actionism, pluralism. The end result of all this has been the decline of the mainline churches--both numerically and spiritually. Evangelicals, fundamentalists, and Pentecostal moved to center stage as modernism has been forced into retreat. In characterizing the mainline denominations during these five decades, Sweet notes: "With everything gone, there was little reason for people to stay." Sweet gives much attention to the relationship between the denominational leaders and the church members, were growing increasingly distant. This led to the leadership taking stands without considering the beliefs and feelings of the people in the pews, which then resulted in a growing distrust by the members of their leaders. Sweet describes these developments as a loss of mastery and mandate--that is, the loss of mastery of the common touch and mandate of the common faith.

Grant Wacker, *Uneasy in Zion: Evangelicals in Postmodern Society*

To most of us, the desire to have cultural world view alternatives is to look toward our faith. To understand the growth of Evangelicalism one must look at the big picture as seen in the social transformations (particularly since WWII) brought about by mass communication and high technology. Evangelicalism as we know it today is a cultural form which grew out of a developing America.

Grant Wacker, *Searching for Norman Rockwell: Popular Evangelicalism in Contemporary America*

Evangelicals thrived even when Hemingway wrote because they understood that Godliness is not passed through the loins of Godly parents, but must be rekindled in the hearts and minds of each generation.

David F. Wells, *God in the Wasteland: The Reality of Truth in a World of Fading Dreams*

Wells in convinced that Modernity is now the Tempter seducing human pride to betray itself through a pawn-like participation in "an ironic recapitulation of the first dislocation in which God's creatures replaced their Creator and exiled Him from His own world" (p. 14).

Notes:

Lesson Twenty-Four Test

Discussion Questions: (100 Points)

A. What does Hemingway mean when he says, "Abstract words such as glory, honor, courage, or hallow were obscene beside the concrete names of villages, the numbers of roads, the names of rivers, the number of regiments and the dates"?

B. It is raining constantly in *A Farewell to Arms*. What effect does this have in the novel?

C. What narrative technique does Hemingway employ? Why?

D. Frederick Henry is not an hero, he is an anti-hero. Explain.

E. A foil is a character who resembles the main character in all respects except one--the one trait that the writer wants to highlight. Give an example of a foil.

Lesson Twenty-Four Test Answers

Discussion Questions: (100 Points)

A. What does Hemingway mean when he says, "Abstract words such as glory, honor, courage, or hallow were obscene beside the concrete names of villages, the numbers of roads, the names of rivers, the number of regiments and the dates"? *To the Realist writer Hemingway hyperbole implies hypocrisy; to the taciturn Naturalist writer Hemingway verbosity is a camouflage for the horror that is life.*

B. It is raining constantly in *A Farewell to Arms*. What effect does this have in the novel? *Nature, like life, is malevolent. Notice how often Naturalist writers use dreary landscapes and weather.*

C. What narrative technique does Hemingway employ? Why? *First person omniscient allows Hemingway to participate in the action without being obligated to tell what anything else thinks (not that it really matters to the self-centered Frederick Henry).*

D. Frederick Henry is not an hero, he is an anti-hero. Explain. *Valor, courage, and nobility are insulting to Henry. He makes decisions out of his own need and subjectivity.*

E. A foil is a character who resembles the main character in all respects except one--the one trait that the writer wants to highlight. Give an example of a foil. *Rinaldi (foil to Henry) and Ferguson (foil to Catherine) are two.*

LESSON TWENTY-FIVE

Readings Due For This Lesson
Students should have read *A Farewell To Arms*, Ernest Hemingway

Reading Ahead

Students should read *The Unvanquished*, William Faulkner (Lesson Twenty-Six)

Suggested Weekly Implementation

Day One	Day Two	Day Three	Day Four	Day Five
1. Students will rewrite graded essays from last week and review Lesson Twenty-Four test. 2. Students should have read the required reading(s) *before* the assigned lesson begins. 3. Teacher may want to discuss assigned reading(s) with student. 4. Teacher shall assign the required essays. Choose two or three. The rest of the essays can be outlined, answered with shorter answers, or skipped.	1. Student should begin reading(s) from next lesson. 2. Student should outline essays due at the end of the week. 3. Students should answer one or two of the essays that are not assigned as formal essays.	1. Students should write rough drafts of assigned essays. 2. The teacher should correct rough drafts.	Student will write final copy of essays due tomorrow.	1. Essays are due. 2. Students should take Lesson Twenty-Five test. 3. Read *The Unvanquished* by William Faulkner.

Hemingway...

Biblical Application

Catherine and Henry openly, without apology, sin. What does the Bible say about fornication? Is there any justification for their actions? *The wages of sin is death. There is no justification for sin.*

Literary Criticism

A. Who is the narrator of this story? What effect does this form of narration have on the story? *Henry tells the story. I find him to be a particularly immature and an unreliable narrator. His Naturalistic, self-centered view point makes every interpretation suspect.*

B. Hemingway writes in a journalistic *style*--or the way a writer presents his material. Give examples of this style and contrast it to the style that we read in *The Scarlet Letter*. *Hemingway writes in an active voice, straightforward style. He uses very few adjectives and modifiers. This is a typical Naturalistic and Realistic writing style. Hawthorne, on the other hand, deliberately wrote with rich metaphors and language. He was trying to reach for reality beyond the sensual setting.*

Critical Thinking

A. Critics have suggested that Hemingway calls his character Henry because he wants to compare him with Henry Fleming in *The Red Badge of Courage*. Compare and contrast these two literary characters. *I think that they are remarkable the same: both are captured by fate. Both have a "farewell to arms" experience and then embrace a Naturalistic vision. Perhaps Henry Fleming does not experience the heartbreak that Frederick Henry does–but in a Naturalistic world everything is happenstance anyway.*

C. Hemingway uses several characters--e.g., Rinaldi and Ferguson--to develop his main characters. These characters are called *foils*. Tell how Hemingway uses these foils. *They develop Henry's lackluster character. They show that he is really a pretty good guy–although he appears to be pretty wimpy to this reader! Catherine Barkley develops Henry in several ways: she calls forth his "who really cares" Naturalistic side. She is a monolithic character who barely changes. She dies the way she lives: with an "I'm going to die," she says. "I'm not afraid. It's just a dirty trick." The priest reminds me of the priest on the old television program M*A*S*H. He is powerless in the face of life's dilemmas and never objects to Henry's nihilistic immortality. I like Helen Ferguson most of all. She represents conventional Judeo-Christian morality. So, to Hemingway, she is an antagonist.*

E. Hemingway's vision was deeply impacted by social Darwinism...*Ironically Henry is wounded for no reason in his dugout. With no purpose Catherine dies. This is pretty hopeless. It also reflects a "survival of the fittest" motif. Actually, I would argue that the philosopher Nietzsche offers a fairly comprehensive picture of Frederick Henry and his creator, Ernest Hemingway. A contemporary of Darwin, he also advanced the cause of Naturalism. Nietzsche coined the phrase "God is dead." He says the only reality is this world of life and death, conflict and change, creation and destruction. For centuries, religious ideas have given meaning to life in the western world; but as they now collapse, Nietzsche observed, humanity faces a grave crisis of nihilism and despair. While I vociferously disagree with Nietzsche's vision, I like Nietzsche's honesty. His prophetic view is refreshing. Nietzsche took the hopeless vision of Naturalism and Social Darwinism to its natural conclusion. Nietzsche saw that a world where only power prevailed, a world without Christianity would inevitably lead to totalitarianism and destruction. He saw, then, in the late 19th century that inevitably western culture would create an Adolf Hitler or Joseph Stalin. The basic character of life in this world is what Nietzsche called the "will to power." He admired those who were strong enough to face this reality: for they alone could live joyfully. But this "modern superman" lived without God and without any hope of salvation. Nietzsche is basically a Naturalist. Man is fundamentally only an animal who has developed in an unusual way. The "will to power" brings about new forms of competition and superiority, and can lead to a "superman" humanity. Here is a passage from Nietzsche that reflects this Naturalism: When we hear the ancient bells growling on a Sunday morning we ask ourselves: Is it really possible! This, for a jew, crucified two thousand years ago, who said he was God's son? The proof of such a claim is lacking. Certainly the Christian religion is an antiquity projected into our times from remote prehistory; and the fact that the claim is believed - whereas one is otherwise so strict in examining pretensions - is perhaps the most ancient piece of this heritage. A god who begets children with a mortal woman; a sage who bids men work no more, have no more courts, but look for the signs of the impending end of the world; a justice that accepts the innocent as a vicarious sacrifice; someone who orders his disciples to drink his blood; prayers for miraculous interventions; sins perpetrated against a god, atoned for by a god; fear of a beyond to which death is the portal; the form of the cross as a symbol in a time that no longer knows the function and ignominy of the cross -- how ghoulishly all this touches us, as if from the tomb of a primeval past! Can one believe that such things are still believed?--from Nietzsche's Human, all too Human Some philosophers and their theories are so bizarre that their theories can be easily rejected (e.g., Darwin and evolution). But Nietzsche unnerves me. While he is wrong in his assessment of Christianity, his discernment about the future of Western culture is uncanny. The British historian Paul Johnson (Modern Times, p. 48) writes: Among the advanced races, the decline and ultimately the collapse of the religious impulse would leave a huge vacuum. The history of modern times is in great part the history of how that vacuum is filled. Nietzsche rightly perceived that the most likely candidate would be what he called the 'Will to Power,' which offered a far more comprehensive and in the end more plausible explanation of human behavior than either Marx or Freud. In place of religious belief, there would be secular ideology. Those who* *once filled the ranks of the totalitarian clergy would become totalitarian politicians. And, above all, the Will to Power would produce a new kind of messiah, uninhibited by any religious sanctions whatever, and with an unappeasable appetite for controlling mankind. The end of the old order, with an unguided world adrift in a relativistic universe, was a summons to such gangster-statesmen to emerge. They were not slow to make their appearance..*

Challenge Questions

There is no absolute truth in Henry's world except that there is no absolute truth.

Gertrude Himmelfarb...*If one can do whatever one wishes there will be consequences. Catherine and Henry learn this fact too late. But, as far as we can tell, they learned nothing. Henry departs in the rain. There is no truth, no rules, only feelings.*

D. Hemingway argued that no new novel had been written since Twain wrote *Huckleberry Finn*. In what ways are *A Farewell* and *Huckleberry Finn* similar? *Both novels employ realism. Characters are both on a journey to no where. Nature, too, has a malevolent, ubiquitous presence.*

For Further Enrichment

Military Casualties in World War I 1914-1918	
Belgium	45,550
British Empire	942,135
France	1,368,000
Greece	23,098
Italy	680,000
Japan	1,344
Montenegro	3,000
Portugal	8,145
Romania	300,000
Russia	1,700,000
Serbia	45,000
United States	116,516
Austria-Hungary	1,200,000
Bulgaria	87,495
Germany	1,935,000
Ottoman Empire	725,000

A. Write a report on World War I. *World War I, 1914-1918, was initially a European War. Americans wanted nothing to do with it. Once committed to going to war, though, in 1917, America intended to make the world–using Woodrow Wilson's words–"safe for democracy."*

Virtually no one wanted to go to war in 1914 and it was not clear whose side to join anyway. Americans were sympathetic toward England and her allies but millions of Americans were of German descent (including my own relatives). Support for the allies was never a forgone conclusion. However, by 1917, unrestricted submarine warfare and German mistakes–like the Zimmerman Telegram incident–make American participation on the allied side inevitable. While casualties on the American side were relatively light when compared to other allied casualties–more Americans died in the 1919 flue epidemic–Americans nonetheless were horrified and resolved never again to be involved in foreign wars. This view was further cemented when Woodrow Wilson was humiliated at the infamous Treaty of Versailles. In fact, Congress refused to ratify the Treaty of Versailles and made its own peace with Germany. This movement toward isolationism ushered in the excesses and hedonism of the 1920's.

B. Research Hemingway's life. How autobiographical was this book? *Use keyword: Barron's Booknotes. Hemingway was in World War I as an ambulance driver for the Italians and he was wounded. The real "Catherine," however, claims that she had nothing to do with Hemingway. She found him to be immature!*

C. H. R. Rookmaaker...

    1. PRE-ENLIGHTENMENT (Middle Ages to 18th century). Reflects a belief in an ordered universe, transcendent values, absolute morality. *Puritanism.*

    2. ENLIGHTENMENT ART. (18th century). Reflects Naturalism. Art ceases to reflect transcendent convictions. The seeds of modern art are planted. *Puritanism and beginning of Rationalism.*

    3. IMPRESSIONISM. (19th century). Reflects the sense experience between painter and object. Feelings are important. *Romanticism, Transcendentalism, Naturalism, and beginning of Existentialism.*

    4. ABSURDISM (early 20th century). Reflects a hopelessness for finding such meaning. *Realism and Absurdism.*

D. Compare two beginnings . . . *Hemingway and Crane, both Naturalists, begin their books with unfriendly images of nature and nameless men.*

E. *In the middle of the eighteenth century science and rationalism replaced theology and Scripture. However, in the last decade, many Americans are abandoning their "science" gods. We will see what happens in the future.*

F. Cornelius Plantinga...*Plantinga, Packer, and others yearn for the days of Puritanism. Indeed, with the rise of Absurdism, Naturalism, and Existentialism, sin has been lost in the shuffle. Freud, in particular, with his studies of psychology, placed mankind in a victim position. Karl Menninger in his book Whatever Happened to Sin profoundly affected the modern world and to a measure brought sin back into American culture. Until sin is dealt with adequately nothing with change. And, of course, Jesus Christ with His death on the cross alone adequately dealt with sin.*

Supplemental Resources:

E.R. Dodds, *Pagan and Christian in an Age of Anxiety*
    4th century way of dealing with hostile environment. Christianity triumphed over paganism because Christianity rejected all gods but accepted all people. They promised eternal life in heaven yet they showed love to all persons. In the face of Hemingway's Naturalism, Dodd argued that many Christians experienced a loss of nerve.

Kenneth J. Gergen, *The Saturated Self: Dilemmas of Identity in Contemporary Life*
    The whole concept of identity began with Freud, but Hemingway and other modernist writers explored the concept of self and invited the reader to unprecedented levels of self-centeredness.

Nathan O. Hatch, *Taking the Measure of the Evangelical Resurgence: 1942-1992*
    If there is such a huge resurgence of evangelicalism, why is there a disconnection problem? Hatch examines a time much like the time in which Hemingway lived–when culture was re-examining all presumptions.

John Keegan, *An Illustrated History of World War I*
    Keegan, a British historian, writes the best overall survey of World War I that is on the market today.

George Marsden, *The Soul of the American University*
    Marsden explains why American academic life excludes religion, and argues that since the reasons for this exclusion are not valid, there should be more room for the free exercise of religion in higher learning. Initially, the relegation of region to the periphery of American universities was justified on Enlightenment grounds. Today, however, few believe in pure scientific objectivity and understand that all intellectual inquiry takes place in a framework of presuppositions and moral commitments. We find today the university in a moral crisis. Tolerance and diversity are the preview values, but there is no longer any standard by which limits can be placed on tolerance. This movement gained momentum when Hemingway was alive.

Mark Noll, *The Scandal of the Evangelical Mind*
    Given the "intellectual disaster" of some Christian groups, Noll aims to reconnect evangelicals to their pre-fundamentalist heritage. Noll is bold in asking evangelicals to soften their distinctive themes for the sake of intellectual engagement.

Thomas C. Oden, *Agenda For Theology: After Modernity...What?*
    Oden issues a call to students and others to return to tradition and orthodoxy. Modernity is defined as "A Time, A Mentality, and a Malaise." Major revealing features of modern consciousness are an unrestrained, individual freedom, the goal of which is to liberate one from all restrictions, constraints, traditions, and all social patenting--all of which are self-evidently presumed to be humanizing. (p.47). Modernity has a contempt for other viewpoints. Modernity is reductionistic Naturalism.

Neil Postman, *Amusing Ourselves to Death*

Television is transforming our culture into one vast arena for show business (p. 80). TV is the highest order of abstract thinking that television consistently undermines (p.41). The early church was low tech but high commitment. Clear boundaries. Today we are high-tech and low commitment.

Quentin Schultze, *Televangelism and American Culture*

To examine how and why televanglists are helping to transform American Christianity from a church into a business, from a historic faith into a popular religion based at least in part on superstition. An examination of these trends indicates that marketing and ministry are now close partners. Each influences the other, and not usually for the good (p.11).

Leonard I. Sweet, *The Modernization of Protestant Religion in America*

Hemingway and his expatriate community in Paris turned their back on mainline religion and embraced a hedonistic Naturalism. Factors that contributed to the decline of the mainline churches are: the growth of individualism, high criticism professionalization of the clergy, unwise and unpopular decisions made by denominational bureaucrats, ecumenism, actionism, pluralism. The end result of all this has been the decline of the mainline churches--both numerically and spiritually. Evangelicals, fundamentalists, and Pentecostal moved to center stage as modernism has been forced into retreat. In characterizing the mainline denominations during these five decades, Sweet notes: "With everything gone, there was little reason for people to stay." Sweet gives much attention to the relationship between the denominational leaders and the church members, were growing increasingly distant. This led to the leadership taking stands without considering the beliefs and feelings of the people in the pews, which then resulted in a growing distrust by the members of their leaders. Sweet describes these developments as a loss of mastery and mandate--that is, the loss of mastery of the common touch and mandate of the common faith.

Grant Wacker, *Uneasy in Zion: Evangelicals in Postmodern Society*

To most of us, the desire to have cultural world view alternatives is to look toward our faith. To understand the growth of Evangelicalism one must look at the big picture as seen in the social transformations (particularly since WWII) brought about by mass communication and high technology. Evangelicalism as we know it today is a cultural form which grew out of a developing America.

Grant Wacker, *Searching for Norman Rockwell: Popular Evangelicalism in Contemporary America*

Evangelicals thrived even when Hemingway wrote because they understood that Godliness is not passed through the loins of Godly parents, but must be rekindled in the hearts and minds of each generation.

David F. Wells, *God in the Wasteland: The Reality of Truth in a World of Fading*

Dreams

Wells in convinced that Modernity is now the Tempter seducing human pride to betray itself through a pawn-like participation in "an ironic recapitulation of the first dislocation in which God's creatures replaced their Creator and exiled Him from His own world" (p. 14).

Notes:

Lesson Twenty-Five Test

Discussion Question: (100 Points)

The following is a diagram of Hegelian dialectics that deeply impacted Hemingway's world view. Take 3 ethical issues and employ Hegelian dialectics to solve them. For example, discussions of homosexuality in the courts have evolved to something like this: one side argues that homosexuality is evil and wrong under all conditions (Theory A). Another party argues that homosexuality is no one's business and appropriate according to the will of the people involved (Theory B). An Hegelian compromise would be: homosexual behavior is appropriate as long as the individuals care for each other and are faithful to each other. Of course, the Bible states categorically that homosexuality always has, and always will be sinful! How has our culture justified other ethical issues by Hegelian compromise? Give at least 3 in a 75-150 word essay.

> Hegel believed strongly in the dialectic. He starts with a thesis (a position put forward for argument). Opposed to this is a contradictory statement or antithesis. Out of their opposition comes a synthesis which embraces both. But since the truth lies only in the whole system, this first synthesis is not yet the truth of the matter, but becomes a new thesis, with its corresponding antithesis and synthesis. And so on. Truth, then, is not absolute and always open to interpretation. Truth lies in the "search" in the "system."

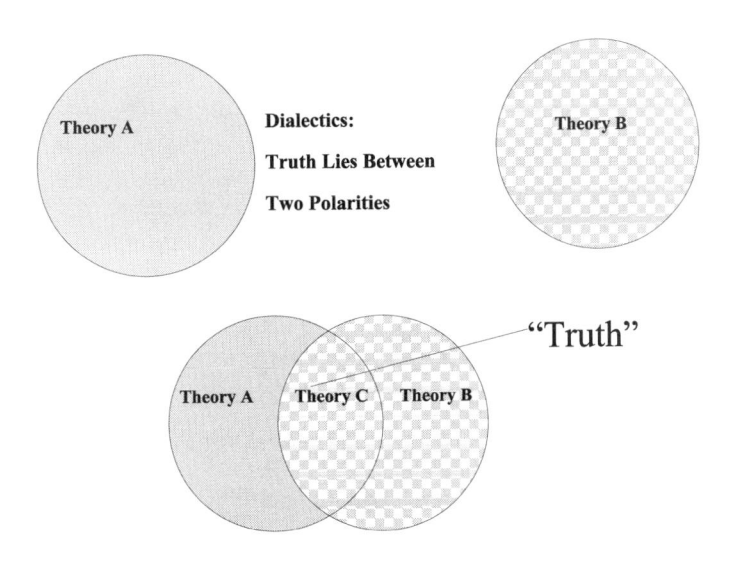

Theory A

Theory B

Dialectics:

Truth Lies Between Two Polarities

Theory A — Theory C — Theory B — "Truth"

Lesson Twenty-Five Test Answer

Discussion Question: (100 Points)

The following is a diagram of Hegelian dialectics that deeply impacted Hemingway's world view. Take 3 ethical issues and employ Hegelian dialectics to solve them. For example, discussions of homosexuality in the courts have evolved to something like this: one side argues that homosexuality is evil and wrong under all conditions (Theory A). Another party argues that homosexuality is no one's business and appropriate according to the will of the people involved (Theory B). An Hegelian compromise would be: homosexual behavior is appropriate as long as the individuals care for each other and are faithful to each other. Of course, the Bible states categorically that homosexuality always has, and always will be sinful! How has our culture justified other ethical issues by Hegelian compromise? Give at least 3 in a 75-150 word essay.

Justification of abortion, which is really murder, is one example. We "compromise" by stating that the woman's choice is most important. Euthanasia (i.e., mercy killing) is another example. We justify the killing of someone because he is in pain, or unhappy, or so on. There are others. The point is, that once we start climbing the slippery slop of dialectic ethics we go nowhere but down.

Lesson Twenty-Six

Readings Due For This Lesson

Students should finished reading *The Unvanquished* ,William Faulkner.

Reading Ahead

Read "Everything That Rises Must Converge," Flannery O'Connor.(Lesson Twenty-Seven).

Suggested Weekly Implementation

Day One	Day Two	Day Three	Day Four	Day Five
1. Students will rewrite graded essays from last week and review Lesson Twenty-Five test. 2. Students should have read the required reading(s) *before* the assigned lesson begins. 3. Teacher may want to discuss assigned reading(s) with student. 4. Teacher shall assign the required essays. Choose two or three. The rest of the essays can be outlined, answered with shorter answers, or skipped.	1. Student should begin reading(s) from next lesson. 2. Student should outline essays due at the end of the week. 3. Students should answer one or two of the essays that are not assigned as formal essays.	1. Students should write rough drafts of assigned essays. 2. The teacher should correct rough drafts.	Student will write final copy of essays due tomorrow.	1. Essays are due. 2. Students should take Lesson Twenty-Six test. 3. Read 20th century short story selections (Lessons Twenty-Seven and Twenty-Eight)

The Unvanquished
By William Faulkner
(Published in 1934)

Book Checkup

__a__ 1.

__b__ 2.

__a__ 3.

__a__ 4.

__b__ 5.

Vocabulary Words

>impunity *(immunity)*
>dispensation *(allocation)*
>cajoling *(coaxing)*
>annihilation *(destruction)*
>inviolate *(hallowed)*

Biblical Application

Faulkner discusses in great detail the whole issue of "family sin." In one novel, Absalom, Absalom, he blames the destruction of an entire family upon the sins of a father. The Snopes--an unprincipled, materialistic family--are the natural result of the sinful South (see *The Hamlet*, *The Town*, and *The Mansion*). Like rats in an empty house, they move in and take over as the moneyed, educated aristocracy self-destructs. In this book, Bayard and the Sartoris family are in a steady, but definite decline. Compare the results of David's sin with Bathsheba and the sin that Faulkner's characters experience. *David committed adultery and then watched his son die and then he had to struggle with another son Absalom. Faulkner argues through his literature that the South–the whole region-- is struggling with the sin of racism. The Snopes represent a type of judgement. The Snopes slowly take the world away from the Southern aristocracy In this novel, Bayard watches the destruction of his world and the rebirth of another. His grandmother and father do not survive the transition.*

Literary Criticism

A. Complete a Book Check-Up sheet.

B. Why is the setting so important to this story? *The "lost cause" drives this novel. Without the pathos that was the American Civil War, this novel would lose much of its energy. The Realistic grandmother confronts the Union general, for instance. As the War progresses, the Colonel loses his Romanticism and replaces it with a raw Realism, devoid of sentimentality. Bayard, too, has his disillusioning moments. The American Civil War is the vehicle that takes the reader to where Faulkner wishes him to go.*

C. What is the point of view? Why does it make this book more effective? *First person--from Bayard. I am not sure how reliable he is. I would not expect his views about slavery to be too open-minded. On the other hand, he is young and unaffected by other events that unfold in this novel. In that sense he is somewhat neutral and somewhat reliable.*

D. Faulkner's prose is so powerful that it seems like poetry. This is accomplished by his puissant imagery. *The chase scene at the end is powerful. Faulkner uses a great deal of stream of consciousness and complex adjectival constructions.*

E. How important is the informal language? How important is the use of a Southern dialect? Are you offended by Faulkner's frequent use of the word *nigger*?
William Faulkner's <u>The Unvanquished</u> is famous for its accurate portrayal of the South, during and after the Civil War. Faulkner develops an interesting, historically accurate story line, and he also involves his characters in situations typical of the reconstruction-era south. This creates a very convincing plot that could be mistaken for events that actually happened. He furthers develops his realistic storyline by incorporating into the book informal language common in the south. Not only does the informal language perfect his novel, it adds several more characteristics to the book. However the language is acceptable for some readers and objectionable to others.

The most common purpose of informal language in The Unvanquished is to make the novel more realistic. Southern vernacular places the final touches in the novel, making the reader believe that he is actually deep within Mississippi. In a more technical sense, the informal language spoken by the characters adds to their depth. As the vocabulary, pronunciation and grammatical form differ from person to person, Faulkner captures this and utilizes it to form a rounder, more fully developed, character. In example of this is found when the slaves refer to their owner as "Marster." This humbles the slave while exalting the owner, painting a very realistic picture of the south. Also, since the original copyright date was 1934, <u>The Unvanquished</u> offers an even more accurate depiction of the south. During the earlier part of the twentieth centaury the south was largely uneducated. Thus it would be incorrect to portray the Satoris plantation using proper grammar and a large vocabulary, as it would detract from the *novel.*

However, in Faulkner's efforts to make <u>The Unvanquished</u> as accurate as possible by including the common southern vernacular, he is forced also to include the offensive term nigger.

> *"That's what marse john and the other white folks is so busy about"*
> *"A nigger?" I said. "A nigger?"*
> *"No," Ringo Said "They ain't no more niggers, in Jefferson nor nowhere else." Then he told me about the two Burdens from Missouri, with a patent from Washington to organize the niggers into Republicans and who Father and the other mean ere trying to prevent it.*
> *"Naw, suh," he said. "This war ain't over."*

Once again, as with all informal language, the use of nigger is intended to add a flavor of the south to the novel. While nigger is considered an offensive term, with the Native American's being called "Timber Niggers," the Irish "Niggers of Europe," and the Arabic Nations as "Sand Niggers," Faulkner clearly had no intentions of being racist. Not once did he ever imply that the usage was correct or not. He merely portrayed the South like it was, knowing that no writing can sanitize the world for its readers. He simply meant no offense, and none should be taken. The use of informal language has many assets. Whether used to add to the setting or to round out a character, it is an important tool that the top writers have captured and utilized. While vernacular is often offensive, one must look beyond its definition to its usage and implied meaning before taking up arms. From chapter one, Faulkner successfully balanced the pros and cons of informal language to create a renowned novel. Combined, Faulkner creates a truly enjoyable read. (Anthony)

Critical Thinking

A. Who is the main character? Granny? Bayard? Colonel Sartoris? Defend your answer. *Bayard. It is from Bayard's viewpoint that the action in the novel unfolds.*

B. The chapter "An Odor of Verbena" has been criticized as being an entirely different story, or a story within a story. They wonder if it really belongs. I disagree. What do you think? *This chapter appropriately develops Bayard's further as a powerful character and the inheritor of the Sartoris reputation. It does belong.*

For Further Enrichment

A. Read the Snopes' trilogy (*The Hamlet, The Town,* and *The Mansion*). Complete a Book Checkup for each book.

B. ...is your response to this quote? If you agree, offer evidence from contemporary books, movies, and television to support your answer. *From history one can find plenty of evidence: Adolf Hitler among others. In totalitarian regimes today, as in the past, Naturalism and Realism spawn dictators.*

Supplemental Resources:

Walter Truett Anderson, *Reality Isn't What It Used To Be*
    Faulkner was the quintessential modern writer who usher into American culture the Postmodern era. Six stories competing in Postmodern era: 1) Western myth of progress; 2) Marxism and Revolution; 3) Christian Fundamentalism; 4) Islamic Fundamentalism; 5) Green; 6) New Age.

Allan Bloom, *The Closing of the American Mind*
  As it now stands, students have a powerful image of what a perfect body is and pursue it incessantly. But deprived of ...guidance they no longer have any image of a perfect soul and hence do not long to have ...the eternal conflict between good and evil has been replaced with 'I'm okay, you're okay.' Men and women once paid for difficult choices with their reputations, their sanity, and even their lives. But no more...America has no-fault automobile accidents, no fault insurance...no consequence choices.

S.D. Gaede, *When Tolerance is No Virtue*
    In our culture, there is considerable confusion about how we ought to live with our differences and a cacophony of contradictory justifications for one approach as opposed to another. All appeal to the need of tolerance, but there is nothing like common argument on what that means. The question our culture raises by nature and development is what is truth and what can we believe? Our culture doesn't know the answers. In fact, we have lost confidence in truth and have come to the conclusion that truth is unattainable. Thus, tolerance moves to the forefront. C. K. Chesterton wrote: Toleration is the virtue of the man without convictions. The Christian Response: A. We need to understand the culture in which we live--one in which relativism is growing which leads to injustice. B. We must know what is right and do it. C. We must seek justice--we cannot turn a blind eye to the injustices related to multi-culturalism. D. We must affirm truth and not tolerate relativism. E. The church must be who it is--it must express its convictions about truth and justice and practice and express tolerance (i.e., love) to the multi-cultural body of Christ.

Minter, David L. *William Faulkner: His Life and Work*

Michael Novak, *Spirit of Democratic Capitalism*
  No political or economic system will survive without a cultural base (i.e., religion).

Ergo, we are in deep trouble in America because no revival is occurring in the Church.

Cornelius Plantinga, *Not the Way it is Supposed to Be: A Breviary of Sin*
    We need a healthy reminder of our sin and guilt. Not only do we need a healthy reminder of how sin affects us personally, we must remember that the truth of traditional Christianity saws against the grain of much in contemporary culture and therefore needs constant sharpening. Christianity's major doctrines need regular restatement so that people may believe them or believe them anew (x)

Dallas Willard, *The Spirit of the Disciplines: How God Changes Lives*
  The disciplines for the spiritual life, rightly understood, are time tested activities consciously undertaken by us as new men or women to allow our spirit ever increasing sway over our embodied selves. They help by assisting the ways of God's Kingdom to take the place of the habits of sin embedded in our bodies.

Notes:

Lesson Twenty-Six Test

Essay: (100 Points)

William Faulkner has retained you to be his ghost writer. He wants you to write a short story, 150 words, exhibiting the style, characterization, plot, and other literary elements that are similar to his own.

Lesson Twenty-Six Test Answers

Essay: (100 Points)

William Faulkner has retained you to be his ghost writer. He wants you to write a short story, 150 words, exhibiting the style, characterization, plot, and other literary elements that are similar to his own.

Presumably the student's story would occur in the south and will exhibit several Faulknerian themes: love, alienation, racism.. In the following short story the narrator is an expatriate, southerner living in the north who visits his mother in the delta:

Larry King was gently scolding Al Gore. CNN Larry King Live was blaring from my mother's opaque Panasonic twenty-five inch screen. Electrons danced across this colander of 21st century entertainment. Cable television munificence clashed with dancing electronic intruders. Bounteous contradictions were everywhere evident.

It did not matter, though, because my mother only accessed one third of her available channels. The effort to ingress more exotic offerings in the upper channels was fatuous anyway. From Mom's perspective, she only needed CNN, the Weather Channel, and the History Channel. Even the local news did not interest her now. This was all the entertainment she needed and, to her, news was entertainment. Mom was dying of pancreatic cancer.

Lying under a crocheted brightly colored afghan knitted by her mother, affectionately called Big Momma by all other generations, mom was obviously defeated by the cancer interlopers who had completely subdued her body and were now skirmishing with her spirit. With her blonde frosted wig slightly askew on her forehead mom very much appeared the defeated warrior.

She needed the bright color in the afghan to tease vigor from her emaciated frame and color from her pallid skin. Big Momma had shamelessly knit bright chartreuse, gold, and pinks into her afghan. Her cacophonic choices doomed the afghan to family coffers or to the most destitute recipient who had no ardor for natural, appealing, subtle hues or had no affordable choice anyway. My mother's body, naturally big boned but until recently pudgy, unnaturally jutted out from loose knitted perimeters. Her angular right knee was lassoed by a frayed portion of Big Momma's much used, little appreciated afghan. It looked like a reptile peeking through the burnished flora of a viscous jungle thicket.

It suited my mother just fine now, though. She felt frayed, tattered, and very old. She also felt used and useless. In the dim hue of Larry King Live the afghan and my mother had a bizarre, surrealistic demeanor that accurately depicted the environs of her crumbling world.

It started with a stomach ache. Ordinary in scope and sequence this stomach ace nonetheless was an aberration in my mother's medical portfolio. Mom simply wasn't sick. Never. Her delusion of immortality was so endemic to her personality that sickness was beyond the realm of her possibilities.

Unfortunately, the stomach ache ended and the anemia began. In most medical communities anemia is a sure sign that something is amiss in the gastrointestinal cosmos. In the Southern Arkansas universe, where my mother lived, medicine was more empathic than empirical and anemia was perceived as too much fried chicken or turnip greens. This diagnosis worked well enough, perhaps better, that conventional interventions, in colds, flu, and the occasional gall bladder attack. However, in the really big things--like pancreatic cancer--normal rural southern medical practice was hopelessly dilatory and inevitably, therefore, nugatory.

My mother, who walked three miles a day and regularly ate chicken gizzards fried in old lard shrugged her shoulders and forgot about the whole thing. In fact, even after Geritol and BC Powders failed, she refused to visit her doctor. To question a doctor-friend's diagnosis was worse than cancer. With confident sanguineness, old Dr. E. P. Donahue, throat reflector protruding from his head, oversized Masonic ring protruding from his left middle finger, pronounced mom to be in remarkably good health. Dr. Donahue, who had delivered all Mom's three boys, was infallible. The medical "pope" as it were, whose edicts, once promulgated, were infallible.

Mom's malady, however, was already fatal. Her stamina and obstinacy propelled her forward for almost a year, but the carcinoma had already ambushed her. No one could not tell, though, because she was in such great health. "My health," my mother ironically shrugged, "killed me."

By the time our family surgeon and good friend Dr. Johnny Joe Jones, one of Dr. Donahue's cardinals, called the hogs with mom one last time before she went into the operating room and opened her up with his scalpel, mom was mellifluent with metastatic carcinoma.

Dr. Johnny Joe was the best surgeon in Arkansas. There was one--Dr. Robert P. Howell--who was as good but tt was rumored that he was a Unitarian. Besides, he enjoyed Jack Daniels too much. That was ok if one sought his services on a Wednesday. He was sober on Wednesdays out of respect for his Assembly of God mother who always went to church on Wednesdays. And it was Thursday.

Trained in Houston, TX--the medical school mecca of the South--everyone wanted a doctor trained in Houston--he must be good if he was from Houston--Dr. Johnny Joe was a brilliant, skilled surgeon. He had assisted in the first heart transplant attempt (the patient died) in Arkansas. He was also a Presbyterian. Everyone knew that the best doctors were Presbyterians who went to medical school in Houston. In spite of one nasty habit--Dr. Johnny Joe chewed Red Chief Tobacco during surgery--he was much sought after. "Wipe my mouth, nurse," Dr. Johnny Joe asked. Dr. Jones loved the Razorbacks. When he had to miss the game he nonetheless kept the radio blaring in the operating room. Once, while removing Mrs. Nickle's appendix, Texas intercepted a pass and ran back for a touchdown. Reacting to this tragedy, Dr. Jones' scalpel cut out Mrs. Nickle's appendix and spleen. No one blamed him.

No, my mother was fortunate to have him. He was pretty busy but since he was a good friend of my mother's old neighbor Josephine Mae Stuart, he agreed to take my mom's case.

Five minutes after Dr. Johnny Joe opened my mother up, he determined that the villainous corporeality had begun in the pancreas but it had progressed too far too quickly and it was not worth anyone's while for him to do anything but remove a particularly nefarious and ripe-with- cancer gall bladder. Deep inside my mother's liver, with his rubber clad left hand, Dr. Johnny Joe had rolled the marble-size tumors between his thumb and index finger. "Wipe my mouth, nurse," He sighed.

Mom's tumor infected gall bladder was sent to Houston for tests but Dr. Johnny Joe had already announced my mother's death sentence. It was over just that quickly. With buck season in full swing. Dr. Johnny Joe was still able to kill a four point later that afternoon. Mom went home to die. Mom did not know that her gall bladder had been removed until she received her hospital bill. She thought it would be impolite to say anything. Dr. Johnny Joe could have taken out her heart and she would have still been grateful.

Southern medicine was like that. Doctors politely did as they pleased. We Northerners want to know what our physicians do. We make them give us forms to sign and we ask for long lectures. We look at their diplomas on their walls and we want to know if they are board certified. All mom wanted was a smile, a nod, and a pat on her hand. "Johnny Joe is a good boy," mom said. "Josephine says he visits his mother every Saturday and he tithes."

For the first time my mother was hedged in. She could not fight this thing. Her chances of survival, Dr. T. J. Jackson, the oncologist, who was a Texas Longhorn fan--a grievous shortcoming only overcome by his obvious doctoring skills--adjudged, were zero. But she never wanted to hear the truth. Neither Dr. Johnny Joe or Dr. Jackson told mom. She did not want to know and they were too polite to tell her. My blood boiled. I smelled malpractice here. Mom only smelled okra gumbo stewing in the kitchen.

It turns out, however, she knew anyway and the okra gumbo probably did her more good anyway. Virginia Maria, her childhood Catholic friend who gambled with her on the grounded riverboats at Greenville, Mississippi, told her, "Nelle, I am so sorry to hear you are going to die. And probably before the July Bonanza Night!"

"I'm sorry to hear that I'm going to miss the July Bonanza Night too," she calmly responded.

As if she was sipping a new brand of orange pekoe tea, to make her family happy, she tried a little chemo-therapy. No one dared die of cancer in 1999 without having a little chemo-therapy. Hospice care was for colored folks, my mom said, who did not have insurance. She meant to have all the medical care Blue Cross and Blue Shield owed her. Unfortunately, it only succeeded in destroying what hair she had left and caused her to discard her last pack of Winston Lights.

"Do you have, Mr. Vice President," Larry King leaned across his desk, "anything else to add."

Although we did not know it, this was the last few weeks of her life. Mom knew it. She had literally moved into her living room. She did not want to die in the backwaters of a bedroom. She did not want to die on the bed she and my father had made love and dreamed dreams that neither lived. She did not want to die on the periphery of life. She wanted to be in the middle of the action. Her living room controlled all accesses to her house. She was the gatekeeper and planned to man her station until she literally dropped dead. A captain at her helm. With her CB radio scanning for police gossip, with practically every light burning, with her television running day and night, mom wanted to feel the ebullience of life until the bitter end. She intended to watch Larry King Live until she dropped dead.

It was Christmas and this was both the last Christmas I would be with my mother on this earth and the first one I had spent with her for two decades. The juxtaposition of these to portentous events seemed strangely ironical to me. I had lost my mother only to reclaim her in death.

I was not proud of the fact that I had not been home for Christmas in twenty-two years. I had too many kids, too many bills, and too little income to justify a two day trip from my Pennsylvania farm to Southern Arkansas. Besides, who wanted to leave the postcard, snowy Pennsylvania Laurel Highlands to spend Christmas along the dirty black railroad ties of the Delta? Who wanted to replace the pristine Mennonite farms of Western PA with the cotton strewn roads of Southern Arkansas?

"I want to tell you a few things, Jimmy (my name), before I join your dad," she said. Mom never said that she was "dying" or even "passing away." She was always going to join dad who had died eighteen years previously.

My mother told me some stories that changed my history. Not that history changed--my history changed. Those hours, those days before she died changed the way I saw my past, and therefore my present and future, forever. I began to write this novel about my mother. But, while she has a ubiquitous presence in my life, I realized I was unqualified to write about her life. I could barely talk about my own. What I discovered really, was that this is a novel about both our lives. Lives that would thrown together and torn apart in ancestral kinship, in hatred, and finally thrown together again in great love. It is also about a land, the South, that we both loved and hated.
(James P. Stobaugh, unpublished novel)

Lesson Twenty-Seven

Readings Due For This Lesson

Students should have read "Everything That Rises Must Converge," Flannery O'Connor.

Reading Ahead

Read "The Tall Men," William Faulkner (Lessons Twenty-Eight).

Suggested Weekly Implementation

Day One	Day Two	Day Three	Day Four	Day Five
1. Students will rewrite graded essays from last week and review Lesson Twenty-Six test. 2. Students should have read the required reading(s) *before* the assigned lesson begins. 3. Teacher may want to discuss assigned reading(s) with student. 4. Teacher shall assign the required essays. Choose two or three. The rest of the essays can be outlined, answered with shorter answers, or skipped.	1. Student should begin reading(s) from next lesson. 2. Student should outline essays due at the end of the week. 3. Students should answer one or two of the essays that are not assigned as formal essays.	1. Students should write rough drafts of assigned essays. 2. The teacher should correct rough drafts.	Student will write final copy of essays due tomorrow.	1. Essays are due. 2. Students should take Lesson Twenty-Seven test. 3. Read 20th century short story selections (Lessons Twenty-Seven and Twenty-Eight)

Twentieth Century American Short Stories

Critical Thinking

A. In what ways are Julian and his mother similar? *They are both intolerant.* Different? *Julian claims to be open minded; His mother makes no claim. S.D. Gaede, When Tolerance is No Virtue. Downers Grove: InterVarsity Press, 1993, argues that in our culture, there is considerable confusion about how we ought to live with our differences and a cacophony of contradictory justifications for one approach as opposed to another. All appeal to the need of tolerance, but there is nothing like common argument on what that means. The question our culture raises by nature and development is what is truth and what can we believe? Our culture doesn't know the answers. In fact, we have lost confidence in truth and have come to the conclusion that truth is unattainable. Thus, tolerance moves to the forefront. C. K. Chesterton wrote: Toleration is the virtue of the man without convictions. The Christian Response: A. We need to understand the culture in which we live--one in which relativism is growing which leads to injustice. B. We must know what is right and do it. C. We must seek justice--we cannot turn a blind eye to the injustices related to multi-culturalism. D. We must affirm truth and not tolerate relativism. E. The church must be who it is--it must express its convictions about truth and justice and practice and express tolerance (i.e., love) to the multi-cultural body of Christ. The reason I say this is because Julian claims to be intolerant but he is also immoral. One cannot be intolerant and immoral at the same time. As bigoted as Julian's mom is, she still is more principled than Julian.*

B. Why is it ironic that both Julian and his mother both focus their dreams on the same things? *They both want to be loved, to be accepted, and affirmed.*

C. What does the title mean? *In the heat of the moment both personalities appear the same. They converge. At the same time, they are very much apart.*

For Further Enrichment

Read other short stories by Eudora Welty, Jesse Stuart, Sherwood Anderson, And Carson McCullers.

Challenge Question

William Faulkner was deeply influenced by the American short story writer Sherwood Anderson. In a one to two page essay, discuss similarities between this short story and "The Tall Men."

The New Englander

Elsie Leander and her girlhood was spent on her father's farm in Vermont. For several generations the Leanders had all lived on the same farm and had all married thin women, and so she was thin. The farm lay in the shadow of a mountain and the soil was not very rich. From the beginning and for several generations there had been a great many sons and few daughters in the family. The sons had gone west or to New York City and the daughters had stayed at home and thought such thoughts as come to New England women who see the sons of their father's neighbour slipping, away, one by one, into the West.

Her father's house was a small white frame affair, and when you went out at the back door, past a small barn and a chicken house, you got into a path that ran up the side of a hill and into an orchard. The trees were all old and gnarled. At the back of the orchard the hill dropped away and bare rocks showed.

Inside the fence a large grey rock stuck high up out of the ground. As Elsie sat with her back to the rock, with a mangled hillside at her feet, she could see several large mountains, apparently but a short distance away, and between herself and the mountains lay many tiny fields surrounded by neatly built stone walls. Everywhere rocks appeared. Large ones, too heavy to be moved, stuck out of the ground in the center of the fields. The fields were like cups filled with a green liquid that turned grey in the fall and white in the winter. The mountains, far off but apparently near at hand, were like giants ready at any moment to reach out their hands and take the cups one by one and drink off the green liquid. The large rocks in the fields were like the thumbs of the giants.

Elsie had three brothers, born ahead of her, but they had all gone away. Two of them had gone to live with her uncle in the West and her elder brother had gone to New York City where he had married and prospered. All through his youth and manhood her father had worked hard and had lived a hard life, but his son in New York City had begun to send money home, and after that things went better. He still worked every day about the barn or in the fields but he did not worry about the future. Elsie's mother did house work in the mornings and in the afternoons sat in a rocking chair in her tiny living room and thought of her sons while she crocheted table covers and tidies for the backs of chairs. She was a silent woman, very thin and with very thin bony hands. She did not ease herself into a rocking chair but sat down and got up suddenly, and when she crocheted her back was as straight as the back of a drill sergeant.

> The first thing that needs to be said is that Anderson's writing is much different from Faulkner's. Faulkner writes in very complicated, long prose, but Anderson writes in much smaller, simpler prose.

The mother rarely spoke to the daughter. Sometimes in the afternoons as the younger woman went up the hillside to her place by the rock at the back of the orchard, her father came out of the barn and stopped her. He put a hand on her shoulder and asked where she was going. "To the rock," she said and her father laughed. His laughter was like the creaking of a rusty barn door hinge and the hand he had laid on her shoulder was thin like her own hands and like her mother's hands. The father went into the barn shaking his head. "She's like her mother. She is herself like a rock," he thought. At the head of the path that led from the house to the orchard there was a great cluster of bayberry bushes. The New England farmer came out of his barn to watch his daughter go along the path, but she had disappeared behind the bushes. He looked away past his house to the fields and to the mountains in the distance. He also saw the green cup-like fields and the grim mountains. There was an almost imperceptible tightening of the muscles of his half worn-out old body. For a long time he stood in silence and then, knowing from long experience the danger of having thoughts, he went back into the barn and busied himself with the mending of an agricultural tool that had been mended many times before.

The son of the Leanders who went to live in New York City was the father of one son, a thin sensitive boy who looked like Elsie. The son died when he was twenty-three years old and some years later the father died and left his money to the old people on the New England farm. The two Leanders who had gone west had lived there with their father's brother, a farmer, until they grew into manhood. Then Will, the younger, got a job on a railroad. He was killed one winter morning. It was a cold snowy day and when the freight train he was in charge of as conductor left the city of Des Moines, he started to run over the tops of the cars. His feet slipped and he shot down into space. That was the end of him.

Of the new generation there was only Elsie and her brother Tom, whom she had never seen, left alive. Her father and mother talked of going west to Tom for two years before they came to a decision. Then it took another year to dispose of the farm and make preparations. During the whole time Elsie did not think much about the change about to take place in her life.

The trip west on the railroad train jolted Elsie out of herself. In spite of her detached attitude toward life she became excited. Her mother sat up very straight and stiff in the seat in the sleeping car and her father

> Individuals displaced from the land are without direction and hope. A similar theme appears in Faulkner.

walked up and down in the aisle. After a night when the younger of the two women did not sleep but lay awake with red burning cheeks and with her thin fingers incessantly picking at the bed-clothes in her berth while the train went through towns and cities, crawled up the sides of hills and fell down into forest-clad valleys, she got up and dressed to sit all day looking at a new kind of land. The train ran for a day and through another sleepless night in a flat land where every field was as large as a farm in her own country. Towns appeared and disappeared in a continual procession. The whole land was so unlike anything she had ever known that she began to feel unlike herself. In the valley where she had been born and where she had lived all her days everything had an air of finality. Nothing could be changed. The tiny fields were chained to the earth. They were fixed in their places and surrounded by aged stone walls. The fields like the mountains that looked down at them were as unchangeable as the passing days. She had a feeling they had always been so, would always be so.

Elsie sat like her mother upright in the car seat and with a back like the back of a drill sergeant. The train ran swiftly along through Ohio and Indiana. Her thin hands like her mother's hands were crossed and locked. One passing casually through the car might have thought both women prisoners handcuffed and bound to their seats. Night came on and she again got into her berth. Again she lay awake and her thin cheeks became flushed, but she thought new thoughts. Her hands were no longer gripped together and she did not pick at the bed clothes. Twice during the night she stretched herself and yawned, a thing she had never in her life done before. The train stopped at a town on the prairies, and as there was something the matter with one of the wheels of the car in which she lay the trainsmen came with flaming torches to tinker it. There was a great pounding and shouting. When the train went on its way she wanted to get out of her berth and run up and down in the aisle of the car. The fancy had come to her that the men tinkering with the car wheel were new men out of the new land who had broken with strong hammers the doors of her prison away. They had destroyed forever the programme she had made for her life.

Elsie was filled with joy at the thought that the train was still going on into the West. She wanted to go on for ever in a straight line into the unknown. She fancied herself no longer on a train and imagined she had become a winged thing flying through space. Her long years of sitting alone by the rock on the New England farm had got her into the habit of expressing her thoughts aloud. Her thin voice broke the silence that lay over the sleeping car and her father and mother, both also lying awake, sat up in their berth to listen.

Tom Leander, the only living male representative of the new generation of Leanders, was a loosely built man of forty inclined to corpulency. At twenty he had married the daughter of a neighboring farmer, and when his wife inherited some money she and Tom moved into the town of Apple Junction in Iowa where Tom opened a grocery. The venture prospered as did Tom's matrimonial venture. When his brother died in New York City and his father, mother, and sister decided to come west Tom was already the father of a daughter and four sons.

On the prairies north of town and in the midst of a vast level stretch of corn fields, there was a partly completed brick house that had belonged to a rich farmer named Russell, who had begun to build the house intending to make it the most magnificent place in the county, but when it was almost completed he had found himself without money and heavily in debt. The farm, consisting of several hundred acres of corn land, had been split into three farms and sold. No one had wanted the huge unfinished brick house. For years it had stood vacant, its windows staring out over the fields that had been planted almost up to the door.

In buying the Russell house Tom was moved by two motives. He had a notion that in New England the Leanders had been rather magnificent people. His memory of his father's place in the Vermont valley was shadowy, but in speaking of it to his wife he became very definite. "We had good blood in us, we Leanders," he said, straightening his shoulders. "We lived in a big house. We were important people."

Wanting his father and mother to feel at home in the new place, Tom had also another motive. He was not a very energetic man and, although he had done well enough as keeper of a grocery, his success was largely due to the boundless energy of his wife. She did not pay much attention to her household and her children, like little animals, had to take care of themselves, but in any matter concerning the store her word was law.

To have his father the owner of the Russell Place Tom felt would establish him as a man of consequence in the eyes of his neighbor. "I can tell you what, they're used to a big house," he said to his wife. "I tell you what, my people are used to living in style."

The exaltation that had come over Elsie on the train wore away in the presence of grey empty Iowa fields, but something of the effect of it remained with her for months. In the big brick house life went on much as it had in the tiny New England house where she had always lived. The Leanders installed themselves in three or four rooms on the ground floor. After a few weeks the furniture that had been shipped by freight arrived and was hauled out from town in one of Tom's grocery wagons. There were three or four acres of ground covered with great piles of boards the unsuccessful farmer had intended to use in the building of stables. Tom sent men to haul the boards away and Elsie's father prepared to plant a garden. They had come west in April and as soon as they were installed in the house ploughing and planting began in the fields near by. The habit of a lifetime returned to the daughter of the house. In the new place there was no gnarled orchard surrounded by a half-ruined stone fence. All of the fences in all of the fields that stretched away out of sight to the north, south, east, and west were made of wire and looked like spider webs against the blackness of the ground when it had been freshly ploughed.

There was however the house itself. It was like an island rising out of the sea. In an odd way the house, although it was less than ten years old, was very old. Its unnecessary bigness represented an old impulse in men. Elsie felt that. At the east side there was a door leading to a stairway that ran into the upper part of the house that was kept locked. Two or three stone steps led up to it. Elsie could sit on the top step with her back against the door and gaze into the distance without being disturbed. Almost at her feet began the fields that seemed to go on and on for ever. The fields were like the waters of a sea. Men came to plough and plant. Giant horses moved in a procession across the prairies. A young man who drove six horses came directly toward her. She was fascinated. The breasts of the horses as they came forward with bowed heads seemed like the breasts of giants. The soft spring air that lay over the fields was also like a sea. The horses were giants walking on the floor of a sea. With their breasts they pushed the waters of the sea before them. They were pushing the waters out of the basin of the sea. The young man who drove them was also a giant.

Elsie pressed her body against the closed door at the top of the steps. In the garden back of the house she could hear her father at work. He was raking dry masses of weeds off the ground preparatory to spading the ground for a family garden. He had always worked in a tiny confined place and would do the same thing here. In this vast open placc he would work with small tools, doing little things with infinite care, raising little vegetables. In the house her mother would crochet little tidies. She herself would be small. She would press her body against the door of the house, try to get herself out of sight. Only the feeling that sometimes took possession of her, and that did not form itself into a thought, would be large.

The six horses turned at the fence and the outside horse got entangled in the traces. The driver swore vigorously. Then he turned and stared at the pale New Englander and with another oath pulled the heads of the horses about and drove away into the distance. The field in which he was ploughing contained two hundred acres. Elsie did not wait for him to return but went into the house and sat with folded arms in a room. The house she thought was a ship floating in a sea on the floor of which giants went up and down.

May came and then June. In the great fields work was always going on and Elsie became somewhat used to the sight of the young man in the field that came down to the steps. Sometimes when he drove his horses down to the wire fence he smiled and nodded. In the month of August, when it is very hot, the corn in Iowa fields grows until the corn stalks resemble young trees. The corn fields become forests. The time for the cultivating of the corn has passed and weeds grow thick between the corn rows. The men with their giant horses have gone away. Over the immense fields silence broods.

When the time of the laying-by of the crop came that first summer after Elsie's arrival in the West her mind, partially awakened by the strangeness of the railroad trip, awakened again. She did not feel like a staid thin woman with a back like the back of a drill sergeant, but like something new and as strange as the new land into which she had come to live. For a time she did not know what was the matter. In the field the corn had grown so high that she could not see into the distance. The corn was like a wall and the little bare spot of land on which her father's house stood was like a house built behind the walls of a prison. For a time she was depressed, thinking that she had come west into a wide open country, only to find herself locked up more closely than ever.

An impulse came to her. She arose and going down three or four steps seated herself almost on a level with the ground.

Immediately she got a sense of release. She could not see over the corn but she could see under it. The corn had long wide leaves that met over the rows. The rows became long tunnels running away into infinity. Out of the black ground grew weeds that made a soft carpet of green. From above light sifted down. The corn rows were mysteriously beautiful. They were warm passageways running out into life. She got up from the steps, and walking timidly to the wire fence that separated her from the field, put her hand between the wires and took hold of one of the corn stalks. For some reason after she had touched the strong young stalk and had held it for a moment firmly in her hand she grew afraid. Running quickly back to the step she sat down and covered her face with her hands. Her body trembled. She tried to imagine herself crawling through the fence and wandering along one of the passageways. The thought of trying the experiment fascinated but at the same time terrified. She got quickly up and went into the house.

One Saturday night in August Elsie found herself unable to sleep. Thoughts, more definite than any she had ever known before, came into her mind. It was a quiet hot night and her bed stood near a window. Her room was the only one the Leanders occupied on the second floor of the house. At midnight a little breeze came up from the south and when she sat up in bed the floor of corn tassels lying below her line of sight looked in the moonlight like the face of a sea just stirred by a gentle breeze.

A murmuring began in the corn and murmuring thoughts and memories awoke in her mind. The long wide succulent leaves had begun to dry in the intense heat of the

August days and as the wind stirred the corn they rubbed against each other. A call, far away, as of a thousand voices arose. She imagined the voices were like the voices of children. They were not like her brother Tom's children, noisy boisterous little animals, but something quite different, tiny little things with large eyes and thin sensitive hands. One after another they crept into her arms. She became so excited over the fancy that she sat up in bed and taking a pillow into her arms held it against her breast. The figure of her cousin, the pale sensitive young Leander who had lived with his father in New York City and who had died at the age of twenty-three, came sharply into her mind. It was as though the young man had come suddenly into the room. She dropped the pillow and sat waiting, intense, expectant.

Young Harry Leander had come to visit his cousin on the New England farm during the late summer of the year before he died. He had stayed there for a month and almost every afternoon had gone with Elsie to sit by the rock at the back of the orchard. One afternoon when they had both been for a long time silent he began to talk. "I want to go live in the West," he said. "I want to go live in the West. I want to grow strong and be a man," he repeated. Tears came into his eyes.

They got up to return to the house, Elsie walking in silence beside the young man. The moment marked a high spot in her life. A strange trembling eagerness for something she had not realized in her experience of life had taken possession of her. They went in silence through the orchard but when they came to the bayberry bush her cousin stopped in the path and turned to face her. "I want you to kiss me," he said eagerly, stepping toward her.

A fluttering uncertainty had taken possession of Elsie and had been transmitted to her cousin. After he had made the sudden and unexpected demand and had stepped so close to her that his breath could be felt on her cheek, his own cheeks became scarlet and his hand that had taken her hand trembled. "Well, I wish I were strong. I only wish I were strong," he said hesitatingly and turning walked away along the path toward the house. And in the strange new house, set like an island in its sea of corn, Harry Leander's voice seemed to arise again above the fancied voices of the children that had been coming out of the fields. Elsie got out of bed and walked up and down in the dim light coming through the window. Her body trembled violently. "I want you to kiss me," the voice said again and to quiet it and to quiet also the answering voice in herself she went to kneel by the bed and taking the pillow again into her arms pressed it against her face.

Tom Leander came with his wife and family to visit his father and mother on Sundays. The family appeared at about ten o'clock in the morning. When the wagon turned out of the road that ran past the Russell Place Tom shouted. There was a field between the house and the road and the wagon could not be seen as it came along the narrow way through the corn. After Tom had shouted, his daughter Elizabeth, a tall girl of sixteen, jumped out of the wagon. All five children came tearing toward the house through the corn. A series of wild shouts arose on the still morning air.

The grocery man had brought food from the store. When the horse had been unhitched and put into a shed he and his wife began to carry packages into the house. The four Leander boys, accompanied by their sister, disappeared into the near-by fields. Three dogs that had trotted out from town under the wagon accompanied the children. Two or three children and occasionally a young man from a neighboring farm had come to join in the fun. Elsie's sister-in-law dismissed them all with a wave of her hand. With a wave of her hand she also brushed Elsie aside. Fires were lighted and the house reeked with the smell of cooking. Elsie went to sit on the step at the side of the house. The corn fields that had been so quiet rang with shouts and with the barking of dogs.

    Tom Leander's oldest child, Elizabeth, was like her mother, full of energy. She was thin and tall like the women of her father's house but very strong and alive. In secret she wanted to be a lady but when she tried her brothers, led by her father and mother, made fun of her. "Don't put on airs," they said. When she got into the country with no one but her brothers and two or three neighboring farm boys she herself became a boy. With the boys she went tearing through the fields, following the dogs in pursuit of rabbits. Sometimes a young man came with the children from a near-by farm. Then she did not know what to do with herself. She wanted to walk demurely along the rows through the corn but was afraid her brothers would laugh and in desperation outdid the boys in roughness and noisiness. She screamed and shouted and running wildly tore her dress on the wire fences as she scrambled over in pursuit of the dogs. When a rabbit was caught and killed she rushed in and tore it out of the grasp of the dogs. The blood of the little dying animal dripped on her clothes. She swung it over her head and shouted.

    The farm hand who had worked all summer in the field within sight of Elsie became enamored of the young woman from town. When the grocery man's family appeared on Sunday mornings he also appeared but did not come to the house. When the boys and dogs came tearing through the fields he joined them. He was also self-conscious and did not want the boys to know the purpose of his coming and when he and Elizabeth found themselves alone together he became embarrassed. For a moment they walked together in silence. In a wide circle about them, in the forest of the corn, ran the boys and dogs. The young man had something he wanted to say, but when he tried to find words his tongue became thick and his lips felt hot and dry. "Well," he began, "let's you and me -- "

    Words failed him and Elizabeth turned and ran after her brothers and for the rest of the day he could not manage to get her out of their sight. When he went to join them she became the noisiest member of the party. A frenzy of activity took possession of her. With hair hanging down her back, with clothes torn, and with cheeks and hands scratched and bleeding she led her brothers in the endless wild pursuit of the rabbits.

    The Sunday in August that followed Elsie Leander's sleepless night was hot and cloudy. In the morning she was half ill and as soon as the visitors from town arrived she crept away to sit on the step at the side of the house. The children ran away into the fields. An almost overpowering desire to run with them, shouting and playing along the corn rows took possession of her. She arose and went to the back of the house. Her father was at work in the garden, pulling weeds from between rows of vegetables. Inside the house she could hear her sister-in-law moving about. On the front porch her brother Tom was asleep with his mother beside him. Elsie went back on the step and then arose and went to where the corn came down to the fence. She climbed awkwardly over and went a little way along one of the rows. Putting out her hand she touched the firm hard stalks and then, becoming afraid, dropped to her knees on the carpet of weeds that covered the ground. For a long time she stayed thus listening to the voices of the children in the distance.

An hour slipped away. Presently it was time for dinner and her sister-in-law came to the back door and shouted. There was an answering whoop from the distance and the children came running through the fields. They climbed over the fence and ran shouting across her father's garden. Elsie also arose. She was about to attempt to climb back over the fence unobserved when she heard a rustling in the corn. Young Elizabeth Leander appeared. Beside her walked the ploughman who but a few months earlier had planted the corn in the field where Elsie now stood. She could see the two people coming slowly along the rows. An understanding had been established between them. The man reached through between the corn stalks and touched the hand of the girl who laughed awkwardly and running to the fence climbed quickly over. In her hand she held the limp body of a rabbit the dogs had killed.

The farm hand went away and when Elizabeth had gone into the house Elsie climbed over the fence. Her niece stood just within the kitchen door holding the dead rabbit by one leg. The other leg had been torn away by the dogs. At sight of the New England woman, who seemed to look at her with hard unsympathetic eyes, she was ashamed and went quickly into the house. She threw the rabbit upon a table in the parlor and then ran out of the room. Its blood ran out on the delicate flowers of a white crocheted table cover that had been made by Elsie's mother.

The Sunday dinner with all the living Leanders gathered about the table was gone through in a heavy lumbering silence. When the dinner was over and Tom and his wife had washed the dishes they went to sit with the older people on the front porch. Presently they were both asleep. Elsie returned to the step at the side of the house but when the desire to go again into the cornfields came sweeping over her she got up and went indoors.

The woman of thirty-five tip-toed about the big house like a frightened child. The dead rabbit that lay on the table in the parlor had become cold and stiff. Its blood had dried on the white table cover. She went upstairs but did not go to her own room. A spirit of adventure had hold of her. In the upper part of the house there were many rooms and in some of them no glass had been put into the windows. The windows had been boarded up and narrow streaks of light crept in through the cracks between the boards.

Elsie tip-toed up the flight of stairs past the room in which she slept and opening doors went into other rooms. Dust lay thick on the floors. In the silence she could hear her brother snoring as he slept in the chair on the front porch. From what seemed a far away place there came the shrill cries of the children. The cries became soft. They were like the cries of unborn children that had called to her out of the fields on the night before.

Into her mind came the intense silent figure of her mother sitting on the porch beside her son and waiting for the day to wear itself out into night. The thought brought a lump into her throat. She wanted something and did not know what it was. Her own mood frightened her. In a windowless room at the back of the house one of the boards over a window had been broken and a bird had flown in and become imprisoned.

The presence of the woman frightened the bird. It flew wildly about. Its beating wings stirred up dust that danced in the air. Elsie stood perfectly still, also frightened, not by the presence of the bird but by the presence of life. Like the bird she was a prisoner. The thought gripped her. She wanted to go outdoors where her niece Elizabeth walked with the young ploughman through the corn, but was like the bird in the room -- a prisoner. She moved restlessly about. The bird flew back and forth across the room. It alighted on the window sill near the place where the board was broken away. She stared into the frightened eyes of the bird that in turn stared into her eyes. Then the bird flew away, out through the window, and Elsie turned and ran nervously downstairs and out into the yard. She climbed over the wire fence and ran with stooped shoulders along one of the tunnels.

Elsie ran into the vastness of the cornfields filled with but one desire. She wanted to get out of her life and into some new and sweeter life she felt must be hidden away somewhere in the fields. After she had run a long way she came to a wire fence and crawled over. Her hair became unloosed and fell down over her shoulders. Her cheeks became flushed and for the moment she looked like a young girl. When she climbed over the fence she tore a great hole in the front of her dress. For a moment her tiny breasts were exposed and then her hand clutched and held nervously the sides of the tear. In the distance she could hear the voices of the boys and the barking of the dogs. A summer storm had been threatening for days and now black clouds had begun to spread themselves over the sky. As she ran nervously forward, stopping to listen and then running on again, the dry corn blades brushed against her shoulders and a fine shower of yellow dust from the corn tassels fell on her hair. A continued crackling noise accompanied her progress. The dust made a golden crown about her head. From the sky overhead a low rumbling sound, like the growling of giant dogs, came to her ears.

The thought that having at last ventured into the corn she would never escape became fixed in the mind of the running woman. Sharp pains shot through her body. Presently she was compelled to stop and sit on the ground. For a long time she sat with her closed eyes. Her dress became soiled. Little insects that live in the ground under the corn came out of their holes and crawled over her legs.

Following some obscure impulse the tired woman threw herself on her back and lay still with closed eyes. Her fright passed. It was warm and close in the room-like tunnels. The pain in her side went away. She opened her eyes and between the wide green corn blades could see patches of a black threatening sky. She did not want to be alarmed and so closed her eyes again. Her thin hand no longer gripped the tear in her dress and her tiny breasts were exposed. They expanded and contracted in little spasmodic jerks. She threw her hands back over her head and lay still.

It seemed to Elsie that hours passed as she lay thus, quiet and passive under the corn. Deep within her there was a feeling that something was about to happen, something that would lift her out of herself, that would tear her away from her past and the past of her people. Her thoughts were not definite. She lay still and waited as she had waited for days and months by the rock at the back of the orchard on the Vermont farm when she was a girl. A deep grumbling noise went on in the sky overhead but the sky and everything she had ever known seemed very far away, no part of herself.

After a long silence, when it seemed to her that she was lost from herself as in a dream, Elsie heard a man's voice calling. "Aho, aho, aho," shouted the voice and after another period of silence there arose answering voices and then the sound of bodies crashing through the corn and the excited chatter of children. A dog came running along the row where she lay and stood beside her. His cold nose touched her face and she sat up. The dog ran away. The Leander boys passed. She could see their bare legs flashing in and out across one of the tunnels. Her brother had become alarmed by the rapid approach of the thunder storm and wanted to get his family to town. His voice kept calling from the house and the voices of the children answered from the fields.

Elsie sat on the ground with her hands pressed together. An odd feeling of disappointment had possession of her. She arose and walked slowly along in the general direction taken by the children. She came to a fence and crawled over, tearing her dress in a new place. One of her stockings had become unloosed and had slipped down over her shoe top. The long sharp weeds had scratched her leg so that it was criss-crossed with red lines, but she was not conscious of any pain.

The distraught woman followed the children until she came within sight of her father's house and then stopped and again sat on the ground. There was another loud crash of thunder and Tom Leander's voice called again, this time half angrily. The name of the girl Elizabeth was shouted in loud masculine tones that rolled and echoed like the thunder along the aisles under the corn.

And then Elizabeth came into sight accompanied by the young ploughman. They stopped near Elsie and the man took the girl into his arms. At the sound of their approach Elsie had thrown herself face downward on the ground and had twisted herself into a position where she could see without being seen. When their lips met her tense hands grasped one of the corn stalks. Her lips pressed themselves into the dust. When they had gone on their way she raised her head. A dusty powder covered her lips.

What seemed another long period of silence fell over the fields. A strong wind began to blow and the corn rocked back and forth. The murmuring voices of unborn children, her imagination had created in the whispering fields, became a vast shout. The wind blew harder and harder. The corn stalks were twisted and bent. Elizabeth went thoughtfully out of the field and climbing the fence confronted her father. "Where you been? What you been a doing?" he asked. "Don't you know we got to get out of here?"

When Elizabeth went toward the house Elsie followed, creeping on her hands and knees like a little animal, and when she had come within sight of the fence surrounding the house she sat on the ground and put her hands over her face. Something within herself was being twisted and whirled about as the tops of the corn stalks were now being twisted and whirled by the wind. She sat so that she did not look toward the house and when she opened her eyes she could again see along the long mysterious aisles.

Her brother, with his wife and children, went away. By turning her head Elsie could see them driving at a trot out of the yard back of her father's house. With the going of the younger woman the farm house in the midst of the cornfield rocked by the winds seemed the most desolate place in the world.

Her mother came out at the back door of the house. She ran to the steps where she knew her daughter was in the habit of sitting and then in alarm began to call. It did not occur to Elsie to answer. The voice of the older woman did not seem to have anything to do with herself. It was a thin voice and was quickly lost in the wind and in the crashing sound that arose out of the fields. With her head turned toward the house Elsie stared at her mother who ran wildly around the house and then went indoors. The back door of the house went shut with a bang.

The storm that had been threatening broke with a roar. Broad sheets of water swept over the cornfields. Sheets of water swept over the woman's body. The storm that had for years been gathering in her also broke. Sobs arose out of her throat. She abandoned herself to a storm of grief that was only partially grief. Tears ran out of her eyes and made little furrows through the dust on her face. In the lulls that occasionally came in the storm she raised her head and heard, through the tangled mass of wet hair that covered her ears and above the sound of millions of rain-drops that alighted on the earthen floor inside the house of the corn, the thin voices of her mother and father calling to her out of the Leander house.

Supplementary Resources

Robert N. Bellah and Frederick E. Greenspahn, *Uncivil Religion: Interreligious Hostility in America*

Harold Bloom, ed., *Modern Critical Views: Flannery O'Connor*

Henry Fairlie, *The Seven Deadly Sins Today*

Gertrude Himmelfarb, *On Looking Into the Abyss*
The first essay, with the same title as the book, describes how in the field of literature the great works are no longer read--or if they are, there are essentially no rules for interpreting them; how in philosophy, truth and reality are considered non-existent. And how in history deconstruction allows the historian to come to any conclusions he

chooses. The second essay continues this line of thought, focusing especially on the freedom taken by authors or professors in recreating events and biographies to suit their ends, which often involves watering down the great individual accomplishments and events of history. This then allows them to place themselves above the people or events they are describing.

Ramsy MacMullen, *Christianizing the Roman Empire A.D. 100-400*
    MacMullen gives us insights on how to do evangelism in an hostile environment.

Brian A Ragen, *A wreck on the road to Damascus: innocence, guilt, & conversion in Flannery O'Connor*

H. R. Rookmaaker, *Modern Art and the Death of Culture*

A. Tanquerey, *The Spiritual Life*

Notes:

Lesson Twenty-Seven Test

Essay: (100 Points)

Write an evaluation of this short story. Be candid in expressing your reactions to the work. Did you like it or not? Support your arguments with specific references to the work. In your essay consider the theme, characters, plot, and other literary elements.

Lesson Twenty-Seven Test Answer

Essay: (100 Points)

Write an evaluation of this short story. Be candid in expressing your reactions to the work. Did you like it or not? Support your arguments with specific references to the work. In your essay consider the theme, characters, plot, and other literary elements.

Answer will vary. This brilliant short story is superb. The characters are economically and precisely created. The plot is well considered; the action flows quickly to a powerful climax. One theme–love and hate are very close emotions– is subtly developed.

Lesson Twenty-Eight

Readings Due For This Lesson
Students should have read "Tall Men," William Faulkner.

Reading Ahead

Read *Emperor Jones*, Eugene O'Neill (Lesson Twenty-Nine), *The Little Foxes*, Lillian Hellman (Lesson Thirty), and *The Glass Menagerie*, Tennessee Williams (Lessons Thirty-One, Thirty-Two, and Thirty-Three).

Suggested Weekly Implementation

Day One	Day Two	Day Three	Day Four	Day Five
1. Students will rewrite graded essays from last week and review Lesson Twenty-Seven test. 2. Students should have read the required reading(s) *before* the assigned lesson begins. 3. Teacher may want to discuss assigned reading(s) with student. 4. Teacher shall assign the required essays. Choose two or three. The rest of the essays can be outlined, answered with shorter answers, or skipped.	1. Student should begin reading(s) from next lesson. 2. Student should outline essays due at the end of the week. 3. Students should answer one or two of the essays that are not assigned as formal essays.	1. Students should write rough drafts of assigned essays. 2. The teacher should correct rough drafts.	Student will write final copy of essays due tomorrow.	1. Essays are due. 2. Students should take Lesson Twenty-Eight test. 3. Read 20th century drama sections (Lesson Twenty-Nine through Lesson Thirty-Three).

Literary Criticism

A. Compare and contrast the world view of the state draft investigator and the marshal. *The state draft investigator is a "by the book" sort of man. The marshal is more flexible. Faulkner is satirizing the intransigent investigator.*

B. Why is Faulkner's title for this story correct? *Once the boys understood their duty they did so with no dispute. They were so "tall" that they could even hug and kiss their parents good-bye.*

C. Describe Faulkner's narrative technique. How does it enhance his story? *Omniscient narration is important to Faulkner's stream of consciousness characterization.*

D. Very little real action occurs in this story yet the plot develops very well. How does Faulkner accomplish this? *Mostly by good writing and lengthy development of internal and external conflict among the characters.*

Supplementary Resources

Robert N. Bellah and Frederick E. Greenspahn, *Uncivil Religion: Interreligious Hostility in America*

Harold Bloom, ed., *Modern Critical Views: Flannery O'Connor*

Henry Fairlie, *The Seven Deadly Sins Today*

Gertrude Himmelfarb, *On Looking Into the Abyss*
    The first essay, with the same title as the book, describes how in the field of literature the great works are no longer read--or if they are, there are essentially no rules for interpreting them; how in philosophy, truth and reality are considered non-existent. And how in history deconstruction allows the historian to come to any conclusions he chooses. The second essay continues this line of thought, focusing especially on the freedom taken by authors or professors in recreating events and biographies to suit their ends, which often involves watering down the great individual accomplishments and events of history. This then allows them to place themselves above the people or events they are describing.

Ramsy MacMullen, *Christianizing the Roman Empire A.D. 100-400*
    MacMullen gives us insights on how to do evangelism in an hostile environment.

Brian A Ragen, *A wreck on the road to Damascus: innocence, guilt, & conversion in Flannery O'Connor*

H. R. Rookmaaker, *Modern Art and the Death of Culture*

A. Tanquerey, *The Spiritual Life*

Notes:

Lesson Twenty-Eight Test

Essay: (100 Points)

Write an evaluation of this short story. Be candid in expressing your reactions to the work. Did you like it or not? Support your arguments with specific references to the work. In your essay consider the theme, characters, plot, and other literary elements.

Lesson Twenty-Eight Test Answer

Essay: (100 Points)

Write an evaluation of this short story. Be candid in expressing your reactions to the work. Did you like it or not? Support your arguments with specific references to the work. In your essay consider the theme, characters, plot, and other literary elements.

Answer will vary. The story moves very quickly with a hint of humor–yet the reader is struck again and again with the great irony of the situation. It is a remarkable story!

LESSON TWENTY-NINE

Readings Due For This Lesson
Students should have read *Emperor Jones*, Eugene O'Neill.

Reading Ahead

Read *The Little Foxes*, Lillian Hellman (Lesson Thirty), and *The Glass Menagerie*, Tennessee Williams (Lessons Thirty-One, Thirty-Two, and Thirty-Three).

Suggested Weekly Implementation

Day One	Day Two	Day Three	Day Four	Day Five
1. Students will rewrite graded essays from last week and review Lesson Twenty-Eight test. 2. Students should have read the required reading(s) *before* the assigned lesson begins. 3. Teacher may want to discuss assigned reading(s) with student. 4. Teacher shall assign the required essays. Choose two or three. The rest of the essays can be outlined, answered with shorter answers, or skipped.	1. Student should begin reading(s) from next lesson. 2. Student should outline essays due at the end of the week. 3. Students should answer one or two of the essays that are not assigned as formal essays.	1. Students should write rough drafts of assigned essays. 2. The teacher should correct rough drafts.	Student will write final copy of essays due tomorrow.	1. Essays are due. 2. Students should take Lesson Twenty-Nine test. 3. Read 20th century drama sections (Lesson Thirty through Lesson Thirty-Three).

Literary Criticism

Discuss in detail how O'Neill builds suspense in this play. *Brutus Jones is alone in his fears. Using the sound of drums and flashback O'Neill keeps us on the edge of our seat. From the moment Brutus enters the forest, he enters a surrealistic journey back in time to his own past.*

Critical Thinking

A. There are several layers of conflict in this play. Comment on the several kinds of conflict that arise in this play. *Jones vs. Jones, Jones vs. slaveholders, Jones vs. his subjects.*

B. Find several instances of Naturalism in this play. *The pervasive sense of nature and fate are powerful in this play. The forest is foreboding and evil. There is no moral structure that holds the world together. In fact, it is the abandonment of that faith structure that doomed Brutus.*

Supplementary Resources

Molefi K. Asante, and Mark T. Mattson,. *Historical and Cultural Atlas of African-Americans*
    The single best resource of the African-American experience in America. It is full of pictures, graphs, and timely articles.

Robert N. Bellah, and Frederick E. Greenspahn, *Uncivil Religion: Interreligious Hostility in America*
    Bellah and Greenspahn are gifted sociologists who employ their ample skills to analyze cross-racial religious controversy in America–one of the most lamentable chapters in our history.

Andrew Billingsley, *Black Families in White America*
    A very scholarly book that nonetheless is important to this area. Billingsley argues that the African-American family is the key to the slave's survival and the maintenance of African-American culture.

John W. Blassingame, *The Slave Community*
   Blassingame, like Billingsley, argues for the efficacy of the African-American slave family.

David Blankenhorn, Jr., *Fatherless America: Confronting Our Most Urgent Social Problem.*
   A scathing criticism of the American social welfare system. David Blankenhorn, in his revolutionary work of cultural criticism, asks an anti-modern, almost heretical question: "So the question is not, *What do men want?* but rather, *What do men do?*" Blankenhorn goes where very few social historians dare to go before: he argues that men should be, very simply, good fathers--no matter how hard it is, or how foolish it may seem. "In a larger sense, the fatherhood story is the irreplaceable basis of a culture's most urgent imperative: the socialization of males." (p. 65). American children need fathers, American society needs fathers.

Ashley Bryan,, *Sing to the Sun*, *The Story of Lightning and Thunder*, *Climbing Jacob's Ladder: Heroes of the Bible in African-American Spirituals*, *Turtle Knows Your Name*, and *All Night, All Day: A Child's First Book of African-American Spirituals*
   The foremost African-American cultural historian in America. Using children's books as a vehicle, Bryan inspires his reader with fresh insights of African-American culture.

John Dawson, *Healing America's Wounds*
   Dawson explores the consequences of racism on American society and offers scriptura/biblical solutions.

Robert William Fogel and Stanley L. Engerman, *Time on the Cross: The economics of American Negro Slavery*
   Fogel and Engerman argue persuasively that slavery was very profitable–which assured its duration.

Kenneth M. Stampp, *The Peculiar Institution: Slavery in the Ante-Bellum South*
   A seminal work on African-American history. The serious historian starts here.

Notes:

Lesson Twenty-Nine Test

Essay: (100 Points)

Agree with the following essay. In your paper state the central thesis of this essay and discuss how the author supports his argument. Then, agree or disagree with his conclusion.

    By the time O'Neill, who was white wrote Emperor Jones, within the African-American community the marriage of race and power was secure. Equality was no longer a goal: empowerment was. Now the movement wanted more than a piece of the pie--they wanted to be in charge. After so much misery and given the failure of white America to address the needs of the African-American urban community, who can blame them? Now African-Americans wanted to be both away from whites and in charge. Brutus manifested this marriage of power and separatism.

    This encouraged a permanent state of rage. "Anytime you make race a source of power," a Black Power leader wrote, "you are going to guarantee suffering, misery, and inequality. . . we are going to have power because we are black!" (Vincent Harding, Hope and History). Many African-Americans today, influenced by black nationalism, argue that the distribution of power in American society has become the single issue of overriding importance to the upward progress of African-Americans. From 1965 to the present every item on the black agenda has been judged by whether or not it added to the economic or political empowerment of black people. In effect, Martin Luther King's dialogue of justice for all--whites and blacks--has been cast into the conflagration of empowerment (Theodore Cross, The Black Power Imperative). The triumph of black nationalism made black anger an indelible part of the racial reconciliation quest. Thus, Brutus, on his island paradise finally felt he had it all: he was in charge and separated from whites.

    Black nationalism was mostly nonviolent. However, some African-American leaders were very angry. To these people, gradualism was anathema. It suggested that races could coexist together at the very time when many were suggesting that the races should remain separated. In The Fire Next Time (1962) James Baldwin wrote of the "rope, fire, torture, castration, infanticide, rape . . . fear by day and night, fear as deep as the marrow of the bone." By 1970, many African-American thinkers, religious leaders, social workers, and politicians were outraged. In fact, hatred and unforgivingness ran so deeply in African-American culture that the struggle became the end itself--instead of a means to an end.

    The theme that O'Neill explored in his play is as alive today as it ever was. Today, the politics of difference has led to an establishment of "grievance identities." The African-American community has documented the grievance of their group, testifying to its abiding alienation.

While predominantly white colleges and universities now enroll a majority of the more than 1.3 million black college students, the fact is there is not much race mixing really occurring. Racism divides and conquers still. One African-American student confessed, "We have a campus of 25,000 students and there is no mixing across cultural and racial lines . . . even during a campus rally for racial unity all the blacks cluster together and all the whites cluster together."

No one can deny that the Civil Rights initiatives in the 1960's broought substantial improvements to the African-American community. As a result of these encouraging developments, many black Americans developed what some historians call a "black revolution in expectations." African-Americans no longer felt that they had to put up with the humiliation of second-class citizenship. This progress was short lived and incomplete. White privilege--who basic under-pinings are based on the myth of racial homogeneity and white supremacy--mitigated all progress.

The real demon here, however, is unforgivingness. Clearly it destroyed Brutus; clearly it will destroy anyone in its path. (James P. Stobaugh)

Lesson Twenty-Nine Test Answers

Essay: (100 Points)

Agree with the following essay. In your paper state the central thesis of this essay and discuss how the author supports his argument. Then, agree or disagree with his conclusion.

The author argues that Brutus and his contemporaries, while they have every reason to be angry and unforgiving, ultimately this destroys the person exhibiting the unforgivingness. This is a biblical principle. I agree with the author.

LESSON THIRTY

Readings Due For This Lesson
Students should have read *The Little Foxes*, Lillian Hellman.

Reading Ahead

Read *The Glass Menagerie*, Tennessee Williams.

Suggested Weekly Implementation

Day One	Day Two	Day Three	Day Four	Day Five
1. Students will rewrite graded essays from last week and review Lesson Twenty-Nine test. 2. Students should have read the required reading(s) *before* the assigned lesson begins. 3. Teacher may want to discuss assigned reading(s) with student. 4. Teacher shall assign the required essays. Choose two or three. The rest of the essays can be outlined, answered with shorter answers, or skipped.	1. Student should begin reading(s) from next lesson. 2. Student should outline essays due at the end of the week. 3. Students should answer one or two of the essays that are not assigned as formal essays.	1. Students should write rough drafts of assigned essays. 2. The teacher should correct rough drafts.	Student will write final copy of essays due tomorrow.	1. Essays are due. 2. Students should take Lesson Thirty test. 3. Read *The Glass Menagerie*, Tennessee Williams.

379

Literary Criticism

Describe in great detail the relationship of Horace and his wife Regina. This relationship is a key element of the play.
Horace represents the monied, educated, but steadily declining South. He embraces abstract, absolute truth. Regina, on the other hand, is a Philistine, self-serving woman who represents the New South.

Critical Thinking

B. Find several instances of realism in this play. *The best examples of Realism are reflected in dialogue and characterization.*

Biblical Application

Compare Regina Giddens to Jezebel. *Both are completely pragmatic. Both manipulate their spouses and invite them to places of unbelief and immorality.*

Challenge Question

A. Faulkner, Hellman, Williams, Welty, Ransom, and other great writers came from the South. Why do you think so much great literature has come out of the South in this century? *Some have argued that in the post-Reconstruction struggle the South grew strong and educated.*

B. Hellman's plays... *A popular book several years ago was Jonathan Livingston Sea Gull. That is the way many Americans want to live their lives--anything goes, live free, no rules. But as we see in these literature selections, the wages of sin is death . . . in Christ though there is eternal life.*

Supplemental Resources:

Steven H. Bills, *Lillian Hellman, an Annotated Bibliography*

Mark W. Estrin, ed. *Critical Essays on Lillian Hellman*

Doris V. Falk, *Lillian Hellman*

Lillian Hellman, *Pentimento: A Book of Portraits*

Richard Moody, *Lillian Hellman, Playwright*

Carl Rollyson, *Lillian Hellman: Her Legend and Her Legacy*

Notes:

Lesson Thirty Test

Complete the following checklist: (100 Points)

NAME OF PLAY:
NAME OF AUTHOR:

I. BRIEFLY DESCRIBE: (10 Points)
   PROTAGONIST--
   ANTAGONIST--
   OTHER CHARACTERS USED TO DEVELOP PROTAGONIST--
   DO ANY OF THE CHARACTERS REMIND ME OF A BIBLE CHARACTER? WHO? WHY?

II. SETTING: (10 Points)

III. TONE: (10 Points)

IV. BRIEF SUMMARY OF THE PLOT: (20 Points)

   IDENTIFY THE CLIMAX OF THE PLAY.

V. THEME (THE QUINTESSENTIAL MEANING/PURPOSE OF THE BOOK IN ONE OR TWO SENTENCES): (10 Points)

VI. AUTHOR'S WORLD VIEW: (20 Points)
   HOW DO YOU KNOW THIS? WHAT BEHAVIORS DO(ES) THE CHARACTER(S) MANIFEST THAT LEAD YOU TO THIS CONCLUSION?

VII. WHY DID YOU LIKE/DISLIKE THIS PLAY? (10 Points)

Lesson Thirty Test

Answers

Complete the following checklist: (100 Points)

NAME OF PLAY: *The Little Foxes*
NAME OF AUTHOR: Lillian Hellman

I. BRIEFLY DESCRIBE: (10 Points)
   PROTAGONIST– *Horace*
   ANTAGONIST-- *Regina*
   OTHER CHARACTERS USED TO DEVELOP PROTAGONIST– *Addie, Cal, Birdie, et al.*
   DO ANY OF THE CHARACTERS REMIND ME OF A BIBLE CHARACTER? WHO? WHY? *Regina = Jezebel*

II. SETTING: (10 Points) *Southern United States in the early 20th century*

III. TONE: (10 Points) Serious

IV. BRIEF SUMMARY OF THE PLOT: (20 Points) *Regina, represented the corrupted old south, destroys her gentile, but alcoholic husband Horace.*

   IDENTIFY THE CLIMAX OF THE PLAY. *When Horace realizes that the "Reginas" of the world now control his world (at the end of the play).*

V. THEME (THE QUINTESSENTIAL MEANING/PURPOSE OF THE BOOK IN ONE OR TWO SENTENCES): (10 Points) *The story of the decline of a civilization.*

VI. AUTHOR'S WORLD VIEW: (20 Points)
   HOW DO YOU KNOW THIS? WHAT BEHAVIORS DO(ES) THE CHARACTER(S) MANIFEST THAT LEAD YOU TO THIS CONCLUSION? *Both exhibit Naturalism (a sense that there is no control in the universe).*

VII. WHY DID YOU LIKE/DISLIKE THIS PLAY? (10 Points) *Answers will vary.*

LESSON THIRTY-ONE

Readings Due For This Lesson
Students should have read *The Glass Menagerie*, Tennessee Williams.

Reading Ahead
Students should read *A Separate Peace*, John Knowles (Lesson Thirty-Four).

Suggested Weekly Implementation

Day One	Day Two	Day Three	Day Four	Day Five
1. Students will rewrite graded essays from last week and review Lesson Thirty test. 2. Students should have read the required reading(s) *before* the assigned lesson begins. 3. Teacher may want to discuss assigned reading(s) with student. 4. Teacher shall assign the required essays. Choose two or three. The rest of the essays can be outlined, answered with shorter answers, or skipped.	1. Student should begin reading(s) from next lesson. 2. Student should outline essays due at the end of the week. 3. Students should answer one or two of the essays that are not assigned as formal essays.	1. Students should write rough drafts of assigned essays. 2. The teacher should correct rough drafts.	Student will write final copy of essays due tomorrow.	1. Essays are due. 2. Students should take Lesson Thirty-One test. 3. Read *The Separate Peace*, John Knowles

Literary Criticism

A. Describe in detail the characters in this play. *Amanda is a fading Southern Belle. Laura is the poor spinster. Tom is the harried brother/son. Jim is the "gentleman caller."*

B. What is the conflict? *In Amanda's world to be unmarried is to be without valuable identity.*

Critical Thinking

A. Why does Williams use the quote from E. E. Cummings on his title page? Do a report on E. E. Cummings. *Answers will vary.*

B. Why does Williams title his play "The Glass Menagerie?" *The characters of this play are similar to the Laura's glass menagerie collection.*

C. Describe the dreams of Laura, Amanda, and Jim. Do any of them fully attain their dreams? *No, not really.*

Biblical Application

Compare the way that Amanda handles disappointment with the way that Joseph handles disappointment. *Amanda does not believe in a benevolent, omnipotent God. She, therefore, languishes in hopelessness. Joseph, in spite of bad things happening with regularity, remains hopeful because of his faith in God.*

Supplemental Resources:

Barron's Booknotes, *The Glass Menagerie*
    Excellent student and teacher guide to this play.

L. A. Beaurline, "TGM: From Story to Play." *Modern Drama 8*

The Glass Menagerie (1987) Video
    A wonderful video version of William's most famous play.

Presley, Delma E. *The Glass Menagerie: An American Memory*

Thomas Siebold, ed., *Readings on the Glass Menagerie*

Donald Spoto, *The Kindness of Strangers: The Life of TW*

Notes:

Lesson Thirty-One Test

Complete the following checklist: (100 Points)

NAME OF PLAY:
NAME OF AUTHOR:

I. BRIEFLY DESCRIBE: (10 Points)
   PROTAGONIST--
   ANTAGONIST--
   OTHER CHARACTERS USED TO DEVELOP PROTAGONIST--
   DO ANY OF THE CHARACTERS REMIND ME OF A BIBLE CHARACTER?
WHO? WHY?

II. SETTING: (10 Points)

III. TONE: (10 Points)

IV. BRIEF SUMMARY OF THE PLOT: (20 Points)

   IDENTIFY THE CLIMAX OF THE PLAY.

V. THEME (THE QUINTESSENTIAL MEANING/PURPOSE OF THE BOOK IN ONE OR TWO SENTENCES): (10 Points)

VI. AUTHOR'S WORLD VIEW: (20 Points)
   HOW DO YOU KNOW THIS? WHAT BEHAVIORS DO(ES) THE CHARACTER(S) MANIFEST THAT LEAD YOU TO THIS CONCLUSION?

VII. WHY DID YOU LIKE/DISLIKE THIS PLAY? (10 Points)

Lesson Thirty-One
Test Answers

Complete the following checklist: (100 Points)

NAME OF PLAY: *The Glass Menagerie*
NAME OF AUTHOR: *Tennessee Williams*

I. BRIEFLY DESCRIBE: (10 Points)
  PROTAGONIST– *Tom*
  ANTAGONIST-- *Amanda*
  OTHER CHARACTERS USED TO DEVELOP PROTAGONIST– *Jim, Laura*
  DO ANY OF THE CHARACTERS REMIND ME OF A BIBLE CHARACTER? WHO? WHY?

II. SETTING: (10 Points) *Urban South*

III. TONE: *Serious*

IV. BRIEF SUMMARY OF THE PLOT: (20 Points) *Amanda, her daughter Laura, and her son Tom languish in a Depression era apartment in a southern city. Laura, who is obsessed with a glass menagerie, is content to live her days in safe reticence. Amanda, however, wants much more. She is thrilled, then, when she hears Tom will be bringing to dinner a "gentleman caller." However, again, her hopes are to be dashed.*

  IDENTIFY THE CLIMAX OF THE PLAY. *When Jim shares his good news.*

V. THEME (THE QUINTESSENTIAL MEANING/PURPOSE OF THE BOOK IN ONE OR TWO SENTENCES): (10 Points) *This is a story about broken promises and dreams.*

VI. AUTHOR'S WORLD VIEW: (20 Points)
  HOW DO YOU KNOW THIS? WHAT BEHAVIORS DO(ES) THE CHARACTER(S) MANIFEST THAT LEAD YOU TO THIS CONCLUSION? *Naturalism*

VII. WHY DID YOU LIKE/DISLIKE THIS PLAY? (10 Points)

Lesson Thirty-Two

Readings Due For This Lesson

Students should have read *The Glass Menagerie*, Tennessee Williams.

Reading Ahead

Students should read *A Separate Peace*, John Knowles (Lesson Thirty-Four).

Suggested Weekly Implementation

Day One	Day Two	Day Three	Day Four	Day Five
1. Students will rewrite graded essays from last week and review Lesson Thirty-One test. 2. Students should have read the required reading(s) *before* the assigned lesson begins. 3. Teacher may want to discuss assigned reading(s) with student. 4. Teacher shall assign the required essays. Choose two or three. The rest of the essays can be outlined, answered with shorter answers, or skipped.	1. Student should begin reading(s) from next lesson. 2. Student should outline essays due at the end of the week. 3. Students should answer one or two of the essays that are not assigned as formal essays.	1. Students should write rough drafts of assigned essays. 2. The teacher should correct rough drafts.	Student will write final copy of essays due tomorrow.	1. Essays are due. 2. Students should take Lesson Thirty-Two test. 3. Read *The Separate Peace*, John Knowles

Challenge Questions

A. Read another T. Williams play and compare it to this one. *One play with which to compare The Glass Menagerie could be A Streetcar Named Desire. Blanche Dubois, the protagonist in the play, is a a fading Southern belle. She has just lost her ancestral home, Belle Reve, and her teaching position as a result of promiscuity. In some ways, those, she reluctantly participated in this behavior to survive (that is not a justification for the behavior). Blanche was described by Tennessee Williams as moth-like. She is a refined, cultured, intelligent woman who is never willing to hurt someone, but she is at the mercy of the brutal, realistic, Naturalistic world. Stanley Kowalski is a common, working man who is simple, straight forward and tolerates nothing but the unembellished truth and lives in a world without refinements. He is common, crude and vulgar. He is the opposing force to Blanche''s struggles and her world of illusion. Stella Kowalski is Blanches's younger, married sister who lives in the French Quarter of New Orleans. She has turned her back to her aristocratic upbringing to enjoy common marriage with a brute. She has abandoned any Romantic notions. Stella is caught in between the two opposing worlds of Blanche and Stanley.*

B. Is Amanda Wingfield more like Regina Giddens or Horace Giddens? *I think she is more like Horace. I find her to be harmless but tragic.*

C. Pretend that Anne Bradstreet, Ralph Waldo Emerson, Nathaniel Hawthorne, Stephen Crane, Ernest Hemingway, and Tennessee Williams have an imaginary conversation about ...Complete the following chart:

	Anne Bradstreet	Ralph Waldo Emerson	Nathaniel Hawthorne	Stephen Crane	Ernest Hemingway	Tennessee Williams
God	God is alive, all powerful, and very interested in human affairs.	Nature is God. The Holy Spirit is Human intuition.	Same as Anne Bradstreet although he embraced nature (small letter n)	If there is a God He cares nothing about people.	See Crane.	See Crane.
Bible	The Bible is the inspired Word of God.	Good stories.	Same as Bradstreet	Bad stories that are for fools.	See Crane.	See Crane.

Salvation	Salvation comes through faith in Jesus Christ.	Within Nature's fold one will find salvation (a sort of Nirvana)	Same as Bradstreet	There is no salvation.	See Crane	See Crane
Nature	Nature is neutral.	Nature is god.	Nature is important because it represents God's work	It is neutral.	It is malevolent.	It is evil.
Fate	A loving God controls our futures.	Nature and human will control the future.	God is in control.	Fate is like rolling dice. No one is in control.	See Crane.	See Crane.

Supplemental Resources:

Barron's Booknotes, *The Glass Menagerie*
    Excellent student and teacher guide to this play.

L. A. Beaurline, "TGM: From Story to Play." *Modern Drama 8*

The Glass Menagerie (1987) Video
    A wonderful video version of William's most famous play.

Presley, Delma E. *The Glass Menagerie: An American Memory*

Thomas Siebold, ed., *Readings on the Glass Menagerie*

Donald Spoto, *The Kindness of Strangers: The Life of TW*

Notes:

Lesson Thirty-Two Test

Discussion Questions: (100 Points)

A. Some critics argue that *The Glass Menagerie* is a savage attack on 20th Century American culture. Agree or disagree and support your argument from the text.

B. Some critics argue that Williams is no Naturalist–in fact, they argue, he is a Theist (not necessarily Christian)–or at least a "moralist"–in the same tradition of Hawthorne. Agree or disagree and support your argument from the text.

C. The play has seven scenes. The first four take place over a few days' time during the winter season. The remaining scenes occur on two successive evenings during the following spring. Since the play contains no formal "acts," a director can prescribe an intermission at any time. How would you divide the play if you were directing a performance?

D. Laura is one of the most pathetic figures in American literature. Is she really that physically crippled? Or is she more emotionally crippled?

E. How credible is Tom as a narrator? As a character in the play?

Lesson Thirty-Two Answers

Discussion Questions: (100 Points)

A. Some critics argue that *The Glass Menagerie* is a savage attack on 20th Century American culture. Agree or disagree and support your argument from the text. *Williams felt that our facile culture enslaved Americans to dreams that could never occur. Everyone–Tom, Jim, Amanda, and Laura (to a lesser degree)–were motivated by visions of reality that were not real at all.*

B. Some critics argue that Williams is no Naturalist–in fact, they argue, he is a Theist (not necessarily Christian)–or at least a "moralist"–in the same tradition of Hawthorne. Agree or disagree and support your argument from the text. *Williams is a sentimental Naturalist but I see no evidence he holds to any higher moral structure. Certainly does not.*

C. The play has seven scenes and the first four take place during the winter. The remaining scenes occur on two successive evenings during the following spring. Since there are no formal "acts," a director can prescribe an intermission at any time. How would you divide the play if you were directing a performance? *Answers will vary.*

D. Laura is one of the most pathetic figures in American literature. Is she really that physically crippled? Or is she more emotionally crippled? *She is more emotionally thatn physically crippled.*

E. How credible is Tom as a narrator? As a character in the play? *Both as a narrator and a character in the place he exhibits self-centeredness that fractures his credibility as a narrator and character.*

Lesson Thirty-Three

Readings Due For This Lesson
Students should have read *The Glass Menagerie*, Tennessee Williams.

Reading Ahead

Students should read *A Separate Peace*, John Knowles (Lesson Thirty-Four).

Suggested Weekly Implementation

Day One	Day Two	Day Three	Day Four	Day Five
1. Students will rewrite graded essays from last week and review Lesson Thirty-Two test. 2. Students should have read the required reading(s) *before* the assigned lesson begins. 3. Teacher may want to discuss assigned reading(s) with student. 4. Teacher shall assign the required essays. Choose two or three. The rest of the essays can be outlined, answered with shorter answers, or skipped.	1. Student should begin reading(s) from next lesson. 2. Student should outline essays due at the end of the week. 3. Students should answer one or two of the essays that are not assigned as formal essays.	1. Students should write rough drafts of assigned essays. 2. The teacher should correct rough drafts.	Student will write final copy of essays due tomorrow.	1. Essays are due. 2. Students should take Lesson Thirty-Three test. 3. Read *The Separate Peace*, John Knowles

Answers will of course vary.

Supplemental Resources:

Barron's Booknotes, *The Glass Menagerie*
    Excellent student and teacher guide to this play.

L. A. Beaurline, "TGM: From Story to Play." *Modern Drama 8*

The Glass Menagerie (1987) Video
    A wonderful video version of William's most famous play.

Presley, Delma E. *The Glass Menagerie: An American Memory*

Thomas Siebold, ed., *Readings on the Glass Menagerie*

Donald Spoto, *The Kindness of Strangers: The Life of TW*

Notes:

Lesson Thirty-Three Test

Rewrite *The Glass Menagerie* as if it was a Christian moral drama. Keep the same setting and characters, but present them, and the plot, in appropriate roles.

Lesson Thirty-Three Test Answer

Rewrite *The Glass Menagerie* as if it was a Christian moral drama. Keep the same setting and characters, but present them, and the plot, in appropriate roles.

Answers will vary.

Lesson Thirty-Four

Readings Due For This Lesson
Students should have read *The Separate Peace*, John Knowles.

Suggested Weekly Implementation

Day One	Day Two	Day Three	Day Four	Day Five
1. Students will rewrite graded essays from last week and review Lesson Thirty-Three test. 2. Students should have read the required reading(s) *before* the assigned lesson begins. 3. Teacher may want to discuss assigned reading(s) with student. 4. Teacher shall assign the required essays. Choose two or three. The rest of the essays can be outlined, answered with shorter answers, or skipped.	1. Student should begin reading(s) from next lesson. 2. Student should outline essays due at the end of the week. 3. Students should answer one or two of the essays that are not assigned as formal essays.	1. Students should write rough drafts of assigned essays. 2. The teacher should correct rough drafts.	Student will write final copy of essays due tomorrow.	1. Essays are due. 2. Students should take Lesson Thirty-Fourtest.

Literary Criticism

A. Describe some of the internal conflict. *Gene struggles throughout the novel with his jealousy towards Finny. Later, he feels guilty (after he injures Finny). This is the source of much internal conflict for Gene. Finny begins almost too late to admire the friend he has in Gene; this is evidence of his internal conflict. This is the primary internal conflict that Finny exhibits. Finny, however, as a character, is not as developed as Gene. There are other examples of internal conflict in every character--especially as the characters (foils) relate to the mock trial at the end of the novel.*

B. Gene is the narrator . . . *The reliability of the narrator, particularly in this novel is critical. One wonders, at times, if Gene is reliable. The philosopher Kant warns us that we can create a moral imperative to do almost anything. One wonders, after the fact, if Gene has not created a reality that suits his own moral imperative. The notion that he could have injured his best friend is unthinkable! On the other hand, Gene's winsome personality, sincerity, and intelligence disarm the reader and invites him to believe Finny. It is your call!*

C. Did Gene cause Finny to fall from the tree? *That is the million dollar question! In my opinion: absolutely! Did he mean to do so? Well, I am not sure . . . but he did it.*

D. How important is the setting? *The setting of a novel is, quite simply, where and when the story takes place. Another way of describing it is "spirit of place," the atmosphere generated by descriptions of the environment and the characters' relationship to it. In Devon School, John Knowles has created a setting rich in evocative detail. And, of course, the time of the novel is also very important: World War II.*

E. Give one or two themes of this novel. *Honesty, Mutability.*

Supplemental Resources:
John Knowles, *Indian Summer*
    Out of print, this book by Knowles exhibits the same moral dilemmas and strong characterizations.

John Knowles, *Peace Breaks Out*
    The Sequel to *A Separate Peace*.

Notes:

Lesson Thirty-Four Test

Essay (100 Points)

In an 150-300 word essay create a sequel to *A Separate Peace* being careful to keep the integrity of the story and characters in place.

Lesson Thirty-Four Test Answer

Essay (100 Points)
In an 150-300 word essay create a sequel to *A Separate Peace* being careful to keep the integrity of the story and characters in place.

Answers will vary.

Credits, Permissions, and Sources

Efforts have been made to confirm to US Copyright Law. Any infringement is unintentional, and any file which infringes copyright, and about which the copyright claimant informs me, will be removed pending resolution.

Most of the literature cited in this book is in the public domain. Much of it is available on the Internet, through the following sites:

Carnegie Mellon University English Server (http://eserver.org/poetry/paul-revere.html)
    Henry David Longfellow, "Paul Revere's Ride" and "The Psalm of Life"

Classical Short Stories: The Best of the Genre (http://www.geocities.com/short_stories_page/index.html)
    Stephen Crane, "The Blue Hotel" and "The Open Boat"
    Sherwood Anderson, "The New Englander"

Fire and Ice: Puritan Writings (http://www.puritansermons.com/toc.htm)
    Edward Taylor, "Meditations I"

Infomotions, Inc. The Alex Catalogue of Electronic Texts (http://www.infomotions.com/alex/).

Stephane Theroux. Classic Reader (http://classicreader.com/)
    Mary Shelley, Frankenstein
    Jack London, *The Call of the Wild* and "To Build a Fire"
    Edgar Allan Poe, "The Tell-Tale Heart" and "The Fall of the House of Usher"
    Emily Dickinson, "Emancipation, " "I'm Nobody! Who are You?," and "Love's Baptism"
    Nathaniel Hawthorne, *The Scarlet Letter* and "Great Stone Face"
    Frank Norris, "McTeague"
    Herman Melville, *Moby Dick* and "I and my Chimney"
    Charles Darwin, *Origin of the Species*
    Edwin Arlington Robinson, "The Pity of the Leaves"
    T. S. Eliot, "The Love Song of J. Alfred Prufrock"
    George Bernard Shaw, *Pygmalion*

University of Virginia. Browse E-Books by Author (http://etext.lib.virginia.edu/ebooks/Wlist.html).
    Stephen Crane, *The Red Badge of Courage*
    H. G. Wells, *The Invisible Man*
    Walt Whitman, "O Captain! My Captain!"
    Herman Melville, *Billy Budd*

The Works of Ralph Waldo Emerson (http://www.rwe.org/)
    Ralph Waldo Emerson, "Days," "Snowstorm," and "The Rhodora"